TRANSFORMATIONAL TRENDS IN GOVERNANCE AND DEMOCRACY

National Academy of Public Administration

Terry F. Buss, Series Editor

DATE DUE

Edited   na Guo

D0224543

Trai   *itury*

Edited by   Kinghorn

Edited   F. Buss

F   *e*

Edited   F. Buss

Reengin   *Century*

I.   *it*

DEMCO, INC. 38-2971

Innovations in Human Resource Management: Getting the Public's Work Done in the 21st Century

Edited by Hannah S. Sistare, Myra Howze Shiplett, and Terry F. Buss

Expanding Access to Health Care:

About the Academy

The National Academy of Public Administration is an independent, nonprofit organization chartered by Congress to identify emerging issues of governance and to help federal, state, and local governments improve their performance. The Academy's mission is to provide "trusted advice"—advice that is objective, timely, and actionable—on all issues of public service and management. The unique source of the Academy's expertise is its membership, including more than 650 current and former cabinet officers, members of Congress, governors, mayors, legislators, jurists, business executives, public managers, and scholars who are elected as fellows because of their distinguished contribution to the field of public administration through scholarship, civic activism, or government service. Participation in the Academy's work is a requisite of membership, and the fellows offer their experience and knowledge voluntarily.

The Academy is proud to join with M.E. Sharpe, Inc., to bring readers this and other volumes in a series of edited works addressing current major public management and public policy issues.

The opinions expressed in these writings are those of the authors and do not necessarily reflect the views of the Academy. To access Academy reports, please visit our Web site at www.napawash.org.

Expanding Access to Health Care

A Management Approach

Edited by Terry F. Buss
and Paul N. Van de Water

NATIONAL ACADEMY OF
PUBLIC ADMINISTRATION

TRANSFORMATIONAL TRENDS IN
GOVERNANCE AND DEMOCRACY

M.E.Sharpe
Armonk, New York
London, England

Library of Congress Cataloging-in-Publication Data

Expanding access to health care : a management approach / edited by Terry F. Buss and Paul
N. Van de Water.
    p. ; cm— (Transformational trends in governance & democracy)
Includes bibliographical references and index.
    ISBN 978-0-7656-2332-4 (cloth : alk. paper) — ISBN 978-0-7656-2333-1 (pbk. : alk. paper)
1. Health insurance—United States. 2. Health services accessibility—Economic aspects—
United States. 3. Medical care, Cost of—United States. 4. Health care reform—United States.
I. Buss, Terry F. II. Van de Water, Paul N. (Paul Nicholas) III. National Academy of Public
Administration. IV. Series.
    [DNLM: 1. Health Services Accessibility—economics—United States. 2. Health Care
Costs—United States. 3. Health Care Reform—United States. 4. Insurance, Health—
economics—United States. W 76 E96 2009]

    RA412.2.E96 2009
    362.10973—dc22   2008042189

Printed in the United States of America

The paper used in this publication meets the minimum requirements of
American National Standard for Information Sciences
Permanence of Paper for Printed Library Materials,
ANSI Z 39.48-1984.

∞

| EB (c) | 10 | 9 | 8 | 7 | 6 | 5 | 4 | 3 | 2 | 1 |
| EB (p) | 10 | 9 | 8 | 7 | 6 | 5 | 4 | 3 | 2 | 1 |

Contents

Preface and Acknowledgments   vii

Introduction
Terry F. Buss and Paul N. Van de Water   ix

**Part I. Management Issues and Policies in Health Insurance
     Market Reforms**

1. Restructuring Health Insurance Markets
    Elliot K. Wicks   3

2. Designing Regional Health Markets
    Cori E. Uccello, John M. Bertko, and Catherine M. Murphy-Baron   35

3. Creating a Level Playing Field for Public and Private Plans
    Bryan Dowd   51

4. Regulating Private Health Insurance
    Timothy Stoltzfus Jost   73

5. Paying One's Fair Share for Health Coverage and Care
    Jill Bernstein   99

6. Refiguring Federalism: Nation and State in Health Reform's Next Round
    Lawrence D. Brown   125

7. Recent Changes in Dutch Health Insurance: Individual
    Mandate or Social Insurance?
    Kieke G.H. Okma   144

Part II. Administering Health Insurance Programs and Reforms

8. Administering a Medicaid-plus-Tax-Credits Initiative
    Lynn Etheredge, Judith Moore, Sonya Schwartz, and Alan Weil   165

9. Administering Health Insurance Mandates
    C. Eugene Steuerle and Paul N. Van de Water   182

10. Designing Administrative Organizations for Health Reform
    Paul N. Van de Water   201

11. Individual Health Insurance Plan Information: Too Much
    and Too Little
    Michael Wroblewski   224

Part III. Controlling Costs Under Health Care Reform

12. Controlling Health Care Costs
    Mark Merlis   241

13. Simplifying Administration of Health Insurance
    Mark Merlis   267

Part IV. Using Performance Management to Enhance Health Care Reform

14. Management and Performance of Federal Health Care Programs
    F. Stevens Redburn and Terry F. Buss   289

15. Performance-Based Management Under Ryan White: The
    BPHC Initiative
    Nicole Rivers, Sandy Matava, and Terry F. Buss   301

Part V. Empirical Studies

16. Expanding Access to Health Care for Hispanic Construction Workers and
    Their Children
    Xiuwen Dong, Knut Ringen, and Alissa Fujimoto   321

17. Expanding Access to Health Insurance for Children: The State
    Children's Health Insurance Program, 1997–2007
    Christen Holly and Daniel P. Gitterman   344

18. Did Medicaid/SCHIP Crowd Out Private Insurance Among
    Low-Income Children?
    Adetokunbo B. Oluwole and Dennis G. Shea   362

About the Editors and Contributors   391

Index   395

Preface and Acknowledgments

This is the ninth in a series of edited books, Transformational Trends in Governance and Democracy, capturing the latest thinking in public management. The books collectively represent what we believe are fundamental, transformational trends emerging in governance and democracy. Each book addresses the critical questions: How is governance or democracy being transformed? What impact will transformations have? Will forces arise to counter transformations? Where will transformations take governance and democracy in the future?

The National Academy of Public Administration (NAPA) sponsors the book series, in partnership with M.E. Sharpe, Inc., as part of its mission to engage the discipline in debate about pressing issues of the times. In this book, the Academy has also partnered with the National Academy of Social Insurance (NASI) and the Robert Wood Johnson Foundation. Many of the chapters in the series have been contributed by Academy fellows, NASI members, and staff. We have drawn on leading researchers, practitioners, and thinkers representing different views on the issues addressed in the series. The views expressed are those of the authors and not those of the academies, the study panel, or the foundation. The books are available at http://www.mesharpe.com.

Acknowledgments

NASI and NAPA would like to thank the Robert Wood Johnson Foundation (RWJF) for its generous support of our project over the past two years. We would like to thank Andrew D. Hyman, senior program officer at RWJF, Jenna Dorn, president of NAPA, and Margaret Simms, president of NASI, for their support and encouragement. NAPA fellows (designated with an asterisk), NASI members (designated with a dagger), and other health care experts participated in a study panel that reviewed many of the chapters in this book, in addition to guiding the project and assessing its findings and conclusions. They include: Robert A. Berenson, MD,† panel cochair, senior fellow, Urban Institute; William A. Morrill,* panel cochair, senior fellow, ICF Consulting; Kenneth S. Apfel,*† professor, School of Public Policy, University of Maryland; Beth C. Fuchs,† principal, Health Policy Alternatives; Thomas R. Hefty, president, Kern Family Foundation; Feather O. Houstoun,* president, William Penn Foundation; Robert E. Hurley, associate professor, Department of Health

Administration, Medical College of Virginia; Jack Lewin, MD, chief executive officer, American College of Cardiology; Catherine G. McLaughlin,† professor of health management and policy, School of Public Health, University of Michigan; Sallyanne Payton,* William W. Cook Professor of Law, Law School, University of Michigan; Michael C. Rogers,* executive vice president, corporate services, MedStar Health; Raymond Scheppach,* executive director, National Governors Association; and Mark D. Smith, MD,† president and CEO, California HealthCare Foundation. In addition to NAPA fellows and NASI members and staff, the project benefited from consultations and participation from experts in the health care field, including Darcie Corbin, Rosemarie Day, Walton Francis, Janet Holtzblatt, Timothy Jost, Jerry Mashaw, Mark Merlis, Steve Redburn, Thomas Stanton, and Cori Uccelo. The great amount of time the fellows and experts committed is much appreciated. Without these contributors, the project would never have been realized. Last but not least, we would like to thank the experts who contributed chapters to this book. They reflect the highest quality of thinking in the field.

Introduction

The U.S. health care system faces well-known problems: 47 million people without health insurance coverage, rapidly rising costs that consume 16 percent of the country's economic output, and uneven quality of care. The Institute of Medicine has demonstrated that "the lack of health insurance for tens of millions of Americans has serious negative consequences and economic costs not only for the uninsured themselves but also for their families, the communities they live in, and the whole country." Even many people with health coverage are experiencing serious problems paying for the rapidly rising costs of health care coverage and health insurance.

The National Academy of Public Administration (NAPA) and the National Academy of Social Insurance (NASI) partnered with the Robert Wood Johnson Foundation to undertake a sweeping analysis of the management and administrative issues that arise in expanding health coverage. The project identified the core administrative functions that need to be performed in ensuring access to health coverage, described how these functions are performed at present and under proposed alternatives, drew lessons from experience in the United States and abroad, and assessed suggested administrative and management approaches designed to facilitate the improvement or expansion of health care coverage. Analysts evaluated approaches to expanding health coverage in terms of their economy, effectiveness, equity, innovation and responsiveness, and legitimacy.

The health care issue may well dominate the domestic policy agenda for the new administration and Congress taking office in 2009. The intent of this book is to draw together some of the best thinking on the health care issue in one place, not as a exercise in advocacy, but rather to lay out the issues in a balanced way so that policy makers, researchers, and citizens can find their way through the complex issue of health care reform. The study panel's final report, published separately by NAPA and NASI, summarizes the project's findings (see www.nasi.org).

Many of the chapters in this volume were originally produced as lengthy, unpublished working papers in support of the NASI-NAPA study panel. These working papers have been revised and shortened for inclusion in this volume. They, and many others not included in this book, are available in full, with appendixes, at www.nasi.org.

Although the chapters here emphasize management, all address health care policy—that is, how it is structured—as well. We believe, and the analysis in this book bears out, that health care policy in large part determines how health care will be managed.

The authors focus on how the health insurance market, including both private and public programs, can be made to work better—that is, more efficiently, effectively, and equitably—as the market now stands or under various reforms through greater attention to management issues. The focus, then, is on a rather limited federal role with a much greater role for states, employers, private insurers, and, of course, consumers.

We have divided the chapters into five separate but interrelated parts. In Part I, we look generally at how the current health care system works and the reforms that might be necessary to expand coverage, improve accessibility, and promote equity. In Chapter 1, "Restructuring Health Insurance Markets," Wicks looks at structural and administrative issues revolving around rating rules, standard benefits, reinsurance, cafeteria plans, and insurance exchanges, all of which can take on very different forms under health care reform. In Chapter 2, "Designing Regional Health Markets," Uccello, Bertko, and Murphy-Baron narrow Wicks's focus somewhat, applying the same kind of structural and administrative concerns to regional health markets. In Chapter 3, "Creating a Level Playing Field for Public and Private Plans," Dowd considers how to structure competition between a government-run health insurance plan and private plans. In Chapter 4, "Regulating Private Health Insurance," Jost, focusing on the five areas identified by Wicks, analyzes the role of regulation in the health insurance system at present, then looks at how this role might change under different kinds of reforms at the state and federal levels. To complete the overview of the health insurance system as it now stands and how it might be reformed, Bernstein, in Chapter 5, "Paying One's Fair Share for Health Coverage and Care," looks at how health insurance is paid, carefully examining tax and insurance premium systems and cost sharing through deductibles, copayments, and coinsurance. Brown, in Chapter 6, "Refiguring Federalism," adds his analysis of public health care programs such as Medicaid and the State Children's Health Insurance Program—both in the United States and in other countries with federal systems—as they relate to intergovernmental responsibilities for coverage of low-income people. The health care system in the Netherlands has been touted by some as a possible model for the United States. Okma, in Chapter 7, "Recent Changes in Dutch Health Insurance," assesses this prospect against the decades-long process required to develop and implement the Dutch system.

Part II assembles chapters recounting in greater detail issues about how administration of major health insurance reforms would work in practice. Etheredge, Moore, Schwartz, and Weil, in Chapter 8, "Administering a Medicaid-plus-Tax-Credits Initiative," review the administrative issues involved in launching and managing a tax-incentive program associated with Medicaid. In Chapter 9, "Administering Health Insurance Mandates," Steurele and Van de Water look at the administrative issues to be considered in employer- or individual-based health coverage mandates. In Chapter 10, "Designing Administrative Organizations for Health Reform," Van de Water provides a sweeping overview of federal agencies and programs, looking for administrative models that might be adopted under several health coverage reforms. In Chapter 11, "Individual Health Insurance Plan Information," Wroblewski addresses the consumer perspective: How can insurance providers offer consumers enough critical information on health care policies without overwhelming them with complexity, volume, and obfuscation?

Part III focuses on cost controls needed to make health insurance reforms affordable and accessible. Most of the health care reforms and management options relating to them will not work well unless health care costs are brought under control. Merlis, in Chapter 12, "Controlling Health Care Costs," offers an overview of major options that might reduce health care costs generally and under various reforms. Then, in Chapter 13, "Simplifying Administration of Health Insurance," Merlis focuses more on cost savings through simplified administration.

Many informed observers believe that performance management and budgeting practices ought to be embedded in any health care reforms undertaken to expand coverage and access. In Part IV, Redburn and Buss, in Chapter 14, "Management and Performance of Federal Health Care Programs," look at the George W. Bush administration's management agenda as applied to the ten largest federal health care programs with an eye toward improving the initiative in the next administration. Rivers, Matava, and Buss, in Chapter 15, "Performance-Based Management Under Ryan White," show how performance management and budgeting of federal programs works at the local level, where health care services are delivered.

Finally, in Part V, we selected three empirical studies that address several issues under health care reform. In Chapter 16, "Expanding Access to Health Care for Hispanic Construction Workers and Their Children," Dong, Ringen, and Fujimoto show the extent to which a minority population remains without health insurance coverage under the current health care system. In Chapter 17, "Expanding Access to Health Insurance for Children," Holly and Gitterman look at the correlation between state program administrative models and caseloads and retention under State Children's Health Insurance Program (SCHIP). Finally, in Chapter 18, "Did Medicaid/SCHIP Crowd Out Private Insurance Among Low-Income Children?" Oluwole and Shea provide an innovative empirical study of public programs—Medicaid/SCHIP—on the private health insurance market.

Terry F. Buss
Adelaide, Australia

Paul N. Van de Water
Washington, DC

Part I

Management Issues and Policies in Health Insurance Market Reforms

1

Restructuring Health Insurance Markets

ELLIOT K. WICKS

States and federal legislators are considering major policy changes to make health insurance more affordable and to expand health care coverage. Often this involves changes in the structure of health insurance markets, such as establishing risk pools or insurance exchanges for certain populations and altering the rules for selling coverage in the individual and small-group markets. This chapter examines structural changes that might be made to expand coverage, with special focus on six administrative issues that must be addressed: changes in rating rules, high-risk pools, standard benefit plans, reinsurance, Section 125 plans (Internal Revenue Code "cafeteria plans"), and insurance exchanges.

The Purpose of Health Insurance

It is useful to begin by recalling the fundamental purpose of health insurance. People buy health insurance to ensure that the cost of paying for medical services will not be a barrier to receiving necessary care and to protect themselves against the financial catastrophe of incurring a very large medical bill that they could not afford to pay from their own resources. When they buy health insurance, people choose to incur a small, certain loss—the insurance premium—to protect themselves against the possibility of incurring a very large, unpredictable loss—the cost of paying for very expensive medical care. In other words, people pool their risk, but this form of protection is sustainable only under very specific conditions: Insurance works only so long as most people in the pool incur expenses far below the amount they pay in premiums so there will be enough money to cover the few people who incur large losses.

The role of health insurers is to design and sell health insurance policies that provide financial protection, but the market does not always perform as intended, especially for people whose risk of needing health services is relatively high. If every person bought health insurance and had identical coverage—the same covered services, the same limits, and the same cost-sharing structure—the role of insurers would be very different and most of the problems related to the functioning of insurance markets would disappear. Such a system would be essentially a system of social insurance, like Medicare, where everyone is automatically covered, the benefits are essentially identical, and everyone pays the same premium rate. Of course, this is not a description of the current private health insurance system. Under competitive pressures in a voluntary market, where people may or may not buy coverage, insurers face strong incentives to develop many different benefit structures and coverage options to try to attract the most profitable business. They find it profitable to segment the market by risk: If other insurers are pooling high-risk and low-risk enrollees and charging them one rate, a competitor can gain business by pooling only low-risk enrollees and offering them a lower rate. For similar reasons, insurers have incentives to structure their benefit plans to be especially attractive to lower-risk people and to avoid the highest-risk individuals.

Of course, once one insurer adopts these tactics, others must follow to remain competitive. If this process remains unchecked by legal constraints, the result is extensive segmentation of the market by risk, where coverage becomes unafford-able for many higher-risk individuals. Of course, the proliferation of coverage options and the mechanisms insurers must employ to differentiate people on the basis of risk add to insurers' administrative costs and create burdens for the people who buy coverage. Legislators and others who seek to restructure the insurance market hope to ameliorate some of the problems while still retaining the private insurance system.

Characteristics of a Well-Functioning Market

Next I compare a well-functioning market with the market operating today.

Efficiency

One desirable characteristic of an insurance market is that it would operate efficient-ly—that is, administrative costs, including transactions costs for consumers and providers, would be minimized. Costs associated with reviewing the characteristics of people applying for coverage, determining eligibility for coverage, and setting prices for categories of applicants—referred to as medical underwriting—would be minimized, since resources used for medical underwriting have no benefits for consumers. Marketing costs would be a small portion of the total premium.

Reasonable Choice

A well-functioning market would offer people a choice of different insurance ben-efits packages and delivery systems—health maintenance organizations (HMOs), preferred provider organizations (PPOs), indemnity plans, and so on. Benefit options would be sufficient to allow people to choose a plan that suited their preferences but not so numerous as to make choice confusing. Consumers would have objective information in a form that would make it easy for them to make intelligent choices as they compared coverage options and plans.

Useful Competition

A well-structured market would promote useful competition among insurers so they were motivated to minimize the cost of coverage and provide timely, efficient, and effective customer service. Competition would induce insurers to reduce not only administrative costs but also the underlying costs of medical expenses. No insurers would be so dominant that they could have control over the market. Insurers would receive a return on investment sufficient to induce them to continue in business, but profits would not be excessive.

Pooling Risk

Market rules would ensure pooling risks to spread them broadly and fairly and not result in high-risk people facing unaffordable premiums. No one who could afford to pay for average-priced insurance would be priced out of the market because of their higher-than-average risk. To the extent that market segmentation exists, it would not threaten the basic insurance principal of having low-risk people subsidize the medical expenses of high-risk people.

Comparing Reality to the Ideal

Comparing present insurance markets to the ideal shows that performance often falls short. Administrative costs are a relatively high proportion of premium costs, especially in the individual market but also in the small-group market. Marketing costs also tend to be high in these markets because each sale adds only a few enrollees. The number and variety of insurance benefit plan options are far more numerous than necessary to meet consumer needs and, along with the complexity of benefit structures, make informed choice difficult. Few people can go to a single source to see and compare all the options. Consumers bear the burdens of trying to keep track of bills and submit claims, worrying about coordination of benefits, and generally trying to ensure that they are getting the financial benefits to which they are entitled. Family or job status changes create a risk that people will fall between the cracks in insurance coverage or even be denied coverage entirely. In states that allow risk rating in the small-group and individual markets, competitive pressures force insurers to devote resources to identifying the relative risk posed by different applicants. In such circumstances, the rewards for being effective at risk segmentation may be as great or greater than those associated with controlling underlying medical costs. As a result, higher-risk people, especially in the individual market, may be priced out of the market, so the basic risk-pooling function of insurance is impaired.

In most states, a small number of insurers account for a very high proportion of the business in the individual and small-group markets—not the picture of a classic competitive market. Market domination by only a few insurers has been common in many states for a number of years, but recently the degree of market concentration has increased greatly, reflecting, in part, a wave of mergers. For employment-based and individually purchased health insurance, WellPoint and UnitedHealth Group each hold 14 percent of shares of the national market, and Blue Cross plans control 32 percent of the overall market. Concentration is higher in many state and regional markets. According to one recent study, the two largest insurers have at least half the enrollment in forty states (out of forty-four for which data were available), and they hold at least three-quarters of the enrollment in fifteen states.

Deficiencies have prompted some critics to call for wholesale reform, often arguing that only something like a single-payer system can fully address such deficiencies. But the opposition to such massive change is fierce, and such a system brings its own set of problems. Likely, in the near future we will continue to have a system composed of multiple insurers offering competing plans. If that is so, the policy question is, What are the options for streamlining the administrative structure of the present system and bringing its performance closer to the ideal?

Major Options for Structural Change

In this chapter I look at rate compression, high-risk pools, standardized benefit plans, public reinsurance, Section 125 plans, and insurance exchanges or purchasing pools. Although I discuss the policy justification for each approach, my emphasis is on administrative issues.

Rate Compression

In the absence of legal constraints, insurers segment people by risk, creating large premium differences between high-risk and low-risk people. Most states have placed some limits on risk rating in the small-group market—although the limits vary from state to state—and a few have done so in the individual market. Some states have required insurers to use a pure community rating in one or both of these markets, so that everyone pays the same rate for similar coverage regardless of health status or any other personal characteristics. In states with the least restrictive rate rules, the rate-variation ratio can be as much as 10:1 in the small-group market, and the highest-risk people in the individual market may be denied coverage entirely. The purpose of rate compression, of course, is to broaden the sharing of risk to make coverage more affordable for higher-risk groups and individuals. The problem with this solution is that rate compression, while making coverage less expensive for higher-risk people, makes it more expensive for lower-risk people. In the absence of a mandate—a requirement that everyone have coverage—the higher premiums may cause some lower-risk individuals or groups to drop coverage and discourage others from acquiring it in the first place. If the exodus is too great, there will be too few people in the risk pool whose medical expenses are substantially less than their premiums. The average cost of medical claims will rise, forcing the insurer to raise the premium, which causes other people with below-average risk to leave the risk pool. The result is a spiral of adverse selection and a continually deteriorating risk pool.

Experience suggests that this phenomenon of adverse selection against the market as a whole is less of a problem in the small-group than in the individual market. It is much easier for an individual than for a group to assess when he or she is most likely to need expensive medical care and to buy coverage only when that need is imminent and to go without coverage at other times.

The policy challenge, then, is how far to go in compressing rates. States have chosen different paths, and their experiences can be a useful guide for those considering whether to move toward greater rate compression. In general, rate compression has seemed to work reasonably well in the small-group market in helping to make coverage more affordable for high-risk groups, but it has not increased the overall rate of coverage. In the individual market, the problems have been greater because of adverse selection against the market as a whole, created when low-risk people drop out.

From a purely administrative standpoint, rate compression does not pose significant new challenges for most states since they already have an administrative structure in place to enforce their current rating rules. The federal government does not now impose rating restrictions in either the small-group or the individual market, but even if this policy were to be changed, it is likely that the responsibility for enforcing the law would fall on the states. To enforce rate limits, states must be able to review individual insurers' procedures and policies and to collect and analyze premium data to ensure that they are complying with the rating restrictions.

If a state adopts a pure community rating, allowing no variation based on any rating factors, the administrative task is much simpler than when insurers are permitted to use a variety of rating factors. For example, it is not unusual for states to allow rate differences based on some combination of health status, age, gender, geography, industry, health-related behaviors, and class of business, typically with different limits attached to each factor. When there are multiple rating factors and different limits on the extent to which insurers can vary rates based on each factor, both compliance with and enforcement of the law become very complicated and therefore more expensive.

One way to simplify the administrative burden and to make the rating restrictions more comprehensible, while still allowing any degree of variation in premium thought to be advisable, is to set an *overall limit* on the amount by which the rate can varied based on *all factors in combination*. For example, if a state decided that no high-risk group should have to pay more than four times the rate paid by the lowest-risk group, the state would stipulate that whatever rating factors were used, the maximum rate variation for all factors in combination could not exceed a ratio of 4:1. Besides being simpler, this approach makes less important the choice about which particular rating factors insurers are permitted to use. Under this approach, state regulators would find it easier to determine whether an insurer is complying with this requirement rather than with one that allows insurers to vary rates based on multiple factors, each with its own limit. Under the latter circumstance, it is sometimes difficult to determine even what total rate variation is the theoretical maximum. Taking this approach also allows states to move gradually to greater rate compression—for example, starting with a ratio of 5:1 and moving to 3:1 by reducing the ratio by 0.5 each year for four years—which will help reduce sticker shock for low-risk people and may make them less likely to forgo insurance.

High-Risk Pools

Rate compression is a way to make coverage more affordable for high-risk people, but it is a tool most commonly used in the small-group market, since, if employed in the individual market, it is more likely to produce adverse selection against the market as a whole. The tool more frequently used in the individual market is a high-risk pool. Like rate compression, it is a way of subsidizing high-risk people. The idea is simple: A mechanism is used to identify people whose risk profile is so high that they could almost surely not afford to pay a premium that would fully cover their risk. These people are then offered coverage with a specified benefit package through a special risk pool composed of just high-risk people. They pay a premium that is higher than what "normal-risk" people would pay for such coverage but still not sufficient to cover their full expected medical claims. The shortfall represents a subsidy that has to be funded from some source, typically some kind of surcharge on insurers but sometimes, and preferably, from broader-based revenue sources. Implementing a high-risk pool raises a number of policy and administrative issues.

Eligibility

An obvious question is how to determine who will be eligible, or, to put it another way, how will high-risk people be identified? Most states have given insurers great discretion in deciding who will be denied individual coverage, allowing them to deny coverage to anyone they judge to be especially high risk. In California, an approach is being considered that would leave insurers no discretion: the state would develop a questionnaire that all insurers would administer to applicants, and insurers would be permitted to deny coverage only to those people who "failed" the test. Everyone who "passed" would have guaranteed coverage. This approach has the advantage of predictably limiting the number of people who will fall into the high-risk category, as well as providing uniform treatment for applicants regardless of the insurer to which they apply.

Some states require the individual to show that he or she has been turned down for coverage by more than one insurer. Denial of coverage does not by itself make one eligible for a high-risk pool in most states. States frequently also require that the person not have available any source of group coverage, including Consolidated

Omnibus Budget Reconciliation Act (COBRA) coverage. In some instances a denial is defined to include having available only individual coverage that excludes some major medical conditions. Some states also allow a person to be eligible if the cost of the only coverage that is available exceeds a specified high dollar amount.

This approach involves many administrative issues, mostly related to verifying eligibility. Someone has to verify that the person has no other coverage available, has been denied coverage, or can find only coverage that excludes some condition or is too expensive. For some of the information, the only reasonable verification may be the applicant's self-report, subject to penalty for false statements, though some states require written proof of having been denied coverage in the form of a letter from the insurer. If written proof is not required, some agency will need to audit a selection of applications to ensure that there is at least a credible threat of a penalty for providing false information.

States have a limited funding pool on which to draw to provide the subsidies inherent in this approach. Questions then arise regarding what to do when the fund is nearing depletion. States may establish waiting lists, which obviously involves some administrative issues related to notifying people initially that they are on a waiting list and then notifying them again if the funding allows more people to be covered, presumably with a recheck of eligibility. Some states have chosen to make the eligibility requirements more restrictive when funding limits are being reached, which requires a procedure for making this change. Presumably, most high-risk pools will be governed by a board that has the authority to make limited policy changes within legislatively set constraints.

Role of Insurers

A high-risk insurance pool involves all of the normal functions that insurers perform: enrollment, determining eligibility and maintaining eligibility rolls, disenrolling those who do not pay premiums, collecting premiums, and verifying and paying claims. But for this high-risk population, case management may be important to control costs.

In most instances, it would not be cost-effective for states themselves to perform all of these functions. It would normally be wiser to contract out these tasks to insurers, who already have in place the necessary administrative apparatus, and to pay them an administrative fee. If the state is at risk for medical claims that exceed the expected amount for the risk pool—that is, the state is the insurer (as is the case in Maryland)—then the state would presumably contract with a single insurer to perform the administrative functions. However, if insurers are at risk, either in whole or in part, then the insurer or insurers would presumably perform these functions for their own enrollees and recover the cost from the premium paid by their enrollees plus the state-supplied subsidy. From a state's standpoint, it would obviously be safer to have the insurers bear the risk of expenditure overruns because the fund that finances the subsidies is normally a fixed amount and thus cannot be easily or quickly increased if there are cost overruns. Of course, insurers would charge a higher premium for assuming the risk. In addition, if there are multiple insurers participating, there has to be a mechanism in place to permit people to make an informed choice among participating plans and to transfer from one to another from year to year. Presumably, the state would need to fill this role.

Preexisting Conditions

The purpose of a high-risk pool is to provide coverage on a guaranteed-issue basis to people who could not otherwise get affordable coverage because of their poor health status. People often find themselves in this position because of a preexisting medical condition. However, if the high-risk pool accepts people without any preexisting-condition limits, it encourages people to postpone buying coverage when they are healthy, knowing they can go to the high-risk pool if they develop a serious condition. The result could be even greater-than-expected adverse selection against the pool, which could threaten its financial viability. Some states have addressed this issue by including preexisting-condition restrictions but making them shorter than what insurers typically impose—for example, three or six months rather than a year or two.

If there are preexisting-condition limits, someone has to have responsibility for collecting and verifying the information that applicants supply regarding these conditions. Commonly, applicants are asked to self-report such data.

Setting Premiums

Four factors are inextricably linked: the number of people who are eligible for the risk pool, the scope of benefits, the amount of funds set aside for the risk pool, and the size of the premium. If more people are eligible for the pool, more funding will be required for subsidies, and the fund will have to be larger, other things being equal. If coverage is more comprehensive, the subsidy cost will be higher, other things being equal. If the premium is lower (making coverage more affordable), the premium subsidy is greater and more funding will be required, other things being equal. Varying any one of the four factors will have implications for the other three. Policy makers will need to keep this fact in mind when setting premiums.

States typically have determined that a person in the high-risk pool should pay no more than 125 percent to 200 percent of the "standard rate," which is essentially the rate a person of "normal" risk would pay. The question is what rating factors should be used in establishing the standard rate. Based on age alone, medical expenses can vary by a ratio of at least 3:1 between young adults age twenty to twenty-four and adults just under age sixty-five. So it would make little sense to charge people in the high-risk pool a premium that is, say, 125 percent of the average rate for the normal *population as a whole*. That could result in a sixty-two-year-old in the high-risk pool paying less than someone of the same age buying coverage in the normal individual market. It would seem more sensible to make the rate equal to 125 percent of the rate for a person of average risk *in the same age cohort*. A case might also be made for also using geography as a rating factor in determining the standard rate if geography is used as a rating factor for the non-high-risk population. From an administrative standpoint, the task is to determine what the standard rate is, using real-world data, and then to make sure that the premiums in the high-risk pool are the agreed-upon multiple of the standard rate.

Funding the Pool

High-risk pools spread risk more broadly to make coverage more affordable for high-risk people. The ideal source of funding for providing such subsidies would be one that is as broad as possible and generates revenues from the population on the basis of ability to pay. General revenues are probably the source that best meets this test. But most states have looked to sources other than general fund revenues to finance the high-risk pool subsidies, presumably because it is politically difficult to raise the taxes that produce general revenues.

Frequently, states assess insurers to provide the funding. From the standpoint of fairness and equity, if this is the course states choose, the ideal approach would be to assess all insurers based on their *total* share of the market, not just their share of the individual market. If the assessment is just on individual-market business, the cost is passed back just to people buying in the individual market, where costs are already higher for comparable coverage than in other markets. That would defeat the purpose of having the high-risk pool, which is to avoid having lower-risk enrollees absorb costs of claims generated by high-risk enrollees. In other words, the approach is not consistent with broad risk sharing or making individual coverage more affordable. Even assessing all health insurers fails to spread risk over all who have coverage, since those covered by self-insured plans would not contribute. Some policy makers have contemplated assessing the third-party administrators who administer health plans for self-insured companies based on the number of covered lives under the plans. Though desirable from the standpoint of equity, this approach could be challenged as inconsistent with Employee Retirement Income Security Act (ERISA) requirements, which limit states' ability to regulate employer health benefit plans.

From an administrative standpoint, if states look to insurers to fund the high-risk pool, the states will have to collect and audit information about insurers' revenues, perhaps for different markets separately, depending on how the assessment is spread. Most states collect and analyze such information, so little additional administration would be required. The more-challenging task will be to monitor outflows from the pool fund to ensure that funding will be adequate and, if shortfalls seem likely, to decide how to remedy the problem—whether to change eligibility requirements, modify the benefit package, establish waiting lists, try to increase the size of the fund, and so forth.

Standard Benefit Plans

A number of states have adopted, or at least considered, the policy of limiting the number of benefit plans that could be sold in the individual or small-group market. Instead of allowing each insurer to offer dozens of different plans, a state entity would define a few standardized benefit plans that all insurers and health plans would offer (with additional differences to reflect the different nature of HMOs, PPOs, and indemnity plans). New Jersey, for example, limited the number of benefit plans in the small-group market to six options, and California is now considering legislation that would require all individual market insurers to offer just five standardized plans. Such a policy is designed to make it easier for consumers to compare options and make an informed choice about which offers the best value. When people are faced with too many options, probably more than six or seven, they have difficulty making the "best" choice. They resort to simplifying procedures or choice—limiting tactics that are not consistent with economists' notions of rational decision making. Thus it could be argued that consumers would be better off—in the sense of being able to make a choice that best meets their tastes and preferences—if they had fewer choices. At a time when there is increasing agreement about the kinds of health insurance protection that people need, it is hard to believe that meeting people's needs and preferences requires the degree of choice that is the rule in the individual and small-group markets. The difficulties involved in having too many choices are presumably the reason that Medicare limits the number of benefit plans that supplemental insurers may offer to Medicare enrollees.

If limiting options enhances consumers' ability to make well-informed choices, it is also an effective way of promoting beneficial competition among insurers. When consumers can make valid judgments about the relative value of the plans offered by each insurer, insurers have much stronger incentives to compete on the basis of price, quality, and service. That, in turn, gives them incentives to encourage participating providers to be more efficient and to improve quality.

Finally, limiting the number of plans reduces potential for risk segmentation. People tend to choose different kinds of plans depending on their health status. For example, those with poorer health status tend to choose coverage that is more comprehensive, has lower cost sharing, and gives greater choice of providers. Insurers know how to tailor benefit plans to attract lower-risk populations, and if there is no constraint on the degree to which they can vary the benefit structure, they can be very creative in devising plans that achieve their desired enrollee mix.

From an administrative standpoint, the challenge is less in enforcing a requirement to offer standard plans than it is in defining what benefits should be in the standard plans. All benefit plans have two elements: the medical services covered and the amount of consumer cost sharing (including coverage limits). The more medical services are covered, the greater the protection for insured people but the higher the premium; the greater the amount of consumer cost sharing, the lower the premium but the greater the financial risk to the insured person. Of course, deciding on the optimum trade-off is why defining standard benefit packages is difficult.

At least in general terms, there seems to be increasing agreement about the kinds of medical services that should be covered to provide good protection, although there are still many areas of controversy around the edges. Few would argue that coverage that does not include hospital care, physician services, radiology and laboratory services, prescription drugs, and substance abuse and mental health services is adequate. There is still much disagreement about what limits there should be on some services, especially outpatient mental health services. Also, there is a great deal of disagreement about how much consumers should be expected to pay out of pocket. This is especially true now that the idea of consumer-driven health plans has become popular. Advocates argue that benefit plans that include large deductibles and copayments are desirable as a way of giving consumers financial incentives to be cost conscious when consuming medical services.

Standard plans will need to include different levels of cost sharing in recognition of the fact that some people will not be able to afford the most generous plans, whereas others will prefer plans that offer the maximum financial protection. In fact, it may be desirable to have all plans offer the same covered medical services and have them vary only with respect to cost sharing.

There is the additional problem that different kinds of delivery systems are inherently structured to use different kinds of cost sharing. HMOs are essentially closed-panel plans, so that services from nonpanel providers are not covered at all (except in emergency situations); patients using out-of-plan providers pay 100 percent of the cost. Moreover, HMOs have typically been designed around the idea that physicians, not patients, should have primary responsibility for ensuring that the care provided is cost-effective, and so they may have no deductibles and only relatively small copayments at the point of service. PPOs have varying cost-sharing requirements depending on whether patients seek care from participating or nonparticipating providers. Indemnity plans have no panel of providers, and so the cost-sharing requirements are the same regardless of which providers patients choose. Standardized plans will probably have to have different cost-sharing provisions for each of these delivery types, even when the covered medical services are the same.

Defining standard plans is a challenge because changes in medical technology may make it desirable to change the covered benefits. However, most of the technological advances occur within a category of covered services. For example, new imaging technologies may be developed that have not previously been covered, but these fall within the larger category of radiological services. The decision about whether or under what circumstances a new technology, or even an existing expensive technology, will be covered has generally been left up to insurers to decide, though their decisions have sometimes led to disputes that have produced court challenges. Letting insurers make separate and different decisions about such new technologies, however, introduces a degree of complexity in the benefits they offer that makes it more difficult for consumers to compare plans to determine which offers the best value. However, having the regulators make such decisions would require a procedure for gathering expert opinion and a decision-making process that would have to be able to withstand the scrutiny of critics.

A final issue is whether insurers will be required to offer plans that are completely identical to the standard plans or whether instead some flexibility will be permitted by allowing them to offer actuarially equivalent plans. (Two benefit plans are actuarially equivalent if they have the same value in terms of the claims the insurer expects to have to pay.) There are several problems with this approach. First, the state regulators must have some method for verifying that the plans meet the test of being actuarially equivalent. This is often done by accepting the certification of the insurer's actuary. Second, allowing this kind of flexibility opens the door for plans to tailor their benefit packages to attract lower-risk enrollees, unless the degree of flexibility is strictly constrained. But if it is so constrained, what is really gained by allowing any deviation from the standard plan? Certainly, allowing greater flexibility adds to administrative complexity: What level of deviation from the standard plan would be considered acceptable, and who would make that decision?

States have typically assigned the responsibility for defining standard benefit plans to a specific board, requiring them to seek expert advice and public opinion before making their decisions. The most ambitious of such efforts was the process that Oregon followed in the late 1980s in trying to establish a ranking of possible covered services based on a combination of cost-benefit assessment by experts and public input. Elements of the outcome of that process, the Oregon Plan, are still used today for the Medicaid program. Most other states have employed less-comprehensive approaches to defining standard benefit plans.

Once the standard plans are defined, the ongoing administrative task should be somewhat minor, since it is relatively easy for regulators to determine whether health plans are conforming to the requirements simply by reviewing their benefit plans.

Public Reinsurance

A high proportion of people who lack health insurance cite cost as the reason for being uninsured. Lowering insurance premiums would cause more people to acquire coverage, although the research shows that only a relatively large price reduction would produce a significant influx of new people to insurance markets. In essence, the only way to produce large premium reductions is by providing subsidies. Typically, proposals for subsidies target lower-income people or perhaps small, low-wage employers. Another option is to subsidize insurers—an approach inherent in the notion of publicly funded reinsurance. The basic idea is simple: If insurers were given a guarantee that claims costs in excess of a specified amount would be subsidized by government, they could be expected to lower premiums by approximately the amount of the subsidy.

Although public and private reinsurance are similar, they have different effects. Both provide an extra layer of protection against unexpectedly high claims costs. But since insurers are paying for private reinsurance from their own resources, for the system as a whole, insurers' costs are not reduced, and so no significant premium reduction would be expected, with one exception: When they buy reinsurance, insurers do not need to set aside so much in reserves to protect themselves against the possibility of having to pay for a costly case, so then can offer somewhat lower premiums because capital is freed up. Publicly funded reinsurance has a different effect: The claims costs paid by the public program are not costs to the insurers, and so they can lower premiums in the aggregate by the amount of the subsidy. The larger the subsidy, the larger the likely premium reduction.

In essence, public reinsurance involves socializing risk—that is, shifting a portion of the risk and the cost from the private sector to the public sector. Such a policy has advantages besides the obvious one of making insurance generally less expensive for buyers. It also protects insurers from some of the worst consequences of adverse selection. Even if they end up with a disproportionate number of high-risk people who then incur high costs, they do not have to bear much of that cost. Being relieved of this risk should make insurers somewhat less reluctant to take on higher-risk individuals or groups (although they still might avoid them because they are more likely to incur costs below the point where the reinsurance takes effect). Moreover, since insurers do not have to set aside as much to cope with the possibility of adverse selection, they can be expected to reduce their premiums by an amount approximately equal to the expected subsidy.

It is not clear what approach insurers would use in lowering premiums in this instance. Reinsurance should make them more willing to take on high-risk enrollees because they are no longer high risk for the insurer. Insurers could pass on the cost reduction in the form of lower premiums for just higher-risk applicants. However, because higher-risk enrollees are more likely to incur costs in general, including costs below the threshold for reinsurance, it is more likely that insurers would reduce premiums more or less across the board, making coverage somewhat more affordable for everyone.

Such subsidized reinsurance would also reduce year-to-year premium variations because insurers would be less concerned about the fact that some change in an insured group's characteristics would increase the probability that the group would incur high-cost medical claims.

The advantage of this government-financed reinsurance approach is that it spreads risk very broadly, across the whole tax-paying population, and it does not compel insurers, enrollees, employers, or anybody else to do anything. The market is left to work. The disadvantage is that it is not efficient in the sense of having a given allocation of government monies produce the largest possible expansion in the number of insured people. The dollars would not be spent in a target-efficient way because much of the subsidy would go to people who are already buying coverage with their own money. Premiums can be expected to decline across the board, for everybody purchasing insurance. Most people benefiting from the lower premium are people who are already buying insurance and who thus are paying for the high-cost cases with their own money when they pay premiums. Government dollars would thus mostly substitute for private dollars. This result is undesirable if the overriding objective is to produce the greatest reduction in the number of uninsured with the fewest dollars. It may be desirable if the objective is to spread risk in the broadest possible way and to move toward a social insurance model like Medicare.

The reinsurance subsidy can be kept lower and the target efficiency greatly improved by limiting the reinsurance program only to groups that generally cannot afford current coverage and among whom a high proportion is uninsured. For example, the reinsurance might be available only for coverage provided to small firms that employ predominantly low-wage workers. These firms often do not buy coverage because of the cost, and thus many employees of such firms lack coverage. Reinsurance subsidies available only to this group would not produce much substitution of public dollars for private dollars already being spent. Reinsurance limited to certain groups would, of course, affect the rates for only those groups, not the market as a whole.

Public reinsurance can take several forms. One is for the reinsurance to cover some or all of an insurer's *aggregate* claims for a defined population in excess of a specified amount. Another approach allows insurers to identify, within a short time after initial enrollment, certain small groups or individuals within a group that they wish to reinsure. In essence, this approach amounts to a high-risk pool for high-risk small groups. This differs from traditional reinsurance because the insurer has to identify high-risk enrollees or groups *before the fact,* that is, before costs are incurred.

But the approach most commonly considered is for the reinsurance to cover a portion of the costs of the really high-cost cases. Reinsurance would pay all or a large portion of the costs incurred by any insured individual during a year beyond some threshold. For example, the insurer might be responsible to pay all the costs up to $50,000, and then the government would pay a large proportion of the costs thereafter, for example, 90 percent. Such a policy would provide substantial subsidies for insurers. Less than 1 percent of the U.S. population incurs medical costs above $50,000 per year, but these few account for approximately 28 percent of total expenditures. Another option would be for government to pay a portion of costs for the highest 1 percent or 2 percent of cases. Such an approach has the advantage of having an in inherent inflation adjustor.

Instead of having all expenditures above a certain level reinsured, there could be a corridor of costs for which government is responsible—above a specified amount, government pays, but above another higher amount, the insurer reassumes full responsibility. This is the approach taken by Healthy New York. The argument for this approach is weak if the prime objective is to protect insurers against high risk. But it does help to limit government's exposure and creates stronger incentives for insurers to manage the extremely high-cost cases. Typically, whether there is a corridor or not, the insurer would still be responsible for a portion of the costs even when the reinsurance threshold is reached, so that the insurer would have an incentive to contain costs of the expensive episodes of illness. The incentive to manage costs is obviously greater the larger the insurer's share of the cost.

This government subsidy would allow insurers to offer reduced premiums, since they would not pay for much of the high-cost care their enrollees need. The lower the threshold point where reinsurance takes effect, the lower the premium that insurers will charge but, of course, the larger the cost to government. For example, Healthy New York reinsurance covers 90 percent of costs between $5,000 and $75,000, and represents one-quarter of the insurers' total medical spending.

From an administrative standpoint, reinsurance may be heavily resource consuming in the stage of setting up the program, but once the program is under way, the burdens should be fewer.

Reinsurance can work smoothly only if the reinsurance applies to a standardized benefit package, including identical cost sharing, offered by all the insurers. Otherwise, it would be very hard to determine whether insured individuals passed the reinsurance threshold because their illness was especially severe and therefore costly or because their coverage was especially comprehensive. Another problem is that an episode of care can be expensive because an insurer does not do a good job of managing the care of a very sick patient. Reinsurance could reward such an insurer. In any case, the reinsuring agency would have to have a system in place to verify insurers' expenses.

A significant task will be to determine what kind of threshold-level and risk-sharing arrangement will yield costs to the state consistent with the budget for the program. This requires, among other things, predicting how many uninsured people will be induced to buy coverage because of the subsidized premium and how many people whose health care has been directly or indirectly financed publicly might take up private coverage because of the reduced cost, thus reducing costs to the state. The cost can obviously be manipulated by altering the threshold, the corridor of risk sharing, the level of risk sharing, and the number of people who are eligible. An agency probably needs to be assigned the responsibility for monitoring and overseeing the reinsurance program and to have some flexibility in changing the threshold and cost-sharing parameters to ensure that the program is achieving the desired objectives. The need for such flexibility became apparent in the case of Healthy New York when the initial parameters proved to be more restrictive than necessary. Fewer-than-expected enrollees were higher risk, and so the state decided to lower the reinsurance threshold to lower premiums by a greater amount to attract more enrollees.

In many ways, the administrative tasks of operating a reinsurance system are like those insurers generally perform, apart from the enrollment functions. The state would obviously need to be able to verify insurers' reports of claims costs that exceed the threshold. The state may also want to ask insurers for early warnings of cases that are expected to pass the threshold as a way of ensuring that the health plan is taking adequate steps to manage the care to keep costs under control. A system for paying insurers would be needed. All of these functions can be performed efficiently only with adequate data collection and computing capabilities. States may find it more cost-effective to select an experienced private vendor to perform these functions.

Section 125 Plans

Under federal tax law, employers are allowed to establish so-called Section 125 plans, often referred to as cafeteria plans or salary-reduction plans. Employees agree to reduce their salary by a specified amount and to have their employer put that amount into an account from which employees can draw to pay for certain expenses, in this case medically related expenses, including insurance premiums. The practical effect of this sleight of hand is that the money in the account is considered to be an employer contribution rather than employee income and is therefore not taxable, so that employees can pay for the benefits covered by the account with pretax dollars, thereby reducing the net cost to them. Savings from not paying federal or state income taxes or payroll taxes can be as much as 40 percent, depending on the employee's tax bracket. So, for example, a family policy that might cost an employee $10,000 a year if the employee had to pay with after-tax dollars might cost a net of only $6,000 after the tax savings. The employer benefits as well because there is no employer payroll tax due on the amount the employee puts in the account. The savings to the employee is realized even if the employer contributes nothing to the health insurance premium, although employer-paid premiums are also not subject to tax.

Several states are considering requiring employers to establish Section 125 plans; Massachusetts already has such a law in force. Requiring employers to offer Section 125 plans is an attractive policy because states can reduce the cost of coverage for employed people who have to buy insurance as individuals because their employer offers no coverage, but without mandating employers to contribute to coverage or having the state come up with any new money. The cost of the employee savings is borne by the federal government in the form of forgone tax revenues.

Apart from the modest administrative cost of establishing and operating such a plan, the burden on the employer is minimal. The employer would have to withhold the amount employees designate and then transfer the appropriate amount from the employee's account for the premium payment. Such a policy is likely to be more effective in reducing the number of uninsured if it is combined with subsidies for lower-income employees or a purchasing pool or insurance exchange to provide a cost-effective source of coverage for people who have such accounts and use them to purchase individual coverage.

Although a requirement to establish Section 125 plans is not technically a restructuring of insurance markets, it certainly is designed to make insurance more affordable, and it works best when combined with some of the insurance market reforms previously discussed.

From an administrative standpoint, mandating Section 125 plans is not an especially burdensome task. Obviously, employers have to be informed of the requirement; they have to report that they have complied; and the state must verify that there is a plan in place that meets state requirements. This would require cross-checking with the state agency that has records of all businesses in the state, presumably the agency that administers business taxes. The federal requirements for establishing Section 125 plans are modest; employers do not even have to file their plans with the IRS. If the state decides to exclude certain employers, as Massachusetts does for employers with ten or fewer employees, or to allow employers to not include certain employees in their plans, such as part-time or temporary employees, the state would need to issue regulations to spell out the exceptions. Massachusetts has a Web site that contains the information that employers need to know to comply with the requirement. A requirement to establish Section 125 plans should not run afoul of ERISA limitations on states' authority to regulate employer health plans because the Department of Labor does not consider Section 125 plans to be ERISA plans.

Insurance Exchange

The idea of having small employers or individuals join together to purchase health insurance is not new, but the concept has been reinvigorated as a result of its inclusion as a key element in the Massachusetts reforms. The basic principle of collective purchasing underlies not only the Massachusetts Health Connector but a host of similar past efforts: health insurance purchasing cooperatives (HIPCs), insurance exchanges, alliances, and purchasing pools. The idea of having small purchasers come together to purchase as a group seems attractive because large employers generally fare better than small employers or individuals when they purchase health coverage. Because they represent a large number of potential enrollees, large employers have purchasing clout and thus can negotiate for better prices and improved quality and service. Their large size allows insurers to realize administrative economies of scale, which translate to lower premiums. The thinking is that if many small employers or individuals could join together to form an entity to represent them in purchasing coverage from insurers, they could realize savings comparable to what large employers enjoy.

Such a purchasing entity (hereafter referred to as an exchange) offers several other potential advantages. Because the exchange contracts with several insurers, *individual employees* within a firm can enroll in any participating health plan rather than all being forced to accept the insurer their employer would have chosen if the employer had conventional coverage. If the exchange accounts for a large share of the small-employer market, coverage portability is increased because employees may not need to switch health plans when they change jobs. And the fact that employees individually select plans every year and can readily switch from one to another means that insurers are in direct head-to-head competition at every open enrollment, which creates stronger incentives for insurers to compete to offer high-value coverage. The environment for this managed competition is strengthened in that the exchange can provide information in a format that makes it easier for enrollees to compare the relative value of competing plans, especially if the benefit structures are standardized.

The real-world experience with stand-alone exchanges strongly suggests that merely establishing such an entity is not by itself an effective strategy for bringing more people under the health insurance umbrella. Even if an exchange could realize its full potential for reducing the costs of coverage, the reduction would not be enough to cause large numbers of the uninsured to newly acquire coverage. Thus, an exchange should be viewed as a part of a more-comprehensive approach to coverage expansion, which almost certainly must at minimum include some form of subsidies to make coverage more affordable for low-income and lower-middle-income people.

Experience with exchanges for small employers has not been especially encouraging. In the early 1990s a number of states passed legislation that resulted in the formation of exchange-like entities. Although some experienced modest success for a time, ultimately almost all failed, including the ones in North Carolina, Florida, Texas, Colorado, and California. They had trouble recruiting sufficient numbers of enrollees. Insurers were sometimes reluctant to participate and, even when they did, often abandoned ship when they realized how few employers sought coverage through the exchange. Exchanges often experienced adverse selection, primarily because they were a magnet for tiny, relatively high-risk employers. Ultimately, few exchanges were able to offer coverage at a price any lower than what employers could find outside the exchange. So the primary benefit was that individual employees within a firm could choose different health plans from those participating in the exchange rather than being forced into the plan selected by their employer.

Some private exchanges started before the wave of the early 1990s and without benefit of state legislation operate successfully, notably CBIA in Connecticut and COSE in Cleveland. Some others have been started since—for example, HealthPass in New York City—but most account for a tiny portion of the potential small-group market. Some other exchange-like organizations that operate as part of a subsidy program of one kind or another exist; nearly all have limited enrollment.

Experience makes clear that it is important to structure an exchange in a way that will make it effective. I turn now to those structural issues.

Size

Perhaps the most important lesson from experience is that exchanges have to be large to realize their potential advantages. Large exchanges can more readily attract and retain health plans because there is enough business to make it worth insurers' while to participate. They have enough visibility and market presence to make them an attractive option for small employers. They can realize economies of scale. And with significant market share, they can negotiate more effectively with insurers, if they choose to take that approach.

The size problem is something of a dilemma. Unless they are large, exchanges have difficulty offering an attractive price because they do not represent enough business to negotiate favorable prices and they cannot realize economies of scale to reduce costs. Unless they can offer a lower price than the outside market, exchanges will have difficulty attracting sufficient numbers of enrollees to become large. Probably the most successful examples of large exchange-like entities are government employee plans. Government exchanges have a unique advantage in reaching critical mass size: Because they have a captive audience—government employees—they do not have to attract customers, and for all practical purposes, their low-risk enrollees do not have the option of going outside the exchange to get lower prices because they would lose the employer contribution. So government employee plans are much less likely to suffer adverse selection. Prime examples are the Federal Employees Health Benefit (FEHB) Program and CalPERS, the public employees plan in California, which serves not only state employees but employees of municipalities as well. Because of their size, these exchanges have no trouble recruiting health plans, and they use their market power to influence the levels of service, the kinds of products insurers offer, the prices at which they offer those products, and even the nature of the delivery of medical care.

One way to ensure that an exchange achieves sufficient size is for government to make it the only option for certain populations. For example, a state that provides subsidies to lower-income people could require that they use the exchange as their source of coverage. If as a result of its large size, the exchange achieves administrative cost reductions, the benefit of requiring use of the exchange is that more of the subsidy dollars are spent for the delivery of medical care rather than for administrative costs. Another option is for the state to require that all who purchase as individuals or all employers below a particular size—perhaps those with twenty-five or fewer employees—use the exchange. This approach seems sensible for people purchasing in the individual and small-group markets because premiums in conventional markets include disproportionately high administrative and marketing costs, costs that might be reduced if purchases were made through the exchange. They are also in the poorest position to get information that allows them to make valid price-value comparisons among health plans, a problem the exchange can ameliorate by being a source of objective information provided in a format that makes plan-to-plan comparisons relatively easy. While policy makers may be reluctant to adopt a plan that involves this level of coercion, the approach does not limit consumer choice in any significant way, since a number of health plans would be available to choose from, and health plans still have an opportunity to compete for the same total market.

Price Taker or Negotiator?

In designing the exchange, policy makers must decide whether the exchange will simply be a price taker or instead will assume the role of active buyer and will negotiate with health plans. From an administrative standpoint, the simplest approach would be for the exchange to solicit bids, accept whatever price is offered by any insurer choosing to participate, and let competition for enrollees be the disciplining force to ensure that prices are reasonable. The other approach is for the exchange to actively negotiate with health plans, aggressively seeking to attain more-favorable offerings, which is the approach that most large employers use. Being a negotiator is a more-complicated role, requiring the exchange to be active rather than passive and to be able to command the information and develop the skills to be effective at negotiation. And to have real bargaining power, the exchange must have the authority to decide not to contract with a health plan that does not offer a reasonable price. Of course, it will always be difficult for an exchange to exclude a health plan that accounts for a large share of the people currently enrolled.

Public or Private?

One of the key issues to be addressed is whether the exchange will be a private or a public agency. The case for having an exchange be private is that it could be more flexible, more entrepreneurial, and quicker to react to changing circumstances. For example, private agencies generally have greater latitude in terms of hiring and terminating personnel and changing policies without undue delay. In addition, small employers tend to be wary of government and may be more hesitant to acquire coverage from a public agency than a private entity. A private entity is also likely to face less skepticism and wariness from agents and brokers. Public organizations may also have a harder time justifying expenditures for marketing, including payment of sales commissions.

A private exchange could be either a for-profit or a nonprofit organization, although the potential for realizing substantial profits may not be large, and given the view of an exchange as serving the public interest, there might be some skepticism about assigning the role to a for-profit organization.

If the exchange is to be a private entity, state government could still retain considerable control. It could issue a request for proposals to select a contractor, or it could certify an entity to serve as the exchange. In either case, the state could require that the exchange have a governing board that would ensure accountability to the people the exchange is designed to serve. This would give the state some of the advantages of both a private and a public entity.

If the exchange is to be a private entity initiated through legislation, then someone within either the governor's office or an executive branch agency would need to be responsible for starting the process of establishing the exchange. Whichever choice is made, the people responsible must have considerable flexibility and not be unduly hampered by bureaucratic restrictions. Criteria would need to be developed as a basis for choosing the organization to be the exchange. Then it might be necessary to prepare and issue a request for proposals to elicit responses from parties willing to serve the function.

One of the issues to be concerned about with this approach is that there may not be an existing entity that is appropriate or willing to perform the functions of the exchange, either because none is prepared to take on the task or because qualified entities (like insurers or brokers) have a conflict of interest. (It is important to make the distinction between the exchange being a private entity and having the exchange contract with a private entity for certain nonpolicy functions, such as administration of premium collection and distribution, maintaining eligibility files, etc.)

The case for a public entity is related to issues of coordination and control, confidentiality, accountability, and the capacity to serve the public interest. If the exchange is established as part of a larger reform, the functions assigned to the exchange would likely be interwoven with other processes and policies that are under state control, for example, determining who is eligible for subsidies, which involves gathering confidential information about income, family size, work status, and so on. Especially if the exchange is not a public entity but is responsible for administering the subsidies, safeguards should be in place to ensure that confidentiality is protected and that the exchange is acting responsibly, efficiently, and effectively in handling large sums of government money. Ensuring that the exchange's activities are consistent with and further the total system reform goals would probably be easier if the exchange were a government entity or at least an entity that is clearly accountable to serving the public interest and is subject to government oversight.

If policy makers assign the exchange responsibilities to government, they must then decide whether to locate the exchange in an existing agency or to create an independent entity. The advantage of assigning responsibility to an existing agency is there would already be people on board who could begin work, and not all procedures would need to be invented anew. However, a new entity might be less constrained by existing procedures and cultures and more ready to experiment and be innovative. An independent government entity governed by a board representing the interests of the people the exchange serves would help to give the exchange an identity separate from existing institutions and provide a more-flexible structure for moving quickly and being able to adapt to changing circumstances. Massachusetts chose this approach in assigning the exchange role to the Health Connector. The exchange should have wide latitude and as much flexibility as possible with respect to the way it carries out everyday procedures, free of civil service and procurement procedures usually required of government agencies, though always subject to the approval of its governing board.

The composition of the governing board of the exchange is important. While the initial impulse might be to include all the stakeholders on the board to help ensure that they buy into the process, the counterargument is that the exchange should mainly represent the *buyers* of health care, namely, employers, employees, and unemployed individuals.

Start-up Issues

Once operations are fully under way, it would be possible to finance operations of the exchange through an administrative fee added to the premiums. Initially, however, funding will have to come from elsewhere. Experience with other purchasing pools suggests that several millions will be necessary to fund the start-up. Assuming funding has been solidified, the first task will be to identify the entity to be the exchange if this is not specified in the legislation. If the exchange is to be a private entity, criteria will need to be developed to choose an organization, and someone will have to be assigned responsibility to research possible candidates and to make the selection. This is a several-month process.

A related step is to appoint a governing board, the composition of which will be specified in the enabling legislation if that is the impetus for the establishment of the exchange.

The third step is to develop a job description for an executive director, do an executive search, and then hire an executive director. This responsibility would most logically be lodged in the governing board, though if the exchange is a public entity, the task might be assigned to an existing government or to the governor's office. Supporting staff will need to be hired or transferred as well, although the executive director would be expected to take primary responsibility for this task. Once the initial staff is in place, a first order of business will be to prepare a work plan and spending plan for the first year and ideally a tentative budget plan for the second and third years.

The exchange will need legal advice on indemnification of staff and board members and making sure the exchange activities are consistent with federal law, especially ERISA.

Major Tasks

What follows is a discussion of the major tasks the exchange must perform before it can begin enrolling people. A number of the tasks will have to be performed simultaneously, and some of them will need to be repeated in future years.

Those who have been through the task of beginning an exchange have found that once the exchange is formed, if all goes very smoothly, it takes at least a year of intense work to complete the necessary tasks before the exchange can start enrolling people.

Choosing a Plan Administrator and Defining the Plan's Tasks

Plan administration refers to specific tasks that the exchange must perform—specifically those that involve enrolling people in health plans, collecting premiums from employers and individuals (along with subsidies from government if they are part of the reform), transmitting payments to appropriate health plans, providing customer service to employers and individual enrollees, and coordinating functions with insurers. The plan administrator is not a policy-making entity but instead performs the routine but very important tasks just described. The administrator's role is similar in many ways to the role that third-party administrators play in administering self-insured employer health plans.

Most of these functions are performed by insurers themselves, with the help of agents and brokers, but they would become the responsibility of the exchange or its contractor. The process is more complicated if individual employees, not their employers, can separately choose from any of the participating health plans. A firm employing five people might have employees enrolled with five different carriers. This complicates the premium-determination process for each employer as well as the process of maintaining eligibility files and distributing premiums to health plans.

Past exchanges have typically chosen to contract for administrative services with firms that specialize in this kind of administration, evidently deciding that it was not practical or cost-effective to try to develop the required expertise in-house, especially today, given the need for sophisticated computer technology and Web-based access for enrollees, employers, insurers, and the exchange itself. Developing such systems is expensive, and there are substantial economies of scale. Having an experienced administrator that is used to working with insurers to implement the individual-choice system is also important, since insurers may have little experience with this model, especially in the context of the small-group market. Smaller employers seldom offer multiple health options.

People with experience in administering exchanges emphasize that it is important that the plan administrator have a cooperative relationship with health plans and that the administrator be able to listen to the problems raised by health plans and work to accommodate them whenever possible. Retaining the good will of health plans is important to the success of the total effort, since they tend to be wary of dealing with exchanges. The insurers need to view the administrator as a partner rather than an adversary, according to people involved in past exchange start-ups.

Given the fact that insurers already perform most of the administrative functions that the exchange must undertake, it might seem obvious to hire a health plan as the administrator. However, the exchange should approach this solution cautiously. The unsuccessful Texas exchange tried this approach and discovered that other insurers were concerned that the administrating insurer would gain a competitive advantage by obtaining access to competitors' information, and they did not trust the administrator to be fair in making decisions that had financial repercussions. At the very least, such an approach creates the perception of a conflict of interest.

If the exchange is established as a result of legislative mandate, the state employees' health plan might be seen as a likely candidate to serve as the exchange's administrator. Although state employees' health plans perform many similar functions, the exchange has unique responsibilities. The administrative process involves collecting premiums from many employers, each of whom may have employees enrolled in several health plans. Maintaining eligibility rolls for such a system is obviously more difficult than maintaining those for the present state employee system. These functions require mechanisms, processes, and computer technologies that the state probably does not have, and developing them and interfacing that system with insurers' systems would likely be expensive and time-consuming and could be difficult to accomplish in a timely way.

However, an advantage of using the state employees' plan as administrator is that the state develops expertise and thus does not become a captive to an outside vendor. If a vendor proves unsatisfactory, it is not a trivial or easy task to switch to a new vendor.

I am not aware of any state that uses the state employees' plan as an exchange for small employers or individuals, although a number of states offer coverage to municipalities and school boards as well as state employees.

Experience shows that it is important to have the plan administrator on board before trying to recruit health plans. The administrator can help to sell the idea to insurers. Health plans have generally not been eager to participate in exchanges, and one element they are concerned about is the administrative aspects of the new program. They have to be convinced that they can trust the plan administrator to properly maintain eligibility files and properly allocate premium revenues. They have to trust that they are getting paid what they are due and that they are not paying claims that are not valid. Insurers are more likely to participate if they are confident of the administrator's expertise and integrity. Thus, the decision about who administers these functions needs to be made before approaching health plans to seek their participation.

Getting Participation of Health Plans

Recruiting and maintaining participation of health plans has proved to be a challenge for previous exchanges. Insurers are not always eager to enter into an arrangement that gives their customers greater bargaining power. They also worry about becoming victims of adverse selection, especially when the exchange allows individual employee choice: Insurers feel better protected against adverse selection when they can be assured of getting whole groups rather than just some individuals within the group, since there is some spreading of risk even within small groups. One way to relieve insurers' concerns is to establish arrangements that protect them against adverse selection. Examples include reinsurance and risk adjustment.

The best way to ensure that health plans will participate is to structure the exchange so that a large portion of insurers' potential pool of business goes through the exchange. Under such circumstances, insurers cannot afford to exclude themselves.

Experience with other exchanges indicates that it is highly desirable to consult with health plans early in the process. They will have concerns about the new system and how it meshes with their normal way of doing business, for example, what changes in their administrative processes will be required and what that will cost. They are especially likely to be worried about adverse selection, as noted earlier. They may have reservations about having to offer a new benefit package, especially since that normally requires a filing with the regulatory authorities. In short, health plans need to be reassured that they can profitably participate in the new system.

As noted, exchanges can take one of two approaches in contracting with health plans: either accepting all comers or choosing only those that offer high-value bids. If the decision is to selectively contract, the exchange will have to decide how many plans should be included in the exchange and what characteristics they should have. Getting desirable, prestigious plans in the exchange may be more of a problem than keeping unwanted plans out. If the number of plans wanting to participate is large, how many should be selected? The number should be large enough to ensure real choice, especially if some of the health plans do not have broadly overlapping provider networks. People do not like to be forced to change providers, so it is desirable to offer enough choices that few people are forced to change providers in order to purchase through the exchange. In addition, the number should be large enough to engender vigorous price competition. In making plan choices, consumers give weight to price differences; thus, plans have incentives to compete on price.

A case could be made for limiting the number of plans, however, to reduce the complexity of choice for consumers and the administrative costs for the exchange. Moreover, if the number of plans is relatively small, each plan has the potential to enroll many people, creating a situation where the health plans have strong incentives to offer an attractive price to gain business.

Even if the exchange chooses to limit the number of participating health plans, it should always keep open the option of allowing additional plans in. In fact, this should be the expectation, and whenever rebidding is done, nonparticipating plans should be encouraged to bid. The exchange should avoid the situation of becoming a captive of the health plans that currently participate.

Designing Benefit Packages

Plan design has two elements: medical services covered and extent of consumer cost sharing. Although there is a growing consensus about most of the medical services that should be included in a comprehensive benefit package, there is still disagreement about marginal services. Every provider group wants its services included as part of the minimal package. How to structure cost sharing is also controversial. Advocates of consumer-driven plans favor high deductibles and copayments to encourage consumer cost consciousness. Others view such plans as providing inadequate protection and as leaving consumers excessively exposed to financial hardships. Of course, if the exchange is part of a reform that includes subsidies, the more generous the minimum benefit package, the greater the cost to the state of financing the subsidies.

Whatever the decision regarding the comprehensiveness of the benefit structure, the advice from exchange officials who have been through this process is to involve the health plans in the early stages. They will have ideas about the specifics of plan design. It will be important to know the direction in which the market as a whole is going with respect to benefits even if the exchange decides to set its own course, and the health plans will be able to provide that context. The insurers will also need time to adapt to the exchange's requirements; doing so may involve some administrative burdens for the insurers, and they will probably need to file their plans with insurance regulators.

Another policy decision involves how many different benefit packages the exchange should offer. On the one hand, if the exchange offers only a few standardized plans, consumers will have an easier time comparing the relative values of the plans offered by different insurers, which creates a favorable environment for vigorous competition. Each year, each individual can compare all of the plan offerings and choose the one that offers the best value. So insurers have strong incentives to compete on price, service level, and quality. But this works well only if individuals assessing the options can easily and meaningfully compare the various offerings. If the benefit packages are not standardized or even if there is an excessive number of standardized plans, the task of comparing the value of the different plans is much more difficult; there are just too many variables to keep in mind. The evidence shows that when people are faced with too many options, they resort to choice-limiting techniques that are not consistent with economists' view of rational decision making.

On the other hand, people value choice, and some variation in benefits may be desirable. One way to achieve elements of both is to have every insurer offer the standard set(s) of benefits, but then allow them to offer add-ons—for example, dental or vision coverage—priced separately from the main benefit plan. It is important that such "riders" be separately priced so that potential enrollees are still able to compare different plans' standardized benefits base without the riders.

Recruiting Agents and Brokers

Experience with previous exchanges shows that agents and brokers play a crucial role in attracting business to the exchange. Because small employers do not have specialized personnel to negotiate and administer a health insurance plan, they depend heavily on the advice and expertise of their insurance agents and brokers. If agents and brokers do not bring the exchange to an employer's attention, the employer is unlikely to buy coverage from the exchange. In addition, if agents and brokers are not part of the exchange's marketing plan, they are likely to be hostile, which will hurt the exchange's ability to attract small employers. Disgruntled agents and brokers may also steer higher-risk people to the exchange, which would exacerbate any adverse selection that the exchange might experience. The exchange offers some features that can help agents and brokers sell coverage, particularly the individual-choice feature. Both employers and employees like the fact that if the employer chooses to buy coverage from the exchange, the employer does not have to force employees into any particular plan. This feature of exchange coverage also makes it easier for employers to contribute to employee health premiums on a defined-contribution basis, thereby making it somewhat easier for employers to limit their cost exposure as premiums rise. Partly for these reasons, employers are less likely to switch to a new carrier at the end of a plan year, which means that the agent enjoys higher retention rates and lower servicing costs.

Once again, experience shows that it is important to involve brokers and agents early in the process—to sell them on the idea and to educate them about the product and the potential markets. The exchange will need to make software available to the agents so that they can easily and quickly provide price quotations to employers.

Marketing and Education

Experience shows even though the exchange is offering coverage with advantages for employers and employees, this is no guarantee that large numbers of employers will take up the offer. Of course, the situation is different if there is an individual mandate in force, requiring people to buy coverage, especially if subsidies are available only to people who purchase through the exchange. If the mandate is not part of the reform package, the exchange will need to have a marketing strategy to bring in as many employers as possible to be assured of being large enough to realize administrative economies of scale and to have bargaining power with health plans.

Past exchanges have tried a variety of marketing approaches, and there is no clear evidence that one particular approach is most effective. Some of the more-successful exchanges have had relationships with organizations already known and trusted by businesses, such as chambers of commerce. The exchange will need to hire a marketing firm to develop a strategy that suits the exchange's environment. The conclusion other exchanges have reached is that they need more money than they have had to carry out a really effective marketing campaign.

Rating Practices

An important issue for the exchange will be the degree to which it restricts insurers' ability to vary premium rates based on history or on the characteristics of insured individuals and groups. Advocates of exchanges sometimes see the exchange as a mechanism for offering more-affordable coverage for higher-risk individuals and groups. They support the exchange as a vehicle for pooling risk—bringing together higher-risk and lower-risk people and spreading the costs evenly among them through some form of community rating. Unfortunately, the exchange cannot be more lenient in its risk-rating practices than the rest of the market. Essentially, the exchange must adopt the same rules for determining the conditions under which people will be allowed into the risk pool and the prices they will pay based on their risk. If the insurers outside the exchange rate on the basis of age, location, and prior claims experience, for example, the exchange insurers must do the same. If the exchange adopts more lenient rules—for example, using community rating while the rest of the market rates on the basis of individual or group risk—the exchange insurers will end up with a disproportionate share of high-risk enrollees. High-risk people would get a better deal by buying exchange-based coverage because they will not be penalized for being higher risk, while lower-risk people can get a more favorable price by going outside the exchange, where the price they pay is based on their lower risk. Under these conditions, the exchange would become a victim of adverse selection: Its claims costs and thus its premiums would rise, the lower-risk people would leave to get a better deal outside the exchange, and the exchange could become financially unviable.

Similarly, if those buying coverage outside the exchange are subject to exclusions and waiting periods for prior conditions, the exchange should follow the same practices. The rules change *in a system in which everyone is mandated to have coverage,* as is the case in Massachusetts. There is no need to have preexisting-condition exclusions or waiting periods inside or outside the exchange. These are in place at present to prevent people from waiting until they become ill or know they need expensive services to enroll in a health plan. Under a mandate, people cannot delay getting coverage in this way; they will normally have continuous coverage. Likewise, community rating becomes practical for the market as a whole. Even though rates would increase for lower-risk people as they decrease for higher-risk people, the lower-risk people do not have the option of dropping out of the market, which is what creates adverse selection against the market in a voluntary environment.

As noted earlier, one way to avoid adverse selection against the exchange is for the exchange to enroll a population that does not have the option of going elsewhere for coverage. If an exchange is established as part of a reform that includes subsidies, and subsidies are available only to people who use the exchange as their source of coverage, the exchange could adopt more lenient rating rules for those eligible for subsidies. If the subsidies are relatively large and available only through the exchange, people who are eligible for those subsidies, even low-risk individuals, will always get a better deal by staying with the exchange.

Although exchanges are thought of as sources of coverage for small employers and perhaps individuals, some analysts have advocated allowing larger employers to opt for exchange-based coverage. The advantage from the exchanges' standpoint would be that the inclusion of these firms would enhance the exchange's bargaining power with insurers. But if the participation of larger firms is permitted, the question arises about how they should be rated. The danger is that if the exchange-based coverage is favorably priced relative to the market as a whole, the exchange would be most attractive to larger firms with a disproportionately high-risk population. Including them in the risk pool on the same basis as other employers could cause an increase in average premiums. Thus, it may be desirable for the exchange to permit them to participate but to require that they pay a premium that reflects the risk of their unique population rather than pooling them with the entire exchange population.

Risk Adjustment

If the exchange adopts the same rating rules as those that apply outside the exchange, the exchange as a whole will be reasonably protected against adverse selection. This does not mean that individual insurers participating in the exchange will not attract enrollees of different levels of risk. Adverse selection for some insurers can be the result of chance, a reputation for being good at treating particular serious illnesses, differences in marketing practices, and so forth. Of course, if some participating insurers enroll a disproportionate share of less-healthy people, their costs will be high and they will not be able to compete unless this disadvantage is somehow offset.

Risk adjustment can offset the effects of enrolling a favorable or unfavorable mix of enrollees. Money is transferred from insurers that enroll a disproportionate share of lower-risk enrollees to those that enroll a disproportionate share of higher-risk enrollees. A perfect risk-adjustment mechanism would completely eliminate any economic disadvantage to enrolling higher-risk people or any advantage to enrolling lower-risk people. It would eliminate incentives for insurers to seek out low-risk enrollees and avoid higher-risk enrollees. Of course, there is nothing approaching a perfect risk-adjustment mechanism because no system can predict the level of medical expenditures a particular population will incur. But even a "good" approach can give insurers greater confidence that they will not be put at a severe economic disadvantage if they attract older, sicker enrollees.

A discussion of the administrative issues involved in developing and putting in place a risk-adjustment mechanism is far beyond my scope here. To a considerable extent, the degree of difficulty will depend on the intricacy and sophistication of the mechanism for measuring risk differences. There is a trade-off between administrative simplicity and accuracy in predicting medical expense.

A National Exchange

To this point, the discussion of exchanges has assumed that they would be established at the state level. However, many analysts and policy makers who have proposed programs for national health reform have also included exchanges as a critical element of their plans. In fact, the success of the Federal Employees Health Benefits Program has led some to suggest that this national exchange be opened up as a source of coverage for people besides federal employees.

Although some of the administrative and policy issues that arise in establishing state-based exchanges apply to national exchanges, the order of magnitude is so different that many of the issues, problems, and solutions have to be rethought. A thorough discussion of how to address all the issues is beyond the scope of this chapter, but it is useful at least to identify the key issues and to show the nature of the problems related to establishing an exchange at the national level.

Problems will differ depending on whether national reform includes an individual mandate requiring everyone to have some form of coverage. Under a mandate, the number of people getting coverage would be much larger, which obviously would add to the administrative challenge. There are other differences as well.

Risk-Rating Challenges

From a policy perspective, perhaps the biggest challenge is to avoid having the exchange become a victim of severe adverse selection. If the exchange is open to any employer or any individual, people will choose the exchange if the cost for comparable coverage is cheaper than what they would have to pay elsewhere. From the standpoint of political acceptance, it is difficult to envision how the federal exchange could charge substantially higher premiums to higher-risk people than to lower-risk people. The exchange would almost certainly have to provide coverage on a guaranteed-issue basis and adopt some form of community rating that did not result in higher-risk or older people paying substantially more than those who posed a lower level of risk. Otherwise, it would fail to correct some of the major deficiencies of the current insurance system, which is presumably the point of undertaking the reform. Many states do have rating rules that allow substantial variance in premiums depending on the risk of the individual or group seeking insurance. Under those circumstances, higher-risk individuals and groups would find the federal exchange to be less costly and would gravitate to it, leaving it with a disproportionate share of high-risk enrollees and raising the cost of providing coverage well above that of the average for the nation. Unless the federal government were willing to subsidize this adverse selection, coverage through the exchange could become unaffordable for many people, and the purpose of having the exchange would be thwarted.

The danger of attracting high-risk individuals would be acute if any employee could opt out of employer coverage and take his or her employer's contribution to the federal exchange. Employers would have incentives to encourage or even offer financial incentives to high-risk employees to do that to improve the risk profile of the group and lower the employer's health insurance bill.

Even if the federal exchange were to adopt rating rules that allowed variation based on the risk of the applicant, rating rules in some states would allow more variation, again making the federal exchange a more desirable source of coverage for high-risk people from those states. This problem would likely arise whether or not an individual mandate were in force unless federal policy makers required all states to adopt uniform risk-rating laws for health insurance. Then, as long as the federal exchange used the same risk-rating standards, it would not be likely to become the victim of severe adverse selection. Without a mandate, however, rating laws would have to permit some rate variation based age, at minimum; otherwise, low-risk individuals would likely often not buy coverage because of the high cost relative to their expected expenditures for medical services. Of course, if a mandate were in force, they would not have this option, so it would be possible to impose community rating on the entire national market. Such a policy could cause severe sticker shock for lower-risk individuals and groups and for those in geographic areas with low medical costs.

From an administrative standpoint, if the exchange employed any kind of risk rating, that would add to the administrative burden. However, if age and geographic location were the only rating factors, the task would not be especially difficult.

Eligibility for the Exchange

Another major policy issue with implications for administrative complexity would be who is permitted to use the national exchange for coverage. If it is open to anyone, the size of the administrative task is obviously greater than if only a portion of the population can use the exchange. One option would be to make it the source—perhaps the sole source—of coverage for individuals (perhaps only those without access to employer coverage) and small firms (perhaps those with twenty-five or fewer employees). If it were so limited, the exchange would have to employ a mechanism to ensure that the applicants met the eligibility criteria. Another option would be to make the exchange the source of coverage for all those who receive subsidies designed to make private insurance more affordable. This policy would make it less likely that the exchange would experience adverse selection.

The administrative tasks of an exchange include the following:

- *Education.* Providing potential applicants with information about the insurance policy and health plan options along with information to compare cost and quality of competing health plans and their provider networks.
- *Enrollment.* Enrolling individuals and/or groups and maintaining enrollment rolls.
- *Premium administration.* Collecting premiums and distributing proper amounts to health plans based on their enrollment.

The federal government has experience with these tasks through Medicare and the Federal Employees Health Benefits Program, but the administrative tasks would be larger and different for a national exchange with the whole population as potential enrollees. Just getting the information about options out to the entire population would be a major challenge. How could everyone be contacted? It would presumably be possible to have the post office deliver information to every mailbox.

Maintaining enrollment information as people move, change names, die, move from employer to employer, drop out of the labor force, and so forth would be a massive undertaking, perhaps not different in character from what large insurers do but certainly on a much larger scale. In addition, insurers are usually dealing with employer groups with a defined membership, where the employer has accurate information on who is in the group along with their contact information.

How would premiums be collected? When employers use the exchange as a source of coverage, presumably the employer would send in both the employer and employee share. A different approach would be needed for people who enrolled as individuals. What would the exchange do if a premium is simply not paid? How would the exchange know if the employer went out of business or just failed to pay, and how would the rights of the individual employee be protected in either case?

Perhaps none of these potential problems is different from those a state-based exchange would have to face, but the magnitude of the task makes the administrative challenge more difficult. Some decentralization of administration might be a good way to address this challenge. If the federal exchange is coupled with a requirement that all citizens acquire coverage—an individual mandate—the tasks are even more complicated.

Conclusion

Policy makers and analysts tend to agree that the small-group and individual insurance markets often do not perform particularly well. Along with all insured people, people in these markets bear the burden of paying the high premiums that reflect ever-increasing costs of medical care. For people in these markets, coverage is even pricier than for those buying in the large-group market. In addition, high-risk people are especially vulnerable to being priced out of the market.

The problem of controlling health care costs requires solutions that go well beyond structural reforms of insurance markets. Even if insurance markets worked better, it is likely that the underlying costs of medical care would remain too high to make insurance affordable for many people. For such people, only substantial subsidies of some form or other will make the purchase of coverage feasible. Alternatively, some structural changes in the insurance markets may help to alleviate the cost problem for people who are in the higher-risk categories and make the markets function more smoothly and efficiently, with some prospect for improved cost control. I have examined six such strategies. While all show some promise of dealing with parts of the problem, it is evident that they will be much more effective in adding to the number of people with coverage if they are combined in creative ways. From an administrative standpoint, it is critical that any such combination be considered as a whole, because the administrative and structural elements need to be coordinated and crafted with careful attention to their interactions, both to enhance the chances for success and to avoid unnecessary administrative burdens and duplication.

2

Designing Regional Health Markets

Cori E. Uccello, John M. Bertko, and Catherine M. Murphy-Baron

Many proposals to expand health insurance coverage rely on the creation of regional health markets to provide a centralized place for purchasing coverage. As envisioned, these regional health markets would offer insurance plans from one or more insurers to individuals and small groups. Creation of these new markets could also entail changing the rules on how health insurance is offered and regulated. For instance, the newly enacted health insurance plan in Massachusetts combines the state's individual and small-group markets and creates a new regional health market through a connector mechanism. The Health Connector, an independent public authority, serves as an additional marketplace for individuals and small employer groups. The Health Connector defines—for the regional health market—what coverage is offered, determines what subsidies are provided, establishes criteria for insurers to participate, creates coverage-comparison and enrollment tools, and reviews insurer performance. How well these arrangements can increase affordable health insurance coverage depends on how these mechanisms are designed and administered. This chapter discusses, from an actuarial perspective, issues that need to be considered when designing regional health markets.

Pooling Issues

Risk pooling is the mechanism that insurers use to spread the costs of medical care. Risk pools are large groups of individuals (or employer groups) whose medical costs are combined in order to calculate premiums (American Academy of Actuaries 2006). Some individuals are expected to have high medical costs and others low medical costs in a given year. Individuals also have costs that vary over time; low-cost individuals in one year may move to high-cost status in a later year, due to the onset of a new disease, an accident, or a flare-up of a chronic disease. Pooling the risks allows costs of the unhealthy to be subsidized by the healthy. Indeed, a cross-section of risks is essential for a viable insurance pool. In general, the larger the risk pool, the more predictable and stable premiums can be, because costs of those with very high health care spending can be spread over other individuals in the pool, with little impact on the premium. In contrast, an individual with high costs in a small pool can significantly impact the average costs of that group, resulting in claim fluctuations from year to year.

On its own, however, creating large risks pools will not necessarily lower premiums. Premiums reflect the relative risk and cost of pool participants. If a pool has a disproportionate share of less-healthy participants, it will have higher premiums. If it is comprised more of healthier participants, it will have lower premiums. Therefore, if a pool attracts those with higher expected claims—in other words, adverse selection—premiums could increase dramatically.

Pools created as a by-product of membership in a group formed for reasons other than obtaining health insurance tend to be less subject to adverse selection than pools created specifically to obtain health insurance. For instance, a large employer often creates its own health insurance pool to provide coverage to its workers. Workers join the pool as an incidental benefit of employment. The employer makes most of the decisions regarding the level and choice of benefits, limiting the decisions (and thereby the ability to select benefits adversely) of individual workers.

In contrast, when people purchase coverage in the individual health insurance market, the resulting insurance pools are formed to obtain health insurance coverage, not as an incidental by-product of other reasons for the group's formation. Therefore, risk pools made up of those in the individual health insurance market are much more subject to adverse selection—people are more likely to purchase coverage if and when they think they will need it. Premiums reflect the expected experience of the group as a whole, although premiums can vary across individuals within the pool (e.g., by age, gender, area, or health status) depending on insurer practices, state laws, and regulations. Whenever permitted, insurers exclude applicants with the worst health conditions, producing lower premiums for other applicants.

In between these two extremes are insurance pools comprised of small and medium-size employers. The employers are not large enough to form their own pools, so insurers combine groups to form a larger pool. Although there is less potential for adverse selection compared to that in the individual market, small employers, especially those with fewer than, say, ten employees, can still select against insurers by moving into and out of the insurance market and from carrier to carrier. Premiums for small groups are based on the combined experience of the pool but can vary among groups, again based on insurer practices, state laws, and regulations.

With respect to regional health market insurance pools, it is important to consider risk-pool size, and also how membership in the pool is comprised. For example, if two pools have the same total number of members, claim costs for the pool covering fewer groups (but having more members per group) will likely be more stable than the one covering many groups (but having fewer members per group). A large-group pool is formed based on a very small number of purchase decisions. Small-group and individual pools are formed based on scores of separate purchase decisions. Each of these decisions presents an opportunity for adverse selection.

Adverse Selection

When health insurance is voluntary and is not merely the incidental by-product of other processes, it is subject to adverse selection based on asymmetric knowledge of health conditions. That is, those in poor health (who have this knowledge) are more likely to purchase coverage, and to purchase more generous coverage in particular. As a result, premiums increase to cover the impact of this selection. As premiums are set higher to reflect the higher costs of enrollees, even fewer new applicants or existing healthy enrollees are willing to pay them, further increasing the selection effects and the average premium per enrollee. Increasing overall participation in regional health market plans, in particular among those with average or lower-than-average claim costs, would be one of the most effective ways to minimize adverse selection. That way, there will be enough healthy participants over which to spread the costs of those with high health care costs. Potential options to help address adverse selection include:

- *Mandating coverage.* Adverse selection is caused in large part because health insurance is voluntary. Individuals compare the perceived value of the coverage to premiums and expected out-of-pocket payments. Those who do not believe that health insurance provides enough value (expected payment of medical costs) for their premium dollars do not purchase coverage. Healthy individuals choose not to participate if they do not believe they will get any benefits from participating. Mandating that individuals purchase health insurance will address this issue. Massachusetts, for example, has mandated that its residents be covered by health insurance, and those who are not must pay a penalty. For such a mandate to be effective, significant penalties and enforcement mechanisms may be required.
- *Premium subsidies.* By reducing the net premium costs faced by consumers, premium subsidies increase the number of eligible individuals who expect their likely benefit from the program to exceed the premium cost. This would increase enrollment, as was the case for Medicare Part D membership, which was highly subsidized.
- *"Default" enrollment.* Making enrollment in a regional health plan the default option (i.e., individuals desiring not to be in the program would have to take a step to opt out) would increase enrollment. Medicare Part B enrollment operates this way. It would not be appropriate to designate a particular plan in the regional health market as the default plan, however. Instead, methods would need to be developed to assign individuals who do not choose a specific plan to the various plans.
- *Penalty for delay.* Mandating that health coverage be available on a guaranteed-issue basis would ensure that all individuals have access to coverage, regardless of health status. However, this requirement could encourage people to delay purchasing insurance until they expect to incur health costs or to drop

coverage when they do not believe they need it, only to purchase it again later when they have new health care needs. Limiting guaranteed issue to an initial open enrollment period (perhaps with infrequent short future periods), or providing some other meaningful penalty for late enrollment (e.g., higher premiums, lower benefits, or long waiting periods for coverage), would encourage individuals with low health care spending to consider their future needs and protect themselves by purchasing and retaining coverage.

• *Risk adjustment.* In the absence of universal coverage, some degree of adverse selection is inevitable. Risk adjustment or other types of risk sharing, such as reinsurance arrangements, can reduce the incentives an insurer might have to avoid enrolling high-risk individuals.

Regional health markets could also be subject to adverse selection if the rules governing the issue and premium rating for plans in the market are different from those for plans that are operating outside of the regional market.

Issue and Rating Rules

Issue and rating rules attempt to balance the somewhat competing goals of access to health insurance and premium affordability. These rules vary by state, sometimes dramatically. A new regional health market's issue and rating rules, and how these rules compare to existing state rules, impact enrollment, adverse selection, and premiums.

Insurance can be issued on a guaranteed-issue basis or it can be underwritten. With guaranteed issue, everyone who applies for insurance coverage must be accepted, regardless of health status. The advantage of this method is that unhealthy individuals have access to coverage that they might otherwise be denied. However, guaranteed issue alone will not ensure that coverage is affordable for the unhealthy if premiums are allowed to vary by health status. In the absence of an individual mandate, guaranteed issue gives individuals an incentive to put off purchasing coverage until they have immediate health care needs. This would exacerbate adverse selection, and, in turn, increase premiums.

Allowing insurers to underwrite would remove some of the perverse incentives arising from guaranteed issue. Insurers could deny coverage to applicants they deem to be at risk for high health care costs or to exclude certain conditions from coverage. This may encourage individuals to purchase coverage while they are still healthy, especially if their premiums reflect their good health status. However, allowing insurers to decline coverage will leave many without access to health insurance. And unless there is a separate and adequately funded high-risk pool for those who would otherwise be denied coverage, allowing for underwriting may be incompatible with the imposition of an individual mandate.

There are three general approaches to premium rating—pure community rating, modified (or adjusted) community rating, and health-status rating. With pure community rating, each individual is charged the same premium, regardless of expected medical costs. Premiums cannot vary by age, gender, or health status. Premiums can vary by family composition (e.g., single versus family coverage), and in some instances premium variations by geographic area are allowed. Among rating methods, pure community rating spreads the risks most broadly and has the highest degree of cross-subsidization, with the healthy risks subsidizing the costs of the unhealthy risks. In other words, pure community rating lowers the premiums for the high risks and raises them for the lower risks. This can work to exacerbate adverse selection and produce higher premiums for all participants, however, especially if coverage is on guaranteed-issue basis without an individual mandate. Such a degree of cross-subsidization can also be considered unfair to younger members, who generally have lower levels of pay and would pay a higher percentage of income to be covered. A second consideration in pure community rating is whether there should be any financial incentives or penalties used to promote healthier lifestyles (e.g., smoking cessation or weight loss).

Under modified community rating, premiums cannot vary by health status, but they can vary by other factors, for example, age and gender. Everyone with the same demographic characteristics faces the same premium, regardless of health status. This reduces cross-subsidization of risks to some degree and can reduce adverse selection, relative to pure community rating.

Under health-status rating, individuals can be charged different premiums, not only based on demographic characteristics, such as age and gender, but also based on health status, at least at the time of issue. Even with health-status rating, however, there may be limitations regarding how much the premiums for one individual can vary from those of another. Under health-status rating, there is less spreading of risk between the healthy and the unhealthy, and premiums charged are more closely correlated to an individual's own expected risk. Healthy individuals face lower premiums than do those who are unhealthy. This reduces adverse selection but may make premiums less affordable for those in worse health.

When designing the insurance issue and rating rules of a regional health market, it is also important to understand how these rules compare with a state's current rules, particularly those applicable to the individual and small-group markets. This is true if the regional health market will operate alongside a state's already existing market, rather than in place of the current market. State rules cover the spectrum, from guaranteed issue to fully underwritten, and from pure community rating to health-status rating. In addition, the rules applicable to the individual market could differ somewhat from those applicable to the small-group market. (Federal law, however, requires policies in the small-group market to be sold on a guaranteed-issue basis.)

If the issue and rating rules of the regional health market differ from those in the existing state market, either the regional market or the existing market could be adversely affected. If the regional health market rules are stricter, that is, if they have more limits, than those in the existing state market, individuals in worse health will tend to migrate to the plans in the regional health market. For instance, if a regional health market operates under guaranteed-issue and pure-community-rating rules, but the existing state rules allow for underwriting and health-status rating, then those in worse health will find it easier to obtain coverage—and perhaps more affordable coverage—in the regional health market. Over time, the regional health market premiums will increase to reflect this, leading to more adverse selection in the regional health market, threatening its viability. The opposite could occur if the regional health market's rules are less strict than those in the existing state market.

Another consideration is how the regional health markets define a small group and how this definition would compare to the state's definition. Most states define small groups as those having two to fifty employees, but some define small groups to include "groups of one." This can have implications due to the guaranteed-issue rules in the small-group market. If individuals are allowed to define themselves as a group of one and qualify as a small group, they can gain access to guaranteed-issued coverage. This can drive up the premiums of small-group coverage due to adverse selection. Similarly, if the regional health markets permit individuals to qualify for small-group coverage on a guaranteed-issue basis, those plans will be subject to increased risk of adverse selection if the existing state rules require small groups to have at least two employees.

Benefit Package Requirements for a Regional Health Market

Setting the benefit package requirements is one of the most challenging tasks for implementing a regional health market. The desire to offer comprehensive coverage must be balanced with the need to make the benefit plan affordable both to consumers and to the government, which will likely subsidize coverage for at least some participants. Many factors need to be considered.

Minimum Benefit or Standard Benefit Package

To ensure that plans offered in the regional health market offer a reasonable level of coverage, either a minimum benefit package can be specified, or insurers can be required to submit bids on a standard benefit package. Both options have advantages and disadvantages. With a minimum benefit package, qualified insurers may submit a bid either for the exact minimum benefits, or for actuarially equivalent minimum benefits (e.g., substituting copays for coinsurance with the same actuarial value), or for a package with enhanced benefits that exceed the minimum benefit package. For instance, Medicare Part D requires a minimum benefit package.

The minimum-benefit-package approach has the advantage of allowing for flexibility in the design and delivery of benefits that may reflect members' preferences for certain benefit combinations. For example, many people prefer known copays (e.g., a $20 copay for an office visit) to the uncertainty of the costs of a deductible and coinsurance for the same visit. In addition, an insurer can tailor benefits to quickly reflect the need to better manage certain services, for example, increasing the copay for emergency room visits while offsetting that cost increase by reduced copays for primary care visits. A major disadvantage of this approach is that it may be difficult for consumers to compare benefits across benefit packages. However, all benefit packages would be actuarially certified to meet or exceed the minimum benefit level.

Mandating that only a standardized benefit package may be offered would facilitate plan comparisons; rather than choosing among different benefit designs, consumers would choose plans based on cost, provider networks, customer service, and care management requirements. Some government purchasers, such as CalPERS, use a standardized benefit approach for their purchasing decisions. Disadvantages include the lack of flexibility, as insurers must offer only the standard package and cannot readily change benefit provisions to meet cost challenges or changes in medical practice patterns. Like Medigap, which had its benefits standardized in the early 1990s, benefit packages may become obsolete. Similarly, standardized benefits may not meet consumer preferences—some may prefer and may be able to pay for benefit enhancements.

A third option is a hybrid: Qualified insurers would always be required to offer the standard package but would be allowed to offer enhanced benefit packages that exceed the standard. No insurer would be allowed to offer a package that was below the standard plan.

Regardless of whether standard benefit plans or minimum benefit requirements apply, the issue of supplemental benefit options arises. If the benefit plan has large cost-sharing requirements, some participants may wish to purchase supplemental benefit insurance. Issues that would need to be considered include whether there should be rules for the types of supplemental benefits offered (e.g., whether there should be at least some minimum cost sharing), whether offering supplemental options would be limited to connector-qualifying bidders or whether nonqualified insurers could also offer packages, and how the connector would minimize the possible risk selection that might occur with supplemental offerings.

What Services Are to Be Included?

An important but potentially contentious issue is what services are to be offered and at what cost-sharing levels. The need to keep benefit packages affordable may require the use of high deductibles or high coinsurance. However, the question of whether all services are to be covered remains. To keep costs reasonable, some services may need to be excluded from coverage. For instance, some mandated benefits, such as in vitro fertilization, are quite costly and could potentially be a target for exclusion. In addition, benefits could exclude treatments not proven through evidence-based medicine criteria, especially for high-cost but unproven treatments. Ancillary benefits such as dental or vision care services might also be excluded.

Another way to determine which services should be included is to consider the value of some amount of first-dollar or low-cost limited services. The value of providing certain preventive care benefits (e.g., mammography, immunization) is generally accepted. Beyond those benefits proved by evidence-based-medicine, there are arguments in favor of including a limited package of primary care services that would be provided with low copays (e.g., a certain number of primary care visits per year or a full package of well-child visits). Higher-cost services, such as a visit to an emergency room or a hospital admission, would still be subject to the benefit package deductible. In theory, use of proven preventive care or primary care services in place of expensive hospital-based treatments might result in lower costs.

What Part of the Market Should Serve as a Guide for Benefit Packages?

Since a regional health market will likely serve those in the individual or small-group markets, it may be reasonable to look to the current benefit packages actually chosen, not just offered, today in these markets. The individual market might be characterized by the choice of high-deductible preferred provider organization (PPO) plans for the most part, with deductibles ranging from $1,500 to $5,000. While the small-group market also has high-deductible packages, these deductibles are frequently somewhat lower, most often in the $1,000 to $2,500 range, than those in the individual market. Last, because affordability is a key issue, and a connector generally will not serve the large-group market, the richer benefit plans with lower cost sharing common in the large-group market may not be fiscally feasible or needed.

Spending as a Percentage of Income

It is also important to consider how much participants should be expected to spend, as it has implications for the amount of government subsidies for low-income participants as well as affordability for those not subsidized. Linda Blumberg et al. (2007) recommend that benchmark affordability standards reflect total out-of-pocket health spending (including premiums, deductibles, coinsurance, and copays) as a share of income for privately insured people with incomes above a set minimum (e.g., 300 percent of the federal poverty level). Then, for lower income levels, spending above this share could be subsidized. This method can also be used to help set benefit package requirements: Working backward from an acceptable level of spending, a level of benefits for a minimum or standard benefits package can be determined.

Risk Sharing

Insurers face many financial risks. As discussed, they face the adverse selection risks associated with overall participation rates in the regional health market.

They can face plan-specific adverse selection as well; that is, their plans could attract a less-healthy group of participants relative to other plans. Plans can also be subject to risks associated with pricing the plan inadequately. A major goal of implementing regional health markets is to reduce the number of uninsured. However, it may be difficult for insurers to price plans targeted to the uninsured given that they lack data on health spending for the uninsured. Moreover, future spending by the newly insured could increase once they obtain coverage, but it is unclear how large that increase would be. Understating premiums could result in large losses to private insurers. Overstating premiums could result in large gains to the insurers, could reduce participation in the plan, or both. In addition to these risks, insurers can also face the risk of incurring unexpected high-cost claims.

Each of these risks can result in financial losses for an insurer. If risks are too high, insurers will opt not to participate in the market. Risk-sharing provisions, such as risk adjustment, risk corridors, and reinsurance, can be used to mitigate some of these risks and thus encourage insurer participation. These provisions are used in the Medicare prescription drug program to limit financial risks that insurers bear. Similar mechanisms could be used in a regional health market.

Risk Adjustment

Even if adverse selection is minimized as a whole, a plan could end up with a disproportionate share of insureds with high health care costs. If plan premiums do not reflect this, the plan could be at risk for large losses. As a result, plans could develop strategies to avoid enrolling less-healthy individuals. Risk adjustment could be used to adjust the payments to all plans in the regional health market to take into account plan participants' health status. Risk adjustment helps to make payments to competing plans more equitable and can reduce the incentives for competing plans to avoid individuals with higher-than-average health care needs. Risk adjustment may also help stabilize the experience among private plans, causing less disruption for plan participants.

Risk-adjustment mechanisms have been developed for use in the Medicaid and Medicare programs. Although currently not used widely in the private insurance market, they could be adapted for use in a regional health market. With risk adjustment, payments would flow from plans that disproportionately enroll individuals with low expected health costs to those that enroll a higher percentage of individuals with high expected costs. Risk-adjusted payments could be based on demographic information (e.g., age, gender), as well as health indicators (e.g., health status, diagnoses) and health care usage (e.g., inpatient or outpatient claims, prescription drug usage). Importantly, however, although risk adjustment can help account for the differences in participant health status across plans, no current risk-adjustment system is designed to compensate each competitor for the full financial effects of adverse selection.

Risk Corridors

Risk corridors can be used to mitigate pricing risk by limiting an insurer's potential losses. More specifically, the government would provide a subsidy if losses exceed a certain percentage. Risk corridors can also be used to limit an insurer's gains to avoid windfall profits—plans would pay the government if their gains exceeded a certain percentage. In a typical arrangement, a best estimate of the plan's premium would be made. Gains or losses inside a risk corridor around that estimated level would be the full responsibility of the insurer. Additional gains or losses beyond the risk corridor would be shared with or borne by the government. Risk corridors may be more appropriate during the first few years of a new program, when less expenditure data are available. However, as more data become available on the health spending patterns of the newly insured, the ability to accurately set premiums should increase, thereby reducing the need for risk corridors. Note that risk corridors do not necessarily have to be two-sided, protecting against both over- and underestimates of premiums. They can be one-sided, to limit only an insurer's losses but not its gains (or vice versa). With two-sided corridors, however, insurer gains could be used by the government to subsidize insurer losses.

The Medicare Part D prescription drug program contains symmetric risk corridors and provides an illustration of how they could work in a regional health market. Prescription drug plans set their target premium. In 2006 and 2007, if actual plan costs came within ±2.5 percent of the target, the plan bore the loss or kept the gains. If actual costs fell outside the 2.5 percent corridor, the government shared in the gains or losses. In other words, the government paid the plan if costs were more than expected, and the plan paid the government if costs were lower than expected. The government bore 75 percent of the spending between ±2.5 and 5 percent of the target and 80 percent of the spending that was ±5.0 percent of the target. Over time, the Medicare Part D risk-sharing thresholds widen and the government risk-bearing percentages decrease.

It is not clear, however, that risk corridors are needed for regional health insurance markets, because pricing risk might not be a significant concern. Private insurers have a great deal of data on and experience with pricing health insurance plans. In comparison, potential Medicare prescription drug plans had less to go on when pricing stand-alone prescription drug plans. Even though fewer data are available on the health spending patterns of the uninsured, insurers may be able to estimate based on spending patterns among the insured with similar characteristics. Nevertheless, risk corridors could encourage competition in new regional health markets by limiting the downside risk for insurers entering this market, especially during the early years.

Reinsurance

Reinsurance is another option to limit insurers' downside risk. Two types of reinsurance are available: aggregate reinsurance, which provides protection against pricing risk, and individual reinsurance, which provides protection against unexpected high-cost claims.

Under aggregate reinsurance, the government would pay all or a percentage of claims once a plan's aggregate claims paid exceeded a predetermined threshold. This threshold is typically expressed as a percentage of aggregate expected claims (e.g., a first-year aggregate limit might be 102 percent of projected incurred claims). Government-subsidized aggregate reinsurance protection is similar to a one-sided risk corridor—insurers would keep all of the gains if actual claims were lower than expected but would bear the losses only up to a certain point if spending was greater than expected. Aggregate reinsurance may be easier to administer than risk corridors, but it may not address the incentives needed to tightly manage the costs of high-cost claimants. However, pricing risk might not be a significant problem for plans in a regional health insurance market, meaning aggregate reinsurance may not be necessary.

Individual reinsurance protects plans from unusually high claims from individual participants. Health insurance spending can be quite skewed, with a very small share of insureds incurring very high health care costs. Plans that cover one or more of these individuals could incur financial losses. Under government-subsidized individual reinsurance, the government would pay all or a percentage of claims once an individual enrollee's claims exceeded a predetermined threshold, typically expressed as a dollar amount, such as $50,000. Individual reinsurance could protect the plan against financial losses from unexpected high claims. In addition, it could lower plan premiums by reducing the amount insurers already build into the premium to cover expected high claims, as long as the government does not charge its costs back to the insurance industry via assessments or other taxes. The amount of premium savings depends on the threshold level set. Any premium savings would be on a one-time-only basis, however, unless other measures were taken to control the growth in health costs.

It is also important to note that insurers already have access to private reinsurance. The difference here would be that rather than paying reinsurance premiums to a private reinsurer and then getting reimbursed for any high-cost claims, the government would simply reimburse the plan for any high-cost claims. Also, although reinsurance would reduce the cost to insurers of high-cost individuals, it would not increase access to health insurance for individuals who insurers deem uninsurable, if underwriting is allowed. Reinsurance thresholds of $50,000 or even much lower would still expose insurers to very high claim costs, much higher than average premiums. Therefore, insurers would continue to have an incentive to avoid these risks.

Competition Under a Connector System

As in Massachusetts, regional health markets could use a connector to serve as the marketplace and link between insurers and individuals and small groups. It is important to define not only how plans compete within the connector, but whether and how plans in the connector compete with plans outside the connector. There are numerous possible models for creating competition under a connector system (see below). (All have advantages and disadvantages, but a full discussion is beyond the scope of this chapter.)

Model 1: Winner Takes All

In both the private and public sectors, there are models where most of the insurer competition takes place before a plan is offered to beneficiaries. In the private-sector monopoly model, some very large employers have chosen what is sometimes called "total replacement," under which the employer (and its consultant) sets up a competition among qualified bidders before a contract year. The winner of the bid then becomes the only insurer to offer insurance to the beneficiaries. In the public sector, the TriCare program for military retirees and dependents chooses regional monopoly winners this way. A slightly different version of this model is to announce ahead of time that there will be a limited number of winning bidders (e.g., three in a region).

Among the advantages are fierce competition during the bidding process to be that sole winner (or one of a limited number of winners). In addition, the winning bidder has fewer worries about the possibility of adverse selection from participants, as long as there is nearly universal coverage. Disadvantages include the lack of choice for beneficiaries regarding provider networks or service and reduced ability for losing bidders to be prepared for future competitions (e.g., no experience and no infrastructure in the region). Also, providers might be concerned that the winning bidder would have too much power in payment-rate negotiations.

Model 2: Any Qualified Bidder

Rather than restricting the competition to the bidding period as in Model 1, a much different model would allow any qualified bidder to offer insurance coverage. Qualification might include meeting minimum standards for provider networks, solvency funds, member service capabilities, and other requirements. The minimum qualification would be intended more as consumer protection than as a hurdle to keep bidders out of the market. However, no insurer would be allowed to offer insurance that did not meet the qualifications and agree to abide by connector rules. The Medicare Part D program for stand-alone prescription drug plans operates on an any-qualified-bidder basis.

Advantages include more consumer choice, intense competition to secure members during open enrollment periods, possibly a greater emphasis on service and cost efficiency, and an easier ability for new qualified insurance company entrants each year. In the absence of standardized benefit-design requirements, one disadvantage may be the greater potential for confusion about a multitude of offerings, one of the complaints about the Medicare Part D program. Other potential disadvantages include the possibility that existing local insurers might dominate the market from the start. In addition, multiple bidders create more work and administrative cost for the connector and providers.

Model 3: Inside the Connector and Outside Competition

A variation of Model 2 would be competition both from insurers within the connector and from insurers outside the connector. Qualified insurers would be offered by the connector and would have the advantages of the connector's infrastructure and visibility, but would also be required to abide by common rules. Some insurers (possibly smaller insurers and those without large regional membership) might prefer to be allowed to continue to offer current insurance benefit plans without all the rules of the connector.

Advantages include greater choice for citizens and more market competition. Disadvantages might include much greater complexity for beneficiaries and more difficulty in making value comparisons. It may be more difficult to regulate the market and provide a level playing field for all insurers in the region. If insurers in the connector must follow different rules regarding issue, rating, or benefit plan requirements compared to insurers outside the connector, the insurers subject to rules that are more advantageous to less-healthy individuals will be selected against. Although risk adjustment can help mitigate adverse selection, this will be difficult if insurers outside the connector do not participate in the risk-adjustment process.

Treatment of Existing Insurance Markets

Traditionally, the commercial marketplace is divided into three basic types of insurance markets: individual, small group, and large group. Regional health markets create a fourth, which can affect the existing markets, especially the individual and small-group markets.

While the aim of a regional health market program is to provide a place for individuals who currently do not have insurance to purchase affordable insurance, some of the individuals who enter this new market will come from the current individual and small-group markets. Generally, a regional health market is directed at individuals rather than groups, so it is likely that the individual market will be affected the most. Whether this has a positive or negative impact on the existing markets and risk pools depends on the risk profile of the individuals who move. The move may result in financial losses to insurers in the existing marketplace, which could ultimately lead to insurers opting not to participate in any market. It may be necessary to provide some risk sharing either in the short term or permanently to maintain a viable market.

The number of markets can be reduced by consolidating the existing markets, as in the Massachusetts Health Connector. Effective July 1, 2007, Massachusetts combined the individual and small-group markets, which previously had separate regulations, into one market. The impact of such a market merger varies by carrier depending primarily on whether the bulk of the carrier's business is individual or small group. A study commissioned by Massachusetts to examine the impact of merging the individual and small-group markets estimates that individual market premiums will decrease approximately 15 percent and small-group premiums will increase about 1.0 to 1.5 percent (Gorman Actuarial 2006). Impact will vary substantially by carrier, ranging from a reduction of 2 to 50 percent for individual market carriers and an increase of 1 to 4 percent for small-group carriers.

As the impact is not consistent across carriers, the short-term impact to some carriers may be harmful. For example, a carrier with a large number of individual policyholders, but little or no small-group business, may need to reduce premiums by as much as 50 percent to compete in the new market and retain its current membership levels. However, the risk profile of the carrier's existing business has not changed, so a 50 percent drop in premium means the carrier would be operating at a loss until it can attract new policyholders with a better risk profile.

Potential Administrative Cost Reductions for Regional Health Markets

In theory, regional health markets could reduce insurers' administrative costs, with two important caveats. First, the regional health market rules are of critical importance. The connector and its governing board must insist on a level playing field for all qualified insurers and must provide both incentives for administrative cost reduction and disincentives for retaining status quo costs. Without sufficient effort, current cost structures are likely to be retained. Second, the challenge of "wringing out" costs is substantial—changes in business models and processes need to occur, restructuring and downsizing of insurer workforces are likely, and investment in new kinds of infrastructure needs to be made. For each large qualified insurer, investments may be considerable.

Administrative costs can vary considerably in the private health insurance system. Although the average percentage of premiums for administrative costs and profit or contribution to surplus (i.e., the part of premiums not paid out in claims to providers) is around 15 percent, this ranges from a low of perhaps 5 to 6 percent for very large employer groups to 30 to 35 percent in the individual market. The challenge is to create a model and incentives for insurers in a regional health market to reduce administrative costs. Cost reductions will not accrue, however, if the regional health market becomes just one more layer of infrastructure.

Types of Administrative Costs and Savings Opportunities

Distribution costs, which cover the cost of advertising, member acquisition, and commissions to agents and brokers, represent one of the largest cost-reduction opportunities, especially for individual coverage. Initial commissions for individual health products are around 20 percent, declining in subsequent years. If the connector can serve as the entire plan comparison, sales, and enrollment mechanism, then much of this cost could potentially be eliminated. For instance, the travel industry has seen this kind of structural change, as either airline Web sites or Internet travel agencies have greatly reduced or eliminated commissions on most airline tickets. Many travel agents today work on a fee basis and provide additional value to travelers who have needs for complex trips. Under Medicare Part D, some drug plans obtained millions of beneficiaries directly (i.e., without commissions) through either the Centers for Medicare and Medicaid Services Web site or their company Web sites. Agents would likely still provide valuable services in a regional health market environment, but possibly under separate fee arrangements.

Billing and enrollment services provide another area for administrative cost savings. These services include setting up the electronic membership databases, providing valid membership cards, billing either individual enrollees or their employers, and answering related queries from members and employers. Enrollment, contract-issue, and billing costs may require from 0.5 to 2 percent of premiums, depending on the size of the contract (e.g., an individual contract, a small-employer contract, or a large-employer contract). Qualified regional health market insurers would still likely issue ID cards, but much of the enrollment might go through the connector Web site with more electronic funds transfer billing. Note that some of the cost savings could be offset if insurers are required to pick up some of the connector's costs for enrollment and billing. Nevertheless, for those enrollees who can make maximum use of the Web site and electronic funds transfer, the annual reduction in billing costs could be significant. Some insurers in today's markets are now charging for paper enrollment and billing if Internet or electronic-funds-transfer billing procedures are not used.

Underwriting, especially for individual health insurance, is a similar-sized amount, perhaps 0.25 to 1 percent of premiums. In a guaranteed-issue market (if this is one of the rules of the regional health market), much of this cost might be eliminated.

Most other administrative areas are unlikely to enjoy cost reductions, however. Claims adjudication, antifraud activities, regulatory compliance, and other related administrative functions are likely in the range of 5 to 7 percent of premiums, depending on factors such as the size of the member premium (lower premium contracts may have higher percentage expenses) and the amount of capitation involved. These administrative costs are unlikely to change, except to the extent that insurers participating in the regional health market gain significant membership and are able to lower the percentage attributable to fixed costs (e.g., amortizing computer systems over a larger membership base).

Another category of costs unlikely to change is associated with care coordination (including disease management, utilization review, and quality assurance and measurement) and provider network management (including contract negotiations with physicians, hospitals, and drug manufacturers). Together, these costs may range from 1 to 2 percent of premiums but are frequently offset by the savings that can be generated and also may provide considerable benefits for the insured members. Costs for customer service and information technology support, which together amount to between 1 and 2 percent of premiums, would also likely remain unchanged under a regional health market, unless a connector took over customer service functions.

A last major category involves taxes, fees, and underwriting profit or contribution to surplus. Taxes are likely to remain unchanged for insured products: Most states have premium taxes in the 2 percent range. Other taxes include federal and state income taxes or guaranty fund assessments, also likely to be unchanged, although some guaranty funds may diminish or disappear. However, additional assessments on health insurers in the form of premium taxes or guaranty fund assessments could be possible, depending on how the regional health market funds premium subsidies, administrative costs, and government risk-sharing provisions.

Underwriting profit or contribution to surplus does not include investment income or other profit, which can vary for companies and regions. The industry average of after-tax underwriting gains is likely to be in the range today of 3 to 4 percent but can vary widely.

Conclusion

A goal of creating regional health markets is to make insurance more available and affordable. Whether this goal is met depends in part on how those markets are structured and the rules that govern them. Although creating new and larger risk pools could result in more predictable and stable premiums, in a voluntary market, unmanaged adverse selection could thwart attempts to provide affordable coverage. Therefore, efforts to establish regional health markets should consider options to minimize adverse selection as well as risk-sharing arrangements. In addition, the issue and rating rules need to be designed carefully to balance the goals of health insurance availability and affordability, and these rules should make sense within the context of the rules applying to any markets competing with the regional markets. The rules governing benefit package requirements, how insurers are chosen to participate in the regional health market, and how the connector's administrative costs are funded can also affect the market's viability.

References

American Academy of Actuaries. 2006. *Wading Through Medical Insurance Pools: A Primer.* Washington, DC: American Academy of Actuaries.

Blumberg, Linda J., John Holahan, Jack Hadley, and Katherine Nordahl. 2007. "Setting a Standard of Affordability for Health Insurance Coverage." *Health Affairs* Web exclusive: W463–W473. http://content.healthaffairs.org/cgi/search?andorexact fulltext=and&resourcetype=1&disp_type=&author1=blumberg&fulltext=&pubdate_ year=2007&volume=&firstpage= (Accessed November 17, 2008).

Gorman Actuarial, LLC. 2006. "Impact of Merging the Massachusetts Non-Group and Small Group Health Insurance Markets." Paper prepared for the Massachusetts Division of Insurance and Market Merger Special Commission, Gorman Actuarial, LLC, Marlborough, MA.

3

Creating a Level Playing Field for Public and Private Plans

BRYAN DOWD

This chapter considers some design features of a health care reform proposal that would make a government-run health insurance plan available to all. The details of any health care reform proposal are important, and the details of this proposal still are under development. However, some details are available and discussed here.

Analysis begins with a description of the problems in health insurance markets that reforms might address. It then considers a specific reform proposal: offering a public plan and competing private plans in a government-run purchasing pool. The Medicare program provides an important precedent for such a system and offers a practical guide to problems and opportunities offered by such a mixed public and private system. Analysis then turns to application of the mixed public and private system to the commercial insurance market, discussing likely problems and ways to resolve them.

An important assumption underlying this analysis is that public and private plans have inherent advantages and disadvantages, and neither type of plan needs to be favored with special subsidies or regulations. Both plans can be offered on a relatively level playing field. The best judges of the advantages, disadvantages, and economic value of each plan are not politicians, bureaucrats, or policy analysts, but consumers supported by good data systems.

In this analysis, *the commercial health insurance market* means the market for health insurance faced by people who are not currently enrolled in Medicare, Medicaid, government-subsidized high-risk pools, or another public insurance program. For example, the nonelderly disabled population that is enrolled in Medicare would not be part of the commercial insurance market as discussed here; nor would the low-income individuals enrolled in Medicaid; nor would the age-entitled Medicare-enrolled population, even though many Medicare beneficiaries are enrolled in private health plans (the Medicare Advantage [MA] program, private supplementary policies, or private Part D drug coverage plans).

Problems in the Commercial Insurance Market

Economists distinguish between problems of efficiency and problems of fairness. The purpose of the division is to understand the steps that are necessary to address a problem. There is not a one-to-one mapping from problems to the categories of efficiency and fairness. A single problem can raise issues of both efficiency and fairness.

A good example is the most prominent problem in U.S. health insurance: the uninsured. Forty-seven million Americans did not have any type of health insurance coverage during 2006 (U.S. Census Bureau 2007). Lack of insurance is, in part, attributable to and results in inefficiencies, and also represents a problem of fairness.

Advocates of consumer-directed health plans with large deductibles have argued that traditional health insurance policies are poorly designed, encouraging inefficient consumption of health care services, which leads to inefficiently high health insurance premiums, increasing the proportion of the population with inadequate coverage. Other analysts cite the relatively higher administrative costs of private health plans compared to public fee-for-service Medicare as a form of inefficiency. Inefficiently high administrative costs would lead to higher premiums, making insurance unaffordable for more individuals. Advocates of single-payer reform believe it would be more efficient for federal government to exercise its massive purchasing power to extract deeper price discounts from the health care industry, including physicians, hospitals, and drug companies.

There also is concern that the lack of truly portable universal health insurance coverage can lead to *job lock,* that is, individuals remaining in a suboptimal job simply to maintain health insurance coverage for themselves or their family members. *Suboptimal* in this case means that the individual's utility, determined in part by his or her marginal revenue product (the effect of an additional hour of labor on output times the market price of one unit of the output), would be higher in another job. The job with the higher marginal revenue product might not offer health insurance, and if it does not, even the higher wages that accompany the individual's increased earning power in the new job might not be enough to cover the cost of similar coverage obtained in the *nongroup* insurance market. An additional problem is that transition to the small-group or nongroup market could entail a reassessment of the individual's risk (or the risk of an insured family member), or greater risk of reassessment if the individual's or family member's health status changes.

These problems impact both efficiency and fairness. *Efficiency* problems can be summarized as follows: An inefficiently high number of people have an inefficiently low level of insurance, including no insurance. This problem is accompanied and in part caused by inefficient production of health insurance coverage, both in administration and in product design. Friction in transitions in the health insurance market may lead to some inefficiency in the allocation of people to jobs (job lock).

The *fairness* dimension of the problem definition suggests the following: Some individuals, including children, lack health insurance for reasons beyond their control, and those individuals do not have the same ability to realize their full potential, holding other factors constant, as insured individuals. This situation violates both process fairness and equal treatment of equals.

A Proposal for a Mixed Public and Private Insurance System for the Commercial Health Insurance Market

Although this analysis addresses a generic proposal to add a universally available, government-run health insurance plan to the commercial health insurance market, a specific proposal to that effect currently is being circulated. The proposal is by Jacob Hacker (2007) of Yale University, whose work on the proposal was sponsored by the Economic Policy Institute.

The primary problem identified in the proposal is the lack of "health security," which Hacker defines as (1) periods of uninsurance that affect a significant proportion of Americans and (2) the high cost of health care. Hacker also mentions the adverse impact of high health care costs on businesses and the costs of uncompensated care borne by people with insurance. The proposal has the following general features:

1. "Every legal resident of the United States who lacks access to Medicare or good workplace coverage would be able to buy into[1] the 'Health Care for America Plan' [HCAP], a new public insurance pool[2] modeled after Medicare. Every enrollee would have access to either an affordable Medicare-like plan with free choice of providers or to a selection of comprehensive private plans";
2. "A requirement that employers (and the self-employed) either purchase coverage comparable to HCAP for all their workers or pay a relatively modest payroll contribution (6 percent of payroll) to fund HCAP coverage for all their employees";[3] and
3. "A requirement that Americans who remain without insurance take responsibility for their and their families' health by purchasing private coverage or buying into the HCAP" (3).

The proposal includes mandates for employers and individuals. Specific features of HCAP include:

1. Coverage of physical and mental health services as well as prescription drugs.
2. Point-of-purchase cost sharing and "strict limits on total out-of-pocket spending" (3).
3. "For those enrolled in the plan at their place of work, anyone whose income was below 200% of the poverty level would pay no additional premiums. (The poverty line in 2006 was roughly $10,000 for an individual and $20,000 for a family of four.) The maximum monthly premium—phased in between 200% and 300% of the poverty level—would be $70 for an individual, $140 for a couple, $130 for a single-parent family, and $200 for all other families" (4). Premiums would not vary with age, region, or health status.

4. Out-of-pocket premiums for private plans and for HCAP would be treated as they are under current tax law.
5. The remainder of the premium would be paid "by employers," who would be "eligible for transitional subsidies that would ensure that no firm faced a substantial new burden" (4).
6. Employers could offer supplements to HCAP benefits.
7. Enrollment in HCAP would be open to any legal U.S. resident without good workplace coverage.

Estimated *total* savings from the plan (as opposed to savings only for employers, insured individuals, the government, etc.) come from several sources, including:

1. "Concentrated purchasing power" in the large HCAP (5).
2. Lower administrative costs in HCAP relative to private insurers.
3. "[I]mprovements in the quality and cost-effectiveness of medical care" (7).

Hacker rests his argument on "the time-tested idea of social insurance, the notion that major financial risks should be pooled as widely as possible across rich and poor, healthy and sick, young and old" (2). But there is no general agreement on the characteristics of social insurance.

Mixed Public and Private Health Insurance: Lessons from Medicare

Advocates for a health care system based on private plans and a universally available government-run plan often appeal to the Medicare program as a successful basis for their proposal. A brief review helps put the discussion of design issues into perspective.

A Brief History of Private Plans in Medicare

Medicare is the most prominent U.S. example of a mixed system of public and private health plans. Three types of private health plans are associated with the Medicare program. The first is private supplementary, or Medigap, policies that cover services and cost sharing not covered by the Medicare entitlement. The second is Medicare Advantage (MA) plans, which replace the government-administered fee-for-service (FFS) Medicare plan with private coverage. The third is stand-alone Part D drug coverage plans that offer optional coverage of outpatient prescription drugs to Medicare beneficiaries.

The history of private plans in Medicare begins in the earliest days of the program with private plans paid on a fee-for-service basis (Dowd, Feldman, and Christianson 1996). Beginning in the 1970s, advocates of health maintenance organizations (HMOs) were arguing in favor of competitive markets for private health plans, and in some cases, extension of those systems to Medicare. The more recent history of private plans in Medicare usually is dated from 1982 to 1985, which marked the introduction of capitated private plans on a wide scale under the Medicare Competition Demonstration. Congress incorporated capitated private plans into the program before the evaluation of the demonstration was complete, which may have contributed to a number of design flaws that have proved difficult to correct.

During the late 1980s and early 1990s, private plans were providing generous supplementary benefits including free prescription drug coverage to beneficiaries in areas with high FFS Medicare costs. However, there was general dissatisfaction with the payment system for private plans, including inadequate risk adjustment and wide variations in payment levels even in contiguous counties.

Both Private Plans and FFS Medicare Have Advantages

Dowd, Feldman, and Coulam (2005–6) have argued that FFS Medicare and private MA plans have advantages, but they need to be carefully scrutinized. FFS Medicare guarantees the availability of *health insurance coverage* nationwide, but not necessarily access to *providers* willing to treat Medicare patients (although about 90 percent of doctors and almost all hospitals participate). FFS Medicare has considerable market power in negotiating prices with health care providers[4] and, depending on how they are counted, lower administrative costs as a percentage of total claims expense.

FFS Medicare also has a demonstrated track record of provider payment initiatives, such as diagnosis-related groups for inpatient services and the resource-based relative value scale for physician services adopted by many private health plans. Studies of care for chronically ill beneficiaries generally favor FFS Medicare over private health plans.

Private MA plans enjoy more freedom in their contracts with providers. The importance of this freedom was demonstrated recently when both courts and Congress prevented the Centers for Medicare and Medicaid Services (CMS) from competitively bidding its contracts for durable medical equipment and clinical laboratory services. Even though private plans' provider fees often are higher than Medicare's (Medicare Payment Advisory Commission 2004), private plans are free to pursue competitive contracting that is more likely to produce efficient price levels than government-administered prices.

MA plans are less constrained in their ability to initiate care-management interventions than other plans. Unfettered by distinctions between Parts A, B, and to a large extent D, they coordinate care easily across a continuum of treatment sites and modalities. Although Hacker appears to believe that the HCAP public plan would deliver more cost-effective health care than private health plans, there is not a great deal of evidence from Medicare to support that belief. Studies of the provision of preventive care, for example, favor private

MA plans over FFS Medicare. FFS Medicare recently began experimenting with disease management strategies, whereas Welch et al. (2002) reported that 99 percent of private plans had employed some type of disease-management programs in 2000. Recent demonstrations of disease management in Medicare have been so unsuccessful that CMS is contemplating ending the demonstration (Abelson 2008).

The relative advantages of either FFS Medicare or MA at any point in time may be temporary. For example, regional PPOs in Medicare have resulted in private health plans being at least nominally available throughout the country, and in addition to disease management and competitive bidding for some types of services, FFS Medicare is experimenting with pay-for-performance systems similar to those of private plans.

Lack of a Level Playing Field in Medicare

The Medicare program does *not* feature a level playing field between private health plans and FFS Medicare. Under current law, FFS Medicare must offer free choice of providers, whereas MA plans are able to practice selective contracting and can require a referral to see a specialist. In addition, FFS Medicare must (1) be offered in all locations, (2) accept all enrollees at any time they apply, (3) and cover only services listed in the entitlement, which might preclude covering some cost-effective preventive care. FFS Medicare is prohibited from offering a one-stop shopping product that includes basic Medicare coverage and (optional at extra cost) supplementary coverage and Part D coverage, all administered and financed by the federal government. FFS Medicare also reports detailed claims data, while MA plans do not.

Private plans also face some legislatively imposed cost disadvantages relative to FFS Medicare. To level the effect of those constraints, FFS Medicare would have to (1) abide by all administrative reporting requirements imposed on MA plans, including submission of adjusted community rate reports; (2) abide by the same quality reporting requirements, including Health Effectiveness and Data Information Set measures; (3) be subjected to the same penalties imposed on private plans for submitting incorrect data; and (4) declare service areas for FFS Medicare (presumably encompassing the entire United States) and ensure adequate access to providers in those service areas.

There are three policy options regarding these disparities. First, some restrictions could be removed. For example, free choice of provider could be removed from the Medicare entitlement, allowing FFS Medicare to use the same contracting approaches as private plans, perhaps as plan options within FFS Medicare. Alternatively, premiums for disadvantaged plans could be subsidized to neutralize their legislatively imposed cost disadvantages. Finally, the disparities could continue to be ignored, and consumers could be left to decide which plans will survive and which will not.

Paying Private Plans in Medicare

One of the most difficult areas in the Medicare program has been designing a payment system for private health plans. In the early 1980s, private plans began to receive capitation payments for Medicare beneficiaries. Despite good advice to the contrary (Dowd, Feldman, and Christianson 1996), those capitation payments were set as a function of average expenditures in FFS Medicare in the beneficiary's county of residence. The extraordinary variation in average FFS spending across counties (even in the same general market area) led to significant variations in private plan capitation rates. Private plans' costs did not vary as much as FFS costs, and thus private plans in high-payment areas had significant amounts of surplus revenue. Private plans could return the surplus revenue to the government, or possibly hide it in inflated cost estimates, but competition among private plans forced them to convert the surplus revenue into supplementary benefits, which varied in direct proportion to their payments (McBride 1998). Because massive reviews of the literature found the quality of care in FFS Medicare and private plans to be roughly equal (Miller and Luft 1997, 2002), the policy concern in the 1990s was that FFS Medicare was being protected from direct price competition with private plans, leading to wasted government expenditures.

The arbitrary benchmark of FFS spending was replaced in the 1997 Balanced Budget Act legislation with an arbitrary cap of 2 percent payment increases per year, which led to the withdrawal of private plans from markets where restricted payments were not sufficient to maintain their competitive position in the market. Further administrative tinkering with payments in the early 2000s led to the establishment of "floor" counties with minimum payment levels that were higher than FFS spending levels. The concept of floor counties was extended in the 2003 Medicare Modernization Act legislation to the point that overpayment of private plans became the dominant policy concern.[5]

The Medicare Payment Advisory Commission has recommended a return to the pre–Balanced Budget Act payment policy—setting private plan payments equal to FFS spending in each county. That would restore the differentials in private plan payments across counties, as well as the differentials in supplementary benefits offered by private plans. An important difference, however, is the ease with which private plans now can offer Part B premium rebates as part of their supplementary benefits. The expected result is that beneficiaries in areas with high FFS spending now receive not only more generous coverage from private plans than beneficiaries in high-payment areas, but also cash payments. It is difficult to see how this approach addresses the problem of wasted government spending.

Dowd, Feldman, and Christianson (1996) recommend a payment approach that eliminates government waste and bickering over whether private or public plans are being unfairly subsidized. The approach is to have private plans and FFS Medicare submit capitation bids, and then set the government's contribution to health-plan premiums for Medicare beneficiaries equal to the lowest bid submitted by a qualified health plan in each county. Demonstrations of this "competitive pricing" or "premium support" approach to plan payment were first mandated, then stopped by Congress in the late 1990s (Dowd, Coulam, and Feldman 2000). Another demonstration has been mandated for 2010.

Designing and Running a Mixed Public and Private Health Insurance System in the Commercial Insurance Sector

Why Offer a Government-Run Health Plan in the Commercial Insurance Market?

The purpose of offering a government-run health plan in the commercial insurance market must be stated carefully because it will become the operational equivalent of the entitlement restrictions in the Medicare program, and the entitlement restrictions will determine the rules governing public and private health plans in the mixed system. Presumably the purpose of any health care reform proposal is to address the problems of market failure and fairness identified earlier in this analysis (or new ones that might be identified by different analysts). This analysis assumes that the purpose of the proposed reform is to offer individuals in the nongroup insurance market the opportunity to purchase group-like health insurance coverage that would have the following features.

Protection Against Having One's Health Risk Reassessed After an Illness or Injury

One of the most valuable features of large-group employment-based health insurance is the guarantee that employees will have access to health insurance premiums that protect against higher premiums due to the onset of serious illness or injury as long as they remain on the job. Large employers are able to provide an insurance product (either one plan or multiple plans) that offer their employees not only community-rated premiums (and thus protection against risk redefinition) but also the opportunity to switch among community-rated health plans during open enrollment periods.

Protection is very limited, however, and can be withdrawn if the employee changes employers. The Health Insurance Portability and Accountability Act has helped in that situation, as long as the employee maintains continuous coverage and moves to another firm that offers community-rated health plans. However, the act carries no guarantee that employment-based coverage will be universally available or that the premiums will not increase if the person changes jobs or is unable to work.

The absence of long-term protection against risk reassessment is a topic of legitimate concern and, if understood correctly, might provide the most stable pillar of a proposal for a new type of government activity in the commercial health insurance market. The problem applies primarily to individuals who lose or are threatened with loss of their group insurance policies.

An Ironclad Guarantee of Portability of Coverage and a Community-Rated Premium from One Job to Another (or from Employment to Unemployment)

Portability of coverage, in this analysis, means that the consumer is guaranteed continuous coverage at a premium that reflects average health expenditures in the consumer's pool if he or she moves his or her residence to any part of the United States. It does not mean that premiums will be invariant with respect to the *average* level of health care spending in the pool of which the consumer is a member, nor invariant with respect to average levels of health care spending in one part of the country versus another; nor does portability imply continuous enrollment in exactly the same health plan or even the same *type* of health plan. In its loosest form, portability might not even imply premiums that are constant across age-groups, since aging is a foreseeable risk, and it might allow for premiums that vary with income, as well.

Lower Marketing and Underwriting Costs than in the Individual Health Insurance Market, Presumably Resulting in More Affordable Premiums

Although there is some controversy regarding the ability of the nongroup market to offer guaranteed protection against having one's risk reassessed in the event of serious illness or injury (Pauly and Nichols 2002), it is not controversial to assert that marketing and underwriting costs are higher in the individual market than in the group market. If it were possible to offer group-like coverage to individuals through some mechanism, the cost of any given level of coverage could be reduced.

Other Possible but Controversial Purposes

Beyond these simple but important purposes, there are secondary purposes that might be proposed. Is the purpose of the government-run plan to ensure the availability of a health plan that features unfettered access to all providers, as in FFS Medicare? Is unfettered access to providers an essential feature of a health plan or an amenity for which some consumers are willing to pay, while others choose lower-cost plans with restrictions on provider access? In other words, if unfettered access to providers increases the cost of the public plan in HCAP, should HCAP receive public subsidies to neutralize that additional cost from the consumer's perspective?

In the Medicare program, FFS Medicare with a supplementary policy is the domain of higher-income beneficiaries, while MA plans with limited provider access have enrolled a plurality of lower-income and minority beneficiaries who are not eligible for Medicaid (Dowd et al. 1994; Thorpe and Atherly 2002). Unfettered choice of provider thus appears to be treated as an amenity in the Medicare program. This analysis takes the same perspective, assuming that group and staff-model HMOs and preferred provider plans are as valid care-delivery models as open-access plans.

Is the purpose of the government-run plan to amass enough individuals in a health plan so that larger price discounts can be extracted from health care providers? Although advocates of government-run plans tout the advantages of bulk purchasing power, monopsony purchasing can be inefficient. FFS Medicare's pricing power does allow it to ignore local market pathologies such as provider pricing power where those pathologies exist (Dowd et al. 2006–7), and thus in some concentrated provider markets, FFS Medicare may offer the efficiency advantage of bilateral monopoly. However, a better approach would be local enforcement of antitrust laws.

If the purpose of a government-run health plan is to deliver a more efficient mix of health care services to the population than private health plans, then evidence from FFS Medicare in the areas of preventive care and disease management is not encouraging.

These secondary objectives are worthy of additional empirical research. Because they are more controversial, however, they are not the focus of this analysis.

Specific Design Features

What health plan characteristics would be necessary to achieve the goals of a mixed public and private system? Which characteristics should be required of all health plans, and which should remain flexible? As noted, this analysis is based on the premise that public and private health plans have some intrinsic advantages and disadvantages, and neither type of plan needs to be favored with special subsidies or regulations. However, public and private plans may face different challenges in implementing different design features, and both plans will be disciplined by the intersection of their own ideas regarding plan design with cost structures and consumers and providers with whom they contract.

Government Pool or Government Health Plan?

In theory, the objectives of universally available coverage and premium stability that covers transitions between the individual and group health insurance markets, per se, could be accomplished without introducing a new government-run health plan. Both objectives could be achieved by introducing only an insurance pool, most likely run by the government, that offered multiple community-rated private health plans to enrollees with annual open enrollment periods that allowed plan switching without reassessment of health risk.

The multiple health plan pool as a model has worked well for large employers for decades, and the problems of risk adjustment appear largely to have been sorted out. From the consumer's perspective, the plan would appear similar to the Federal Employees Health Benefits (FEHB) Program. The choice of health plans would vary depending on the region of the country, but every area would have at least one plan available. Premium stability would require consumers to abide by the rule that stabilizes group-insurance pools: continuous participation. Another key difference between employer-sponsored and nongroup insurance is that the former provides the individual with guaranteed issue, while the latter is individually experience rated (i.e., medically underwritten).

Standardization of the Benefit Package

Any system that promotes competition among health plans must wrestle with the question of the benefit package. Is it best to have a standardized package of benefits on which all plans base their prices, or should plans be able to offer any benefits they like? Even among advocates of health plan competition, opinion is divided on this issue. Some analysts believe that a standardized benefit package makes it easier for consumers to compare health plans, and reduces the temptation for plans to use benefit packages to attract good risks. Others note that not all consumers have the same preferences, and forced uniformity of benefits reduces consumer welfare.

Certainly precise standardization has the potential to limit competition. For example, requiring staff-model HMOs to charge coinsurance rather than copayments created difficulties in the past, because physicians in staff-model HMOs often were salaried, and no fee schedules existed. Medicare has approached the problem by allowing private plans' benefit packages to be actuarially equivalent to FFS Medicare benefits. What about larger differences in benefit packages, for example, consumer-directed health plans with large deductibles? Hacker would require employers to offer a benefit package as good as that of HCAP, thus ruling out large-deductible plans. An operational definition of *as good as* that is realistic, much less efficiency enhancing, can prove elusive, however. Even the strictest interpretation of *standardized benefits* fails to include some of the most important features that distinguish one health plan from another, such as the size of the provider networks, the inclusion of specific providers such as specialty or tertiary hospitals, and the location of clinics. Erring on the side of maximum consumer choice, with contingency plans to deal with any problems arising from variation in plan benefit levels, would seem to be the prudent course of action. Two areas requiring further thought are risk segmentation and rules for setting employer or government contributions to premiums, as discussed below.

Equal treatment of plans with varying levels of consumer cost sharing requires equalization of the tax treatment of premiums and out-of-pocket spending at the point of purchase (e.g., coinsurance, copayments, and deductibles). One approach that has advantages for fairness and efficiency would be to replace the current tax deduction of employer-paid health insurance premiums with a refundable, advanceable tax credit used to pay either premiums or qualified out-of-pocket health expenditures.

A related issue is whether public and private plans would have to abide by the same rules regarding approval of new medical technology. Pauly (2005) believes that any serious attempt to make health care more affordable must incorporate some approach to the adoption of costly new technology. He is not optimistic that competition among plans can produce an efficient rate of growth in the adoption of new technology in the current market environment, though the mid-1990s may have provided some evidence that it is technically feasible. Pauly cites legal obstacles as one of several constraints that may prevent health plans from making efficient allocation decisions. Health plans may be unwilling to make even efficient allocation decisions if they run the risk of being portrayed unilaterally as cost-driven rationers of technology. While *requiring* all health plans to adhere to the same payment rules for new technology could inhibit what little innovation might take place, *allowing* all plans in a market area to adopt the same payment policy regarding a new technology (though not necessarily the same *prices*) without fear of antitrust action might provide a way to avoid the risks of unilateral decisions by individual plans.

The approach to benefit standardization in Medicare has been to specify a basic minimum benefit package, but to allow beneficiaries to purchase different types of additional coverage, either through supplementary policies, MA plans, or Part D coverage. One of the lessons learned from that experience is that the basic benefit package, once specified, is difficult to change, making an allowance for supplementary coverage even more important. Even so, FFS Medicare is disadvantaged relative to MA plans by not being able to offer one-stop shopping—a single product that covers the basic entitlement benefit package, supplementary coverage, and outpatient prescription drug coverage. Hacker's proposal would allow private plans to offer coverage that was more (but not less) generous than HCAP.

Hacker's proposal also would allow employers to offer supplementary coverage to HCAP. Although this feature addresses the problem of diverse consumer preferences, there is a well-known problem with supplementary coverage in Medicare. Because Medigap policies often reduce the point-of-purchase cost sharing for services covered by Medicare, care becomes cheaper, and demand for care increases. Medicare pays approximately 80 percent of the increased cost due to Medigap coverage, but beneficiaries' premiums reflect only the 20 percent covered by Medigap. The result is a spillover cost from privately financed Medigap policies to tax-financed Medicare.

It is unclear whether supplementary insurance for HCAP would reduce the point-of-purchase price of health care services in the same way as Medigap insurance. If so, and HCAP premiums were paid entirely by enrollee premiums, the spillover problem would be reduced, since the increased cost of HCAP attributable to supplementary insurance would be borne "internally" by HCAP enrollees. However, HCAP premiums for low-income enrollees are publicly subsidized, presumably from tax revenue. Thus, there would be an increased income transfer both from non-HCAP enrollees to HCAP enrollees who purchase supplementary insurance, and from HCAP enrollees without supplementary insurance to HCAP enrollees with supplementary insurance. These transfers could be addressed by taxing HCAP (or supplementary insurance) premiums.

Advertising and Consumer Information

Standardized benefits are one approach to improved consumer information, but not the only approach. There has been remarkable progress in the availability of consumer information about varying types of health plans and health care providers in recent years. At the simplest level, employers nationwide have developed clear, concise summaries of health plan information that are distributed to employees at open enrollment. These summaries minimally contain information about coverage, provider networks, and premiums, but in some cases have results from surveys of provider quality and consumer satisfaction, as well. However, there are limits to this information. As the *Guide to Health Plans for Federal Employees* points out, "We cannot deal with every single coverage nuance or difference. . . . Nor can we assure that all plans will make identical medical necessity decisions in close cases" (Francis 2007).

At the national level, the production of similar information for Medicare and the growing availability of consumer information about the quality of providers are encouraging developments. CMS's detailed information on the Part D plans, including formularies, pharmacy locations, and estimated savings by plan, all produced in an eighteen-month time frame, stands as one of the remarkable technological achievements in the history of consumer health care information.

Even if only a small portion of consumers access information about plans and providers, it might be enough to discipline the market. Health plans also can incorporate information about the quality of providers into the provider network decisions. The widespread availability of quality information also can engender a response by providers even if the effect on consumer choice is ambiguous.

A level playing field implies that the same consumer information should be available for both public and private health plans. That information should be tailored and relevant to the consumers' local market area even if some of the plans, for example, the public plan in HCAP, are available nationwide.

Consumer information should take two forms: standardized information of the type made available by large employers to their employees, and plan-generated advertising. Both public and private plans should be allowed to advertise. Other government agencies that find themselves in competition with the private sector are allowed to advertise, and many have large advertising budgets (e.g., the U.S. Postal Service). Advertising must, of course, be truthful, and the ironclad rule regarding advertising of the government-run health plan is that the entire cost of advertising must be built into the government plan's premiums. If marketing pathologies are suspected, such as marketing designed to encourage the enrollment of low-risk individuals, those practices first should be analyzed to determine why the enrollment of low-risk individuals is profitable—for instance, a flaw in the risk-adjustment system—before simply prohibiting them.

Risk Selection and Risk Adjustment

The objective of risk adjustment is to have out-of-pocket premiums of competing health plans faced by consumers reflect the efficiency with which care is delivered, rather than a component of enrollee health status that is not attributable to membership in the health plan.[6] A second objective is to reduce the health plan's incentive to expend resources on efforts to attract only good risks.

The relationship between plan design and risk selection is not a new topic. Concerns over risk selection were rampant in the 1980s and 1990s. One analyst during that period referred to risk selection as the Achilles' heel of all competitive approaches to health insurance markets (Robinson et al. 1991). Risk adjustment appears to elicit less concern today. It is possible that the potential problems of biased selection simply were overemphasized in a population of working adults with plan switching limited to annual open-enrollment periods. The technology of risk adjustment has also improved considerably. As Ginsburg (2008, 683) writes, "Indeed, with the state of risk adjustment having progressed, risk selection that occurs when differences in benefit design are offered would not be as large a problem."

In the Medicare program, private plans were concerned that the risk adjusters of the 1990s were triggered by utilization data, particularly hospital admission data, and they felt their efforts to reduce unnecessary hospitalizations were being penalized. The problem seems largely to have been resolved when CMS allowed the health plans to have a stronger hand in the design of the risk-adjustment system, resulting in triggers that did not rely as heavily on traditional sources of utilization data.

Currently, concerns about risk selection seem confined to situations in which health plans are dramatically different, as in the case of large-deductible plans versus traditional full-coverage plans. Hacker emphasizes this point in his proposal, ruling out the health savings accounts that accompany large deductible plans and "threaten to further fragment the health insurance market."

The Choice Environment

Working from the premise that both public and private health plans have intrinsic advantages and neither requires artificial advantages in the market, then any restriction on consumer choice between the two types of plans needs careful justification. Although Hacker's proposal allows choice between HCAP (either the HCAP health plan or the HCAP multiple health plan pool) and employer-sponsored insurance at the employer level, the HCAP health plan and other employer-chosen plans would not be offered alongside each other to employees.

There are several possible justifications for prohibiting the side-by-side offering of the HCAP health plan and employer-sponsored private plans in the same firm, though none of them necessarily are convincing. The first involves the calculation of the HCAP premium. Should there be one HCAP premium for the entire country, as in the Hacker proposal, or should the premium reflect geographic differences in health care costs, or expected health care expenditures of other subgroups of enrollees? Part B FFS Medicare premiums are constant for beneficiaries nationwide, meaning beneficiaries and other taxpayers in (relatively low-cost) Minnesota subsidize the premiums of beneficiaries in (relatively high-cost) Miami. I know of no efficiency- or fairness-based defense of those subsidies, yet they are retained and expanded to the commercial health insurance market in Hacker's proposal.

Should the HCAP premium vary by industry? For example, the expected health expenditures for employees in the logging industry might be quite different than those for employees in the banking industry. Setting HCAP premiums equal for everyone establishes a system of subsidies across firms whose employees might have very different levels of risk. Are those subsidies desirable or do they mitigate the economic incentives for risky industries to improve the working conditions of their employees? What private plans will be offered in the HCAP pool? Will they be limited to plans that can serve the entire country, or will local private plans be allowed in the HCAP pool? Health care costs vary substantially across the country. If the public HCAP health plan were offered alongside local private plans, either in the HCAP pool or alongside plans offered by the employer, and the HCAP plan was required to charge only one premium averaged across the entire country, then it seems unlikely that anyone would join the HCAP health plan in areas with lower-than-average costs.

A good reason to subject the public HCAP health plan to competition with private plans is that the market could help determine the efficient set of benefits for the HCAP plan. Do most consumers really want unfettered access to physicians (comprehensive provider panels and no referrals needed for specialists) if such access results in a substantial increase in premiums? Do they want first-dollar coverage at higher premiums, or some level of point-of-purchase cost sharing? One way to answer these questions, of course, is to look at the choices that consumers have made in the current commercial health insurance market (albeit often under the effect of prices distorted by the tax deductibility of premiums and out-of-pocket spending). Another way to answer the questions is to test various designs of HCAP against one another and against the designs of private plans in a level-playing-field choice environment with no special subsidies for the HCAP plan.

In the HCAP multiple health plan insurance pool, should the government limit the number of competing private plans? Although the notion of having two tiers of competition, one for health plans to gain entry to the government-run pool and one for the enrollment of individual consumers, may be intuitively appealing, I know of no evidence that two-tier competition produces lower premiums than open competition; one study comes to the contrary conclusion (Vistnes, Cooper, and Vistnes 2001). The long-run equilibrium in the Part D market will be very instructive in this regard. Will the market continue to support fifty different plans in a market area, or will the equilibrium number of plans with any significant enrollment be much smaller?

Mandatory Participation and Default Enrollment

An interesting question is whether purchase of health insurance should be mandated, as in Massachusetts. Mandatory coverage solves the problem of adverse selection (consumers waiting until they are sick to purchase insurance), although medical underwriting already makes the adverse-selection strategy difficult to implement. Mandatory coverage has the additional advantage of forcing irresponsible uninsured consumers who are able to pay for health care services to do so, but collection agencies hired by health care providers serve a similar purpose. Mannheim and Court (2008) warn that legislative mandates requiring individuals to purchase insurance from private health plans with no "escape clause" (e.g., the option not to drive if one wants to avoid the mandate for automobile insurance) might be unconstitutional, whereas a mandate to purchase insurance from a public health plan would not.

Proposed mandates often apply to employers as well as employees. In the Hacker proposal, for example, employers would have the option of offering private health plans or contributing to the cost of HCAP for their employees. As long as costs are the same under the two systems, it is likely that the results will be similar, since the cost of the employer's mandated contribution to premiums (whether toward a plan offered by the employer or toward HCAP) would come out of the employees' total compensation. It also is likely that the effect of the mandate on low-wage employees would be the same, inducing the substitution of capital for labor. Whether employer and employee mandates have similar economic consequences for employees depends on the tax treatment of premiums.

One effective way to detect noncompliance with a mandate is to require proof of insurance anytime a person visits a health care provider. Uninsured individuals then can be assigned to a health plan. Mandatory assignment can become a contentious issue, depending on the likely health status of noncompliers. It might be the case that noncompliers are young healthy individuals who believe that they do not need health insurance or low-income individuals in poor health for whom the premium subsidy is inadequate. In a multiple health plan pool, it would be possible to assign noncompliers randomly to one of the participating health plans.

The Employer's Contribution to Premiums

The employer's contribution to premiums, though a misnomer, is an important topic because the structure of the employer contribution can alter the total cost of health insurance in the firm. The reason that *employer contribution* to premiums is a misnomer in economic theory is that the employee's total compensation is determined by his or her marginal revenue product. Competition in the market for the output of the firm prevents the employer from paying the employee more than his or her marginal revenue product, and competition in the market for labor prevents the employer from paying less. Total compensation can take the form of either taxable wages or (generally tax-exempt) fringe benefits such as health insurance, but more of one type of compensation must be offset by less of another type. This is the reason why economists often are not concerned that rising health care costs will put U.S. firms at a disadvantage relative to foreign competitors. An increase in the cost of health insurance will lead to a decrease in wages or other fringe benefits, but not to an overall increase in the cost of production.

However, this theoretical result does not preclude employer interest in finding cheaper ways to provide the health insurance benefit. In order to retain employees, the employer must maintain the market equilibrium level of employee happiness or utility. Suppose that employee happiness is a function of taxable wages and the characteristics of the health insurance policy (or policies) offered by the firm. *Characteristics* in this case refers to level of coverage, quality of care obtained from participating providers, and other similar characteristics, but not the *cost* of the insurance product. If the employer (and employees) can find a way to offer a new health insurance product that maintains the same level of employee happiness as a previous product but at lower cost, then that firm will be able to offer higher wages and thus gain an advantage in the market for labor. So employers do care about the cost of health insurance products, even though they do not actually pay the cost of insurance.

Vistnes, Cooper, and Vistnes (2001) reviewed several different strategies of offering multiple health plans to employees, including a single health plan and multiple plans with different methods of employer premium contributions. They found that total costs were minimized when the employer offered multiple health plans and set a level dollar contribution to premiums.

It is possible, of course, for employers to structure premium contributions so that employee enrollment choices *do* affect employer costs. Suppose that an employer sets its contribution to premiums at an equal percentage of the premium for each plan, and does not adjust wages or other fringe benefits when employees choose more expensive plans. In that case, the employer's labor costs will rise when employees choose more expensive plans. If HCAP and employer-sponsored private plans were offered side by side, it would be important to consider the employer's incentives regarding employee choice of plan. If the employer's costs were reduced by enrolling high-risk employees in HCAP, for example, then the employer's incentive would be to structure the contribution to premiums to encourage enrollment of high risks in HCAP. One way to neutralize an employer's incentives is to require the employer to make the same risk-adjusted contribution to premiums for both HCAP and private health plans.

A practical question regarding the employer premium contribution arises when benefit levels are very different from one plan to the next. This problem becomes especially acute when large-deductible health plans are mixed with traditional health insurance products. The way the problem is resolved can have the effect of distinguishing health plan features that are considered essential from those that are considered amenities. If the employer sets a contribution to premiums based on the lowest-cost plan in the choice set, regardless of its features, then the cost-increasing features of more-expensive plans that are not shared by the least-expensive plan implicitly are deemed amenities, rather than essentials, and employees must purchase those plan features with out-of-pocket dollars.

The Employee's Contribution to Premiums—Tax Effects

The tax treatment of employer and employee premiums is an important part of any health insurance proposal. Presumably, any employer contributions to health insurance costs would be deductible from corporate income taxes as a cost of doing business, and under Hacker's proposal employer contributions to health plan premiums would continue to be exempt from the employee's personal income and FICA taxes.

Employee-paid premium contributions to HCAP would be taxed as other employee-paid premiums under current law. This strategy almost certainly would ensure, holding other factors constant, that the wealthy would remain in private plans while the poor would join HCAP. Hacker acknowledges, "Thus, enrollees in the Health Care for America Plan would mostly be current beneficiaries of Medicaid and S-CHIP, low-wage employees, and the working uninsured, as well as early retirees, contingent workers, and the self-employed" (Hacker 2007, 5).

Setting Provider Payment Rates in the Government-Run Health Plan

The controversy over provider-fee discounts obtained by a large payer with price-setting ability has been mentioned at several points. As in the case of administrative costs, the goal of provider fees is not to minimize them but to find the efficient level. The efficient level is the point that equalizes the supply of, and demand for, the services of health care providers. As discussed by Nyman (2003), one difficulty is that in markets with insurance, the level of demand for an insured service is likely to include a component of inefficient moral hazard. Should provider fees be set to supply that inefficient level of demand?

Another problem is that pricing decisions by a large payer can affect the supply of services to enrollees in smaller health plans in complex and often nonintuitive ways. For example, if the large price-setting plan reduces its provider-fee levels, it might seem obvious that providers would raise their prices to other health plans. However, if the large plan lowers its fees, providers should want to see *more* patients from the smaller health plans, and the way to do that is for them to *lower,* not *raise* their prices to patients in those smaller plans. Analysts who believe the opposite should ask themselves if they believe that providers would *lower* their prices to smaller plans if the larger plan *raised* its fees.

Are smaller health plans placed at a disadvantage in the market for provider services relative to Medicare? Should providers be required to serve enrollees of private health plans for the same fees as FFS Medicare (or the public plan in HCAP)? If FFS Medicare's fee discounts are cost-justified because FFS Medicare patients are cheaper for providers to treat than the patients of smaller health plans, then inefficiency in FFS Medicare price discounts would be limited to any inefficiency associated with incomplete risk adjustment. If FFS Medicare's discounts are the result of monopsony pricing power, then extending that pricing power to private plans would increase the level of inefficiency.

Taking FFS Medicare as an example, we could ask what it would mean to require providers to serve private plans' enrollees for the same fees as FFS Medicare's beneficiaries. As in other markets, private plans are free to demand any level of discount they like from providers, and providers are free to accept or reject the offer. Presumably, mandating FFS Medicare fee levels for private plans would mean the provider who failed to grant FFS Medicare discounts to private plans would become ineligible to serve FFS Medicare beneficiaries. In areas where such a mandate had any teeth, the result would be de facto price controls, and there is no guarantee that FFS Medicare's fee levels are efficient (Dowd et al. 2006–7). The same concern extends to all forms of price controls, including all-payer fee schedules determined administratively rather than by the market.

FFS Medicare fees vary only by the geographic practice cost indicator, and that adjuster takes only the price of inputs to the practice of medicine into account, not market conditions like variations in demand or supply of health care services. FFS Medicare fees might be inefficiently high in some markets and inefficiently low in others. Pricing by private health plans provides an independent check on the efficiency of FFS fees. The lack of responsiveness of FFS Medicare fees to local market conditions as well as the lack of any well-specified process for monitoring the effect of FFS Medicare fees on provider access by Medicare, Medicaid, or commercially insured patients does not provide support for the concept of efficient price setting by the government. However, greater flexibility in Medicare fee setting could open up the process to greater political manipulation.

Who Should Run the New System?

There are two levels of administration to consider in any mixed public and private insurance system: (1) Who should run the public health plan (if there is one); and (2) who should set the rules for the overall system?

If a new government-run plan were established, it would be necessary to consider exactly what *government-run* means. Although policies for FFS Medicare are set by Congress and CMS, claims payments and many quality assurance tasks are administered by private or quasi-private firms. In theory, there is no reason why many of the administrative tasks of the government-run health plan, including disease management, utilization review, marketing, and provider contracting, could not be subcontracted to the private sector. Although CMS would be an obvious candidate to administer a government-run plan, particularly if many of the costs of administration were fixed costs already incurred in the administration of FFS Medicare, it might be difficult for CMS to adapt to, or incorporate, a new system that relied much less heavily on government administration. Otherwise, there might be some advantage to establishing a new independent agency free to innovate and whose performance could be compared to that of CMS.

Assigning administrative responsibility for the entire mixed public-private system is a much more difficult question, and one with a long history, even in the purely private sector. When fully insured HMOs first were offered by employers alongside the employer's self-insured plan, there was concern that employers were establishing premium contribution rules to favor selection of the self-insured plan by good risks.

Throughout the history of private plans in the Medicare program, there have been charges that portions of Congress and CMS were hostile to private plans, and the design of the Tax Equality and Fiscal Responsibility Act (TEFRA)-risk and Medicare+Choice systems, with their restrictions on premium rebates, their uneven reporting requirements for private plans versus FFS Medicare, and the insistence on an HMO-only competitive pricing demonstration in the 1990s, gave those charges some credibility. Periodically, there are proposals to establish a relatively free-standing entity, modeled after the Securities and Exchange Commission or the Federal Reserve Board, to administer a mixed public and private health insurance system in Medicare. Today, in contrast, some claim that CMS is favoring private plans over traditional Medicare (Berenson and Goldstein 2007). Advocates of managed competition often hold up FEHB as a successful example of a quasi-private system in which multiple health plan choices are offered to employees. Although the employer is the federal government, the health plans in FEHB are private, and unlike FFS Medicare, which is micromanaged by Congress, FEHB is managed in a relatively autonomous manner by the Office of Personnel Management. However, the stakes would be much higher in a mixed public-private system for the entire commercial insurance sector, and it seems unlikely that such a system could avoid the political micromanagement that has plagued the Medicare program.

Conclusion

The position that public and private plans each have some intrinsic advantages that do not require artificial support leads to the recommendation that they be offered on the same terms to consumers. Difficulties arise when analysts attempt to impose asymmetric constraints on either set of plans, or plan designs that have not been vetted by the market; requiring the public plan to contract with all willing providers in a market area or to offer unrestricted access to specialists are examples. If the cost increases associated with such restrictions are worth less to consumers than the costs themselves, then advocates of those restrictions will find that they have to impose further restrictions to keep the public plan from being rejected by consumers. The result is an endless array of adjustments designed to favor either public or private plans.

A simpler approach would be to equalize all rules and all subsidies (e.g., premium subsidies for low-income consumers) across public and private plans. Undoubtedly, the result will be some level of inefficiency and some features that will be considered unfair, but the alternative is the somewhat tortured history of private plans in the Medicare program, which cycles from one set of restrictions and overpayments to another.

Notes

1. In fact, they would be *mandated* to enroll in HCAP.

2. In the Hacker proposal, the term HCAP appears to be used to refer to both a government-run health plan (like fee-for-service [FFS] Medicare) and a government-run pool that would feature both the HCAP plan and a selection of private health plans.

3. Employers would have to choose between offering their own health plan (or set of health plans) to their employees or offering the HCAP pool, which would include both the government-run plan and a selection of private plans.

4. While its large market share has allowed Medicare to extract significant price discounts from providers, that advantage must be considered in light of the fact that monopsony can be inefficient. That point might be easier for advocates of bulk purchasing power to grasp if we change "FFS Medicare" to "UnitedHealthcare." FFS Medicare's payments to providers need careful monitoring because FFS Medicare is large enough to affect marketwide supply behavior (Dowd et al. 2006–7).

5. Interestingly, analysts who object to the overpayment of private plans express no concern regarding overpayments to FFS Medicare in areas where FFS Medicare's costs are substantially higher than those of private plans.

6. This topic is more complex than most analyses recognize. For example, most analysts would agree that a health plan should not be held responsible for the diabetes of a new enrollee, but what about an enrollee who has been in the plan for thirty years and develops diabetes?

References

Abelson, Reed. 2008. "Medicare Finds How Hard It Is to Save Money." *New York Times,* April 7.

Berenson, Robert A., and Melissa M. Goldstein. 2007. "Will Medicare Wither on the Vine? How Congress Has Advantaged Medicare Advantage—And What's a Level Playing Field Anyway?" *St. Louis University Journal of Health Law and Policy* 1 (1): 5–43.

Dowd, Bryan E., Robert Coulam, and Roger Feldman. 2000. "A Tale of Four Cities: Medicare Reform and Competitive Pricing." *Health Affairs* 19 (5): 9–29.

Dowd, Bryan E., and Roger Feldman. 1992. "Insurer Competition and Protection from Risk Redefinition in the Individual and Small Group Market." *Inquiry* 29 (2): 148–57.

Dowd, Bryan E., Roger Feldman, and Jon Christianson. 1996. *Competitive Pricing for Medicare.* Washington, DC: American Enterprise Institute Press.

Dowd, Bryan E., Roger Feldman, and Robert Coulam. 2005–6. "FFS Medicare in a Competitive Market Environment." *Health Care Financing Review* 27 (2): 113–26.

Dowd, Bryan E., Roger D. Feldman, John Nyman, and Robert Town. 2006–7. "Setting Prices in FFS Medicare." *Health Care Financing Review* 28 (2): 97–112.

Dowd, Bryan E., Ira Moscovice, Roger Feldman, Michael Finch, Catherine Wisner, and Steven D. Hillson. 1994. "Health Plan Choice in the Twin Cities Medicare Market." *Medical Care* 32 (10): 1–18.

Francis, Walton. 2007. *Guide to Health Plans for Federal Employees.* Washington, DC: Consumer's Checkbook.

Ginsburg, Paul B. 2008. "Employment-Based Health Benefits Under Universal Coverage." *Health Affairs* 27 (3): 675–85.

Hacker, Jacob. 2007. "Health Care for America: A Proposal for Guaranteed, Affordable Health Care for All Americans Building on Medicare and Employment-Based Insurance." Economic Policy Institute Briefing Paper 180. www.sharedprosperity.org/bp180/bp180. pdf. (Accessed 18 November 2008).

Mannheim, Karl, and Jamie Court. 2008. "Not So Fast on the Health Insurance Mandates." *Los Angeles Times* (March 24). www.latimes.com/news/opinion/commentary/la-oe-court24mar24,0,659180.story. (Accessed 1 August 2008.)

McBride, Timothy. 1998. "Disparities in Access to Medicare Managed Care Plans and Their Benefits." *Health Affairs* 17 (6): 170–80.

Medicare Payment Advisory Commission. 2004. *Report to Congress.* Washington, DC: Medicare Payment Advisory Commission, March.

Miller, Robert H., and Harold S. Luft. 1997. "Does Managed Care Lead to Better or Worse Quality of Care?" *Health Affairs* 16 (5): 7–25.

———. 2002. "HMO Plan Performance Update: An Analysis of the Literature, 1997–2001." *Health Affairs* 21 (4): 63–86.

Nyman, John. 2003. *The Theory of Demand for Health Insurance.* Stanford, CA: Stanford University Press.

Pauly, Mark V. 2005. "Competition and New Technology." *Health Affairs* 24 (6): 1523–35.

Pauly, Mark V., and Len M. Nichols. 2002. "The Nongroup Health Insurance Market: Short on Facts, Long on Opinions and Policy Disputes." *Health Affairs* Web exclusive (October 23): W325–W44. http://content.healthaffairs.org/cgi/search?andore xactfulltext=and&resourcetype=1&disp_type=&author1=pauly&fulltext=&pubda te_year=2002&volume=&firstpage= (Accessed 17 November 2008).

Robinson, James C., Harold S. Luft, Laura B. Gardner, and Ellen M. Morrison. 1991. "A Method for Risk-Adjusting Employer Contributions to Competing Health Plans." *Inquiry* 28 (2): 107–16.

Thorpe, Kenneth E., and Adam Atherly. 2002. "Medicare + Choice: Current Role and Near-Term Prospects." *Health Affairs* Web exclusive (July 17): W242–W252. http://content. healthaffairs.org/cgi/search?andorexactfulltext=and&resourcetype=1&disp_type= &author1=thorpe&fulltext=&pubdate_year=2002&volume=&firstpage= (Accessed 17 November 2008).

U.S. Census Bureau. 2007. *Income, Poverty, and Health Insurance Coverage in the United States: 2006* (August). www.census.gov/prod/2007pubs/p60–233.pdf. (Accessed 1 August 2008).

Vistnes, Jessica P., Philip F. Cooper, and Gregory S. Vistnes. 2001. "The Effect of Competition on Employment-Related Health Insurance Premiums." *International Journal of Health Care Finance and Economics* 1 (2): 159–87.

Welch, W. Pete, Christopher Bergsten, Charles Cutler, Carmella Bocchino, and Richard I. Smith. 2002. "Disease Management Practices in Health Plans." *American Journal of Managed Care* 8 (4): 353–61.

4

Regulating Private Health Insurance

Timothy Stoltzfus Jost

This chapter examines the role of health insurance regulation and the role it could play in a reformed health care system. It explores the nature of health insurance and alternative approaches to its regulation. It considers the status of state, then federal health insurance regulation, describing the development of regulation and examining arguments about regulatory interventions. Finally, it considers how health insurance should be regulated in a reformed health care system, as well as where authority for insurance regulation should reside.

The Health Insurance Relationship

At its core, the insurance relationship is based on a contract under which the insured pays money to an insurance company with the understanding that should losses described in the contract occur later, the insurer will cover the loss. The insurer pools risk, collecting premiums from many insureds, only a few of whom will recover their full premium, at least in the short run. The insurer, however, is at risk of paying out large sums of money for the benefit of a few in the short run, and for the benefit of many more in the long run.

This relationship is problematic. First, its viability depends on the financial capacity of the insurer to respond to claims, the total of which could exceed the total premiums received. Second, the insured depends on the insurer's good faith and efficient business practices for the prompt and fair payment of claims. In the short run at least, it may be in the financial interest of the insurer to delay payment of claims and to dispute questionable claims, or even to refuse to pay legitimate claims. Third, an insurance contract is a complex instrument, drafted by the insurer. Few terms, if any, are negotiated. The insured is dependent on the insurer for ensuring that the contract meets the reasonable expectations of the insured for coverage being purchased and does not contain terms that can be used unfairly to deny coverage later. Finally, the insured is dependent on the marketing practices of the insurer to understand the nature of the insurance product being purchased and to avoid unreasonable expectations about coverage.

The insurance transaction is complicated by problems of adverse selection and moral hazard. The applicant knows more about the extent and nature of the risk the applicant faces than does the insurer, and is more likely to secure insurance if that risk is perceived to be greater than normal. The insurer, therefore, has to worry about being taken advantage of by applicants who expect to make claims. Adverse selection, moreover, not only makes it more likely that persons at high risk will purchase insurance, but also that they will purchase more complete coverage than those who perceive themselves at low risk. Thus, adverse selection not only affects the market as a whole, but also disadvantages specific insurers or policies offering more comprehensive coverage. Insurers respond to the threat of adverse selection by carefully assessing the risks they insure, by denying coverage to high-risk applicants in some instances or charging them higher rates in others, and by attempting to shed themselves of bad risks once selected (practices known as cherry-picking). Insurers can also refuse to insure preexisting risks, impose waiting periods before certain risks are covered, or scrutinize applications for potential misrepresentations once a claim is made.

Moral hazard refers to the fact that once a risk is insured it is more likely to be incurred. For example, an insured driver may drive less carefully; a person with health insurance may smoke more or exercise less. Once insured, a person is more likely to incur a loss, particularly if the insured has some ability to cause the insured loss and the possibility of recovering a payment from the insurer that exceeds the true extent of the loss; for example, an insured shipowner scuttles a ship to collect on the insurance policy.

The health insurance transaction poses its own problems beyond those in other insurance. First, it is very difficult, if not impossible, to fully specify in advance the coverage of a health insurance contract. There are simply too many products and services potentially covered by a health insurance contract to describe what is covered and what is not. Typically, policies have used terms such as *medically necessary services,* but under such policy language, everything depends on who decides what is necessary and what procedures are followed in making and reviewing that determination. Second, because of the complexity of health and health care, it is often difficult for the insured to understand in advance the extent of coverage needed. In particular, insurance applicants are unlikely to comprehend the nature and extent of the risks against which they are insured, and are likely to use heuristic devices to choose the extent of coverage to purchase. An applicant may, for example, purchase insurance for a particular kind of cancer from which the purchaser's aunt has died, but forego coverage for another condition that is much more likely to occur.

The market dynamics of the health insurance transaction are also unusual. In most markets, sellers are attentive to their high-use customers. Businesses have reason to cater to those who demand a high volume of their products or services to keep their loyalty and to secure return business. Precisely the opposite is true in health insurance markets. Insurers lose money on individuals or groups who need extensive and expensive health care services and thus face an incentive to underserve these insureds and to encourage them to disenroll or even to cancel coverage if possible. This is true if the insurer is limited in its ability to charge higher premiums for high-risk insureds by state law, but even an insurer who can charge risk-based premiums may underestimate the true cost of a policy and attempt later to shed itself of its obligations. Of course, an insurer cannot ignore the reputational effects it may suffer if it consistently underserves its insureds, but an insurer that provides excellent service to its low-cost insureds (providing hassle-free coverage for primary and preventive care, for example), or even for its otherwise healthy insureds who periodically experience higher-cost episodes, such as sports injuries or normal maternity care, may well be able to get away with providing inferior coverage or service for rare but very high-cost events, such as organ transplants.

Serious agency problems also attend health insurance markets. First, most Americans receive health care coverage either through their place of employment or through a government program. Ultimately, all health insurance is paid for by individuals, if not directly through premiums then as taxpayers or as employees who receive less in wages and in other benefits because of the cost of health insurance. Persons insured through a government program or through their place of employment, however, are unlikely to be aware of the cost of their insurance coverage, and depending on how costs are distributed among employees or taxpayers, may have little responsibility for that cost. Tax subsidization of employment-based insurance further removes insureds from the cost of insurance. Risk of moral hazard may, therefore, be enhanced in employment-based or public insurance.

Because most private health insurance is purchased by employers (or provided directly by self-insured employers), this affords advantages. Insured employees benefit from employer expertise in purchasing, as well as from economies of scale. Insurers also face less of a risk of adverse selection from employment-based policies (at least those that insure large employers) because the primary insureds are healthy enough to work, employment is sought because of factors other than the desire for insurance for an anticipated risk, and the size of employment-based pools decreases insurer risk from any one individual. Insurers can afford to give employers a better rate than they would give individuals, where risk of adverse selection is higher.

However, employers that provide health benefits are purchasing (or self-insuring) a policy to cover all of their insured employees, and may not secure the coverage most valuable to any particular employee. Also, employers must be concerned about the cost of insuring their employees, and this concern may overshadow other concerns such as difficulties their employees may encounter with claims processing or generosity of coverage, especially for uncommon conditions. Insurance coverage is also less stable because it is employment based. While individuals often have long-term relationships with their auto, home, or life insurers, they are likely to change health insurers whenever they change jobs, and employers often change insurers from year to year as they look for the best bargains in the market. Finally, insureds play little role in negotiating employment-based insurance contracts and may not ever see the insurance contract itself, much less understand its terms.

When insureds need health care services, they encounter another agency problem. Although individual insureds usually decide whether or not to seek health care products and services, once they decide to do so, the scope of the products and services they receive is often out of their hands. Physicians and other health care professionals and providers determine what is ordered and provided. Patients often do not fully understand what services they need, much less how much those services cost. Rather, professionals and providers determine what services are provided (with some input from the patient), and often these same professionals and providers are paid for those same services. Risk of moral hazard is, therefore, enhanced in health insurance transactions. Insurers and managed care organizations must address this, and often provide the only real oversight of health care utilization and cost.

Finally, health insurance is unusual because health care is perceived to be different from other products and services, and health risks as different from other risks. Public insurance programs cover health risks for large populations, and support for health care access for all is widespread. For individuals, health care transactions are fraught with fear and anxiety. Life and limb can be at risk. Objective economic judgments are difficult under these circumstances. Indeed, individuals may demand lower levels of cost sharing than they might be comfortable with for other forms of insurance to avoid having to make economic trade-offs under stress.

Governance of Health Insurance

Given these characteristics of insurance in general and of health insurance in particular, how should insurance be governed? A number of possibilities are conceivable.

First, health insurance could be left completely unregulated, governed only by markets. The insurer and insured would negotiate the terms and price of coverage. Presumably the insurer would insist on full disclosure of known risks, charging a premium proportionate to the risk and imposing limitations of coverage necessary to protect itself against adverse selection and moral hazard. If the insurer was subsequently unwilling or unable to cover claims, it would suffer reputational injury and thus have a harder time finding customers in the future, but would experience no other consequences.

This approach, of course, does little to help the individual insured whose claim is denied unfairly or in breach of the insurance agreement. At the very least, therefore, the market needs to be supplemented by judicial oversight. Breach-of-contract lawsuits are common in insurance law. Insurers draft insurance contracts that would be expected to give them an advantage in contract litigation. Recognizing the imbalance of bargaining power in these transactions, however, the courts have come to the aid of the insured through the common-law doctrine of *contra preferentum*—construing the contract against the insurer where it is ambiguous— and the doctrine of protecting the reasonable expectations of insureds. Some states have also permitted punitive damages in bad faith breach-of-contract actions against insurers who have blatantly violated their contractual obligations.

Common-law rights of insureds can also be supplemented by statutory rights enforceable through private litigation. These can take the form of general consumer-protection statutes or can address particular insurance abuses, such as unfair statutes for claims settlement practices. Such statutes can set basic standards for insurer obligations. They can make it likely that insurance contracts offer the terms insureds are likely to expect or that insurers treat insureds fairly. They can also encourage insureds to protect their rights through litigation by offering statutory penalties or attorneys' fees for prevailing insureds.

Private litigation has significant limitations, however. First, it is very costly, time-consuming, and inefficient. Unless a great deal of money is involved, it rarely pays for an insured to hire a lawyer and sue an insurer for a claim denial. Given the time it takes for a case to be resolved, moreover, litigation rarely meets the insured's immediate need for service or for payment for a service. Because insurers draft contracts, which the insured often never sees before a claim is made, insureds face an uphill battle. Moreover, insurers are "repeat players" in litigation, while insureds are not, so insurers are in a superior position to understand and control litigation. For all of these reasons, insurers have good reason to discount the likelihood of losing, or even facing, litigation, and thus relying on litigation is unlikely to optimally protect insureds.

High costs and inefficiencies of litigation can be avoided through alternative dispute resolution. Both state and federal governments require health insurers to offer internal review mechanisms, which provide a quick and inexpensive approach to clearing up mistaken or ill-considered claim denials. Virtually all states also provide for external review of managed care claim denials. External reviews, often binding, do not necessarily require insureds to hire lawyers and must be resolved within reasonably tight time frames. They provide an efficient approach to ensuring that insurers live up to their commitments.

Claims review is in some instances handled by private entities. Some managed care contracts expressly require arbitration of claims disputes, while some state statutes provide for the use of private contractors for external review. Fairness concerns arise when the insurer is permitted to choose the contract interpreter and enforcer, but unbiased private review entities may assist in providing efficient dispute resolution.

Private accreditation organizations can also provide a form of nongovernmental standardization and regulation of insurers. The National Council for Quality Assurance, for example, accredits managed care organizations, providing standards with which accredited organizations agree to comply and offering insurance purchasers a means of identifying organizations that accept these standards, and even, through the application of the Healthcare Effectiveness Data and Information Set Act measures, a means of comparing the performance of accredited organizations.

However, private dispute resolution and accreditation, and even litigation, are unlikely to deal successfully with insurers guilty of out-and-out fraud. This is a serious problem, particularly during times when insurance premiums are increasing rapidly. A Government Accountability Office (2004) report covering the years 2000–2002 found 144 entities that sold bogus insurance in every state to fifteen thousand employers covering two hundred thousand insureds, leaving $252 million in uncovered claims, only 21 percent of which had been recovered at the time of the survey. Insurance scams during 1988–91 left four hundred thousand people with more than $123 million in unpaid bills (Kofman et al. 2006). Ensuring the financial responsibility of insurers and preventing or sanctioning marketing and claims-processing fraud are the responsibility of government regulation.

Regulation, however, can take different forms. Some administrative regimes, for example, operate through ex-post case-by-case adjudication and enforcement. The administrator simply waits until a statute is violated and then takes enforcement action, either through administrative adjudication or through litigation. Beyond this, administrators can promulgate regulations that expand and elaborate on a statutory scheme. In some instances, promulgating regulations requires explicit authorization; in other instances, it is assumed to be within the general power of the regulator. Some regulators also offer advisory opinions or rulings, interpreting general regulations in the context of specific circumstances.

Finally, a regulator can become actively involved in supervising regulated entities, ensuring compliance with solvency and reserve requirements as a condition of granting licensure; reviewing prefiled insurance policies and rates before use; examining the regulated entity and auditing its books; or requiring regular reports. This form of oversight can be very prescriptive and intrusive and can involve the regulator deeply in the operation of the regulated entity. With respect to some activities such as ensuring solvency, however, it might prove the most useful form of regulation. What follows examines emerging forms of insurance regulation, first at the state and then at the federal level.

State Health Insurance Regulation

Early Regulatory Efforts

By the time health insurance came into common use in the 1930s, authority in the states to regulate insurance was well established. State regulation of insurance dates back to the eighteenth century, and state jurisdiction over insurance regulation was confirmed by the Supreme Court's decision in *Paul v. Virginia,* which held that insurance was not sold in interstate commerce, and thus not subject to federal control (*Paul v. Virginia,* 8 Wall.168 [1869]). In 1944, the Supreme Court reversed itself, holding that insurers were engaged in interstate commerce and thus governed by the federal antitrust laws (*United States v. Southeastern Underwriters Association,* 322 U.S. 533 [1944]). Congress adopted the McCarran-Ferguson Act, ceding jurisdiction over regulation back to the states except where Congress explicitly provided otherwise. The federal government did not play a role in insurance regulation until the 1970s.

State regulation has long been coordinated by the National Association of Insurance Commissioners (NAIC), founded in 1871. NAIC model statutes and regulations often form a template for the laws and regulations adopted by the states, and thus bring uniformity and national character to insurance regulation. The NAIC has an ambiguous status, in part a private trade association and in part a support center for government officials, but also dependent on the insurance industry for financial support through fees it collects for database filings and for technical support and advice.

Financial Responsibility

From the beginning, states regulated commercial health insurance as part of the larger life and accident insurance industry. This regulation focused on the financial responsibility of insurers, long a concern of state insurance regulation. Insurer solvency remains a serious concern of the states, and lies at the heart of their objections to recent proposed federal legislation that would free health insurers from state regulation, discussed later in this chapter. Insurers are required to meet specific capitalization requirements as a condition of initial licensure and to maintain reserves sufficient to meet their ongoing obligations. Insurers must regularly file audited financial reports with the states and are subject to periodic examinations and audits by state insurance departments. States have proceedings in place to manage insolvent insurers (often through transferring their obligations to ongoing insurance concerns) and have solvency guarantee funds to cover the obligations of insurers that become insolvent.

Application of health insurer financial accountability requirements has long been problematic with respect to some forms of managed care organizations. The federal Bankruptcy Code expressly excludes insurance companies from its coverage, leaving the issue of insurer solvency to the states (Bankruptcy Code § 109[b] [2]). It was for a time arguable that traditional staff-model health maintenance organizations (HMOs) were service providers rather than insurers, and subject to oversight by the bankruptcy courts rather than by state insurance regulators, but the Supreme Court's pronouncement in 2002 that HMOs are insurers would seem to settle this issue (*Rush v. Parham,* 536 U.S. 355, 371 [2002]). When provider-sponsored organizations and integrated delivery systems became common in the 1990s, they similarly contended that they should not have to meet the same financial responsibility requirements as insurers, because their contractual obligation was to provide services rather than to carry financial risk. The practice of "downstreaming" risk through capitated payment of providers or professional groups (which in turn may be at risk for payment of other health care products and services) further complicated the issue of financial responsibility of managed care organizations, when many risk-bearing physician groups went bankrupt in the late 1990s. States have responded variously to the problem of risk-bearing providers, imposing financial responsibility requirements on risk-bearing providers, requiring insurers to assume responsibility for the obligations of downstream risk bearers who default on those obligations, and requiring providers to hold consumers harmless when risk bearers fail to compensate them for their services.

Other Traditional Regulatory Concerns

Financial responsibility was not the only concern of traditional insurance regulation. Regulators required insurers in the emerging health insurance industry to incorporate into their policies "standard provisions" that had been formulated to govern the insurance industry long before health insurance became a significant line of business. These provisions dealt with issues such as time limits for making claims and proof of loss. Insurers were also prohibited from engaging in unfair or deceptive advertising and marketing practices. All states required insurers to file health insurance policies and most required filing of rates, but state approval was not required before policies or rates went into effect. States retained the right to disapprove policies that were "unjust, unfair, inequitable or misleading" but rarely interfered with health insurance underwriting or rate-setting practices, believing that market control was adequate. States also imposed premium taxes on commercial insurers, which served as a significant revenue source. Finally, coordination of coverage where multiple policies might cover the same risk has long been addressed by statute and regulation, as well as by contract. But in general, as long as insurers remained solvent, paid premium taxes, met filing requirements, and avoided outright fraud, they were quite free to conduct their businesses as they saw fit.

From the beginning, Blue Cross and Blue Shield plans were regulated somewhat differently from commercial plans. The Blue plans argued that they were non-profit service benefit plans rather than for-profit insurance plans, and thus should not be required to meet the capitalization and reserve requirements imposed on commercial insurers or to pay premium taxes. In fact, they functioned for a time much like public insurers, offering open enrollment to all applicants and charging community-rated premiums. Recognizing their role, most states adopted special laws authorizing "health services plans," with many of these laws reducing the financial responsibility requirements imposed on the Blue plans and freeing them from premium taxes. In exchange, however, the Blues were subject to public service requirements. Some states, for example, required the Blue plans to have substantial public representation on their boards. Blue plans were required to file a description of their benefit structures and a majority of states required that these be approved by the state. Some states required Blue plans to provide free choice of provider. Half of the states required regulatory approval of Blue Cross and Blue Shield reimbursement or fee schedules. Two-thirds of states required prior approval of Blue Cross and Blue Shield rates, while most other states regulated rates through subsequent disapproval provisions. Some states required community rating. As hospital cost inflation became a problem in the 1950s and 1960s, a few states used their rate-making power to force Blue Cross and Blue Shield plans to become more assertive in attempting to control hospital prices, setting the stage for greater regulatory involvement in insurance-rating practices later in the twentieth century.

Coverage Mandates

Although regulators were long content to allow the market to determine the actual terms of insurance policies, by the middle of the twentieth century, some states began to look more closely at the actual coverage health insurance policies afforded. In 1949 California adopted a Minimum Benefits Law that prohibited the sale of health insurance policies unless the policy's benefits were "sufficient to be of real economic value" to the insured. The law also imposed several more specific regulatory requirements on insurance policies, and was supplemented by even more specific regulations. This legislation was not reproduced outside California, although the NAIC did briefly consider the minimum coverage issue, and some states did interpret their rate-approval powers to include the assurance of a reasonable relationship between premiums and benefits.

Beginning in the 1950s, a number of states limited the ability of insurers to cancel, and in some instances, to refuse to renew health insurance policies. Prior to that time, insurance policies contained clauses allowing the insurer to cancel at any time with five days' notice and a pro rata return of premiums collected, a provision subject to abuse. Most of these laws simply prohibited cancellation during the term of the policy or required advance notice of nonrenewal, but North Carolina required up to two years' notice of refusal to renew (depending on the length of time the policy had been in force), and New York prohibited nonrenewal of policies that had been in force for at least two years. The New York law also permitted insureds who had lost employee coverage to convert from group to individual policies.

In the 1970s and 1980s, state coverage mandates—statutes requiring health insurers to cover specific persons, services, or providers—became much more common. Among the earliest mandates were laws requiring insurers to cover the newborn children of insureds, which were enacted in all but six of the states by 1980, and laws requiring coverage of handicapped dependents; the services of optometrists, psychologists, and chiropractors; and alcoholism treatment, all of which became common in the 1970s and 1980s. Coverage mandates continued to spread during the 1990s and through the early 2000s. Some have been enacted now in all or virtually all states (mammography screening, minimum maternity stay, chiropractors, adopted children) and some in only a few (acupuncturists, naturopaths, grandchildren, morbid obesity care). Some mandates require insurers only to offer applicants specific forms of coverage; others require coverage actually to be provided. A third of the states impose more than forty coverage mandates, and all but two impose more than twenty.

A number of arguments are offered in support of mandates. Some are justified as assuring the availability of public goods or preventing negative externalities. Examples include vaccine coverage mandates, which help reduce the prevalence of communicable diseases, and emergency care coverage mandates, which prevent insurers from shifting to hospitals the cost of emergency care that hospitals are required by law to provide. Some mandates address adverse selection. If insurers are allowed to exclude coverage for high-cost but uncommon conditions (or even some common but avoidable conditions such as pregnancy), persons who need coverage for those conditions will be forced to deal with a limited pool of insurers, who will then need to charge more for coverage. Some mandates protect insureds from opportunistic behavior on the part of insurers interpreting vaguely worded contracts (for example, exclusions of "experimental care"). Others acknowledge the "bounded rationality" of insurance purchasers confronted with a choice among complicated and technical insurance contracts, stepping in to protect those consumers against significant risks they might not consider.

Coverage mandates evoke visceral opposition from insurers and their trade associations, business associations, and promarket advocacy groups. These groups argue that mandates increase the cost of insurance, both directly by raising premiums and indirectly by increasing moral hazard. The increased cost of insurance, they argue, causes more businesses to self-insure, because, as is explained further below, the federal Employee Retirement Income Security Act (ERISA) permits self-insured employee benefit plans to escape state mandates. Insofar as self-insurance is inefficient, especially for small businesses, this is likely to decrease the value of insurance. The increased cost of insurance causes other employers to simply drop insurance, thus increasing the number of uninsured. Alternatively, mandates cause employers to decrease employees' wages to pay for the mandate. Mandate opponents also argue that mandates are not rational responses to real problems, but rather an irrational reaction by legislators to highly publicized anecdotes or the product of lobbying campaigns by highly organized and well-funded provider groups and disease organizations. Finally, many mandate critics base their opposition on normative grounds—government should not compel individuals or firms to enter into contracts that they themselves do not choose.

Although most studies show that mandates increase the cost of insurance and reduce coverage, not all do (Monheit and Rizzo 2007). Some studies even show that some mandates reduce the cost of coverage, because they permit the substitution of less-expensive for more-expensive forms of care, while other studies show that, while coverage mandates may increase cost, they do not significantly reduce employer offers of insurance coverage.

Although economic logic compels the conclusion that mandates will increase premium cost and decrease coverage, there are several reasons why these results may not follow ineluctably. First, there is some evidence that small businesses (most affected by mandates, since large businesses self-insure and mandates often do not apply to nongroup policies) have a low elasticity of demand. Small businesses either offer insurance or do not, but they are not likely to drop or add insurance in response to small fluctuations in cost. Moreover, most mandated benefits (such as acupuncture) have very minor effects on insurance cost, and those that have major effects on cost, such as mental health coverage mandates, involve services that employers are likely to cover in any event. If insured employers are offering mandated benefits, mandates do not affect their costs. In fact, large self-insured employers often offer mandated benefits even though they are not affected by the mandates, because of ERISA, and attempts by states to allow small businesses to buy mandate-free bare-bones policies have had few takers. Third, it may be that employees value mandated benefits and thus are willing to absorb the cost. Surveys show that employees express themselves willing to forgo taxable wages in exchange for health insurance coverage at levels approximating the median cost of health insurance coverage.

In response to the concerns of mandate opponents, a number of states have taken steps to limit mandates. Eighteen states have adopted laws requiring that new proposed mandates be subjected to cost-benefit analysis, while an additional eight states also review mandates retroactively to study their effects. A number of states have adopted laws that excuse very small businesses from coverage mandates, allowing them to purchase bare-bones policies. It is not clear how effective these laws have been, but it appears that the lobbying of mandate opponents is succeeding—very few new mandates have been adopted since 2001, while some mandates have been repealed.

Small-Group and Individual Market Underwriting and Rating Reforms

States invariably differentiate in health insurance regulation between large groups (usually more than fifty members), small groups (three to fifty members), and the nongroup market (covering individuals and individual families). It has long been understood that the large-group health insurance market functions rather well, but that the small-group and nongroup (individual) markets do not. Virtually all large employers offer health insurance to their full-time employees, and some even to their part-time employees. Small employers are much less likely to offer health insurance to their employees, and the nongroup market has remained marginal, covering only a fraction of the uninsured who are not members of groups.

From the perspective of insurers, the small-group market is problematic and the nongroup market even more so. Small groups vary significantly in their risk profiles and present a substantial threat of adverse selection, while these problems are even greater within the individual market. Insurers have traditionally responded by being cautious in underwriting small groups and individually denying, canceling, or refusing to renew coverage for particularly high-risk groups and individuals; charging high premiums to other groups and individuals that seem to pose heightened risk (and low premiums to healthy groups and individuals); increasing rates sharply from year to year as the risk profile of an initially healthy group deteriorates; charging a risk premium to give them ample cushion when faced with significant underwriting uncertainty; and using preexisting-condition clauses, waiting periods, or postclaim underwriting (revisiting the insurance application after a claim is filed to seek a means of canceling the policy) to protect themselves against adverse selection. The administrative costs of carrying out these strategies increase the cost of small-group and individual policies, which are already much higher than those of large groups because of additional marketing costs and agent commissions.

In many states, the problems of the small-group and individual markets were addressed in part by the Blue Cross and Blue Shield plans, insurers of last resort. The Blue plans were for a time more likely to have open enrollment and community-rated premiums and to be subject to state rate regulation in exchange for tax subsidies. Over time, however, the Blues moved to experience rating and became less willing to take on applicants unacceptable to other insurers.

Starting at around 1990, states began to enact small-group market reforms. The most common of these were guaranteed-issue and guaranteed-renewal laws, which required insurers that sold policies in the small-group market to insure all applicants and to renew policies upon expiration. Another very common reform limited preexisting-conditions exclusion clauses. In 1996, as is discussed below, guaranteed-issue, guaranteed-renewal, and preexisting-condition limitation reforms were adopted at the national level by the Health Insurance Portability and Accountability Act. Some states adopted laws requiring insurers to offer a standard policy that must be offered to any small group that desires it. Most states also adopted rating reforms, aimed at limiting the disparity of insurance premiums. Rating-band requirements typically limit the dispersion of rates between the worst and best risks covered by a particular plan to a specified ratio (e.g., median plus or minus 15 percent), but because rates can also vary in many states based on other factors, such as age, gender, geographic location, and type of plan, a policy covering a small group of older unhealthy workers in a high-cost area could cost sixteen times as much as a policy covering a group of healthy young workers in a low-cost area, even where rating dispersion is limited. A few states have gone further, requiring community rating, although most of these states do allow some variance based on factors such as age and geographic location. A number of states also limit the extent to which insurers can raise premiums from year to year.

These reforms have been supplemented in a number of states by attempts to broaden risk pooling to lessen the risk of insurers who accept high-risk insureds. States have established risk pools through which small-group insurers can voluntarily share their highest-risk insureds, and some states make participation in risk pooling mandatory. A few states have also established state reinsurance programs through which the state assumes the cost of the highest-risk insureds. Finally, some states have established purchasing cooperatives to allow small groups to shop for health insurance with greater bargaining power and lower transaction costs.

Many states have also adopted reforms in the individual market, but these reforms tend to be less widespread and demanding. The individual market is perceived to be volatile and under threat from adverse selection, and there is concern that aggressive state regulation could destroy the market. As noted, states have long prohibited the cancellation of individual insurance policies, and virtually all states have now adopted guaranteed-renewal provisions in the individual market. Thirty-one states limit use of preexisting-conditions clauses (which are also limited by federal law in cases where an individual converts from the group to the nongroup market after having been insured for eighteen months or more), and a number of states require guaranteed issue. Only ten states limit the range of rating variation, however, while eight states impose some form of community rating. A handful of states also have voluntary or mandatory reinsurance programs. The primary response of about two-thirds of the states to the problem of providing nongroup coverage to high-risk individuals has been to establish state-managed high-risk pools to which individuals can turn if they are denied coverage for insurance in the regular market. The premiums for this coverage are usually quite high—125 to 150 percent of average premiums for comparable insurance—and are thus unaffordable for many high-risk uninsureds. Even so, premiums do not cover the cost of coverage, and are supplemented by state funds or assessments against insurers. Only a half dozen state risk pools have ten thousand participants, and most states have fewer than five thousand members.

State insurance rating reforms have not provoked as much opposition from insurers as have other mandates; indeed, some have been supported by insurers who were concerned about the volatility of the small-group market and welcomed a level playing field. They have, however, been vigorously opposed by free-market advocates and have been received with skepticism by economists. It stands to reason that if insurance premiums are reduced for high-risk groups and individuals, they must be increased for low-risk groups and individuals. Because there are many more low-risk than high-risk groups and individuals, the trade-off for better access for the high risks could be a substantial increase in low-risk uninsureds. In a worst-case scenario, an insurance market could enter a death spiral as more and more low-risk insureds left and high-risk applicants entered the market, making insurance unaffordable not just to low-risk but also normal-risk individuals and groups. Moreover, as higher-risk individuals and groups tend to be older and better compensated than lower-risk individuals and groups, equity issues are raised by transferring the costs of health insurance from the former to the latter.

Again, however, reality is more complicated than theory. Early reports claimed that community rating in the individual market had dramatically increased the number of uninsured in states that required it, but later analysis showed that the reports were badly flawed. In fact, empirical studies tend to show that small-group reforms have on the whole not had much effect, for good or for ill. Some higher-risk groups have been able to get affordable insurance, some lower-risk groups have dropped insurance, but neither effect has been dramatic. Individual market reforms have reduced coverage for low-risk individuals in some states, but comprehensive reforms have increased coverage for at least higher-income high-risk insureds, and again the effect of reforms has not been as dramatic as could have been predicted. High-risk pools in most states have remained small, while purchasing cooperatives have proved unpopular. In fact, insurance coverage at any one time seems to have much more to do with the state of the job market than with the insurance market. Moreover, whatever effects insurance regulation might have had on increasing prices were overwhelmed by the price-lowering effects of the movement to managed care and of vigorous competition in some insurance markets during the 1990s. In any event, few states have adopted market reforms since the late 1990s.

One effect of state reforms, however, has been the proliferation of attempts to avoid them through the formation of ersatz large groups such as multiple-employer welfare exchanges, group trusts, association health plans, and other stratagems. For example, a small-business association can offer group insurance as a benefit to its members, resulting in a group that is large enough to escape small-group rating requirements. Although many are sponsored by legitimate trade associations, many others have been referred to as "air-breather associations" (open to anyone who breathes air). Although most states regulate in-state associations, about half of the states exempt national associations from some or all of the standards that they apply to in-state insurers. Association markets have been volatile, with group associations actively engaging in cherry-picking and charging steep premium increases from year to year, while businesses change associations frequently to obtain lower rates. There is also a long history of scams and fraudulent activity in the markets for association health plans and multiple-employer welfare exchanges.

Managed Care Reforms

A third area of state legislative and regulatory activity, during the late 1990s and early 2000s, has been managed care reform. Prepaid group practices, which later came to be known as HMOs, date back to the early days of health insurance. They were for decades subject to vigorous opposition from organized medicine; indeed, the American Medical Association was criminally convicted of antitrust violations for its attempts to suppress the Group Health Association of Washington, D.C., in 1943. They were also limited by state free choice of provider laws, adopted by a number of states to permit workers' compensation claimants to go to doctors of their choice rather than to doctors chosen by their employers. State anti–managed care laws were partially preempted by the federal HMO legislation of 1974, but only for federally qualified HMOs.

As managed care emerged in the late 1980s and early 1990s, one of its primary strategies was to form provider networks. Steering of managed care plan members to provider networks is probably the most important distinguishing characteristic of managed care. The provider-network strategy allows managed care organizations to negotiate discounts from providers, to require network providers to comply with other practice limitations, and to steer members to providers with lower-cost or higher-quality practice styles, or both. The nature and degree of restrictiveness of networks became the primary factor for distinguishing among the various types of managed care organizations: HMOs, preferred provider organizations (PPOs), point-of-service (POS) plans, and provider-sponsored organizations (PSOs).

When managed care began to appear in the late 1980s, laws regarding free choice of provider were joined by any willing provider (AWP) laws. AWP laws require that any provider who is willing to accept the terms offered by a managed care plan can join its network. AWP laws struck at the heart of managed care and have received attention in the literature. In fact, however, twenty-one states have AWP laws and in fourteen of these states AWP laws apply only to pharmacies and pharmacists. In only five states do AWP laws seem to apply to providers generally. Further, until the Supreme Court decided in *Kentucky Association of Health Plans v. Miller* (538 U.S. 329 [2003]) that AWP laws were not preempted by ERISA, the preemption issue limited their effectiveness. In a few states, however, these laws might have impeded the growth of managed care.

Through the mid-1990s, anti–managed care legislation seemed largely anecdote driven. A 1995 *New York Times* article about gag clauses (clauses in managed care provider contracts prohibiting providers from discussing noncovered treatment options, disparaging the managed care organization, or discussing confidential payment arrangements) provoked universal adoption of state laws banning gag clauses over the next couple of years. Reports of managed care plan restrictions on maternity stays led to the enactment of "drive-through-delivery" laws guarantying a forty-eight-hour hospital stay for normal deliveries by virtually all states and then by the federal government. Managed care plan refusals to pay for emergency room visits deemed unnecessary led to "prudent layperson" requirements, enacted by most states.

By the late 1990s, states became more coordinated and deliberate in their regulation of managed care. Many adopted comprehensive reform statutes that addressed all aspects of managed care plans. Four-fifths of the states adopted external review statutes, giving external review entities authority to review managed care plan coverage determinations. Many states adopted laws limiting the use of gatekeeper arrangements and giving plan members direct access to specialists, including gynecologists and obstetricians for women. States also passed laws limiting managed care provider incentive arrangements, although these laws do not outlaw common forms of incentive arrangements—capitation, bonuses, and withholds—and tend to be largely hortatory in nature. Many states have adopted laws protecting interests of providers in disputes with managed care organizations, limiting without-cause terminations, giving providers procedural protections in termination proceedings, or requiring managed care organizations to pay providers promptly. Finally, twelve states have adopted statutes subjecting managed care plans to liability for negligent denials of coverage that cause injuries to their members.

The intensity of legislative activity brought on by managed care has been truly remarkable. Even Congress seriously considered comprehensive managed care legislation, and probably would have enacted legislation including many of the provisions adopted by the states had not the events of September 2001 intervened. The legislative flood ebbed in that year, but by that time managed care had changed significantly from the mid-1990s, becoming far less restrictive. Networks had become larger and looser, utilization review less frequent and intrusive, provider incentive arrangements less common. Health care costs were also rising rapidly—the cost constraints that managed care brought in the1990s seemed to have faded.

The extent to which a causal connection exists between anti–managed care legislation and the movement toward less-restrictive managed care and accompanying cost increases has been the subject of vigorous debate. Those who are opposed to mandates generally tend to see managed care restrictions as just another form of government meddling in otherwise functioning markets, or more specifically as provider-protection legislation enacted in response to self-interested lobbying. Market forces (and bad press) played at least as important a role as the law in loosening up managed care. Many of the perceived abuses addressed by the laws were never widespread or had been abandoned by the time the laws went into effect. Many of the prohibitions affected the practices only of industry laggards or outliers. Provisions with wider application, such as external review laws, have been invoked rarely and do not seem to have radically changed managed care practice, although in some states they seem to have been used to expand the rights of plan members. The reform most vigorously opposed by the managed care industry, liability for negligent denial of services, was adopted in a minority of states and was then held by the Supreme Court to be preempted by ERISA with respect to employee benefit plans (*Aetna Health Inc. v. Davila,* 542 U.S. 200 [2004]). Like other forms of insurance regulation, therefore, managed care regulation in the end may have not had a dramatic effect, for good or for ill.

Deregulation to Facilitate Consumer-Driven Health Care

Although most state legislative initiatives over the past two decades have tended to increase the regulation of insurance plans, the most recent initiatives have been deregulatory. In 2003, Congress adopted the Medicare Modernization Act, which, among other things, authorized tax subsidies for health savings accounts (HSAs) coupled with high-deductible health plans. The legislation did not preempt state insurance regulation. It did provide, however, that HSA tax incentives would be available only in states that permitted high-deductible health plans to be sold. The Treasury Department gave the states until the end of 2005 to repeal any laws limiting health-plan deductibles below the levels required by the legislation ($1,000 for individuals, $2,000 for a family). Most states rapidly fell into line, repealing legislation inconsistent with the federal requirements. Many states went further, moreover, permitting HMOs to sell high-deductible policies as well. Indeed, most states with an income tax enacted laws permitting state tax subsidies for HSAs to supplement the federal subsidies. No state enacted a law limiting consumer-driven health plans.

The full regulatory implications of consumer-driven health care may not yet be clear. The federal law allows insurers to manage HSAs. Insurers are not regulated by the federal government when they do so but are apparently not regulated by the states either. Allowing unregulated financial institutions to hold large sums of money seems like a recipe for disaster. Most high-deductible plans are currently offered through managed care organizations. Most of these organizations make their networks available to high-deductible plan members and count payments for products and services against the deductible only to the extent they would be covered by the plan. The question will thus arise, Do managed care protection statutes protect plan members while they are still spending the deductible? If a high-deductible health plan refuses to count a member's expenses against the deductible because it deems the service purchased not medically necessary, can the member use the state's external review procedure? Time will tell. Finally, consumer-driven plans are subject to the same questionable marketing and claims practices as are other health insurance plans, and are likely to cause at least as much consumer confusion. Insurance regulators may find, therefore, that they have an important role to play in protecting consumers from consumer-driven health care as it becomes more common.

Federal Insurance Regulation

As noted, insurance regulation was long the task of the states, not the federal government, a situation reaffirmed by the McCarran-Ferguson Act, which acknowledged the authority of the federal government to regulate insurance, but stipulated that federal laws that did not expressly purport to regulate the "business of insurance" should not be interpreted to preempt state laws and regulations that do.

The last half-century, however, has seen a steady expansion of federal authority over health care finance. To begin, the 1954 Internal Revenue Code established that employer contributions to employment-related health insurance plans were taxable to neither the employer nor the employee. This provision, which confirmed earlier administrative rulings by the IRS, was a key factor in the rapid expansion in the mid-twentieth century of employment-related health insurance, which now covers slightly less than 60 percent of Americans. Nondiscrimination provisions of the Internal Revenue Code, which prohibit companies from singling out highly compensated employees for health coverage superior to that afforded other employees in self-insured plans and Section 125 cafeteria plans (which allow employees to exclude from taxation their own share of employment-related health insurance premiums), have gone further to ensure that employment-related health benefits are more or less equally available to all full-time employees of a particular employer (26 U.S.C. §§ 105[h], 125[b]). Subsequent laws, extending tax subsidies to cover health insurance premiums made by the self-employed and for funds deposited in health savings accounts, have underwritten further extensions of health benefits.

In 1965, Congress established two massive public insurance programs, Medicare and Medicaid, which today cover about 80 million Americans and 33 percent of American health care costs. The Medicare program is funded exclusively through the federal government and is administered by the federal government through regional contractors. State law that conflicts with Medicare program requirements—including state regulation of managed care organizations that participate in the Medicare program—is in general preempted by the federal law (42 U.S.C. § 1395w-26[b][3]). For example, there have been numerous complaints of Medicare Advantage plans being marketed in "chronic and blatant" disregard of state consumer protection regulations, but state regulators have been powerless to act in response to these abuses because of federal preemption. The relationship between federal and state authority in Medicaid is more complex, as the program is funded by both federal and state governments and administered by states subject to federal law. Medicaid services are currently provided for most Medicaid beneficiaries through private managed care organizations, which in general are licensed by the states and must meet state solvency requirements, but also must meet extensive federal regulatory requirements (42 U.S.C. §§ 1396b[m][1][C], 1396u-2). Federal standards governing Medicaid managed care organizations explicitly do not preempt more stringent state regulatory requirements (42 U.S.C. § 1396u-2[c][1][B]).

The most important intervention of the federal government into insurance regulation, however, has undoubtedly been the Employee Retirement Income Security Act of 1974, ERISA, which has already been mentioned several times. ERISA was adopted primarily to reform pension law, but it also regulates employee benefits. Section 514(a) of ERISA provides that ERISA "shall supersede any and all State laws" that "relate to any employee benefit plan" (42 U.S.C. § 1144[a]). The purpose of this provision seems to have been to permit employers to offer benefit plans on a national basis without having to adapt their plans to each state in which they operated. Section 514(a) preemption, however, is subject to a number of exceptions, one of which almost swallows the rule. Section 514(b)(2)(A) saves from preemption state laws that regulate insurers. States are thus free to impose a wide range of regulatory requirements on health insurers that insure employment-related benefit plans, including benefit mandates, AWP requirements, and external review (e.g., *Kentucky Association of Health Plans v. Miller,* 538 U.S. 329 [2003]; *Rush Prudential HMO, Inc. v. Moran,* 536 U.S. 355 [2002]).

The "savings clause," however, is also subject to an exception. Section 514(b)(2)(b) provides that states are not permitted to "deem" employee benefit plans themselves to be insurers. The courts have interpreted this provision to mean that states cannot require employers to offer any particular benefits and cannot impose any regulatory requirements at all on self-insured plans (*FMC Corp. v. Holliday,* 498 U.S. 52 [1990]). *Self-insurance* is defined to include almost any situation in which the employer bears some risk, even if the employer has a generous reinsurance plan. This creates two dilemmas for states: First, they cannot extend insurance coverage to those currently not covered through employer mandates (e.g., *Retail Industry Leaders Association v. Fielder,* 475 F.3d 180 [4th Cir. 2007]), and second, if they are too aggressive in requiring health insurers to offer expansive coverage, many employers will simply self-insure, thus escaping state regulation altogether.

Section 514 does not, moreover, fully define the scope of ERISA preemption.

The Supreme Court has read the remedial provisions of ERISA, Section 502, to have their own independent preemptive authority. Indeed, the Court has interpreted Section 502 to effect two kinds of preemption—jurisdictional and remedial. First, the Court reads Section 502 to allow any ERISA plan administrator sued in state court to remove the case into federal court. Second, the Court interprets Section 502 to provide that the only remedy available against an ERISA plan for a denial of benefits or for an interpretation of an ERISA plan is a suit under ERISA. The remedies available under ERISA are very limited—effectively the recovery of the cost of an item or service covered under the plan for which payment is improperly denied. Nevertheless, state lawsuits for recovery of health care costs incurred by the negligent denial or limitation of health care services by a managed care plan are not permitted (*Aetna Health Inc. v. Davila,* 542 U.S. 200 [2004]).

The consequences of the interaction of the various ERISA preemption provisions and their exceptions can be quite bizarre. States can enact laws affecting benefit coverage as long as the effect is indirect rather than direct. They can, for example, enforce hospital rate regulations that require hospitals to charge self-insured health plans more than Blue Cross plans (*New York State Conference of Blue Cross and Blue Shield Plans v. Travelers Ins. Co.,* 514 U.S. 645, 654–662 [1995]). They may not, however, require employers to provide health insurance or to spend any particular amount on health coverage. States can impose virtually any mandate they wish on insured employee-benefit plans but cannot impose any obligations at all on self-insured plans directly. ERISA itself imposes some procedural and disclosure requirements, but virtually no coverage mandates. Persons injured by managed care benefit denials—regardless of how egregiously negligent and contrary to the benefit plan the denial may have been—are not permitted to sue in state court and can recover only, at most, the value of the benefit denied in federal court.

In the past two decades, the federal government has taken several further steps toward regulating insurance markets. First, the Consolidated Omnibus Budget Reconciliation Act of 1986 (COBRA) permits several categories of "qualified beneficiaries" who lose employment-related health insurance benefits through specified "qualifying events" (such as termination of employment or reduction of hours, divorce, or cessation of dependent status) to extend their coverage, in most instances for a period of eighteen to thirty-six months, by paying 102 percent of the premium or cost of the insurance. Coverage continuation requirements had been adopted by a number of states before COBRA, but COBRA extended these requirements to the entire country, including ERISA self-insured plans. Because there is heavy adverse selection against COBRA coverage, this turns out to be one of the most costly insurance mandates.

Second, the Health Insurance Portability and Accountability Act (HIPAA) of 1996 limits the ability of insurers to engage in certain risk-selection practices. It prohibits employment-related group plans from discriminating on the basis of health status in determining eligibility for enrollment or level of premiums for plan members. It thus effectively requires community rating within groups. HIPAA further imposes three limits on the use of preexisting-conditions clauses in employment-related group insurance policies—it imposes a reasonably narrow definition of preexisting condition (excluding, for example, genetic predisposition or domestic violence); it limits to six months the look-back period for determining whether a preexisting condition exists; and in most instances it permits the preexisting-conditions clause to operate for a maximum period of only twelve months. Insurers must reduce this twelve-month period by the length of immediately preceding time periods during which the insured had "creditable coverage" (i.e., another form of insurance, which in many instances completely eliminates preexisting-conditions clauses for individuals changing jobs). HIPAA further requires insurers operating in the small-group market to guarantee issue and renewability, although it does not govern the price at which policies must be offered. HIPAA also requires insurers that operate in the individual market to offer nongroup coverage to persons who lose prior "creditable coverage" under certain circumstances. This final provision applies only in states that do not make alternative provision for covering uninsured individuals. Most states do offer an alternative, usually a high-risk pool, as discussed above. Finally, HIPAA requires insurers who offer individual coverage to guarantee renewal of that coverage, except under certain circumstances, such as nonpayment of premiums.

Other federal laws also affect insurance coverage. Congress has adopted three coverage mandates, requiring insurance plans to provide forty-eight hours of hospitalization for a normal delivery and ninety-six hours for a Cesarean section, to pay for breast reconstruction if they cover mastectomies, and, subject to a number of exceptions, to not apply annual and lifetime limits to mental health coverage that are less generous than those applied to physical health coverage. The Age Discrimination in Employment Act requires employers in general to offer the same coverage or coverage of the same value to their employees regardless of age, while the Pregnancy Discrimination Act requires employee benefit programs to cover pregnancy- and childbirth-related services. The Americans with Disabilities Act prohibits at least intentional discrimination against the disabled in insurance underwriting, although as a practical matter it permits insurers to take health status into account as long as they do so rationally.

Interim Balance Sheet on Health Insurance Regulation

State regulation has attempted to assure the financial responsibility of health insurers, protect consumers from fraud and deception, expand the persons, providers, and services covered by health insurance, make health insurance more available to high-risk insureds, and rein in the excesses of managed care. Federal law has reinforced state efforts to limit risk underwriting but has otherwise limited the reach of state regulation by allowing employee benefit plans to opt out of state regulation by self-insuring. Justifications for many health insurance regulation initiatives over the past three decades have been consumer protection and risk-pool expansion.

However, free-market advocates, economists, and some business and insurance interests have, at every step, challenged insurance regulation as limiting individual choice and increasing the cost of health insurance, which in turn would seem to lead to decreased insurance coverage.

Insurance mandates have not in fact dramatically altered insurance markets for good or for ill. Indeed, regulation has often mimicked market trends. The effect of regulation seems to have been primarily at the margins, expanding coverage for some high-risk applicants, making it less attractive to some healthy applicants, compelling marginal insurers to provide better service than they otherwise might have, providing better coverage for some, keeping or putting some fraudulent insurance arrangements out of business, and discouraging some employers from offering or individuals from purchasing insurance.

Even so, in the end, our experience with insurance and managed care reform would seem to teach us that it is very difficult to make private for-profit insurers behave as anything other than private for-profit insurers. The surest route to profit for an insurer is to attract the lowest-risk applicants available at any given premium. There is always more money to be made by an insurer by managing risk exposure than by trying to manage health care costs. Beyond this, insurers that intend to remain in the market try to provide as generous benefit packages as the market demands and to maintain a reputation for good service, at least to low-cost insureds. Regulatory efforts may budge insurers slightly from these business strategies, but rarely much or for long. This is particularly true in the current environment, in which any insurer, employer, or individual can simply cease to sell or buy insurance if it does not like the opportunities or options available at any given moment in any given market.

Insurance regulation is thus a thankless effort. But regulations that bear little hope of success in purely private markets might take on new importance (for good or ill) in markets where the purchase of insurance is required, supported by public subsidies, or both. If purchaser exit from a market ceases to be an option, regulation to protect purchasers may become more salient, while need for regulation may be more pressing if large sums of public money are involved in the purchase of insurance. Next we turn to the role of regulation in a reformed health care system.

Insurance Regulation Issues in Health Care Reform

What Forms of Regulation Will Health Care Reform Require?

If the United States is to proceed with health care reform, health insurance regulation will no doubt need to change. Needed change will depend on the approach to reform that is chosen. This section considers the various options that are widely discussed for reform and the types of insurance regulation each would necessitate. The next section considers whether insurance regulation reform should take place at the state or federal level.

In the unlikely event that a single-payer system were embraced, insurance regulation would be simplified. Basic health care services would be covered by public insurance, and private insurance would be limited to covering supplemental noncovered services (as in Canada), to allow those who chose to pay for the privilege to get services in more convenient or luxurious settings (as in England), or to cover residual cost-sharing obligations (as in France or under Medigap insurance). This supplementary private insurance would need to be regulated at least to ensure insurer solvency and to protect against fraudulent marketing and claims practices, but further mandates or regulatory interventions would probably be unnecessary.

A second approach to reform would be to require individuals to purchase coverage under the threat of some form of sanction, such as an excise tax. This is the approach taken by the recent Massachusetts reforms and by recent health care reforms in the Netherlands and in Switzerland. Because such a requirement is imposed on individuals rather than employers, it does not raise issues of ERISA preemption; thus, states are free to pursue this course.

If the individual mandate approach to health reform is adopted, several regulatory requirements would seem to be necessary. First, the scope of minimum insurance coverage would need to be established. It makes little sense to require an individual to purchase insurance unless the minimum coverage that must be purchased to comply with the mandate is also defined. If an individual mandate is imposed by a state, required coverage might include all products and services covered by mandates already imposed by the state, although a state with generous mandates might want to consider scaling back. Second, a government implementing an individual mandate would need to make provision for individuals who would not be able to purchase insurance at all or who would not be able to purchase it at affordable rates because they presented an unfavorable risk profile. Many solutions are possible, ranging from high-risk pools to reinsurance to rating-band limitations to community rating. Third, a government implementing an individual mandate might want to establish a purchasing cooperative, like the Massachusetts Health Connector, to organize the market for individual insurance purchase and reduce transactions costs. Fourth, a government implementing an individual mandate would need to continue oversight over financial responsibility (solvency and reserves) and protections against fraudulent marketing and claims practices. Finally, a government implementing an individual mandate might choose to leave in place managed care consumer protections to the extent that these address real problems worth addressing. Adoption of comprehensive reform legislation might provide an opportunity for reviewing existing state managed care legislation and determining which provisions have been helpful and which have not.

If health reform is to be accomplished in part through employer mandates, it will have to be implemented through federal legislation. ERISA prohibits states from requiring employers to provide employee health benefits. Were the federal government to require employers to provide their employees with insurance coverage (or to authorize the states to mandate coverage), a definition of minimal coverage would again be necessary. Some means would be necessary to ensure high-risk small employers access to insurance coverage, either through guaranteed issue and renewal and rating-band limitations, or through reinsurance and risk pooling, or both. A purchasing cooperative might be helpful for reducing the transaction costs of insurance purchasing for small groups, although if participation were optional the cooperative might disproportionately attract high-risk small groups and thus not help much with affordability. Insurer financial responsibility regulation would still be necessary, as would probably be some mechanism for dealing with fraudulent marketing and claims practices. Small groups have in recent years often been the victims of such practices. Finally, states might want to continue in-place managed care regulations.

Any approach to health care reform that intends to achieve universal coverage through the use of private insurance will require some form of public subsidy for the purchase of private insurance, provided through a tax credit, through a voucher, or in some other way. A significant proportion of individuals do not earn enough income to pay the full price of unsubsidized private insurance. Under the individual-mandate, private-insurance-based system recently implemented in the Netherlands, 60 percent of the population receives public subsidies to help cover insurance costs.

Of course, insurance can be made more affordable by allowing it to cover less. Bare-bones, high-cost-sharing policies sold in the individual market to young, healthy individuals can be quite inexpensive. But these policies also leave those who purchase them exposed to considerable financial risk, as well as to the possibility of not being able to afford health care when it is needed. A number of studies have been published in recent years examining the plight of underinsured Americans. Nearly one in six American families spent 10 percent or more of their income (5 percent or more if low income) on out-of-pocket medical costs in 2001–2. These families were more than twice as likely not to obtain needed medical care and half again as likely to delay or have difficulty finding needed care as insured Americans generally. Another study found that adults with health problems with deductibles above $500 (and particularly those with incomes below $35,000 a year) are more likely than those with lower deductibles not to fill a prescription, not to get needed specialist care, to skip a recommended test or follow-up visit, or to have a medical problem for which they have not sought medical care. Patients with high deductibles are also much more likely to have problems with medical bills or medical debt.

Any program to provide public subsidies for private insurance will probably need to ensure that the funds are used to purchase a policy that in fact ensures adequate coverage and will not expose the insured to financial disaster if health problems eventuate. The State Children's Health Insurance Program (SCHIP) program, for example, which in many states subsidizes the purchase of private insurance, stipulates that the funds must be used to purchase health coverage that complies with certain minimum standards, which can be defined with reference to certain benchmark plans, such as Blue Cross and Blue Shield or state or federal employee plans.

An insurance subsidy-based program will also either need some regulation of risk underwriting and premium rating or full risk adjustment of premium subsidies. Simply giving all eligible persons the same level of income-based subsidy without consideration of age or health status would mean that health insurance would be unaffordable for many older and sicker individuals, and probably unavailable at any price to some of them. At minimum, a sophisticated and generous system of risk adjustment of premium subsidies coupled with a guaranteed-issue and renewal requirement would be needed. If insurers are free to set their premiums at any level they believe justified, regardless of the level of risk-adjusted subsidies, insurance may remain unaffordable. Some limitation on risk bands may remain necessary. Reinsurance may also be helpful in assuring that high-risk cases can find affordable insurance.

As with other approaches, insurer financial responsibility requirements and consumer fraud protections will be necessary. A purchasing cooperative not only might improve the functioning of the market, but might also facilitate administration and payment of subsidies.

Finally, a system that involves public subsidies should be accompanied by a regulatory program to limit products and services covered by subsidized insurance. Most countries that have public insurance systems, as well as the Medicare program, have some system for deciding which products and services are covered and which are not. Adoption and dissemination of new health care technologies is one of the causes of the increase of health care costs in the United States. Creation of some means for evaluating the costs and benefits of new health care products and services, with the possibility of making public subsidies available only for insurance plans that do not cover products and services that are clearly not effective, or even cost-effective, might make an important contribution to health care cost control.

At What Level of Government Should Reform Be Carried Out?

Health reform is taking place at the state level. Although states have extensive power to regulate insurance in our federal system, their authority is ultimately limited by ERISA, which not only deprives the states of the power to regulate self-insured employee benefit plans, but also limits the extent to which they can regulate insured plans, since an employer can often choose to self-insure if it finds that state-regulated insured plans are too costly or otherwise unacceptable. ERISA also prohibits states from imposing health-coverage mandates directly on employers and restricts ERISA plan participants and beneficiaries to the very limited judicial remedies available under ERISA when they are denied coverage by an ERISA plan.

One approach to reform, therefore, would be for the federal government to "deregulate" the states by repealing or amending Section 514 of ERISA to give states the authority to regulate all health benefit plans in the state, and even to require employers to offer health insurance coverage. Congress could go a step further and repeal or amend Section 502, allowing ERISA plan participants and beneficiaries to sue employment-based insurance plans under state law.

A number of arguments support giving the states more power to reform health insurance. States are closer to, and thus more responsive to, the needs of their citizens; states are freer to experiment and thus to identify more varied and better solutions to problems than the monolithic federal government; and states are better able to address regional variations in health care. Allowing states to take different approaches also allows persons or businesses with preferences for more or less health care coverage or expenditures a range of options. However, arguments can be made for health care reform at the federal level. The need for health care exists more or less uniformly throughout the country, and it seems unfair for Americans in one state to have excellent health coverage while Americans in another state go without. Allowing health care coverage to vary significantly from state to state also presents the possibility of a form of adverse selection if persons with high-cost health needs move to states with good coverage while businesses that want to minimize health care costs leave for states with low coverage requirements. A "race to the bottom" might occur as states try to attract businesses and shed themselves of unhealthy residents. It might also be harder for provider and disease groups to secure the adoption of inefficient coverage mandates at the national level, where the political process is more visible and less provincial. Finally, the repeal of ERISA preemption seems difficult to imagine politically, as it would be opposed by most business interests and insurers, and even by unions that operate sizable health benefit plans.

An even less attractive option is that offered by the Health Care Choice Act of 2005, which would allow interstate sales of insurance in any state by any insurer licensed in at least one state. This proposal would seem to lead inevitably to a race to the bottom, as states attempted to offer increasingly lenient regulatory environments in exchange for increased access to premium taxes. States would be powerless to guarantee the financial responsibility of insurers located in other states or to police fraudulent marketing or claims practices by those insurers. State regulators in one state would also be unable to compel the regulatory authorities in other states to take action against insurance abuses. A history of fraudulent practices by unregulated insurers counsels against this approach.

If health insurance reform is to take place at the national level, several approaches are possible. One would be national preemption of all state regulation as a means to deregulation. The "deemer" clause would be expanded to cover all ERISA plans, or even all insurance plans, eliminating all state mandates and rating and managed care reforms. Though deregulation is popular in certain quarters, complete deregulation of insurance markets would be likely to lead to even greater disparity in access to care for the rich and the poor, the healthy and the unhealthy, than is currently the case. It would also impose intolerable burdens on providers, particularly safety-net providers, if they were expected to take up the slack in health care provision without compensation. Another alternative would be the establishment of uniform national standards governing state regulation. This approach would lead to greater national uniformity while capitalizing on the regulatory expertise and the greater accountability of state government. One concern, however, is that it poses potential constitutional problems. Federal government may adopt and enforce its own regulations governing interstate commerce or it may offer financial incentives to the states to take regulatory action (as it does through Medicaid), but it cannot constitutionally "commandeer" state officers to enforce federal laws. There are also practical problems with delegated regulation, illustrated by Medicaid. It leaves the federal government exposed to state demands for greater resources and greater flexibility and variation.

Finally, there is the option of federal enforcement of uniform federal standards. This approach would provide all of the benefits of a national approach, while offering none of the benefits of state regulation. It could permit a uniformly regulated national market in health insurance, freeing insurers and employers from having to deal with fifty different state standards and regulators. However, no regulatory infrastructure exists at the national level for regulating insurance, and the creation of such an infrastructure would be a daunting task.

In the end, the best approach would be to develop uniform national minimum standards for health insurance enforced at the state level. States would be given the authority to enforce the national standards against all health plans in the state, including ERISA plans. States would not be required to enforce the national standards, but only in those states that did so would households be eligible for federal tax credits or other subsidies for health insurance for lower-income residents, much as is now the situation with respect to access to federal tax subsidies for HSAs. States that accepted the tax credits for their residents could not apply less-stringent insurance regulation standards than the federal standards. If three or more states banded together, however, they could impose standards more protective of their residents, just as the federal air pollution law has allowed states that prefer air pollution standards more restrictive than the federal standards to adopt the California standards. This approach would achieve national uniformity while allowing some room for state flexibility.

References

Government Accountability Office. 2004. *Unauthorized or Bogus Entities Have Exploited Employers and Individuals Seeking Affordable Coverage.* GAO-04–512T. Washington, DC: Government Accountability Office.

Kofman, Mila, Kevin Lucia, Eliza Bangit, and Karen Pollitz. 2006. "Association Health Plans: What's All the Fuss About?" *Health Affairs* 25 (6): 1591–98.

Monheit, Alan C., and Jasmine Rizzo. 2007. *Mandated Health Insurance Benefits: A Critical Review of the Literature.* Trenton: New Jersey Department of Human Services and Rutgers Center for State Health Policy.

5

Paying One's Fair Share for Health Coverage and Care

JILL BERNSTEIN

Questions about how much people should pay for health insurance and health care can direct discussions down many paths. The ultimate goal is to structure contributions in a manner that ensures access to necessary and appropriate care and is also sustainable for individuals, families, insurers, other payers, and government. Achieving that goal involves issues of resources, incentives, and values. This chapter provides a framework for examining these questions.

Background

The primary focus here is on two broad categories of health care costs borne by individuals and families: (1) paying for coverage, through premiums or taxes, and (2) cost sharing for health services or supplies, consisting of deductibles, fixed copayments, or coinsurance (calculated as a fixed percentage of cost), often with limits on total annual out-of-pocket costs, which are capped at a specific level, or at different levels for different types of health care. Each category of costs can be structured in different ways, varying in amount covered, scope of benefits affected, special protections for vulnerable populations, and other design features. Permutations possible when different cost requirements are combined in insurance plans are legion.

There are also major differences in the administration of payments for health coverage and health costs. People can pay for insurance or for health care through publicly administered systems, generally taxes or fees; through privately administered systems, such as payroll contributions to employer-sponsored health insurance; or through direct payments to insurers, intermediaries, or health care providers. When people use health services or suppliers, they can pay via combinations of insurance (sometimes multiple insurance programs) and various out-of-pocket payments for covered or uncovered health services. This complexity makes it difficult to determine how costs to individuals or families affect access to, or use of, health care. Nevertheless, approaches to structuring premium payments and cost sharing in private and public programs can provide insights for policy makers considering coverage expansions.

What people pay for health care encompasses cost sharing, defined as the amount people pay out of pocket when they use health care. But there appears to be a growing tendency to also use the term to capture enrollees' out-of-pocket "share" of the full costs of coverage. For example, the Bureau of Labor Statistics counts contributions to employment-based insurance premiums paid by employees as a component of cost sharing. Similarly, subsidies to low-income families to help them pay for insurance are sometimes discussed as a form of cost sharing, as in "government and enrollees sharing the costs of coverage." To further confound discussion, surcharges for premiums for high-income enrollees are sometimes called "means testing," a term used when discussing social welfare programs for poor people.

Differences in the scope of the terms *cost sharing* and *income-related* are more than semantic—they reflect different perspectives on the basic goals of health care policies setting out what people should pay. The goals, when structuring costs for individuals or families (hereafter referred to as "people"), fall into three broad policy domains: garnering resources to pay for health care; promoting appropriate and efficient use of health care; and contributing to broader social and political policies.

Generating Resources

Having people pay more for health care reduces costs for other payers, and vice versa. Other things are not, of course, equal. Some things, such as the tax treatment of health insurance, or shifts in enrollment between public and private coverage (often induced by plan changes in the scope of benefits or structure of cost sharing) also affect public and private revenue streams for health care. Nevertheless, how much of the bill is paid by people directly, rather than by third-party payers, is a major point of contention.

However, health care cost increases since the 1980s have been associated with a general shift in the proportion of health care costs covered by insurance (public and private). Between 1985 and 2005 alone, the share of personal health care expenditures paid by people out of pocket decreased from 26 percent to 15 percent. This decline has led some to focus on whether people are overinsured and should, or must, take on a larger proportion of costs over time.

The significance of the decline in the proportion of health costs paid out of pocket is, however, distorted by the magnitude of increases in costs. Personal health care costs, including costs of insurance premiums, have risen faster than wages or inflation (Kaiser Family Foundation and Health Research and Education Trust [Kaiser/HRET] 2007). Health insurance premiums and out-of-pocket spending for health care are a large component of family budgets and a burden to a growing proportion of working Americans.

Public and private payers are asking insured populations to pay more for coverage and the costs of care. Increasing premiums for high-income beneficiaries for Medicare Part B or increasing premiums for state insurance assistance programs for low-income families and low-wage workers generate revenue. States have introduced copayments or income-related premiums into Medicaid and State Children's Health Insurance Programs (SCHIP), in part to generate program savings. Employers faced with increasing health insurance costs have shifted some costs to employees through increased premiums and increased cost sharing. Despite these shifts, employers have continued to pay a large proportion of the premium costs; without the shifts, revenues devoted to employee health insurance would have been far greater. Employers have also restructured cost sharing by increasing annual deductibles and out-of-pocket maximums to slow the growth of health insurance bills.

When evaluating alternative approaches to structuring how people pay for coverage, both employers and taxing authorities need to weigh implementation and administration costs against potential revenue gains. These involve more than financial costs. Administering complex cost-sharing systems could entail significant personnel and systems costs, particularly for small organizations. The need for accountability in public programs could lead to rules and procedures that appear inflexible or arbitrary. Frustrations with complex rules, limits on coverage, or inadequate financial protection from medical costs could increase already high levels of distrust in either public or market-based approaches.

Promoting Efficiency in Health Care

There is a growing body of research as well as a variety of strongly held beliefs focused on how the way people pay for health care affects *if, when, how much, in what form,* and *where* they get care. (Methods designed to influence health care providers are beyond the scope of this review.) Methods of linking evidence-based practice standards to what people pay for health care, however, are fundamentally important for the discussion here. How should financial incentives be structured so that people use health services efficiently? This includes discouraging inappropriate or unnecessary care, but also encouraging people to get the right care, at the right time, in the right place.

One policy discussion focuses on the importance of people understanding how much health care really costs, and exposing them to more of those costs. This should create strong incentives for people to become more informed consumers. This is sometimes referred to as making sure people have some "skin in the game." Another version is to expect people to take on more responsibility for their own health, and in particular for health problems that are a result of lifestyle choices, such as smoking or becoming obese. In addition to shifting costs to some people (e.g., higher premiums for smokers), the increased cost sharing or higher premiums might create greater demand for effective prevention and health care management programs.

Other approaches integrate evidence regarding the effectiveness of medical care and treatment alternatives into consumer decision making. This can be done in a variety of ways, such as adjusting coinsurance for different services to reflect "value" (based on calculations of relative benefits and cost of services), or assigning health plans to different tiers that offer different levels of cost sharing, based on efficiency and other performance measures. The policy goal is not only to use financial incentives to drive consumers to use the right sorts of care, but to use the market to drive providers to compete for patients based on their performance.

Contributing to Broader Social and Political Goals

Restructuring the way that people pay for health care could also affect the political dynamics of government and its role in ensuring the well-being and security of its citizens. Mechanisms for collecting payments for premiums or cost sharing can expand or reduce the roles of government, employers, or the private insurance market. Policy reforms define responsibilities for administering program requirements such as eligibility, collecting revenues, organizing enrollee choice of plans or specific benefit options, or even designing the structure of cost sharing itself.

Some approaches would build on social insurance principles. Income-related premiums or cost sharing tied to income can be structured to increase vertical equity, that is, allocate a greater share of health care costs to those who can afford it. Cost sharing can also be designed to promote horizontal equity, if it links standard cost-sharing protections across plan options that are available to everyone. Reforms could also set the stage for wider application of market-based approaches to providing insurance coverage, with greater emphasis on means testing and personal responsibility for health and health care.

Assuming that the goal is clear, a plan for achieving it will need to include decisions about structuring costs that could provide appropriate vehicles for successful implementation.

Paying for Health Insurance Coverage

The general framework described here begins with paying for insurance coverage, then turns to mechanisms for structuring cost sharing. For each, options have been divided into a set of broad categories intended not to cover every possible approach, or even to be mutually exclusive, but rather to illustrate key differences with respect to how they might contribute to different policy objectives. A discussion of approaches may or may not contribute to each of the three policy goals—resources, efficiency, and political and social fairness.

Collecting revenues to pay for coverage can be administered through public mechanisms, the private market, or a combination of the two. There are significant differences between the two, in terms of the potential to find the revenue needed to pay for comprehensive coverage reforms, administrative costs and burden, potential efficiency gains, and equity.

Public Programs

A variety of public systems collect, or oversee collection of, premiums, fees, or revenues earmarked for programs that provide or pay for health care coverage, in three areas: social insurance models, income tax credits, and means-tested premium assistance.

Social Insurance Models

There are several ways that individual (or family) contributions to pay for health coverage are structured in public social insurance programs. In its simplest form, people pay taxes, such as a payroll tax, health tax, general income tax, or some form of excise tax for health coverage. Medicare requires people to pay both premium contributions for insurance and taxes earmarked for health coverage. Medicare enrollees pay premiums for supplemental health insurance and prescription drug coverage (Medicare Parts B and D), and people enrolled in the Medicare Advantage plans (Medicare Part C) also pay plan-specific premiums.

Because they are universal and mandatory, social insurance programs can, in theory, raise significant revenue; how much depends on how the tax is integrated into the wider array of taxes. Payroll taxes for Medicare (1.45 percent of workers' pay) and Social Security (6.2 percent of workers' pay for the first $94,200) in 2006 amounted to more than federal income tax liability for two-thirds of taxpayers (individuals or households filing jointly). Premiums can also generate significant revenue. Medicare Part B premiums are structured to pay for a quarter of its costs.

Collecting revenues to pay for health coverage for more Americans could be simple if it were integrated into existing payroll and tax systems. Coverage expansions could also draw on existing systems. Social Security coordinates with the Internal Revenue Service and the Treasury Department. The complicated Medicare Part D system was up and running and making progress toward meeting many of its administrative goals in a very short period. But the complexity of the Medicare reforms also illustrates potential administrative problems. Obtaining accurate information and processing the correct premium deductions have proved difficult. Initial glitches resulted in incorrect or missing Part D premium deductions from Social Security checks for about five hundred thousand Medicare beneficiaries (of 4.7 million who enrolled) (Appleby 2006).

There is, however, no off-the-shelf equivalent of monthly Social Security checks from which premium deductions could be made if a Medicare-like system were used to expand health care coverage to working people. Some system for withholding taxes, or for tax credits (discussed below), would need to be in place. If premium contributions were administered through the tax system, there would also be costs related to collecting premiums for the people who would need special payment options—those not filing tax returns. This would be analogous to efforts to process enrollments and payments from people who voluntarily enroll in Medicare.

Structuring contributions (health taxes or premiums) in social insurance models provides an opportunity to achieve greater equity in access to insurance and to health care. Specific design characteristics are important, however. Because the payroll tax for Medicare is not capped, high-income people contribute more, relative to lower-income workers, than they do for Social Security. But payroll taxes also place a greater burden on lower-paid workers, and fixed premiums can take a big bite out of small budgets. Other features of social insurance models contribute to horizontal equity because they generally prescribe a standard premium for all enrollees. In Medicare, for example, the program equalizes premium costs for Part B coverage across markets that might otherwise vary significantly. This equalization can mean that people in high-cost markets pay lower premiums than they would otherwise, but it also means that low-income people in poor or underserved areas have the same coverage as everyone else. This may help equalize access to care across urban and rural areas and across wealthy and poor market areas.

The tax system can also be used to augment revenues for insurance programs through special fees or tax levies or adjustments to premiums that target higher-income taxpayers. Social Security and Medicare both employ tax surcharges for higher-income beneficiaries. Up to 85 percent of Social Security benefits of individuals, or of couples with incomes exceeding certain levels beginning at $25,000 for individuals and $32,000 for couples filing jointly, are subject to taxation. Although the tax affects more than one-third of all Social Security recipients, the bulk of the revenue comes from recipients with incomes over $50,000, and even among those subject to the highest taxation formula the tax represents less than one-fourth of Social Security benefits. Consequently, revenues divided among Social Security and Medicare trust funds are modest. In 2006, Medicare's share of this revenue was $10.6 billion, about 5 percent of Part A income.

In 2007, single Medicare beneficiaries with incomes of $80,000 or more and couples with incomes above $160,000 also began paying more than standard Part B premiums. Premiums are adjusted upward across five income brackets. Over a three-year period, the additional assessment will increase the percentage of the Part B premium paid by high-income beneficiaries from the 25 percent of program costs that applies to other beneficiaries to as much as 80 percent. The Part B income-related adjustment to premiums is expected to affect about 1.65 million beneficiaries enrolled in Part B in 2007 (4 percent). Income-related premiums are expected to generate about $7.7 billion between fiscal year 2007 and fiscal year 2011 (Government Accountability Office 2006), less than 1 percent of the projected total Part B income for that period (about $1.043 trillion).

Administering these income-related premium contributions is inexpensive because much of the infrastructure is in place. The Social Security Administration estimated, for example, that implementing income-related premiums would cost the agency an additional $200 million in administrative expenses between fiscal year 2006 and fiscal year 2010. This includes the costs of educating beneficiaries about the premium provisions, working with the IRS to identify the people who will be required to pay the additional premiums, devising and implementing procedures for beneficiaries who request changes to their adjustment due to changes in financial circumstances, appeals, and so on (Government Accountability Office 2006). The process for requesting adjustments involves filling out an IRS form (Form 8821) similar to other tax withholding forms.

The amount of revenue that can be generated through taxes that target only high-income earners, such as the Medicare income-related premium, is limited, however, because income distribution is skewed. Unless the high-income definition is set in the range most people would think of as middle income, or the tax rates are set very high, the tax does not affect enough people to generate significant revenues. These income-related premium contributions are technically progressive, but if they are applied to premium costs, the redistributive contribution is limited. If the rates are bracketed, the very highest-income taxpayers would not pay more than the merely very high-income taxpayers. And, even at a 100 percent tax rate, the additional liability for high-income taxpayers is capped at the "official" value of the premium.

Social insurance taxes or income-related premium surcharges do not, unless tied to other reforms, provide an obvious means of promoting greater efficiency in the health care system. Even if people with high incomes use health care more inefficiently, it does not necessarily follow that increasing their premium costs would change their preferences. Theoretically, tax rates that effectively eliminate the federal subsidy for a social insurance program like Medicare could lead, instead, to a demand on the part of high-income people to exit the program altogether. That could, in turn, lead to market segmentation and resulting inefficiencies. This is unlikely if there are no alternatives for obtaining coverage, as is the case for Medicare beneficiaries.

Social insurance models can, however, integrate approaches that provide an impetus for greater health system efficiency. The Medicare Advantage (MA) program provides an example of using competition, including premium prices, to focus consumers on plans' costs and benefits, and to stimulate health plans' focus on efficiency or quality of care. Assessing whether this example has been success-ful is difficult, in part because it is difficult to sort out issues of risk selection and variations in benefits. Whether premium competition provides a real impetus to greater efficiency may depend on whether the scope of benefits and out-of-pocket liability are addressed effectively. Differences in benefit design have the potential to allow healthier people (who may be less concerned about out-of-pocket risk) to sort themselves into low-premium plans. This would leave people with greater health risks in higher-cost plans. Low-cost plans would have financial incentives to dissuade potentially high-cost patients from enrolling, to keep their costs down and market advantage in place; high-cost plans can be caught in a spiral of sicker enrollees needing more care, leading to even higher premiums.

Income Tax Credits

Tax credits become part of the health care cost equation when they are applied to purchasing insurance or paying for out-of-pocket health costs. The focus here is on tax credits for individual taxpayers to use for buying insurance, rather than credits for employers to induce them to provide coverage. Variants of tax credits can be applied to the purchase of public or private insurance, in either group (employer-based) or individual insurance markets.

One example is the federal Health Coverage Tax Credit (HCTC), created for older workers who lost coverage as a result of international trade agreements that triggered job dislocations and reductions in benefits in affected industries. The credit pays 65 percent of the costs of health insurance premiums for eligible individuals enrolling in qualified plans. Credits are paid in full to everyone who qualifies and are fully refundable, and individuals can have credits advanced to insurers monthly, before they file their tax returns (or claim the credit when they file their tax returns). Initially touted as a model for larger-scale efforts to expand health coverage (Pear 2004), HCTC has had limited success. Just over one in ten eligible workers were using the credit in 2007 (Dorn 2007). As a model, however, the program is instructive.

In terms of revenue, HCTC is very small, because participation is low. An estimated twenty-one thousand to twenty-six thousand beneficiaries received the credits in 2005 (Dorn 2006). The amount of the subsidies for 2005 ($110 million) was 29 percent of what had been estimated when the legislation establishing the program was passed. Office of Management and Budget projections show that use of the credits is now expected to remain much lower than original estimates. The dollar value of the credits, however, is critically important. On the one hand, the credits represent a large revenue outlay per eligible recipient (roughly $4,600 per recipient in 2005). On the other hand, the single most important factor limiting use of the credits is that coverage is still unaffordable for many workers, even with a 65 percent subsidy (Dorn 2006).

Administrative and regulatory issues are complex. For HCTC, much of the administrative work involved in setting up the program, including coordination between the IRS and Treasury Department, appears to have been efficient. However, the application process is complicated and time-consuming, involving three or more public and private organizations. Systems that have to be put in place to provide advance funding, so that people can get the money they need to enroll in health plans, proved to be difficult and costly. Some of the administrative costs represent starting up an entirely new system. New tax credit approaches might be able to build on this work, but operational and administrative costs remained high years after the program implementation.

HCTC payments must be applied to premiums for qualified plans, defined as employment-related plans that meet federal standards for continuing postemployment coverage or state-qualified health plans. Plans that qualify for HCTC can, however, differ in benefits offerings and medical underwriting (adjusting premiums to reflect risk factors such as age, gender, or health status). Some state-qualified plans offer limited benefits. Many require high deductibles ($1,000 or more), and many have strict limits on maternity care, mental health care, preventive care, or prescription drugs. Underwriting can also lead to premiums unaffordable for people who need insurance (e.g., in one state, in 2004, the 35 percent portion of premium to be paid by a fifty-five-year-old woman with health problems was more than $4,000 [Dorn 2007]).

Tax credits could be integrated into reforms that promote more effective health care delivery. The vehicles would be standards for the participating plans, or adjusting the amount of the credits to provide incentives to enroll in efficient plans, or both. Conversely, without provisions to encourage plans to provide appropriate, effective services, affordability would be the dominant factor driving consumers, as it is in the HCTC model.

Like any other tax policy, credits can be structured to be progressive or regressive. The refundable Earned Income Tax Credit and Child Tax Credit reduced the tax burden for low-income families. Refundable tax credits, because they are linked to income tax rates, are more progressive than payroll deductions.

Means-Tested Premium Assistance

Federal Medicare Savings Programs (MSPs) work with the federal or state Medicaid program to subsidize premiums (and sometimes cost sharing) for low-income Medicare beneficiaries. Federal law directs Medicaid to cover the cost of Medicare Part B premiums and all Medicare deductibles and coinsurance for Medicare beneficiaries eligible for full Medicaid coverage and for some additional low-income beneficiaries. Another category of MSP pays just the Part B premium for people with incomes below 120 percent of the poverty level who do not qualify for the other programs. A separate program provides premium subsidies for the Medicare Part D benefit for low-income beneficiaries. About 7 million beneficiaries are dually eligible for Medicare and Medicaid (including those eligible for any of the MSPs).

Other examples are found among state programs that provide subsidies to low-income people to help them buy health insurance. Some provide subsidies directly to employers, some to individuals to apply to premium payments. The programs providing assistance directly to people for the purpose of buying coverage generally draw on federal Medicaid or SCHIP funds under waivers designed to promote coverage expansions. Premium-assistance programs of some sort have been put in place in more than a dozen states, including Iowa, Illinois, New Jersey, Oregon, Pennsylvania, Rhode Island, Utah, Maine, Vermont, Washington, Oklahoma, and Massachusetts, and others are under development (National Governors Association 2007). Enrollment in many of these programs has been small, with less than 1 percent of the relevant Medicaid or SCHIP populations enrolled. New programs, however, including Maine's Dirigo health reforms and, notably, the Massachusetts program, are broader in scope. In Massachusetts, Medicaid expansions and the state's Commonwealth Care program initially provided premium subsidies covering 135,000 of the lowest-income uninsured residents. In 2007, the state announced plans to expand premium subsidies so individuals earning up to $15,000 per year (up to $31,000 per year for families of four) pay no premium; this is expected to include another 52,000 people (December 2007).

In terms of revenues, premium subsidies represent a small proportion of government's health care outlays. Medicaid expenditures for all Medicare-Medicaid dual-eligible individuals, including MSP programs, represented about 5 percent of Medicaid spending in 2003 (Kaiser Commission on Medicaid and the Uninsured 2005). Premium assistance leveraged through Medicaid or SCHIP waivers for state-based programs is by design "budget neutral" because it is permitted under federal law only if its expected costs will not exceed the costs of coverage for mandated benefits under the federal programs. Programs such as that in Massachusetts, however, do represent new spending. Covering premiums for the additional 52,000 low-income residents in Massachusetts noted above will add an estimated $13 million to the $470 million in subsidies budgeted for fiscal year 2007 (December 2007).

Premium-assistance programs involve more administrative costs, oversight, and burden on participants than tax-based systems. Identifying people who may be qualified for benefits, processing applications, verifying eligibility over time, adjusting subsidies due to changes in people's financial or family circumstances, and ensuring subsidies end up in the right place requires resources. The more complex the subsidy systems, including both eligibility requirements and the structure of the subsidy payments, the higher the administrative costs.

Many means-tested programs include both income and assets in determining eligibility. The MSP programs, for example, have resource limits as well as income limits. The low-income subsidy for Part D drug benefits also includes resource limits (these differ, however, from the resource limits for MSP). The costs involved in determining eligibility for premium assistance are often measured in terms of processing time. Studies in two states found that it took four hours of staff time to process initial Medicaid applications (Summer and Friedland 2002). Arizona eliminated the asset test for MSP in 2001, after a study the state conducted found that the costs of documenting assets was roughly the same as the costs providing benefits to additional program participants enrolled as a result of not verifying assets (Summer and Thompson 2004). An analysis of reform options conducted for New Mexico estimated that program administration costs were $125 per applicant in 2007 (Chollet 2007).

In addition to inefficiencies created by multiple systems often spanning multiple agencies (issues that could be addressed), means-tested premium assistance, by definition, involves obtaining and verifying information from people with limited resources. This results in gaps in participation in eligible populations. Less than half of seniors eligible for Medicaid are enrolled, and that less than one-third eligible for premium assistance through the other MSP programs are enrolled in the programs (Kaiser Family Foundation 2005). About 70 percent of Medicare beneficiaries eligible for the low-income subsidy for Part D drug coverage received the subsidy in January 2007 (Kaiser Family Foundation 2007). This higher participation rate reflects intensive efforts involving identification of eligible beneficiaries on the part of the Social Security Administration, the Centers for Medicare and Medicaid Services (CMS), the Administration on Aging, the states, and a number of advocacy organizations, but also computer-assisted "auto-enrollment" of Medicaid recipients into the plans (Dorn 2007).

Premium subsidies tied to enrollment in efficient health care plans can provide a mechanism for driving health system performance. Some states, including Maine, Oregon, and Pennsylvania, have combined premium-assistance reforms with comprehensive efforts to improve quality and efficiency in the health delivery system. In Washington, comprehensive system reforms enacted in 2007 created sliding-scale premium subsidies for individuals who earn less than 200 percent of the federal poverty level, while other reforms require that plans contracting with the state incorporate specific types of benefits designed to promote better care and improved care management. Other states would prefer to take a very different approach, based on the view that efforts to move more low-income people into private coverage would benefit from more flexibility in benefit design and the structure of enrollee cost sharing. Greater market competition would, in this view, increase system efficiency.

Premium assistance is designed to redistribute resources to low-income people. The extent to which premium assistance equalizes access to coverage depends on the scope of benefits. Subsidizing premiums for a standard benefit, such as Medicare Part B, redistributes resources to low-income beneficiaries. Subsidies to purchase coverage with more limited benefits than are available through public programs, or limiting subsidies to a level that relegates low-income people to a range of second-tier plans, is rather different.

Employer-Sponsored Insurance

The private insurance market is divided among the employer-based large-group market, small-group market, and individual market. The employer-based market provides most private coverage, and many of the innovative strategies for structuring how people can contribute to the costs of coverage have originated in the large-group market. Efforts to bolster the small-group and individual markets, however, also provide some lessons for possible reforms.

Fixed Contributions

Most employment-based insurance involves fixed contributions by employers to cover some proportion of health insurance premiums arranged for their employees. There are, however, ways that employers can adjust premium contributions by employees to reduce their organizations' insurance costs, promote better health and more efficient health care for their workers, or address goals related to attracting and retaining the workers they need.

The goals of employer efforts to structure premium contributions are not the same as the goals of public programs. Employers want to find ways to control the growth of their health insurance costs, and like public programs, they can do that by shifting costs to employees, or by creating financial incentives to use services more efficiently. But they also want to attract and retain a productive workforce. Health insurance as a percentage of total compensation has increased over the past decade (National Center for Health Statistics 2006). As a result, as noted earlier, while employees are paying more, the percentage of premium costs that employers pay has been stable (Kaiser/HRET 2007).

Use of variable premiums by employers is exposing employees to some level of price competition—employees pay more to enroll in a higher-cost health plan. Most firms—87 percent in 2007—however, offer only one type of health plan. About half (49 percent) of covered workers were employed in firms that offer more than one plan (Kaiser/ HRET 2007).

Wage-Related Contributions

Although the practice is not widespread, some private- as well as public-sector employers require higher-wage employees to contribute more in premiums. In 2005, the Kaiser/HRET survey of employer-sponsored health benefits found that about one in ten workers covered by employer-sponsored health insurance were in firms that adjusted premiums by wage rate. Several state governments, including those of West Virginia, Hawaii, New Mexico, Massachusetts, and Illinois, vary premiums by wage level (National Conference of State Legislatures 2006), as does the California State University system for its more than forty thousand employees.

Wage-related approaches vary in design. One large nonprofit association set up a system that divides the workforce into six income brackets. Pretax payroll deductions for health premiums for employees in the lowest-wage bracket (less than $35,000 annual salary) cover about 9 percent of the cost of the premium for the four plan offerings. Employees with salaries over $100,000 pay about 30 percent of the total premium cost. The University of California system uses four income tiers (less than $40,000, $40,000–80,000, $80,000–120,000, and more than $120,000). The University of Rochester recently changed its premium-assessment formula, requiring employees with salaries over $100,000 to pay a higher proportion of premiums, while lowering the contributions for employees earning less than $40,000. The formula was designed to result in university employees paying approximately 20 percent of premiums. Prior to the change, all employees contributed a flat 18 percent of total premium costs for the plan they selected.

That some employers have adjusted premium contributions from pretax wages is noteworthy. There are tax advantages to employers and employees from structuring compensation in the form of benefits rather than wages, because benefits are not subject to payroll taxes (for employers or employees). Assuming benefits are not additions to income, but are traded off against income, then effectively reducing benefits to higher-income employees increases employers' payroll tax liability and increases the proportion of employees' compensation subject to both payroll and income taxes. But because premiums are deducted from pretax income, higher-income taxpayers can take advantage of the rules to offset some of their increased premium costs.

Tiered Premiums

Employers also use premiums as incentives to choose types of coverage, or to change their health behaviors. Some employers are offering premium incentives to employees who enroll in wellness programs or plans that offer programs designed to manage ongoing health problems. In 2007, the Kaiser/HRET survey found that 6 percent of covered workers were employed in firms that vary premiums based on participation in wellness programs, twice as many as in 2005. The increase was entirely among workers employed in larger firms with two hundred or more workers.

Employers, often in collaboration with broader private and public-private initiatives, are also linking premium contributions to enrollment in more efficient health plans. An example is the State of Wisconsin Group Health Insurance program, administered by the state's Department of Employee Trust Funds (ETF). The largest purchaser of health coverage in the state, the program is responsible for coverage for more than 250,000 active state and local government employees and 115,000 retirees and their dependents (Silow-Carroll and Alteras 2007). ETF assigns plans that qualify for participation to one of three tiers, based on the relative efficiency of the plans in delivering a standard set of benefits defined by the state. In addition, the plans are graded on measures of quality, patient safety, and customer satisfaction. Premiums for the highest-rated tier (tier 1) are significantly lower than premiums for lower tiers. Most plans qualified as tier 1 plans in 2007 (Wisconsin Department of Employee Trust Funds 2007). The employee share for most family coverage under tier 1 plans, for example, was $68 per month; for tier 2, $150 per month; and for the single tier 3 "standard" plan, $358 per month.

Whether premium-based incentives can generate savings for employers remains unclear. Even when incentives are large, as in the Wisconsin ETF program, and people choose to enroll in more efficient plans, employers remain responsible for paying the bulk of premium costs. Analysis of savings in the EFT program suggests that slower rates of increase in insurance premium costs in the three years after program implementation may not have differed from the slower rate of premium growth nationally (Silow-Carroll and Alteras 2007).

There are also potentially difficult issues related to the administration of some of the more sophisticated approaches to structuring premium contributions. Adjusting contributions by wage level is straightforward and inexpensive. Employers have expressed concerns, however, that complications arise if couples work at the same company.

Designing systems that include the evaluation of complex health care cost and quality information requires an ongoing commitment of professional and technical resources. Helping employees understand plan options—what to look for, what the measures of quality mean, and so on—can also require considerable resources.

Health care providers, researchers, and employers believe incentives geared to driving enrollment to more efficient plans can lead to more effective care management and prevention of illness (Braithwaite and Rosen 2007; Fendrick and Chernew 2006). These improvements are difficult to measure and might take a long time to materialize (Orszag 2007).

Varying premium rates can also raise issues of fairness. Requiring higher-income employees to pay a larger share of their health insurance premiums is progressive, but this progressivity is diluted by treatment of health benefits as pretax income. In addition, the contribution rate is based on an individual employee's wage rate, not family income. Lower-wage workers with higher-wage spouses could receive a windfall.

Other forms of adjusting premiums also raise some equity concerns. Relating premiums to behavior—for example, requiring higher contributions from employees who do not want to participate in wellness, disease management, or smoking-cessation programs, and the like—could be viewed as a form of cherry-picking, that is, a way to single out and possibly drive less-healthy people from the workforce and out of the employer-sponsored insurance market.

Cost Sharing for Health Care Services

Cost sharing includes (1) crafting designs for copayments and coinsurance and (2) establishing boundaries for financial liability, through deductibles, caps on out-of-pocket payments, or insurance protection from very high medical costs. These are intertwined with coverage and benefit design—that is, how much one has to pay depends on what is covered, under what circumstances, and how much is covered.

Some cautions are necessary. First, discussions about the structure of health insurance coverage and benefits use employer-sponsored insurance as a benchmark. Most private insurance is provided the large-group market. It is important to keep in mind, however, that there is a great deal of variation in cost sharing within the employer-sponsored market. Overall, small employers have more limited resources and fewer options for obtaining coverage for employees, and the coverage they can obtain tends to be more expensive than what can be purchased at the group rates available to large employers. Employees in small firms, therefore, on average, pay higher premiums for coverage that requires more cost sharing (Kaiser/HRET 2007). Second, health insurance available in the small-group and individual markets is less generous and more expensive than coverage in the employer-based group market. Similarly, health insurance programs created to help people who cannot buy insurance in the private market often include limited benefits and charge higher premiums compared to insurance for the large-group market.

Copayments and Coinsurance

Copayments or coinsurance are supposed to do two things: increase the percentage of insurance costs paid by the insured person and counter "moral hazard." As defined colloquially by Mark Pauly, *moral hazard* manifests itself when patients show up in the doctor's office saying, "That's OK doc, the insurance will pay for it" (Pauly 2007).

Nominal fees, such as $10 per visit to a primary care provider, are not viewed as an effective means of dealing with moral hazard. Nevertheless, copayments are the most common form of cost sharing for visits to in-network physicians for people with employer-sponsored insurance. The copayments might be viewed as fees that cover some administrative costs for visits, such as scheduling and record keeping. For out-of-network physician visits, coinsurance is the most common form of cost sharing in employer-sponsored plans. Moreover, coinsurance rates may be quite steep. In 2007, the average coinsurance rate for out-of-network office visits was 33 percent. This approach provides clear incentives for people to choose in-network physicians. Although coinsurance is generally more common in the employer-based group market, health plans sometimes include significant copayments for hospital admissions or outpatient surgery; copayments for emergency room or urgent care services are common. MA plans also employ a variety of both copayment and coinsurance cost-sharing designs for different Medicare-covered services such as durable medical equipment, physical therapy services, and emergency and urgent care, as well as for hospital care and physician visits.

There are two areas where refinements to cost sharing may be undertaken when considering reform: protecting vulnerable populations and linking cost sharing to improved value.

Protecting Vulnerable Populations

Most national health systems that utilize cost sharing waive some cost sharing for segments of the population, as they do for premiums In addition to people below a particular income level, including beneficiaries eligible for Medicaid or several other low-income groups covered by the MSPs, some systems reduce or waive cost sharing for additional populations, including elderly or retired persons, people who are unemployed, or those who have serious health problems.

Establishing limits on cost sharing in insurance plans (discussed below), when focused in particular on plans that serve low-income populations, provides another policy option. The Massachusetts Commonwealth Choice program offers three tiers of insurance products designed to ensure that options are available to people who did not have coverage previously, and, as discussed above, provides subsidies to help low-income people pay for coverage. The level of cost sharing varies across three tiers of plans, but the state also sets limits on the total amount of cost sharing for all products (effective beginning in 2009).

Approaches designed to link cost sharing directly to income have been proposed (see Rice and Thorpe 1993; Gruber 2006; Furman 2007). In government-run programs, the tax system provides a ready mechanism for relating health expenditures to income. Under tax rules, Americans can deduct the amount of medical and dental expenses that is more than 7.5 percent of adjusted gross income. An infrastructure for reporting medical expenses and for adjusting taxable income based on this information is therefore already in place. Proposals have outlined ways that health care expenses could be integrated into tax calculations, using deductible base amounts, or tax credit, with higher-income people eligible to apply smaller offsets.

Promoting Value

Varying cost sharing to improve efficiency or quality of health care can take a variety of forms.

Some plans reduce or eliminate cost sharing for services they want enrollees to use. One large employer, for example, devised an approach to reduce the likelihood that its new high-deductible plan would keep employees from using preventive services. While deductibles as well as cost sharing for many services, including physician visits, increased, most preventive services were exempted from cost sharing. Initial analyses indicated that the use of preventive services did not decline after the new policy was put in place (Busch et al. 2006).

Tiered cost sharing applies the same concepts and many of the same methods as tiered premiums programs such as the Wisconsin ETF model. In Minnesota, the Department of Employee Relations, which buys insurance for about 120,000 state employees and their families, worked with an alliance of health care and professional organizations as well as business groups to craft a value-driven benefits plan called Minnesota Advantage. The system uses detailed information on quality and performance to assign primary care clinics into tiers. Copayments and coinsurance are lower for the higher-rated clinics. There are also reduced copayments for members who participate in a health assessment.

More sophisticated clinical applications of value-based cost sharing are also being implemented, including programs that reduce copayments for specific drugs used to manage serious chronic conditions including diabetes, asthma, and hypertension. A program at the University of Michigan focused on diabetes care extends the concept of tiers by directly linking information on clinical effectiveness to cost sharing to individual patients. Using specialized data applications, the program created differential copayments based on patients' characteristics, reducing copayments for specific treatments that have the highest value for individual patients.

Setting Boundaries for Cost Sharing

While specific copayment or coinsurance designs create incentives related to using particular health care services, the way that costs add up creates another layer of incentives. This can be exceedingly difficult to sort out. Deductibles create the lower bounds of what people (individuals or family units) have to pay for particular services, classes of services, or overall, before insurance kicks in. Out-of-pocket limits create the upper bounds of what people have to pay out of pocket for health care. Maximum benefit limits place upper bounds on what insurance will pay for a particular service, types of services, or altogether, for a year, or for a lifetime.

Deductibles

Deductibles are used to reduce the total amount of risk covered by insurance. Deductibles provide a means of "buying down" the amount of coverage. Use of deductibles has evolved and taken on new roles in different insurance products. Deductibles are most common in loosely structured arrangements such as preferred provider organizations (PPOs), where they are much like coinsurance, tailored to create incentives targeted to different types of services. Some health plans have separate deductibles for hospital care or outpatient surgery rather than copayments. Half of workers in private industry are in plans that have different deductibles for in-network versus out-of-network care. In the same vein, insurers may cover some services without patients having to reach the deductible, for example, preventive services, prescription drugs, or physician office visits, to remove potential barriers to patients seeking appropriate care (Kaiser/HRET 2007).

Deductibles have become larger over time. For example, among workers in PPOs who had a general deductible, the percentage with deductibles of less than $500 dropped from 86 percent in 2000 to 64 percent in 2007, while the percentage with deductibles of $1,000 to $2,000 increased from 1 percent to 10 percent (Kaiser/HRET 2007). This is parallel to, but distinct from, the development of officially designated high-deductible plans.

Employer-sponsored coverage and individuals can, under current law, organize coverage that is built on a framework of high deductibles, coupled with a savings plan that allows people to set aside pretax money to pay for health care until the deductible has been reached. The plans can be offered with health savings accounts (HSAs), or health reimbursement arrangements (HRAs). In 2007, high-deductible health plans (HDHPs) are required to have minimum annual deductibles of $1,050 for self-only coverage ($2,100 for family coverage). HDHPs may provide preventive benefits without a deductible, or at a lower deductible than the HDHP general deductible. People can contribute to HSAs so the savings accounts cover the costs of the deductibles, up to limits specified by law ($2,700 for single coverage, $5,450 for family coverage). Plans can be offered by employers or established through financial institutions by self-employed individuals and some employees of small employers.

The Kaiser/HRET 2007 survey found that 10 percent of firms offered health benefits under HDHP/HRA or HSA arrangements. Five percent of workers with health coverage were in these plans. The average deductible for single coverage in HSA-qualified HDHP plans was $1,923, and the average aggregate deductible for family coverage in HSA-qualified HDHP plans was $3,883. An estimated 3.2 million policyholders and dependents were covered by HDHP/HSAs in 2006 (Kaiser/HRET 2007).

Out-of-Pocket Maximums

Most employer-sponsored coverage includes a cap on out-of-pocket costs. Close to 70 percent of employees are in such plans. The design of these caps varies. The out-of-pocket limits may not include all out-of-pocket costs, such as deductibles, office-visit coinsurance, or prescription drug coinsurance, and out-of pocket limits are more common in some types of health plans than others. HMOs and PPOs are less likely to require general deductibles and less likely to have out-of-pocket maximum amounts (Kaiser/HRET 2007). Plans that require less cost sharing up front may be less likely to have out-of-pocket maximums.

Generally, the maximum amounts for out-of-pocket costs for single coverage in employer-sponsored insurance range from $1,000 to $3,000. But, about a fifth of workers with single coverage have out-of-pocket limits set at amounts greater than $3,000. Out-of-pocket maximums for family coverage are about twice the limits for single coverage, with most set at $2,000 to $6,000, and close to one in five set at some amount greater than $6,000. The statutory requirements for HDHP plans set maximums for annual out-of-pocket expenses at $5,500 for single coverage and $11,000 for family coverage.

The largest single national health plan, Medicare, does not have out-of-pocket caps. If a beneficiary remains in the hospital for more than ninety days and uses up the "lifetime reserve" days, or stays in a skilled nursing facility more than one hundred days, Medicare coverage ends. Beneficiaries are wholly responsible for these costs (which is another reason most seek supplemental coverage). There are no ceilings on Part B coinsurance, and while Part D pays 95 percent of prescription drug costs after beneficiaries reach the limits of the "coverage gap" (requiring $3,850 in out-of-pocket spending in 2007), total liability thereafter is not capped.

Out-of-pocket maximums can play an important role in balancing the positive effects that cost-sharing incentives can have, that is, moderating the unnecessary or inappropriate use of health services, with the negative consequences it can have, creating barriers to appropriate care. The Medicare program asks participating MA plans to include out-of-pocket cost limits in their benefit designs. Plans that set the maximums at or below the amount recommended by CMS are given greater latitude in the design of cost sharing for individual covered services.

From an insurance theory perspective, the reason to have health insurance is to obtain protection from catastrophic, unpredictable medical costs. Health insurance in the United States addresses this potential risk, but with limits. If comprehensive coverage expansions are implemented, consideration will need to be given to catastrophically large health expenses. Federal law and regulation allow insurers' health plans to place dollar limits, as well as limits on utilization, on particular types of care or treatment of certain conditions, as long as the provisions are applied to all plan participants and not directed at an individual based on his or her health condition. Limits can be a dollar maximum per day of care or dollar ceilings on benefits for particular services, such as extended care, home health care, hospice care, or mental health or substance abuse services. In addition, employer-sponsored coverage often includes a lifetime maximum, a dollar amount beyond which benefits end. More than half of workers were in plans with lifetime limits in 2007. The majority of limits were set at $1 million or more. Lifetime limits can be lower in small-group or individual-market insurance products.

The most direct way to deal with catastrophic health care bills is for government to assume the costs. A provision in Medicaid allows states to establish medically needy programs designed to cover people whose medical expenses are very high but whose incomes are above the level that would qualify them for federal assistance. This includes people facing very high recurring expenses related to a disability or serious chronic illness, a catastrophic illness, or an accident. Not all states have medically needy programs, however, and eligibility standards vary from state to state. In 2003, total enrollment in Medicaid medically needy programs was about 3.5 million people, and total spending for the programs nationally was about $27.4 billion. The Veterans Health Administration also takes on the costs of care for veterans unable to afford out-of-pocket costs required from other providers, including a large number of veterans enrolled in Medicare who have no other form of supplemental coverage.

Risk pools and reinsurance schemes designed to stabilize the small employer or individual markets can be designed to offer protection to people with high medical expenses. The Healthy New York program provides coverage for employers of low- to middle-income employees, sole proprietors, and individuals. The state contracts with HMOs directly and provides reinsurance for the people who enroll. Employers and employees or individuals pay a community-rated premium, and enrollees have standard benefits with cost sharing. After the cost of care, including required cost sharing, reaches a specified level, the reinsurance kicks in.

This design would not, however, be easily transferable. First, the state pays for the reinsurance. Second, New York requires all insurers to offer individual coverage to everyone, at the same cost, without regard to health status. In addition to community rating, plans participating in Healthy New York are also required to set a single premium for all program enrollees—sole proprietors, individuals, or workers in small companies. Few states require guaranteed issue or community rating in the small-group or individual insurance markets.

Achieving Policy Goals

If the goal of structuring how people pay for health care is to generate or steer resources to support comprehensive coverage, the available evidence presents a mixed message. Copayments, coinsurance, and deductibles can shift costs from public and private insurers to insured people. The introduction of cost-sharing mechanisms such as high deductible plans and various forms of consumer-directed health plans would appear to raise the ante considerably.

But while there is research on how cost sharing affects health care costs and use of health services, there is not enough evidence to conclude what the likely effects of major changes in the structure of cost sharing would be (Congressional Budget Office 2006). In fact, because many health insurance plans include substantial cost sharing and consumer-directed plans (such as HDHP/MSA plans) include out-of-pocket spending caps, it is not clear that new approaches involve higher levels of cost sharing for the highest health care spenders than employer coverage now does.

How much revenue can be captured by redesigning cost sharing appears to depend more on people's ability to share the costs than on the structure of cost sharing. Most health care spending is concentrated in a small portion of the population. The 5 percent of the population with the highest health expenses accounts for about half of total health care expenses; the lowest 50 percent of health spenders accounts for about 3 percent. This spending is mostly for the treatment of serious diseases, injuries, and chronic illnesses. For more than half of those with the highest spending, the cost of deductibles, copayments, and services not covered by insurance added up to more than 10 percent of family income (Stanton 2006). Higher levels of cost sharing would not affect most people because they do not use much health care, while many of those with the highest levels of spending are unable to afford much additional cost sharing.

Exposure to out-of-pocket costs can also build demand for secondary insurance. As discussed above, Medicare is a prime example. Supplemental insurance, particularly coverage that provides first-dollar coverage, is assumed to reduce incentives to exercise caution when using health services. It also adds to administrative costs by creating additional billing systems, the need to coordinate payments, and other administrative systems.

More cost sharing could also increase the need for and costs of public programs that protect vulnerable populations. People could find that the coverage available to them is not worth the cost of the premiums. This could increase pressure on public programs to expand coverage, or increase subsidies for private coverage. When people are faced with high medical costs not covered by insurance, there is a limit to what most can pay before depleting all their resources. When that happens, costs are absorbed by other payers one way or another.

Costs and administrative burdens associated with cost sharing are harder to estimate than costs related to premiums. Insurers have developed sophisticated systems for processing health insurance claims, including complex cost-sharing provisions.

Technologies including the Internet make it relatively easy to put together insurance packages with menus of cost-sharing options. A new health insurance arrangement introduced by Wal-Mart in September 2007 allows employees to pick from fifty combinations of premiums, deductibles, and so on (Barbaro 2007). In addition, there is a layer of claims processing, appeals, and adjudication that is labor-intensive and burdensome for both consumers and health care providers. Similarly, proposals to link cost sharing to income through the tax system should be much like other special tax provisions (e.g., reporting various forms of income on 1099 forms, or itemizing health care costs on Schedule A). But while the basic structure is in place, including rules for what is and is not a legitimate health expense, auditing and revising cost-sharing information could be more complicated and therefore more expensive than administering income-related premiums.

Value-based systems with tiered cost sharing involve the same start-up costs, research, and so on as tiered premium systems but, again, may involve additional costs. Targeting medical conditions and ranking specific treatment options and explaining them to patients is more difficult than in sorting plans into tiers. In addition, stakeholders have expressed concerns about administrative costs related to preventing fraud or abuse and data privacy (Chernew, Rosen, and Fendrick 2007).

Copayments or coinsurance may be effective means of shifting costs to people who use health care, but they are increasingly viewed as somewhat blunt tools for driving efficiency in the health care system.

There is evidence that cost sharing can promote more effective health care delivery. The Minnesota ETF program avoided any premium increase in 2006, and $20 million in savings were returned to employees in the form of a 4.4 percent reduction total in annual premiums. The program attributed savings to lower-than-expected claims resulting from financial incentives and health promotion and management strategies. Value-based designs reviewed by Chernew, Rosen, and Fendrick (2007), however, were not expected to achieve savings. Copayments were reduced for high-value services specifically to remove barriers to the appropriate use of these services. This results in more, and appropriate, use of some high-cost services. Better care is not necessarily cheaper.

From one perspective, high-deductible approaches promote horizontal equity. Everyone can use their money any way they want to pay for health care. High-deductible plans eliminate the complex, arbitrary array of deductibles, copayments, and coinsurance for medical services or supplies that have evolved in many insurance plans. As structured, however, high-deductible plans with HSAs provide a tax advantage to higher-income people by shifting cost sharing to pretax income. Combined with the tax treatment of HSAs, high-deductible plans could amplify the relative advantage of wealthier, healthier people in the insurance market.

Without additional adjustments or public subsidies, cost sharing has been shown to have negative consequences for people who are poor or are in poor health. Studies of the effects on increased copayments in Medicaid have found that the introduction of even relatively small copayments in Medicaid programs has been associated with adverse outcomes including failure to fill prescriptions, increase in hospitalizations and nursing home admissions, and increase in emergency department visits (Ku and Wachino 2005). Other research has linked increasing premiums and cost sharing in Medicaid and SCHIP to drops in enrollment from the programs, and to problems obtaining medical treatment (Argita and O'Malley 2005). Small increases in copayments (required by supplemental insurance) can also have a significant effect on Medicare beneficiaries' use of outpatient services and filling prescriptions. One study of retired public employees in California found that while increased copayments did not affect hospitalization rates for average beneficiaries, they were associated with more hospital admissions for chronically ill beneficiaries (Chandra, Gruber, and McKnight 2007).

Tiered cost sharing could remove barriers to high-value medical care for lower-income people. Good care would be coupled with lower cost sharing. Approaches that assign providers to tiers based on efficiency and quality, however, could have negative consequences for some disadvantaged populations. At issue is whether the methods used to assess efficiency and quality of care are sufficiently sensitive to differences in patient health status and risk. In these approaches, providers are going to be assigned to tiers based on their success in achieving various goals related to prevention, health promotion, or managing care. They could be penalized for trying to manage the care of people who are less able to contribute to their own health care. If not done well, value-based systems could lead to a sort of medical underwriting, where people who cannot make it to appointments, do not take their medications, and so forth, are undesirable to the plan.

Plotting a Course

Comprehensive reforms to expand health coverage will involve some changes in how, and how much, people pay for insurance coverage and out of pocket for health care. Somewhat surprisingly, there is some convergence in thinking about approaches to structuring premiums and cost sharing here and abroad. Comprehensive state coverage reforms in the United States are hybrid models that draw on the strengths of different approaches to structuring how people pay for care.

Either income or payroll taxes can generate significant revenue in ways that are relatively fair and progressive. Regardless of whether the money comes from payroll tax deductions collected by employers and paid into a government social insurance fund that reimburses health care providers (like traditional Medicare), or from payroll deductions transferred to a government fund that buys down the cost of coverage in the private market, higher-income people pay more for a standard level of coverage.

In addition to having the potential to generate significant revenue—assuming contributions are not distorted by perverse tax code incentives—income-related contributions present minor administrative obstacles. Other tax-based approaches, including surcharges or tax credits, would likely require new administrative systems to deal with advance payments to cover premium costs, adjustments related to changes in income, or family circumstances. Using the tax system to administer some form of income-related cost sharing could also introduce separation between the time people pay for services and when they annually settle up with government.

Premium assistance for low-income people will be part of any coverage expansion. As the experience of the HCTC program and the various MSP programs has demonstrated, there are significant resource costs associated with obtaining, processing, and updating eligibility information. Costs increase when the programs involve multiple public and private entities. When different rules apply in different states, issues of fairness arise as well, because, depending on where they live, people in similar financial or health circumstances may have substantially different options for coverage or financial assistance with out-of-pocket costs. Medicare's experience with the MSP programs suggests that simplifying eligibility criteria as well as using data systems to facilitate eligibility and enrollment procedures could help the assistance programs to work more efficiently. Establishing the subsidy levels also raises difficult issues. The Massachusetts experience, consistent with other analyses, indicates that subsidies may have to be fairly large to make insurance affordable (Blumberg et al. 2007).

Premium competition is compatible with a hybrid social insurance approach as well as with private market approaches. In a social insurance model, health plans that provide the standard level of benefits could offer different configurations of benefits and cost sharing that meet the overall standards. They could also compete on the basis of customer service or operational efficiency that could be translated into lower premiums. This kind of competition is currently in play in MA plans in Medicare, and in the Federal Employees Health Benefits Program. At the margins, consumer choices about accepting risk of out-of-pocket costs could reduce the indiscriminate use of medical services or supplies.

Linking what people pay for health care to improving efficiency and quality of health can also be accomplished in different ways. One approach is to develop standards that would apply to all plans. Information on what works best in clinical care can be used to define what is covered. Treatments, procedures, tests, and other services that are not effective would not be covered in basic insurance packages. This approach has been integrated into a growing number of national health systems, particularly as applied to pharmacy benefits, and in private-sector as well as public insurance programs. As this work progresses, it may be possible to design systems in which care that is appropriate and cost-effective would require little or no cost sharing, while medical treatments, tests, and services that are proven to be effective, but no more effective than less-costly alternatives, would require higher levels of cost sharing.

An alternative approach would be to encourage health plans and insurers to develop their own techniques for using information about medical effectiveness, with appropriate safeguards to ensure that incentives do not create barriers to accessing needed care. Designing systems that are able to integrate incentives to use health care effectively could be important for efforts to control health care costs over time, but concluding that the resulting savings could pay for coverage expansions is not supported by available evidence.

Price competition and cost sharing, with appropriate safeguards, can be compatible with social insurance models for comprehensive health coverage. Underwriting and insurance rating cannot. In social insurance systems, health coverage is community rated, and no one can be excluded from coverage based on health risk. Evidence from small-group and individual insurance market reform initiatives indicates that community rating and related market regulation are critically important if market-based programs are to play a significant role in expanding coverage to people who are poor or in poor health. If insurance carriers are allowed to deny or condition coverage based on health status, or charge some people or groups more than others, markets become segmented. Costs of providing coverage to people who need help paying premiums or cost sharing spiral up, making it harder for government to subsidize those costs.

The effectiveness of any approach to restructuring how people pay for health care coverage or service, with respect to any of the policy goals discussed here—revenue, system efficiency, or promoting social or political policies—will depend on how insurance is defined and regulated. The scope of benefits and financial protection determines whether coverage is "comprehensive." If obtaining the right care at the right time in the right place involves high out-of-pocket spending, or coordinating benefits across multiple insurers, it is difficult to assign responsibility for health care outcomes or efficiency. But if insurance is designed to provide access to appropriate health care, many of the problems of insurance markets, including risk selection, market segmentation, and moral hazard associated with secondary coverage, become far more manageable. If the health care services people need are covered and affordable, health providers have a better chance of being able to promote better health and manage health care effectively. If care that people need is covered and affordable, it is reasonable to hold health providers, working with their patients, accountable.

References

Appleby, J. 2006. "Billing Errors Dog Medicare Drug Benefit Since Its Start." *USA Today* (November 11). www.usatoday.com/money/industries/health/drugs/2006–11–07-medicare-bills-usat_x.htm. (Accessed 15 August 2008.)

Argita, S., and M. O'Malley. 2005. "Increasing Premiums and Cost Sharing in Medicaid and SCHIP: Recent State Experiences." Issue paper. Kaiser Commission on Medicaid and the Uninsured, Washington, DC.

Barbaro, M. 2007. "Health Plan Overhauled at Wal-Mart." *New York Times* (September 19).

Blumberg, L., J. Holahan, J. Hadley, et al. 2007. "Marketwatch: Setting a Standard of Affordability for Health Insurance Coverage." DOI 10.1377/hlthaff.4463. *Health Affairs* Web exclusive: W463–W473. http://content.healthaffairs.org/cgi/search?andor

exactfulltext=and&resourcetype=1&disp_type=&author1=blumberg&fulltext=&pub date_year=2007&volume=&firstpage= (Accessed 17 November 2008).

Braithwaite, R., and A. Rosen. 2007. "Linking Cost Sharing to Value: An Unrivaled Yet Unrealized Public Health Opportunity." *Annals of Internal Medicine* 146 (8): 602–5.

Buchmueller, T.C., and A. Couffinhal. 2004. "Private Health Insurance in France." OECD Health Working Papers 12. Paris: Organization for Economic Cooperation and Development.

Busch, S., C. Barry, S. Vegso, et al. 2006. "Effect of a Cost-Sharing Exemption on the Use of Preventive Services at One Large Employer." *Health Affairs* 25 (6): 1529–36.

Chandra, A., J. Gruber, and R. McKnight. 2007. "Patient Cost-Sharing, Hospitalization Offsets, and the Design of Optimal Health Insurance for the Elderly." NBER Working Paper Series 12972. Cambridge, MA: National Bureau of Economic Research.

Chernew, M.E., A.B. Rosen, and A.M. Fendrick. 2007. "Value-Based Insurance Design." *Health Affairs* Web exclusive (January 30): W195–W203. content.healthaffairs.org/cgi/content/full/26/2/w195. (Accessed 15 August 2008.)

Chollet, D. 2002. "Expanding Individual Health Insurance Coverage: Are High-Risk Pools the Answer?" w2.349v1. *Health Affairs* Web exclusive (October 23). content.healthaffairs. org/cgi/content/full/hlthaff.w2.349v1/DC1. (Accessed 15 August 2008.)

Chollet, D. 2007. "The Role of Reinsurance in State Efforts to Expand Coverage," *Issue Brief* (State Coverage Initiatives, AcademyHealth) V (4) October.

Congressional Budget Office. 2006. "Consumer-Directed Health Plans: Potential Effects on Health Care Spending and Outcomes." CBO Study. Washington, DC: Congressional Budget Office.

December, A. 2007. "Health Plan May Exempt 20% of the Uninsured." *Boston Globe* (April 12).

Dorn, S. 2006. "Take-up of Health Coverage Tax Credits: Examples of Success in a Program with Low Enrollment." Washington, DC: Urban Institute, www.urban.org/url. cfm?ID=411390. (Accessed 15 August 2008.)

———. 2007. "How Well Do Health Coverage Tax Credits Help Displaced Workers Obtain Health Care?" Statement of Stan Dorn, JD, Senior Research Associate, Urban Institute, to the Congress of the United States, Committee on Education and Labor, U.S. House of Representatives, March 26.

Fendrick, A., and M. Chernew. 2006. "Value-Based Insurance Design: A 'Clinically Sensitive' Approach to Preserve Quality of Care and Contain Costs." *American Journal of Managed Care* 12 (1): 18–20.

Furman, J. 2007. "The Promise of Progressive Cost Consciousness in Health Reform." Hamilton Project Policy Brief 2007–05. Washington, DC: Brookings Institution, June.

Government Accountability Office. 2006. "Social Security Administration." GAO-07–228R. Washington, DC: Government Accountability Office, November 17.

Gruber, J. 2006. "The Role of Consumer Copayments for Health Care: Lessons from the RAND Health Insurance Experiment and Beyond." Publication 7566. Paper prepared for the Kaiser Family Foundation, Washington, DC, October.

Kaiser Commission on Medicaid and the Uninsured. 2005. "Dual Eligibles: Medicaid's Role for Low-Income Medicare Beneficiaries." Medicaid Facts. Washington, DC: Kaiser Family Foundation.

Kaiser Family Foundation. 2005. "Medicare: Low Assistance Under the Medicare Drug Benefit." Fact sheet. Washington, DC: Kaiser Family Foundation.

———. 2007. "State Health Facts. Medicaid Medically Needy Program Enrollment, FFY 2003." January. www.statehealthfacts.kff.org/comparetable.jsp?ind=209&cat=4&yr=2 1&typ=1&sort=a&o=a. (Accessed 15 August 2008.)

Kaiser Family Foundation and Health Research and Education Trust (Kaiser/HRET). 2007. *Employer Health Benefits 2007 Annual Survey.* Chicago: Health Research and Education Trust and Kaiser Family Foundation.

Ku, L. and V. Wachino. 2005. "The Effect of Increased Cost-Sharing in Medicaid: A Summary of the Research Findings." Washington DC: Center on Budget and Policy Priorities, Revised July 7.

National Center for Health Statistics. 2006. *Health, United States with Chartbook on Trends in the Health of Americans.* Hyattsville, MD: National Center for Health Statistics.

National Conference of State Legislatures. 2006. "State Employee Health Benefits—Monthly Premium Costs (Family Coverage)." Compiled by Richard Cauchi. 64.82.65.67/health/StateEmpl-healthpremiums.pdf. (Accessed 15 August 2008.)

National Governors Association, NGA Center for Best Practices. 2007. "Leading the Way: State Health Reform Initiatives." Issue brief. Washington, DC: National Governors Association.

Orszag, P., Director, Congressional Budget Office. 2007. Letter to Hon. Pete Stark, Chairman, Subcommittee on Health, Committee on Ways and Means, U.S. House of Representatives, September 5.

Pear, R. 2004. "Sluggish Start for Tax Credits for Insurance." *New York Times* (January 25).

Pauly, M. 2007. "The Truth about Moral Hazard and Adverse Selection." No. 36. Maxwell School, Syracuse University, Center for Policy Research, Syracuse, NY.

Rice, T., and K.E. Thorpe. 1993. "Income-Related Cost-Sharing in Health Insurance." *Health Affairs* 12 (1): 21–39.

Silow-Carroll, A., and T. Alteras. 2007. "Value-Driven Health Care Purchasing: Case Study of Wisconsin's Department of Employee Trust Funds." Publication 1056, Washington, DC: Commonwealth Fund, August.

Stanton, M. 2006. "The High Concentration of U.S. Health Care Expenditures." *Research in Action* Issue 19. Washington, DC: Agency for Healthcare Research and Quality, June.

Summer, L., and R. Friedland. 2002. "The Role of the Asset Test in Targeting Benefits for Medicare Savings Programs." Washington, DC: Commonwealth Fund, October.

Summer, L. and L. Thompson. 2004. "How Asset Tests Block Low-Income Medicare Beneficiaries from Needed Benefits." *Issue Brief* (Commonwealth Fund) (May).

Wisconsin Department of Employee Trust Funds. 2007. *It's Your Choice 2007 Book.* Madison, WI: author.

6

Refiguring Federalism:

Nation and State in Health Reform's Next Round

Lawrence D. Brown

Most Western nations treat health policy (especially, but not only, issues of coverage) as a national responsibility in which subnational governments or regions may be granted a more or less prominent role. The United States, by contrast, has never adopted a national health policy, nor agreed that it ought to do so. In consequence, the fifty states have played three roles: partnering with federal government on programs (e.g., Medicaid and the State Children's Health Insurance Program [SCHIP]), pressuring Washington for a redivision of labor in health affairs, and innovating in health policy in default of national leadership.

This role trilogy was a potent political force in the run-up to the Clinton health reform plan of 1993–94. In the late 1980s, state spending on Medicaid shot up as a result of costs of treating people with HIV/AIDS, new federal coverage mandates, states' Medicaid maximization strategies, the impact of general medical inflation, and increased uninsured residents. The George H.W. Bush administration was disinclined toward bold national measures, and a cadre of states resolved to install systems that would achieve or approach universal coverage and contain costs, mainly via managed care, to boot. In 1988 Massachusetts passed legislation aimed at universal coverage via a play-or-pay approach. Oregon's famous rationing plan (aka prioritization) earmarked savings imputed to the elimination of insufficiently cost-effective services in Medicaid for an expansion of eligibility in that program. In legislation of 1993 Washington coupled an employer mandate with managed competition. Other states—New York, California, Colorado, Vermont, and Florida, for example—deliberated at length on reform but after various and sundry detours came up short. These real and attempted innovations boosted the conviction that health reform was not only imperative but also at long last doable and thereby pushed reform higher on the national agenda. When Bill Clinton advertised his commitment to health reform in his successful presidential campaign of 1992, few doubted that the idea's time had finally come.

By 1994, national reform and most of the states' handiwork were dead. Massachusetts deferred implementation of its plan and then repealed most of it. Oregon added about one hundred thousand residents to Medicaid and then, failing to find big savings by rationing or otherwise, struggled with the program's costs. Washington gutted most of its 1993 reform bill in 1995.To be sure, not all was lost. Minnesota, for instance, quietly layered federal and state programs without employer mandates or managed competition and brought its rate of uninsurance below 10 percent. The Health Insurance Portability and Accountability Act of 1996 gave the federal government a larger role in regulating private health insurance, which heretofore had been left to the states. The creation of SCHIP in 1997 put "catalytic federalism" (Brown and Sparer 2003) on display: Drawing both on Medicaid and on innovative programs of child coverage in states such as New York, Massachusetts, and Florida, the federal government designed a new template that entailed new funding and challenges for the fifty states. On the whole, however, misadventures at both levels of government reaffirmed a sour truth: Health reform initiatives tend to generate much more antagonism among threatened interest groups (especially business, providers, and insurers) than gratitude within the electorate and are therefore a poor investment of political capital. For a decade thereafter, the reform "movement" fell mute while states fine-tuned their "partner" role in Medicaid waivers, the implementation of SCHIP, and other variations on incrementalist themes.

Around 2005, however, history began to repeat itself. The uninsured, rising by roughly 1 million per year, hit 45 million. As in the late 1980s, relentless media attention to the issue powerfully intimated that the status quo was doomed. Meanwhile, growth in Medicaid and SCHIP had lowered the number of uninsured children by about 5 million. By enacting a program to cover all its children, Illinois showed that state health reform was astir again, and Maine and Vermont passed laws that aimed at universal coverage. For a time the media recorded lagging enrollment in Maine's plan, but then reformers everywhere were drawn to Massachusetts, which, Rip Van Winkle–like, rose to reprise the quest for reform abandoned earlier.

Even as the exogenous shock of soaring Medicaid spending had galvanized states in the late 1980s, the prospect of being hanged the next day by waiver-meisters in the federal Centers for Medicare and Medicaid Services concentrated the minds of Massachusetts's leaders on how best to meet Washington's conditions for renewing roughly half a billion dollars in waiver funds, namely, that the state spend less on the safety net and more on coverage for the uninsured. In 2006, Massachusetts passed legislation that combined an individual mandate (all residents are legally obliged to buy "affordable" coverage if it is available), very modest financial penalties for employers who fail to offer coverage, expansion of Medicaid, new income-related subsidies for those who do not qualify for Medicaid, and assorted administrative innovations that would help residents to find and enroll in affordable health plans. As before, New York wondered if it should do something similar, and California too soon joined in. In 2008, as had been the case fifteen years earlier, innovations within the federal "laboratory" signaled to the public and presidential contenders seeking their votes that a plausible plan for national health reform was a precondition for political success. Now, as then, federalism is sometimes said to be a positive, perhaps indeed invaluable, element in the strategic design.

Mandates, Medicaid, Models, and More

States as stimuli to and models for federal policy are one thing; states as partners and participants in federal policies are another. Whereas the Clinton plan of
1993–94 gave the states a major role in organizing and overseeing regional health
alliances (which vanished with the rest of the blueprint), the three main Democratic
presidential contenders in 2008 were rather more laconic on federalism. The main
allusion to the states in Hillary Clinton's plan allowed them "the option of banding
together" to offer regional versions of her Health Choices Menu. Barack Obama
would permit "flexibility for state plans . . . provided they meet the minimum standards of the national plan." The state of the art of health reform on the Republican
side, meanwhile, is pretty well captured by the repudiation by (failed) presidential
aspirant Mitt Romney of the plan for universal coverage he had promoted while
governor of Massachusetts.

In the Clinton episode, an employer mandate, regional health alliances, and managed competition were the centerpieces of a model that was expected to wed Left and
Right, government and market, regulation and competition, into an acceptable reform
package. Today's model features individual and employer mandates, expansion of
Medicaid, new public subsidies geared to income, and savings from information technology, prevention, and much more on lists notable for the absence of managed care.
Whereas the Clinton concoction came out of whole theoretical cloth, the latter-day
stratagems derive from flesh-and-blood legislation that has already inspired emulation
in important states and could become a serviceable national model.

The generalizability (upward to Washington or outward across the states) of this
or other approaches probably turns less on analytical merit than on goodness of
political fit. The Massachusetts plan is arguably highly context dependent. The law
of 2006 was not (merely) the product of superior political enlightenment but rather
a response to a sharp stimulus—possible loss of sizable Medicaid funds in a waiver
under renegotiation with the federal government. The plan supposedly advanced the
presidential fortunes of then governor Romney. Massachusetts coupled a high rate
of private health care coverage with a generous Medicaid program and therefore
began the exercise with a low percentage of uninsured residents. The state enjoys
cohesion and cooperation among health care sectors—this law, like the enactment
of 1988, brought hospitals, physicians, business groups, insurers, and academic
medical centers together in sustained collaboration rarely found in other states.
Continuing federal waiver money, plus new and reprogrammed public funds in a
state sometimes caricatured as "Taxachusetts," cemented a good financial deal for
providers (mainly excepting the safety net), for the business community (penalties
for not covering workers cost less than buying insurance), and for insurers, who
stood to gain new subsidized business. The Massachusetts case calls the federalism
question, pondering how this or a similar approach might fare in other states, or
in a national program in which all states were obliged to participate, is a kind of
litmus test of the prospects for success of the emerging reform project.

Mississippi is not Massachusetts. States that lack the carrot and stick of big federal waivers on the line do not have governors eager to use public program building for the disadvantaged to appeal to a national audience; combine relatively low private-sector coverage with constricted Medicaid eligibility; suffer high rates of uninsurance; house providers, businesses, and insurers with little history of or inclination toward cooperation; and show little taste for crafting new income-related public subsidies for the less affluent; and so may find the emerging reform template distasteful as federal or state policy. Presumed skeptics would be Texas, Oklahoma, New Mexico, Florida, and Arizona (five states in which uninsurance rates run around or above 20 percent and that collectively contain about 40 percent of the uninsured in the United States), and the political economy and health policy tastes of most states probably lie closer to this quintet than to Minnesota, Massachusetts, Maine, and Vermont.

A mandate that all residents of a state (or the nation) buy coverage could be a progressive coup or a regressive affliction—depending on whether Medicaid and public subsidies are generous enough to keep out-of-pocket payments tolerable. The weaker the requirements for employer participation, the longer the fiscal stretch for public programs. But the firmer the bite on employers, the greater the prospects of political opposition by powerful small (and some large) business lobbies. The broader the role of an expanded Medicaid, the bigger the tax burden to meet state shares of whatever intergovernmental matching formula might be adopted. (As Nicole Kazee [2008] points out, 70 federal cents on the dollar is objectively a good deal but may not be so perceived by states accustomed to think of themselves as poor and fiscally beleaguered.) The smaller the role for enlarged Medicaid coverage, the greater the funds that must come from consumers, employers, or new public subsidies, or some combination of the three, that will probably mimic the fiscal politics of Medicaid expansions. Equity objectives go hand in hand with tax issues— the need for new taxes to sustain redistributive programs old and new, the case for repealing tax breaks, and so on—that roil the smooth surface of consensus.

The reform approach on display in Massachusetts and, mutatis mutandis, in the proposals of Democractic presidential party candidates, Barack Obama and Hillary Clinton, is less a model than a laundry list of strategies. The five variables in question—individual mandates, employer requirements, Medicaid expansion, public subsidies, and "savings" from various and sundry sources—invite diverse outcomes that extend from fair and affordable universal coverage premised on newfound solidarity among Americans to a cruel charade that compels the less well-off to pay heavily out of pocket to buy costly coverage dubbed affordable by regulatory fiat or for coverage affordable but inadequate because insufficiently subsidized, with multiple mixed cases in between. The new template reformulates the big health reform questions but does not answer them. The devil, not yet in the details, haunts the design.

In principle the elections of 2008 could launch a universal national health measure that embodies the appeals and virtues of a social insurance–based Medicare program for all or a general revenue-based single-payer system. In practice, however, the states now are probably too heavily entrenched in health policy and too powerful and insistent a political presence to be pushed to the sidelines. For this and other reasons, Medicaid may well be a more plausible foundation for reform than is Medicare. If so, the central reform challenge is to reconcile subnational variation and discretion with a national set of rules that steers between rigidity and indulgence in ways that are substantively workable and politically acceptable.

Though it is not the sole focus of federal-state relations in the health sphere, Medicaid is certainly the most prominent one, and it therefore offers an especially helpful entry into the intergovernmental complexities a reformed system will face. Created in 1965 as a program of "welfare medicine" principally for mothers and children on public assistance, Medicaid has steadily added beneficiaries and services and now covers (with SCHIP) around 60 million Americans on an annual budget of more than $350 billion. Boiled down to basics, the federal-state challenges in the program revolve around ten main issues.

1. Beneficiary categories. In the course of a "gradual and relentless extension" (Smith and Moore 2008, 181), Medicaid covers not only poor mothers and children but also the aged, blind, and disabled; many of the mentally ill and mentally retarded (the program is the nation's most important payer for mental health services); indigent Medicare beneficiaries who qualify "dually" for Medicaid; some temporarily unemployed; victims of intermittent disasters (for instance, Hurricane Katrina); and Americans whose incomes and medical conditions qualify them for long-term care, an extremely costly commitment that the states have at intervals explored "swapping" to the federal government in exchange for assuming other functions. Who "deserves" Medicaid coverage has been a continual subject of debate in the program, which has seen ever-more-organized groups and policy entrepreneurs in and out of Congress seize political opportunities that get benefits for "their" populations ensconced in some corner of the statute.

2. Income thresholds. Medicaid's enrollment has grown not only by the addition of new groups but also by incremental elevation of income limits on eligibility. In both Medicaid and SCHIP, states can opt to exceed federal income thresholds. What the upper federal limits should be for what groups and how far the federal government should agree to match the Medicaid spending of states that want to go further are contentious issues, as skirmishing between President Bush and the Democratic Congress over the latter's proposed expansions in SCHIP illustrated.

3. Mandated/optional benefits. One important federal lever for steering Medicaid in the states is to offer them the option of adding new beneficiaries or new covered services, or both, at their federal matching rate. The federal government can also make options mandatory if political conditions are ripe, and a wave of such transitions—the so-called Waxman two-step—in the late 1980s triggered protests by governors and the National Governors Association (Smith and Moore 2008, 177–78).

4. Delivery patterns. The federal government and states clash and negotiate over the organizational settings in which care for which Medicaid pays is delivered, including the shift from a fee-for-service model to managed care (which now enrolls more than half of Medicaid beneficiaries nationwide); the push for "least-restrictive" care settings for the mentally ill; the drive to reduce the program's alleged "institutional bias" by means of home- and community-based treatment loci; battles over what nursing home variant—intermediate, extended, skilled, and so on—qualifies for payment under what circumstances; and the struggle to formulate and enforce quality standards and patient protections in these and other venues.

5. Safety net. Medicaid, uninsured, or otherwise disadvantaged patients constitute a disproportionate share of the patient mix in some hospitals. To ease the fiscal strain, the federal government offers states (and thence the hospitals) special payments, the amounts and conditions on receipt of which have grown and contracted over the years to the tune of considerable conflict. Some analysts contend that the eternally beleaguered safety-net hospitals need all the help they can get. Others view them as relics of a superseded system, ripe for downsizing, and urge that funds be shifted toward community health centers and other sources of primary and outpatient care. Another camp favors shifting dollars from paying for care to supplying or improving coverage.

6. Fraud and abuse. Fear that a nontrivial fraction of Medicaid's billions goes to providers (or consumers) who cheat the system has inspired congressional inquiries, agency investigations, and closer scrutiny of the financial records of beneficiaries and the billing records of providers. The issue lends itself to (literally) arresting headlines, but the cost-effectiveness of antifraud efforts is unclear, given that antifraud and anti-abuse systems occasionally succumb to fraud and abuse.

7. Matching formulas. Since the program's inception, Medicaid has given all states a federal matching percentage of no less than 50 percent, and more (up to 72 percent) for poorer states. Changes in the formula would have large redistributive implications, and so the allocations have stayed pretty much frozen in place (Smith and Moore 2008, 239). States, however, have annoyed the federal government with perennial fiscal improvisations to raise their share of the match—for example, by imposing taxes on or securing donations from providers, or contriving "intergovernmental transfers" from localities, which then recoup their "losses" with dividends from the larger federal funds drawn down. At times the federal government has proposed to reduce its exposure to open-ended matching of state Medicaid spending by converting the program to a block grant or by imposing caps on federal matching, but the states and their allies in Congress and in the advocacy community have thwarted such initiatives.

8. Compliance enforcement. Because Medicaid covers many complex services for a heterogeneous cadre of beneficiaries, the federal government and states sometimes clash over whether the latter are meeting the program's statutory and regulatory requirements. For example, is the Early Periodic Screening, Diagnosis, and Treatment Program reaching out adequately to beneficiaries and offering treatment for the conditions it finds? (Whether such treatment is required when the clinically indicated services are not included in a state's Medicaid plan has been a matter of federal-state contention.) Are substance abuse treatments for adolescents in Medicaid available and accessible?

9. Flexibility and innovation. As states chafed under federal rules but failed to agree on a fundamental redesign of the program, governors increasingly argued for greater flexibility to introduce innovations within their states. These pleas, especially after welfare reform in 1996 severed the link between eligibility for public assistance and eligibility for Medicaid, persuaded President (and former chafing governor) Bill Clinton to grant federal waivers that permitted states to make changes in coverage (expansions in some states, reduced benefits in others), financing (including limited cost sharing), delivery (for instance, ventures in community-based care), and other features of the program. President (and former governor) George W. Bush has also been generous with federal waivers, leading some observers to worry that such limited national uniformity as Medicaid has had is dissipating into fifty different Medicaid programs.

10. Payment policies. Although the states enjoy broad discretion over how much and how they pay providers, the federal government sometimes limits their freedom. Contested cases in point include the (now repealed) Boren Amendment, which mandated higher payments to safety-net providers, the "upper payment limit" that links Medicaid payments to those made by Medicare for some services, drug rebates, rules governing payment to nursing homes, and required funding for graduate medical education.

Health reform might address these intergovernmental diversities and disparities in one of three main ways. First, much of the problem would disappear (or be much mitigated) by a single-payer, Medicare-for-all plan that took the states largely out of the action. The system would look something like, say, France—one dominant "sickness fund" operating in a unitary (nonfederal) framework. It is sobering to note, however, that roughly 160 million Americans now have health coverage a good deal less uniform across work sites, let alone states, than is the coverage of those on Medicaid or SCHIP. The 47 million uninsured enjoy no uniformity at all. Successful national standardizing of this privatized and federalized system would be no mean policy feat, and excluding or much downsizing the roles of employers and the states would be an equally astounding political coup. Some minimum adequate scope for disparities (which may or may not constitute objectionable inequities) may be unavoidable.

Second, if Medicare for all is out of reach politically, reformers could push for Medicaid for more, ratcheting up the program's strong expansionary dynamics. This implies working one's way down the ten-item list reviewed above to identify opportunities for cost-effective and politically palatable extensions of Medicaid coverage, for instance, Medicaid for all lower-income children or for more working, lower-income adults, or both. How would *lower-income* be defined? What happens to long-term care? Would there be optional coverage for some groups at federal matching rates, or more national mandates? Is managed care to be the, or a, vehicle of choice? Should the federal government mandate the use of, and set standards for, electronic medical records and kindred managerial advances? Will more money go to safety-net hospitals, community health centers, or perhaps to coverage instead of (directly to) caregivers? How much more fraud and abuse (and efforts to deter and detect them) does Medicaid for more imply? Will the federal matching formula for the states change? Will programs such as the Early Periodic Screening, Diagnosis, and Treatment Program be preserved, and if so, on what terms? How much flexibility will be granted to individual states, and on what terms (waivers? making the program more like SCHIP, as some governors prefer?)? How and how much will providers (expected to deliver accessible care of good quality to an expanded Medicaid clientele) be paid? Policy issues and political conflicts that haunt Medicaid today would grow along with the program's enrollment. More of the same battling within political trenches inside the Beltway and state capitols may seem a pitiful and unworthy model of reform, but it may be the best the system can do, and if it were done in a more liberal political environment after the elections of November 2008, this strategy might make a more than marginal dent in the ranks of the uninsured.

Third, reformers reconcile national consistency with subnational (and private-sector) diversity by taking a cue from Canada and promulgating a set of general standards, principles, and criteria that the states must meet to qualify for their share of federal matching funds. These standards would be broader and less constraining than those of a fully national system, but they would require no small measure of averaging among current state practices, and designing them would be easier said than done.

Pessimists who fear that such a project is beyond the capacity of government to master may well be right, but before dismissing it as doomed a priori, critics might pause to note that other Western nations with federal systems have achieved affordable universal coverage while striking a reasonably serviceable and stable intergovernmental balance that addresses health policy conundrums not so dissimilar from those Americans confront. The workings of federalist improvisations elsewhere might therefore have something to say to reformers.

Health Policy and Foreign Federalism

Like the United States, most Western societies are in the process of adjusting relations between central and subnational governments or regional units in the health sphere. France, for example, is a unitary, not federal, system, but looks to regional hospital agencies, created a decade ago, to help design and implement changes in local hospital markets. Sharing of authority and spending between the national government in Rome and local and regional units and enterprises has held center stage in Italy's health policies since it scrapped its social insurance system and adopted a national health service model in 1978. In nations whose constitutions grant formal powers to subnational governments, negotiations between these and the center over which level should do and fund what in the health system are basic parts of the policy furniture.

One European federation—Switzerland—ranks second only to the United States in health spending as a percentage of GDP and per capita. Two others—Canada and Germany—generally vie for third place on the spending charts. That these four federal nations finance health care differently—Canada has a single-payer system, Germany a social insurance regime, Switzerland a variant on so-called consumer-driven health care, and the United States a hodgepodge of private, public, and safety-net arrangements—may even suggest that correlation is not causation, that federalism itself works to push health costs upward. A quick review of the Canadian, German, and Swiss systems pinpoints some challenges and options for U.S. reformers.

Canada

If, as some argue, most-similar systems are the best sources of usable policy lessons for national counterparts, then Canada, which shares a border, a language, and important historical and institutional similarities with the United States, is the first (and perhaps last and only) place U.S. health reformers ought to canvas. Macrosimilarities aside, moreover, the Canadian and U.S. health systems exhibit intriguing variations on two key health policy themes. First, whereas the U.S. Constitution leaves ambiguous how states' rights may constrain federal health initiatives, Canada's explicitly assigns health matters to the provinces. Second, the U.S. and Canadian health systems looked very similar for much of the twentieth century—until the 1970s (late in the game by cross-national standards), when the adoption of Canada's version of Medicare put the two nations on divergent strategic paths.

Provincial debates about public health (especially hospital) insurance commenced around the time of World War I and, particularly in British Columbia and Alberta, moved on and off the provinces' policy agendas in the 1930s. Creation of a federal Interdepartmental Advisory Committee on Health Insurance in 1942 centralized and intensified these debates, but negotiations between the central (formerly known as "dominion") government and the provinces ran aground and adjourned in 1946. The stalemate first broke when Saskatchewan moved in 1947 to create a provincial hospital insurance program. By the end of 1950, four of the ten provinces had broad or near-universal programs of hospital coverage and the federal government came under rising pressure to create the fiscal conditions (i.e., put up the money) that would induce the remaining provinces to consent to enter a new national program.

The Canadian debate of 1956–57 rings familiar to American ears fifty years later: "It was too much, it was too little, it was too soon, it was overdue, it drained the federal treasury, it did not offer enough to the provinces, it was the road to socialism, it was the beginning of a new day, it would not represent any additional expenditure, it would bankrupt the nation" (Taylor 1990, 92). Then, in a decidedly un-American denouement, Canada's Parliament set aside opposition by the insurance industry and chambers of commerce and the lack of endorsement of the Canadian Medical Association and passed the Hospital Insurance Act unanimously in both houses in 1957. A parliamentary political structure does matter: national and provincial prime ministers weighed options and took time before endorsing health insurance breakthroughs in their bailiwicks, but once they resolved to make them happen, party unity carried the day.

Four years later, Saskatchewan launched a bigger battle by adding provincial coverage for physician services, an innovation that triggered a bitter (and finally unsuccessful) physicians' strike but also caught the eye of other provinces which (again) adopted similar measures and sought national funds to help pay for them. This prospect called into question the economic future of existing private, voluntary, and medical society–sponsored insurance plans, so insurance and physician organizations lobbied hard for means-tested benefits in any national plan and urged that a national commission be formed to explore the issue and (presumably) confirm the wisdom of their wishes. As it happened the report of the Royal Commission on Health Services "astounded" (Tuohy 1999, 53) this coalition in 1964 by recommending that public (provincial and central) funds should go directly to pay for care, not for income-scaled subsidies to help citizens meet the cost of private health insurance premiums. This decision, which seems to have gone down politically with remarkable ease, reflected both a principled distaste for private insurance and fiscal pragmatism—income-related subsidies not only introduced an inequitable two-tieredness into the system but also were costly and administratively cumbersome (Tuohy 1999, 55). After the Medical Care Insurance Act passed in 1966, private insurers could not sell coverage that duplicated the contents of the single-payer program and were thus consigned to offering extra (supplementary) benefits—outpatient prescription drugs and long-term care, for example. (In Canada supplementary coverage is largely employer based, while funding for the public plan comes mainly from personal, sales, and corporate taxes at the national level and in combinations and at rates that vary among provinces.)

Despite the singularity of public payment in Canada, the system is often characterized as ten provincial (and three territorial) systems that differ on many counts. What keeps order amid this potential chaos is a list of five criteria (also sometimes called principles, conditions, and standards) the national government requires the provinces to honor as a condition of receipt of its money. (As a constitutional matter, it lacks the power to mandate them outright but can attach them as strings to grants.) As set out in the Canada Health Act of 1984, the criteria declare that provincial health programs must secure comprehensiveness (medically necessary physician and hospital services must be covered); universality (the whole provincial population must be covered); accessibility (physicians may not engage in extra billing and hospitals may not impose user charges); portability (Canadians moving to or traveling in other provinces must be covered by their province of residence); and public administration (provinces cannot delegate management of their health plans to for-profit entities).Contemplation of thirteen subnational health systems bonded serenely by five general principles embodied in eight pages of national legislation may soothe the frayed sensibilities of U.S. reformers, but the evolution of the Canadian system has been conspicuously conflictual all along the way. As noted, hospital insurance was decades in the making, and the addition of coverage for physicians' services sparked quite a brawl. Once Canada's version of Medicare was intact, the provincial and central governments began (and have continued) to clash earnestly and often over which levels will pay how much and how for the health system. Initial arrangements, which had the central government sharing a percentage of provincial health costs, left the former upset about its growing share of provincial overruns and the latter fuming about nitpicking federal audits and rulings. In 1977 cost sharing gave way to "Established Program Financing," which entailed block grants and the yielding of federal tax points in combinations that complicated the disentangling of provincial from federal funding streams. Through much of the 1990s, economic growth slowed and the federal government retrenched. In 1990–91, federal transfers amounted to 33 percent of provincial and territorial health spending, but by 1999–2000 the shares had shifted to 28 percent and 72 percent, respectively (Marchildon 2005, 45.)The provinces bewailed betrayal, the providers deplored underinvestment in the health sector, and the public's satisfaction with the system, hitherto among the highest in Western nations, began to erode. Political leaders got the message, and when the economy revived, so too did federal health care contributions, which in 2005–6 stood at 35 percent federal and 64 percent provincial and territorial (Marchildon 2005, 45). Not all was forgiven, however. The renewed federal largesse in 2000 and after generated "considerable irritation from provincial governments who saw it [the federal government] as trying to gain credit for re-entering an area from which it had withdrawn in an antisocial manner" (Greer 2004, 218). A 2003 survey found that only 42 percent of respondents affirmed that the federal government and provinces worked well together (France 2005, 40). Throughout this fiscal fracas, the provinces have been devolving authority in the hospital sector to new regional and community boards that could admirably fuse planning with local control or could, as Jonathan Lomas (1997, 821) observes, become "sponges for local discontent."

All the same, in contrast to the United States, Great Britain, and various continental nations that perpetually ponder systemic reforms, the Canadian system has been and remains, as Carolyn Tuohy (1999) notes, impressively stable. Evidently, intergovernmental marriages, like the nongovernmental kind, can be, as Greer (2004, 220) writes of the Canadian system, "petty in the moment" but "productive overall." The frictions the system faces are, however, surely more than momentary and arguably more than petty. Allegations by American critics that the Canadian system is one long waiting list widely miss the mark, but such lists (sometimes called the system's Achilles' heel) do sometimes accumulate in some provinces for some services, leading providers, the media, and consumer groups to complain that the system so egregiously underinvests in health care facilities and personnel that citizens are sometimes driven to distraction—or over the U.S. border for care! Indeed, a recent court decision in Quebec that excessive waiting jeopardizes the accessible care the system promises could open the door to the private competition Canada has so far refused to admit. Meanwhile, even as the Right deplores the absence of private competitors in the public insurance plan, the Left denounces the advent of groups of private physicians (some with corporate ties in the United States) on the supply side. And of course the absence of a national requirement that provincial plans fund outpatient prescription drugs and home health care (among other omissions) continues to vex critics who point out the rising (and often out-of-pocket) costs of such services to the public and the disparities that ensue when coverage is left to provincial discretion.

Another camp of critics complains that the system's accommodative and "collegial" (Tuohy 1999) catering to private practitioners (mostly independent and paid fee-for-service, which constitutes 83 percent of physician revenue) and hospitals (mainly private, nonprofit, and paid by global budgets) generates excessive use of services, forecloses opportunities for integration and coordination, and deserves a heavy dose of the managed care (and/or managed competition) in which Canada has to date shown little interest. These aggravations all flow in some measure from the system's costs, which though well below those of the United States, stand high enough and rise fast enough perpetually to distress Canadian leaders.

What insights might the United States take from the success (for so it is by any reasonable definition or measure) of Canada's system? It is tantalizing to picture a federal compact in which the U.S. states, like the Canadian provinces, agree to a fund-sharing formula accompanied by five (or however many) criteria that ensure to all citizens accessible, comprehensive, portable, properly managed health services. The Canadian case also shines light on some possible minefields along the way, however. In the political run-up to Medicare, Canadian employers did not cling on principle to health insurance as a fringe benefit for workers or ideologically bash a big-government takeover of the health sector. Canadian physicians remain independent private practitioners subject to little clinical monitoring or interference, but collegiality is not capitulation by the state: they agree collectively to negotiate their fees with provincial ministries of health and, overall, earn less than U.S. counterparts. Most important, Canada's federal authorities gave private insurers a swift shove to the sidelines of the system and have so far insisted that they stay there. For all the grumbling about the distasteful features of the U.S. health insurance industry, it is not easy to picture U.S. policy makers doing something comparable.

Germany

The German health care system, quite the opposite of single payer, has been since its creation by Otto von Bismark in 1883 a social insurance model, reliant in 1910 on 23,354 occupation-based sickness funds (Leichter 1979, 124), a universe that declined to about 1,000 by 1990, and contains roughly 250 funds, competing and open to all customers, wherever employed. The system draws funds mainly from payroll taxes shared half and half by worker and employer. This financing method has much-noticed limitations: It allegedly discourages the formation and expansion of businesses, is at the mercy of the dependency ratio (given Germany's low birth rates, a shrinking number of workers must sustain benefits for a growing number of beneficiaries over time), and it fails to tap "modern" sources of wealth such as real estate and stock holdings. Germany, therefore, has begun emulating France by infusing more general revenues into the health accounts, blurring the distinction between the Beveridge and Bismarck models. The latest round of German reforms also aims to fill a small but important gap in the fabric of universal coverage—two hundred thousand self-employed residents who were not hitherto eligible for the statutory regime.

The German constitution (Basic Law of 1949) assigns to Germany's federal government responsibility for designing the benefits, eligibility, funding, and payment rules for the public health insurance system. The *Lander* (states), which since unification in 1990 number sixteen, are in charge of planning, building, licensing, and monitoring hospitals. (About half of Germany's acute-care beds are in public-land-owned hospitals; roughly 35 percent are in nonprofit hospitals often run by religious orders; and 15 percent are in for-profit facilities. Hospital physicians are generally salaried, whereas their community counterparts are paid mostly fee-for-service.) The hospitals of course depend on funds from the public insurance system, so the federal and land levels share authority for determining hospitals rates and payments (Altenstetter 1999, 66).

German health care policy honors what Altenstetter and Busse (2005, 125, 138) call the three *S*'s: solidarity, subsidiarity, and self-governance. Solidarity—universal and equitable coverage and the cross-subsidies required to sustain these goals—falls largely to national policy. Subsidiarity—the making and running of policy should be entrusted to local units insofar as possible—honors the turf of the *Lander,* which themselves embody strong regional identities that antedate the creation of the German nation in 1871 and have by no means disappeared (Altenstetter 1999, 54, 81n3). Self-governance adds a distinctively German element to the equation—delegation (within a framework of federal and *Land* rules) of many decisions to national and regional (*Land*-based) associations of sickness funds and national and regional associations of sickness-fund physicians, which bargain over matters of mutual interest, especially the monetary coefficients of medical procedures listed in fee schedules. The result, wrote William Glaser (1978, 110, 109) some years ago, is "national uniformity with provincial flexibility," a model for Americans of how "government can enact the rules and then leave the doctors and sick funds to carry out the program with little government interference." More recently, Altenstetter and Busse (2005, 124–25) characterize the German state (presumably both the federal and *Land* levels) as "regulator, facilitator, and enabler to the parties in corporate self-governance."

Admirers of the German system laud its cooperative federalism, under which national government makes policy and the *Lander* and national and *Land*-based corporatist associations of sickness funds and providers implement it. Critics of German federalism complain, however, that it can make the price of cooperation unacceptably high. The *Lander* have a hand in making as well as implementing policy because they are constituent units of the upper house of the German parliament, the Bundesrat. Legislative proposals go first for debate to this body, which can withhold approval from some statutory categories. A majority party at the head of the federal government may encounter an opposition majority (or no clear party majority) in the Bundesrat, which can stymie legislation and occasionally oblige federal ministers to make policy via federal ordinances.

These structural arrangements give voice to the *Lander:* the views of *Land*-level political leaders and bureaucrats are "known from the very beginning of the federal legislative process." They also prompt critics to lament that the *Lander* are a "cartel" and a "decision trap" (Altenstetter and Busse 2005, 129–30). The *Lander* successfully vetoed plans to put tougher controls on spending for drugs and physician salaries in 1999, have been slow to advance national policies favoring closer integration between the community and hospital sectors of care, and, seeking to maintain a "regionalized landscape" of sickness funds, have lately resisted proposals to consolidate and thus reduce the number of funds (Bode 2006, 202).

Since enacting in 1993 the legislation that gave its population a choice among sickness funds, Germany has flirted with managed competition, a development that piqued the interest of U.S. would-be reformers in the Clinton years. The advent of competition ushered in predictable protections—funds, for example, cannot turn away applicants or tailor premiums to health conditions and are compensated for the risk profiles with which they end up by risk-adjusted payments determined by a federal formula—and equally predictable debates; for example, do the risk adjustment mechanisms "work"? Do the competing sickness funds think they work fairly? Might the new competitive ethos not insidiously undercut solidarity in practice? (For a discussion of techniques of informal risk selection, see Bode 2006, 193–94). Moreover, although the (limited) price-competition scheme has triggered some (limited) switching among funds, the system's de facto unwillingness to break the long-standing norm that any German physician can treat any member of the statutory plan leaves the selective contracting now officially permissible little practiced, at least to date. In Germany, then, managed competition comes unaccompanied by "managed care"—the reverse of the American picture (Brown and Amelung 1999).

The German system holds several lessons for the United States. First, if U.S. employers were to accept mandatory contributions to the coverage of workers and citizens more broadly—a very big *if*—one would expect vigorous complaining by them and their ideological allies about damage to economic growth and the unfitness of social insurance financing in modern times. This implies that a Medicare program continually alleged to teeter near bankruptcy may be hard to expand for all and that general revenues (and the taxes that supply them) will be a crucial and growing component of universal coverage. Second, although German physicians (fee-for-service in the ambulatory sector, salaried in hospitals) retain wide clinical freedom, the collective bargaining with associations of sickness funds that determine their incomes has led to discontent and, of late, strikes, unheard of in the past. Third, the United States too could avert the big government inherent in a single-payer system—so long as its health insurance firms morphed into health insurance institutions (private bodies with a public charter, as the Germans have it), competition among which would be governed by firm rules that, among other things, proscribe preferred risk selection. Fourth, a pervading and sometimes messy federalism can obstruct health reform in Germany, as in the United States, but is less likely to do so if, as in Germany, universal and equitable health coverage is an undisputed duty of the national government and the values of subsidiarity (government close to the people) and self-governance are not allowed to trump solidarity. Uses and limits of federalism in health policy are, in short, context dependent.

Switzerland

The Swiss system is insurance based (unlike Canada); however, the insurance is funded not from the payrolls of workers and firms (as in Germany) but rather from the checkbooks of individual citizen-consumers, who since 1996 have been mandated to buy coverage. The Swiss constitution, like Canada's, officially vests power over health affairs mainly in subnational units, and like Canada's, the Swiss system is highly decentralized. This nation roughly the size of Maryland is sometimes said to have twenty-six different (cantonal) health systems. Like that of the United States, the Swiss political system bristles with veto points—in this case, requirements that major legislation be approved in popular referenda. These high hurdles for system overhauls, breached only in 1911 and 1996, have, as in the United States, brought down promising reform proposals, which then linger on the agenda, awaiting another try on a better day.

Until very recently, scholarly accounts seldom took note of Switzerland. That system is now enjoying at least fifteen minutes of fame because it combines three features of great interest to American reformers, namely, an individual mandate, "consumer driven" insurance (Herzlinger and Parsa-Parsi 2004), and not inconsiderable discretion for and diversity among the cantons. Less frequently remarked upon is the framework of national rules that govern the system. Before 1996, health insurers were allowed to tailor premiums to risks, but now, in an explicit affirmation of solidarity, the national government requires all insurers to offer a basic package of benefits, to set community rates, and to take all applicants. (Medical exams and differential premiums are allowed, however, in supplemental insurance contracts.) That government proscribes for-profit insurance firms; mandates and defines a risk-adjustment formula to level the playing field among insurers; reviews the compliance of insurers with national law; and audits (and can reduce) their proposed rates (European Observatory on Health Care Systems 2000, 29). It also requires that the cantons define eligibility and levels for related premiums for consumers who could not otherwise afford what is offered in their canton (about a third of the population is subsidized, and cantonal policies vary considerably); precludes selective contracting among providers by insurers (except by managed care plans); and sets national fee schedules for payments to providers, the monetary value of which is negotiated in each canton by associations of insurers and associations of physicians and "endorsed" by the cantonal government (European Observatory on Health Care Systems 2000, 15). Swiss citizens do indeed get to choose among insurance plans that compete on price (premiums, size of deductibles, and copayments), choice of provider (health maintenance organizations [HMOs] and other managed care variants are available, though their penetration is low so far), and service amenities (administrative efficiency, quick handling of queries on the telephone, and so on). But, as noted above, the public—national—rules of the insurance game are many and stringent.

Official cantonal duties, as in Germany, center mainly on the construction, running, and (partial) funding of hospitals (249 of which were publicly owned or subsidized and 143 of which were private in 1999) (Herzlinger and Parsa-Parsi 2004, 1215); planning and delivering public health services; and overseeing negotiations on prices between insurers and physicians. The number and type of insurance plans differ among cantons, as of course does the distribution of physicians, hospitals, and other resources.

Some key features of the Swiss system are but a decade old (including the individual mandate and the shift from employer-based to consumer-driven funding), and thoughtful Swiss would remind American enthusiasts that this reformed system remains a work in progress. As in the United States (and Canada and Germany), Swiss policy makers are distressed that health costs are so high (according to the latest Organization for Economic Cooperation and Development data, in 2005 the nation spent 11.6 percent of GDP and $4,177 per capita on health care, second only to the United States on GDP, and, for per capita spending, third behind the United States and Norway). Moreover, out-of-pocket costs are high (in 2002 in Switzerland these ran to $1,149 per capita, as contrasted with $302 in Germany and $281 in France) (de Jong and Mosca 2006, 5) and cantonal spending on health services ranges widely—from $2,452 per capita in the canton of Geneva in 2002 to $1,103 in Appenzell-Innerrhoden) (de Jong and Mosca 2006, 8).

Analysts round up the usual suspects: Switzerland has the highest hospital density and highest concentration of high-tech equipment in Europe (European Observatory on Health Care Systems 2000, 35), a high physician-to-population ratio, an abundance of specialists, high expenses for chronic care, restrictions on selective contracting, too little managed care, an expanding list of mandated benefits, and so on. Some critics charge that efforts to boost efficiency are damaging equity. Insurers cannot legally turn away high-risk applicants, but they can and allegedly do discourage them informally, partly because the national risk-adjustment formula is widely agreed to need work. The financing system is said to be regressive, inflicting on Swiss citizens very high out-of-pocket payments that (incidentally and ironically) have demonstrably failed to curb the rise of spending. Consumer choice among competing insurers has triggered "little switching . . . and little price convergence." Indeed between 1996 and 2000, rates of switching among insurers, already low, declined further, suggesting that amid so many choices consumers find themselves unable to "make an effective selection" (de Jong and Mosca 2006, 12, quoting Frank and Lamirand). The premium subsidies for the less well-off do not keep pace with the costs of coverage—perhaps because this lag may encourage membership in managed care plans, on which some policy makers pin hopes for cost containment. Finally, planning for the number and distribution of hospitals and physicians and for the prevention of illness and promotion of health are said to suffer from lack of coordination among the cantons.

Could the United States "do" the Swiss system? It could indeed, *if* it were willing to couple an individual mandate with a long list of central constraints on health insurers; craft public subsidies that offset the regressive effects of a shift in funding from employer based to consumer driven; create fee schedules as a basis for bargaining with the medical profession over payments; and give states a large say about the size and character of the hospital system, among other reforms. Simply to scan the list is to see that the present and potential goodness of fit between the Swiss and U.S. systems is much more problematic than surface inspection suggests.

Conclusion

The three federal systems scanned here in search of lessons for the United States have distinct financing approaches (single payer in Canada, social insurance supplemented by general revenues in Germany, consumer driven in Switzerland) but all three in their various fashions honor the adage that one must first centralize policy before one can effectively decentralize it. All have achieved universal coverage by including everyone (Canada) in the system or permitting (Germany) or requiring (Switzerland) everyone to join the system. None grants autonomy to business in the offering and funding of coverage: In Canada, business supports the health system (and the rest of the public sector's budget) via general corporate taxes; in Germany, employers have long been obliged by federal law to contribute fifty-fifty with workers into social insurance funds; and Switzerland's 1996 reform largely took business out of the health financing picture per se (employer contributions now come only to 6 percent of the funds in the system).

In all three nations, physicians are largely independent, fee-for-service private practitioners whose fees are set by means of bargaining over nationally designed fee schedules between their associations and either provincial authorities (Canada) or associations of insurers (Germany and Switzerland). In none are managed care organizations an important source of employment for physicians. In all three, subnational discretion applies mostly to hospitals, in the planning, construction, and funding of which the provinces, *Lander,* and cantons play large roles. All three complain of excessive (albeit declining) hospital beds, admissions, and lengths of stay; decry lack of integration between the ambulatory and inpatient sectors; and intimate that the power of subnational units over "their" hospitals is an obstacle to integration and streamlining. All three laud the promise of public health and health promotion to improve the health of their populations and (potentially) the fiscal picture of the health systems, and all three offer mea culpas for not doing more on this score. All three say (and may even believe) that advances in information technology, evidence-based medicine, and health technology assessment will improve their systems in numberless ways.

One of the three, Canada, contemplated retaining insurance firms whose premiums would be offset by income-related public subsidies, concluded that the financial and administrative costs of doing so were too high, and summarily relegated insurers to a market strictly supplementary to the public single-payer plan. The other two have competing sickness funds but constrain their rates, proscribe risk selection, forbid profit making by firms, and mandate benefits. All three (though Canada less so) rehearse the virtues of managed care, but none yet shows much taste for selective contracting, which would trigger pitched battles with physicians long accustomed to treating any patient who selects them.

The good news is that well-working (albeit costly) systems of universal coverage are eminently compatible with federal systems of government. The bad (anyway disconcerting) news is that emulation of their achievements in the United States would require several major departures from its current system. The minimum workable package would include central rules of the game such as Canada's five principles that govern fund sharing between the central government and the provinces; the elevation of health coverage from a fringe benefit of employment to an entitlement of citizens, thus telling business in effect to pay its fair share into national or state budgets or both and then butt out; requirements that physicians accept (hence presumably agree to bargain collectively over) fees set by subnational payers, insurance institutions, or some combination of government and insurers; and constraints on or elimination of business practices now central to profit- or revenue-maximizing firms in a health insurance industry unique among Western nations. Such provisions make sense if the United States decides that universality, equity, and solidarity should be guiding principles of health reform. Within such a context, federalism can be part of orderly arrangements in which subnational units sometimes lead, sometimes follow, and sometimes get out of the way. But refiguring federalism is no reform panacea. The health policy records of other nations have much to say to American reformers, but whether these latter care, and can afford politically, to listen is an open question.

References

Altenstetter, Christa. 1999. "From Solidarity to Market Competition? Values, Structure, and Strategy in German Health Policy, 1883–1997." In *Health Care Systems in Transition: An*

International Perspective, ed. Francis D. Powell and Albert F. Wessen, 47–88. Thousand Oaks, CA: Sage Publications.

Altenstetter, Christa, and Reinhard Busse. 2005. "Health Care Reform in Germany: Patchwork Change Within Established Governance Structures." *Journal of Health Politics, Policy and Law* 30 (February–April): 121–42.

Bode, Ingo. 2006. "Fair Funding and Competitive Governance: The German Model of Health Care Organization Under Debate." *Revue Francaise des Affaires Sociales* (English ed.) 2–3 (April–September): 183–206.

Brown, Lawrence D., and Volker Amelung. 1999. "Manacled Competition: Market Reforms in German Health Care." *Health Affairs* 18 (May–June): 76–91.

Brown, Lawrence D., and Michael S. Sparer. 2003. "Poor Program's Progress: The Unanticipated Politics of Medicaid Policy." *Health Affairs* 22 (January–February): 31–44.

De Jong, Philip R., and Ilaria Mosca. 2006."Changes and Challenges of the New Health Care Reform in the Netherlands: What Should the Dutch Be Aware Of?" Netherlands: Tilburg Law and Economics Center, TILEC Discussion Paper DP 2006–026, October.

European Observatory on Health Care Systems. 2000. *Health Care Systems in Transition: Switzerland.* Brussels: European Observatory on Health Care Systems.

France, George. 2005. "Lights and Shade: Health Insurance, National Standards and Federalism in America." Unpublished paper (March 8).

Glaser, William A. 1978. *Health Insurance Bargaining: Foreign Lessons for Americans.* New York: Gardner Press.

Greer, Scott. 2004. *Territorial Politics and Health Policy: UK Health Policy in Comparative Perspective.* Manchester: Manchester University Press.

Herzlinger, Regina E., and Ramin Parsa-Parsi. 2004. "Consumer-Driven Health Care: Lessons from Switzerland." *Journal of the American Medical Association* 292 (September 8): 1213–20.

Kazee, Nicole. 2008. Personal communication with the author. June 1.

Leichter, Howard M. 1979. *A Comparative Approach to Policy Analysis: Health Care Policy in Four Nations.* Cambridge: Cambridge University Press.

Lomas, Jonathan. 1997. "Devolving Authority for Health Care in Canada's Provinces: 4. Emerging Issues and Prospects." *Journal of the Canadian Medical Association* 156 (March 15): 817–23.

Marchildon, G.P. 2005. *Health Systems in Transition: Canada.* Copenhagen: WHO Regional Office for Europe on behalf of the European Observatory on Health Systems and Policies.

Smith, David G., and Judith D. Moore. 2008. *Medicaid Politics and Policy: 1965–2007.* New Brunswick, NJ: Transaction.

Taylor, Malcolm G. 1990. *Insuring National Health Care: The Canadian Experience.* Chapel Hill: University of North Carolina Press.

Tuohy, Carolyn Hughes. 1999. *Accidental Logics: The Dynamics of Change in the Health Care Arena in the United States, Britain, and Canada.* New York: Oxford University Press.

7

Recent Changes in Dutch Health Insurance

Individual Mandate or Social Insurance?

KIEKE G.H. OKMA

Dutch health insurance changed dramatically in 2006 with the abolition of the sickness fund insurance that had covered wage earners and their dependents for more than one hundred years. In 2005, with surprisingly little opposition, the Dutch Parliament passed a law introducing a new population-wide health insurance that replaced the former public and private systems. As of 2006, all residents of the Netherlands have to take out health insurance with one of forty or so insurers. Insurers have to accept any applicant for the government-determined basic coverage. Half of insurers' income consists of the income-related contribution that employers withhold as earmarked taxation channeled to insurers through a central fund. For the remaining half, insured persons pay a flat-rate premium directly to their insurers, and patients pay modest user fees. Low-income groups can apply for subsidies. The *Wall Street Journal* sees the Dutch model as a triumph of consumerism and "Holland as Model for U.S. Health Care" (Naik 2007). Similarly, the *New York Times* considers the Dutch model (together with that of Switzerland) a good example for the United States because it would "eliminate the role of employers" (Harris 2007). The rapid introduction of the new system is remarkable, as earlier efforts failed because of lackluster political backing, stakeholder opposition, and erosion of popular support (Okma 1997).

What explains the remarkably smooth transition to the new insurance model in 2006? What led to the change? Does it really represent a dramatic break with the past, heralding a new and untested model of social insurance administered by private insurers—or, perhaps, a private insurance system under public regulation? Does it really provide the answer to America's health care problems? How does it work? And what has actually happened after its introduction?

This chapter analyzes the new insurance model and its origins in earlier reform efforts. The chapter details social policy making and the core features of the 2006 health insurance reform, then reviews failed reform proposals of the 1980s and early 1990s. Next, the chapter looks at the changing positions of the main stakeholders in Dutch health care, including managers and organized patient groups. The chapter concludes that rather than a dramatic break with the past, the 2006 health insurance reform represents much continuity in the role of government and other actors in Dutch health care. Rather than replacing existing governance arrangements, the new scheme has led to a complicated mix of self-governance, market competition, and government control.

The 2006 Health Insurance Law

The Health Insurance Law (ZVW) of 2006 requires all legal residents of the Netherlands to take out health insurance. Employers collect part of the insurance contribution as earmarked taxation (in 2008, 7.2 percent of taxable income up to a ceiling of about €30,000). To compensate for risk differences in their portfolios (for example, when they have a relatively high share of elderly or chronically ill patients), insurers receive extra funding for each insured rated as high risk—based on age, gender, disability, and pharmaceutical consumption—so that, in theory, they will focus less on selecting the most profitable clients. Premium levels solely reflect variations in efficiency or quality. For the remaining 50 percent of their income, insurers charge a flat-rate premium to their insured. Premiums may differ between but not within insurance plans. The government pays the contributions for those eighteen years of age and younger. In 2007, low-income families, 37 percent of the population, received a subsidy. Patients pay modest user fees. Out of €50 billion (€3,000, or about $4,200 per person per year) in 2006, €46.4 billion ($65 billion) came out of insurance contributions and tax subsidies, while patients paid €3.9 billion ($5.5 billion) as user fees (less than 10 percent of total health expenditure). On average, insureds paid about €1,000 ($1,400) per year for the ZVW to their insurer, plus about €1,000 for the income-related contribution for the ZVW and €980 ($1,370) for public long-term care insurance.

Health Care in the Netherlands and Europe

European countries share basic principles and goals of their health policy: universal access to health services and insurance, solidarity (sometimes framed as equity or fairness) in sharing the financial burden of illness, and good quality of services (Organization for Economic Cooperation and Development 1994). As the major share of health funding is public, cost control is an overriding concern. Most see patient satisfaction, patient choice, and professional autonomy of physicians as important goals, too.

Nonetheless, there is wide variety in the administrative arrangements for funding and contracting mechanisms of health care. In the United Kingdom, Italy, Spain, and the Scandinavian countries (as well as Canada), the major share of health care funding comes out of general taxation. In Austria, Belgium, Germany, France, Luxembourg, and the Netherlands, social (and, to a lesser degree, private) health insurance systems are the main source. Even in the United States, when the amount of tax subsidies to private employment–related insurance is added to Medicare and

Medicaid and other public programs, the public share of funding is more than 50 percent. Germany (since 1994) and the Netherlands (since 1968) have separate population-wide social insurance systems for long-term care. The two countries also share several institutional features of their funding, contracting, and governance. Both systems are a hybrid between the German Bismarck-type employment-related system and the United Kingdom's Beveridge model of population-wide tax-based health funding. In all countries, patients pay for some services out of their own pocket or face copayments for other services, but in many cases governments exempt certain groups or set limits on how much families must pay.

Three important characteristics set the Dutch system apart: the relatively high share of private funding (at least until 2006; see below), the long tradition of nongovernment provision of care, and the neocorporatist style of social policy making.

Holland's funding model borrowed heavily from Germany's. In 1941, the German occupational forces imposed the Sickness Fund Decree, which required certain groups of low-income wage earners to register with a sickness fund. Since the beginning of the twentieth century, successive Dutch governments had tried to introduce similar legislation but failed to reach agreement over the governance model or, more precisely, over the question of who would dominate the boards of sickness funds: labor unions, employers, and government, or only labor and capital. External imposition of the model (without direct government representation but under tight state control) thus solved the problem.

After the war, the government kept the system in place. By the time it became the base for the formal Sickness Fund Law (ZFW) in 1962, the private insurance market had expanded to cover more than one-third of the population. Following the German example, in a pact with private insurers, the government agreed to keep the share of the public insurance under 65 percent of the population. For more than four decades, until 2005, all changes in policy respected this division (the "peace border"). From 1962 to 2006, about two-thirds of the Dutch population had coverage under the mandatory ZFW for acute medical care in hospitals and for general physicians, prescription drugs, and some other services (in Germany, that share was about 90 percent at the time it introduced social health insurance). The sickness funds, independent administrative bodies that had run the voluntary mutual income protection systems since the late nineteenth century, remained responsible for administering the social insurance. Although private insurance was voluntary, the rate of noninsurance was only slightly above 1 percent of the population, a very low share compared with the United States. This low rate of uninsurance was an important starting point for the new scheme of 2006.

A second important feature of Dutch health care is the dominance of private provision of services. Similar to other Western European countries, the Netherlands has had a long tradition of provision of collective goods by voluntary, nongovernmental organizations. That tradition of public services provided by private actors is still visible today, even while recent waves of mergers have led to the fading of denominational backgrounds. The majority of Dutch hospitals and other health care institutions are owned and run by charities, nonprofit foundations, or religious orders. In spite of the dominance of not-for-profit health care, the system has always included for-profits (e.g., the pharmaceutical and medical aids industry or self-employed professionals).

State intervention in Dutch health care was modest until World War II and was largely limited to public health, consumer protection, and the regulation of health professionals. During the reconstruction and the development of the modern welfare state after the war, successive governments stepped in by mandating sickness fund membership for low-income employees and other groups. The scope and coverage of social health insurance expanded, and so did the role of government in the allocation of resources and planning of health facilities. This also strengthened state control over health care expenditures. However, the management of health facilities remained largely nongovernmental, and most general practitioners, dentists, and physiotherapists continued to practice as self-employed health professionals. In contrast to other European countries, the Netherlands never nationalized its hospitals. Recent policy shifts in the 1990s and early 2000s—inspired as much by a general ideological preference for market competition as by changing demographic and economic conditions—encouraged the expansion of for-profit health care and for-profit health insurance. Dutch hospitals and other actors suddenly have had to behave like market actors, a role they do not always feel comfortable about.

Third, the arena of social policy in the Netherlands is characterized by its own tradition of neocorporatist policy making. In this model, governments share the responsibility for the shaping and outcomes of social policy with organized stakeholders (e.g., labor unions, employers, associations of health care providers and insurers, and organized patient groups). Such associations often had a denominational background. The basic assumption of this interaction was a certain hierarchy in responsibilities. First, individual families had to take care of their own members, and second, the denominational organizations that most Dutch families belonged to (for example, the Roman Catholic or Protestant housing corporations, home care, or other welfare organizations) were to provide support. Only when those two levels failed to meet the basic needs of the members would the state step in as a residual safety net.

In the 1950s and 1960s, the health care system expanded through the creation of a wide array of quasi-independent administrative and advisory bodies, with formal representation of many interest groups. In those bodies, health insurance agencies and providers of care held a dominant position. Ironically, this form of engagement of all the major stakeholders in the shaping and implementation of social policy—sometimes labeled the "polder model"—was vilified in the 1980s as the main cause of stagnating growth and high unemployment. Critics of the "Dutch disease" (the enormous windfall state income from oil and natural gas that had boosted social spending) observed how the polder mentality was bogging down efforts to cut public spending, loosen up labor markets, and increase the efficiency of the economy. Later, the very same model of corporatist policy making was heralded as the "Dutch miracle," when, in the early 1990s, economic growth turned higher (and unemployment lower) than in the neighboring countries in Europe (Visser and Hemerijck 1997). The corporatist system provided veto power to organized interests that enabled them to block or thwart policy proposals they felt were detrimental to their status or incomes. In several instances, those organized interests derailed or slowed down planned or announced health reforms. At the same time, the involvement of a wide array of private organizations contributed to the remarkable stability of Dutch politics.

In the 1980s, inspired by debates on a broader reassessment of the Dutch welfare state, there was mounting criticism of the polder model as a slow and inefficient mode of policy making (Visser and Hemerijck 1997). The Dutch Parliament commissioned a study on the role of advisory bodies in the early 1990s and found that there were several hundreds of expert committees in the domain of health policy alone (Commissie De Jong 1993). The Parliament decided to drastically reduce the number and size of those external bodies and eliminate stakeholder representation altogether to create efficient, expert-only advisory bodies (Okma 1997). The change in volume and functions of the advisory structure also curtailed the scope for organized interests to influence health policy. The easy passage of the 2006 basic insurance law illustrates that the dismantling of the neocorporatist structures had made life easier for governments keen to implement rapid change.

Dutch Health Reform Efforts of the 1980s and 1990s

In 1987, an expert committee headed by the CEO of Philips Electronics, Wisse Dekker, proposed a major overhaul of the health care system (Commissie Dekker 1987). The committee signaled several problems, such as fragmented funding; a lack of financial incentives to consumers, providers, and health insurers to contain the growth of health expenditures or offer good-quality care; and rigid regulations inhibiting a more flexible organization of services. In itself, that analysis was not new: Earlier reports had also pointed to those weaknesses, proposing to integrate public and private insurance (Okma 1997). The Dekker committee proposed an amalgamation of existing funding streams into one mandatory (social) health insurance system for the entire population, covering the risks of both acute medical care and long-term care. It wanted to strengthen the role of sickness funds (and private insurers) as third-party payers in health care and to increase consumer choice. Proposals included free choice of health insurer, reduction of the services covered by the mandatory basic insurance, partial replacement of the income-related contributions by (community-rated) flat-rate premiums, and options for insured persons to accept deductibles or coinsurance in exchange for lower premiums. Further, the committee wanted to reduce the role of government by deregulating the existing planning and fee-setting legislation.

The expert group recommended the introduction of an "internal market" within the framework of social health insurance. This would not eliminate the role of the state in health care altogether, however, as government would determine the coverage of the mandatory health insurance, set the budgets of the health insurers, and monitor health insurance and quality of health services. The responsibility for negotiations over the quantity, quality, and prices of health services was to shift to (competing) health care providers and (competing, but not-for-profit) health insurers, within the framework of social health insurance. The aim was to create a level playing field for sickness funds and private insurance. Consumer choice of health insurer combined with selective contracting would create incentives to improve the quality and efficiency of services as well as contain health expenditures.

At first, the proposals caused much uproar in the world of Dutch health care (Okma 1997). After lengthy debate, Parliament accepted the proposals. The Ministry of Health framed an ambitious four-year implementation plan for 1989 to 1992. In the end, however, it realized only a few (but important) steps. For example, in 1991, it shifted ambulatory mental health care, prescription drugs, and some other services from the public and private health insurance systems to long-term care insurance, which was to become the new social health insurance for all. Further, the government relaxed the rules for planning and setting fees. Local authorities lost control over the opening of new practices of family doctors, and fee ceilings replaced fixed fees for health services. Provincial authorities lost their role in the planning of hospitals and other health facilities. In a later stage, to "compensate" for this loss, provinces were given the task of organizing regional platforms of consumer and patient groups. Other steps included abolition of legal boundaries of the working areas of sickness funds (so that they could expand their activities countrywide and offer insured persons a choice of fund) and introduction of selective contracting of self-employed health professionals by the funds (with the announcement that the mandatory contracting of health facilities would end later). These measures increased the room for insurers to negotiate with providers over the volume, price, and quality of services and to selectively contract with providers.

After the first steps of implementing the reforms in the early 1990s, stakeholder opposition resurfaced, public support eroded, and the political backing became more and more hesitant. After accepting (albeit in adjusted form) the legislation for the second reform phase in 1991, Parliament decided to shelve discussion over the next steps. After general elections in 1994, a new governing coalition consisting of the surprising combination of the Labor Party, Conservatives, and Liberal Democrats stepped into office. For the first time in more than half a century, the Christian Democrats were not part of the government. The governing manifesto of this new "Purple coalition" stated that it would no longer continue the reforms but would shift toward incremental adjustment of the existing system instead. Four years later, the same coalition continued in office, maintaining its policy course.

In December 2001, the Purple coalition stepped down from office over the political fallout of the tragic events in Srebrenica (where a small and insufficiently armed battalion of Dutch soldiers was not able to defend the village's population; as they fled, the Serbian attackers murdered all the five thousand or so male Muslim habitants). The general elections of May 2002 brought sweeping gains for a new party, List Pim Fortuyn, only a few weeks after the murder of its populist leader, Fortuyn. This surprising election outcome brought the Christian Democrats back to power, together with the Conservatives and List Pim Fortuyn. But escalating internal conflicts led to its rapid demise. After the January 2003 elections, in spite of a large electoral gain by the Labor Party, the Christian Democrats and the Conservatives switched partners, replacing List Pim Fortuyn with the Liberal Democrats. This re-created, in fact, the dominant Christian Democrat–Conservative–Liberal Democrat coalition of the early 1980s. The new coalition presented its plans in its governing manifesto in May 2003. In health policy, the program included a striking mix of old and new instruments to control costs and improve efficiency: delisting of services from the public health insurance, new or increased copayments and deductibles, strict budgetary ceilings, and, again, the intention to introduce universal health insurance based on the principle of "regulated market competition" (without defining or explaining that notion in detail). In 2007, Labor again replaced the Conservatives in the coalition with the Christian Democrats; this time, the two parties opted for the conservative Christian Democratic party as a coalition partner.

Changes in political coalitions and the shift from structural reform to incremental policies thus did not kill the basic features of the Dekker reforms. Dutch health policy has shown a large degree of continuity. For example, the budget model for the sickness funds introduced in the early 1990s is still in place today as the base for determining budgets for health insurers. Likewise, the return of the Labor Party to the coalition did not change the introduction of the new health insurance of 2006.

Shifting Decision Making in Dutch Health Care

In contrast to earlier Dekker proposals, the 2006 insurance system excludes long-term care insurance. For this segment of health care, the government proposed to shift some services to basic insurance and the remaining budgets and decision-making power to local authorities. But in 2007, after shifting ambulatory mental care to basic insurance and part of the home care budget to the local level, it announced a moratorium on those changes, and it is not yet clear what categories of services will actually remain under central government control.

The reform legislation of the 1990s introduced entrepreneurial risks to players who previously enjoyed high levels of certainty and income protection. Since 2006, all health insurers, both the former sickness funds and the private health insurers, receive a capitated budget (a fixed amount per insured person) that takes into account certain risk factors such as age, gender, and health status of their insured. That budget replaced the open-ended reimbursement that characterized the former sickness fund model of the early twentieth century and covers about 50 percent of expenditures. In a way, the new budget model restored the status of sickness funds as independent risk-bearing insurers. The new budget model has broken up the wider pool of social insurance by shifting insurance risk (back) to the individual health insurers. Employers withhold the income-related part of the contribution as an earmarked tax, and government does so for welfare recipients and certain categories of insured without income. This payment flows through the tax department into a central fund that administers the budgets of insurers. In addition, insurers charge about 50 percent of their income as flat-rate premiums to their (adult) insured. Insureds younger than nineteen years do not pay this flat-rate premium, as the central fund picks up their payment. In 2007, those premiums were, on average, €1,134 ($1,580) per person per year.

In the late 1990s, there was rising dissatisfaction with growing waiting lists in Dutch health care, especially in the care for elderly and chronically ill patients. To solve this problem, the cabinet drastically increased the funding for health care. As a result, waiting lists shrank, and public spending on health care increased considerably. A few years later, politicians seemed to have forgotten the former episode, focusing on "runaway" public health expenditures (caused, in fact, by explicit policy decisions rather than uncontrollable cost pressures). The government used the cost escalation as one argument in favor of the new ("private") health insurance system. There was seemingly agreement on the problem and the solution, and the return of the Christian Democrats to power meant there was enough political willingness to act.

The rules of the game in social policies changed, but the new rules did not replace the old ones. In the early 2000s, illustrating a certain degree of internal inconsistency in policy (perhaps reflecting a somewhat weak belief in the cost-controlling capacities of market competition in health care), the Dutch government turned its attention, once again, to a reassessment of the benefit package of social health insurance, setting tight budget controls and delisting services, and introducing or increasing deductibles, copayments or user fees, and coinsurance. As in other countries, the introduction or increase of user fees met with fierce resistance, and to soften the impact, the government regularly exempted certain groups, such as the elderly or chronically ill, or reversed the measure altogether. In fact, the story of efforts to reduce the coverage of Dutch social health insurance reads like a catalog of failure.

Government encouraged providers and insurers to compete but, at the same time, kept control over health expenditures and the allocation of public funds. This created an overlay-of-governance model. It also created managerial dilemmas for health care providers and insurers. They have to invest in improving services and expanding market shares, but they face growing uncertainty over future clients and income streams. They have to act as entrepreneurs, but they have to sit down with governments at the national, regional, and local levels to discuss policy results. They compete, but government wants them to collaborate and participate in collective decision making. They have to attract and keep their patients and insured, but they have to please governments and other stakeholders.

Managerial Changes in Dutch Health Insurance and Health Care

Managers in Dutch health insurance have tried different approaches to address those dilemmas. They sought to defend and expand their market shares and to gain strategic market positions by merging with others and improving and expanding (or sometimes contracting) their coverage and services. In general, however, insurers have shown themselves more concerned about keeping their existing clients and attracting new ones than improving the quality and efficiency of care. In the years before and after the introduction of the new population-wide health insurance, insurers spent massive amounts on marketing and advertising in order to maintain or expand market shares. Several set their premiums below cost. Still, on average, premiums rose by about 10 percent in 2007.

Some insurers engaged in efforts to reduce waiting lists and waiting times by contracting with for-profit clinics and pressuring hospitals to work more efficiently. Others offered new services, such as twenty-four-hour call centers for their insured and preferred provider arrangements (the latter never became very popular with Dutch patients). In the latter option, insured face higher charges when they go to a provider outside the contracted network of their health insurance. Some health insurers widened their supplemental coverage by including a variety of preventive services, such as sports clinics or regular checkups. As the latest step, insurers explored forms of integration with health services. This, in effect, led to the creation of some kind of health maintenance organization model, started in the United States in the 1970s, even while the actual expansion of such activities by health insurers is still modest in the Netherlands. In historical perspective, those health maintenance organizations are similar to the nineteenth-century sickness funds that combined income protection with the ownership of health facilities and employment of physicians.

Some health insurers successfully focused on the market for collective insurance contracts to attract new clients. Almost 60 percent of those who changed their health insurance in 2006 did so as members of collective employment-based plans. In 2007, this share had risen to more than 80 percent (while less than 5 percent of the Dutch insured were switching—thus less than 1 percent of the population decided to switch plans as an individual decision). Clearly, there has been a trend toward increased collectivization of health insurance, in a way strengthening and not weakening the employment base of health insurance.

In principle, the abolition of the regional monopolies of sickness funds in 1991 allowed new entrants into the social health insurance field. In practice, however, it fueled a rapid process of mergers and acquisitions that sharply reduced competition. The number of independent sickness funds went down from more than sixty in the early 1980s to thirty in 1999. On average, the funds had three hundred thousand members, but membership ranged from a few thousand to more than 1 million insured. In 1999, there were also about forty private insurers that catered to the remaining 40 percent of the population. After a rapid process of mergers and informal collaboration between public and private insurance, there were forty-three health insurers (both former sickness funds as well as private insurers) in the Netherlands in 2005. Many of those operated as part of broader conglomerates. For example, five main health insurance groups covered 11 million insured, or more than 60 percent of the population in that year. After further consolidations, the two largest conglomerates covered more than 50 percent of the population. The next stage of this development has been the rise of international insurance conglomerates in the European Union, offering both public and private health insurance, a development that is already showing its first appearances in the Netherlands. But some of the foreign firms that tried their hand at offering health insurance in Holland soon left the country again.

Health care managers—like health insurers—have reacted in different ways to the new challenges. On the financial side, hospitals and other facilities have contracted out maintenance and hotel functions and developed arrangements for the collective purchase of medical goods. They built up financial reserves by improving their administration and expanding office hours, realizing economies of scale, and finding substitutes for labor-intensive services. They reined in labor costs by differentiating functions and replacing skilled staff with less-expensive labor. Some hospitals have created for-profit subsidiaries. Others shifted from standardized to customized care, added luxury care, and extended services to become more attractive to patients and health insurers alike. A few providers ventured into new areas of health care–related services, including home care, meals on wheels, and sports clinics.

Like the insurers, providers tried to focus on the most promising market segments by cherry-picking patients (selecting the wealthiest, healthiest, and cheapest groups), for example, in setting up health clinics to provide rapid access for employees. Public polls and debates in Parliament reveal opposition in society to such queue jumping or to services limited to certain groups. In the late 1990s, the Health Minister announced measures to limit the activities of private clinics and to prohibit preferential treatment altogether. A few years later, however, that opposition seemed to have faded. In fact, the Dutch government considered the rise of private clinics as a solution to the problem of long waiting lists, as they added to total treatment capacity. Not all of those centers fared well, and after a few years some closed their doors.

Further, Dutch health care providers—like insurers—strengthened their market position by collaborating or even fully merging with other providers. Many hospitals and other health facilities expanded their activities by developing informal networks and engaging in horizontal integration with similar institutions and vertical integration with nursing homes, retirement facilities, and extramural care in their region. In fact, in several cases, such regional collaboration has sharply reduced the number of independent providers, sometimes eliminating competition altogether and thereby also reducing consumer choice. Providers of care for the elderly and of mental health services have shown themselves to be eager entrepreneurs. In some instances, their activities led to virtual regional monopolies, defeating procompetitive government policies. For hospital care, this has created a tension between the contracting role of health insurers (based on the assumption that they negotiate with competing providers over contracts) and efforts of the Health Ministry to encourage regional collaboration between health care service providers.

The creation of the internal market in Dutch health care did not lead to a reduced government presence. On the contrary, there is wide recognition that competitive markets require extensive regulation and supervision to function fairly well. In spite of announced shifts from supply regulation to demand regulation, both categories of government regulation are now firmly in place. Dutch citizens—like other Europeans—expect government to safeguard access to quality care and to step in if needed. For example, faced with public discontent over the delisting of dental checkups for adults from basic insurance, government reinstated (part of) those services. Government also extended its presence in monitoring health care quality, the development of case-based payment models, and the implementation of information technology.

It is important to note that after the dismantling of the neocorporatist institutions, the Dutch polder-model mentality has not completely disappeared. Associations of health insurers and providers and other organized interests still show remarkable willingness to sit down with government and discuss and implement social policy (while their individual members do not always adhere to such informal agreements). One instrument that still plays a major role is the "covenant." Less than formal law and somewhat more than an informal agreement, covenants are not legally binding, but the government sees them as a convenient way to engage and involve major stakeholders in realizing its goals. For example, when expenditures for hospitals exceeded the budget estimates in 2004, the Ministry of Health framed a covenant with the hospital association and national association of health insurers.

Like other stakeholders, the association of Dutch health insurers has maintained its prominent presence in a wide range of collaborative efforts. In spite of market rhetoric, it has continued to work with government to find a common solution for the problem of the uninsured and other issues. In a political sense, there clearly has not been a major exit from the policy arena in the small country where the leaders of all the main stakeholder groups know each other well and continue to meet.

Uninsured in the Netherlands

The occurrence of uninsured persons has always created a sensitive policy issue in the Netherlands. Traditionally, this number has been very low. Although the 40 percent of the population who were not eligible for social insurance did not have to take out (private) insurance until 2006, the vast majority had actually done so. Only about 1 percent of the Dutch population was uninsured. While health insurance is now mandatory, there are few effective sanctions if a person does not take out insurance. In mid-2007, an estimated 240,000 people were uninsured, and another

200,000 had not paid their premiums for more than six months. At first, the Health Ministry decided that in case someone without insurance needed hospitalization, he or she would not only have to pay the hospital costs him- or herself, but would also have to take out insurance on the spot, retroactively, and pay a fine. But that solution did not appear feasible. (A study by the Central Bureau of Statistics showed that single mothers, young immigrants, and welfare recipients were overrepresented in the delinquent category.) Under the new system, private health insurers can bar someone who has not paid premiums for more than three months, and in 2007, the national association of health insurers announced that its members would start doing so. The government announced it would return to a system where welfare recipients would no longer have to pay the flat-rate premium themselves. Local welfare offices would deduct the monthly amount from welfare income. Further, insurers would keep delinquents insured, but government would try to recover unpaid premiums. Moreover, delinquents would not be allowed to leave their insurer before paying all outstanding amounts. Those measures illustrate that a general mandate to take out health insurance is not easy to enforce.

New Roles for Patients and Consumers in Dutch Health Care

Dutch citizens have taken on new roles in health care, too, but this has hardly resulted in consumer-driven health care. In the 1990s, since the abolition of regional boundaries of sickness funds, almost all of the thirty or so funds expanded their activities countrywide, so that people with social insurance could switch plans. To encourage this mobility, the government sponsored Web sites that enabled consumers to compare health insurance policies. In the early 1990s, the main consumer association in the Netherlands, Consumentenbond, started to publish systematic assessments of costs and quality of health care and health insurance. The weekly *Elsevier* published lists of the "best and worst" hospitals. The national daily *Algemeen Dagblad* gained fame by publishing detailed lists of waiting times for certain medical procedures, encouraging patients to actively shop around when faced with unacceptable waiting lists, and government-sponsored Web sites offer comparative information about health care and health insurance. Nonetheless, this rapid growth in comparative information has had a limited effect on patient behavior. There is some backlash against the rise of consumerism in Dutch health care. Dutch citizens seem rather weary of the bombardment of new information.

Until the early 2000s, mobility of insured persons remained modest. That changed dramatically with the introduction of the basic health insurance of 2006—at least for the first year. Almost 20 percent of insured changed their health insurance in 2006. More than 50 percent did so as members of collective employment-based plans. In 2007, less than 5 percent of the Dutch insured changed plans (more than 80 percent as part of employment-related collective contracts). Thus, interestingly, the new insurance has strengthened rather than weakened the collective nature of Dutch health insurance even while its basic premise is that individual choice will improve the outcome. Some insurers even offered a "collective" contract for insured without access to another group. Insurers do not have to accept every group seeking coverage, however, and some patient groups have been turned down. Insurers are less interested in chronically ill patients than in "normal-risk" patients. The large-scale change of insurer thus seems to have been a one-shot event in 2006, mostly as part of collective employment-based arrangements rather than based on individual choice. In general, people who are part of employment-based collective groups represent better risks for insurance companies. There is an element of risk selection by health insurers and self-selection by insured in this pattern of collective contracting. Thus far, this has not created major problems (it is still a bit early to tell the final outcome of this process). Dutch health insurers traditionally have felt the bounds of social norms that condemn such behavior; they have never applied risk rating that fully reflected the risk of certain groups. The growth of collective contracting has pushed up the premiums for individual coverage. To counteract this trend—as another example of government intervention in the private market—health insurers cannot offer more than a 10 percent discount on collective contracts.

Dutch patients show a high degree of loyalty to hospitals (particularly to hospitals with a religious background) and to the former regional sickness funds. They refuse to go much beyond the first option that seems reasonable (or that they already know well), and they do not have the time, energy or resources to shop around. The bombardment of information provided by government-sponsored or commercial Web sites, newspapers, specialized journals, and other media has not done much to change that satisficing behavior in Dutch health care. Interestingly, the area where consumer action has affected services the most is not acute medical care, but rather long-term care. In this domain, organized patient groups, in particular the "lunatics movement" of psychiatric patients in the 1960s and relatives of patients with mental disabilities, have successfully demanded better services. Advocacy has worked well in this area. In other areas, people have opted out. Since the mid-1990s, long-term care insurance has offered the option for certain categories of patients to take cash benefits or vouchers instead of services in kind. This has allowed them to contract with providers outside the traditional institutions. Within a few years, those vouchers became very popular. By the end of 2003, more than fifty thousand patients had chosen this option, receiving an average amount of more than €20,000 ($28,000) per year. In 2006, the total budget for those vouchers was more than €1 billion ($1.4 billion), or about half of the entire budget for home care—while home care organizations offered care to more than six hundred thousand persons. In acute care, however, Dutch patients express far less interest in exiting the care they are familiar with. Interestingly, government policy focuses on increasing competition in acute care. It seems less convinced of the market power of consumers in long-term care. In 2007, it announced a moratorium on changes in long-term care insurance, and it will keep long-term care insurance under strict central government control.

Conclusion: Change, No Progress?

At the beginning of the twenty-first century, the main actors in the health policy arena—patients, insurers, providers, and governments—have shown a mix of antici-patory and defensive behavior. They anticipated shifts from centralized consensual policy making with strong government control to decentralized decision making and the creation of internal markets. This anticipatory behavior explains much of the smooth transition to the new health insurance system of 2006. Because of this anticipatory behavior, the notions of individualized choice that did not gain last-ing support during the earlier reform efforts became acceptable in the mid-2000s. Rather than heralding a new era of competition, the new system codified rather than modified behavior. The same type of law that in the late 1980s would have been considered an instrument of modification had become an instrument of codi-fication, not because it had changed direction itself, but rather because the context and behavior of the group affected by the law had changed.

A second question this chapter seeks to address is whether the 2006 system implies a dramatic change in Dutch health care. "Yes and no" is the short answer. Yes, because the 2006 legislation effectively ended the more than hundred-year-old tradition of sickness funds, plunging Dutch health care in an uncharted direction. This has prompted health insurers and providers to anticipate and to adjust. Some have improved and expanded (and sometimes limited) the range of their services. Most have sought to consolidate their market positions by mergers and acquisi-tions. Insurers merged mostly at the national level, while providers sought to limit competition by creating new strategic alliances at the regional level, in several cases eliminating competition altogether. The verdict is still open as to whether and to what extent these activities have improved the quality, diversity, and patient friendliness of Dutch health care services. The main actors seem to be focused more on gaining and defending strategic market positions than on increasing consumer choice and improving the quality and efficiency of health care. The strategic be-havior of health insurers and health care providers—anticipating changes in gov-ernment policy—has contributed to the reshaping of the health policy landscape. This has also created new problems. For example, the announced amalgamation of the acute-care and long-term-care insurance systems in the original Dekker proposals encouraged managers to seek vertical integration by merging hospital and outpatient nursing services. In 2006, the government reversed this plan. It left long-term-care insurance out of basic insurance, announcing that local authorities instead of health insurers would have greater say in this field (but again changed its position in 2007). Thus, the integrated providers now face another split in their revenues and have to deal with different negotiating partners. Such turnarounds, not uncommon in Dutch social policy, have made managers of health insurance and health care wary of major shifts in their business. They try new directions but also show much continuity and do not want to break off existing long-term relations. Moreover, the creation of an internal market in Dutch health care has not led to a reduced government presence. In spite of an announced shift from supply regulation to demand regulation, both categories of regulation are in place. Dutch citizens expect a strong public role in safeguarding access to good-quality care and expect the government to step in if needed. For example, faced with rising numbers of uninsured in 2006, the government announced that it was considering the creation of a separate risk pool for the uninsured. In 2007, it took up the earlier suggestion of local authorities to abolish the flat-rate premiums for welfare recipients altogether to avoid the problem of delinquency. Government has also extended its presence in monitoring health care quality, developing case-based payment, and implementing health information technology.

Another factor explaining the high degree of continuity in Dutch health politics is the permanent presence of multiparty coalitions that impose restraints on changes in social policy. Since the early twentieth century, none of the main political parties has ever been large enough to govern by itself. There is always need for a coalition with others, and changes in political coalition do not appear to have much direct impact on health policy. For example, after the presentation of the Dekker reform plans by the Christian Democratic–Conservative coalition in 1987, the next coalition of the Christian Democrats and the Labor Party started to implement the plans in 1989 with only marginal change (for example, leaving long-term-care insurance for a later stage). The 1994 surprise coalition that excluded the Christian Democrats formally abandoned the reform but did not undo steps already taken; actually, it continued most of its predecessor's policies by labeling structural reform as incremental adjustments. When the Christian Democratic Party returned to power, it more or less took up the reform course it had started decades before. The comeback of the Labor Party as coalition partner in 2007 did not stop or reverse the introduction of universal health insurance in 2006.

The third central question is whether the 2006 Dutch health insurance reform might provide a model for the United States. Some elements of the new model, for example, the principle of individual choice, market competition, and decentralized administration by independent health insurers, seem to appeal to some American policy analysts. Alain Enthoven of Stanford University, for example, is convinced that "[t]he lesson for America is that this is what we ought to do" (Naik 2007, A5). According to the *New York Times,* both Switzerland and the Netherlands lead the way for the United States, as they have increased consumer choice and reduced the role of government in health care (Harris 2007). But have they?

It is important to note that there are major differences between the U.S. and Dutch situations. First, even while nominally shifting from "supply control" to "demand control," the Dutch government still plays a major role in health care and is quick to act when outcomes are perceived as unfair. Second, the starting position of the health insurance market was and is different. The Dutch government faces a major political problem when the rate of uninsured threatens to go up from 1 percent to 2 percent of the population. In the United States, 16 percent of the population has no health insurance at all, and perhaps another 15 percent is underinsured. Many proposals to reduce that number would expand private health insurance coverage by subsidizing low-income families. The Dutch experience, on a much smaller scale, shows that offering a fiscal subsidy to low-income groups is not enough to make sure that the most vulnerable groups actually take out health insurance. Third, the Dutch experience shows that rather than eliminating the role of employers, the reform strengthened their role, as most now offer health insurance as part of a wider package of employee benefits. In both Switzerland and the Netherlands, the new "private" systems under strict governmental control added to administrative complexity, and within five years Switzerland reached the peak of health expenditure (after the United States) in the world. In 2007 in the Netherlands, premiums went up on average by about 10 percent, and experts expect further premium increases, as several insurers are in the red—not quite the success of cost control by private markets.

It is also important to note that the (partially implemented) health reforms of the 1980s and 1990s did not replace the existing policy directions or governance models. Some argue that this led to a certain degree of complementarity of governance models that exist side by side. But it might be more accurate to say that the current landscape of Dutch health care and health insurance reveals a complicated mix of competing and sometimes conflicting notions of public and private governance. The partially implemented and sometimes reversed reform measures led to an intricate overlay of state control and deregulation, of patient choice and paternalistic government, of market competition and market concentration, of individual choice and collective action, and of a rapid growth of collective, employment-based health insurance arrangements within a system of universal insurance that seeks to enlarge individual choice. Since 2006, Dutch citizens have not shown much interest in switching their health insurance individually.

It remains to be seen to what extent the egalitarian tradition in Dutch social policies will create barriers to a further shift toward private for-profit health care. Thus far the experience shows that there is little support for greater differentiation in treatment or inequalities in access to health care. The health policy discourse has shifted, but the new orientation toward market competition has clearly not replaced former notions of social solidarity in Dutch society. Efforts to develop commercial services will be successful on only a modest scale as long as basic insurance covers a wide range of services. Efforts to engage in risk selection on a large scale by insurers and providers will likely face strong resistance and evoke government action. It is not yet clear whether this will change with the growing presence of international insurance conglomerates, in particular, when those businesses do not share the traditional business norms in Holland. There is consumerism at the margin, but there is no sign of widespread acceptance of rising inequality in access to health care, and there is no evidence that Dutch citizens are embracing consumer-driven health care. However, they have strong feelings about the quality of long-term care for their elderly and relatives with disabilities and are willing to take an active position (as seen by the rapid growth of the cash-benefit system). The trend toward greater market concentration in health insurance and health care that accelerated in the 1990s has not yet leveled off. Virtual elimination of competition will drive up costs. It will undermine the effectiveness of both market competition and the informal agreements between government and other parties, as dominant players in a particular market have less need to agree with government or others.

The Dutch experience illustrates that health policy making takes place within the constraints of national traditions, national culture, and national institutions. Government policy interacts with the behavior of the groups affected by that policy. This also means that formally stated policies can differ substantially from actual developments. In several cases, even after passing a formal law, the Dutch government changed the actual implementation for a variety of reasons. This confirms the importance of clearly distinguishing announced policy proposals from actually implemented ones. Terms such as *policy, health care reform,* and *consumer-driven health care* are usually not very well defined. Policy proposals that were unacceptable at one time gained support in a later period, as some of the main stakeholders had changed their positions and showed anticipatory behavior. This chapter shows how announced reforms and anticipatory behavior by health providers and insurers alike have reshaped the Dutch health care landscape and opened the way for new directions in governmental policy. Still, new developments were tested by strong popular support for universal access without undue barriers, as well by a strong sense of justice and equality in Dutch society. Both public and private actors feel the restraint of such cultural factors and are quick to assure the Dutch population that innovation will not lead to the erosion of social solidarity. When facing public outcry over development seen as unfair, the government is quick to act and impose restrictions or to reverse its policies.

Note

This chapter draws on a chapter by Kieke Okma and A. De Roo "From Polder Model to Modern Management in Dutch Health Care," in *Comparative Studies and Modern Medical Care: Learning Opportunity or Global Mythology,* ed. Theodore R. Marmor, Richard Freeman, and Kieke G.H. Okma (New Haven, CT: Yale University Press, forthcoming).

References

Commissie De Jong. 1993. *Raad op Maat* [Measured advice]. *Rapport van de Bijzondere Commissie Vraagpunten Adviesorganen.* Kamerstukken II, 1992–1993, 21427, 29–30. The Hague: SDU.

Commissie Dekker. 1987. *Bereidheid tot Verandering* [Willingness to change: report of the Committee on Health Care Reform]. The Hague: Distributiecentrum Overheidspublicaties.

Harris, G. 2007. "Looking at Dutch and Swiss Health Systems." *New York Times* (October 30).

Naik, G. 2007. "Dutch Treatment: In Holland, Some See Model for U.S. Health Care System." *Wall Street Journal* (September 6), A5.

Okma, K.G.H. 1997. "Studies in Dutch Health Politics, Policies and Law." PhD thesis, University of Utrecht, the Netherlands.

Organization for Economic Cooperation and Development. 1994. *The Reform of Health Care.* Health Reform Studies 5. Paris: Organization for Economic Cooperation and Development.

Visser, J., and A. Hemerijck. 1997. *A Dutch Miracle—Job Growth, Welfare Reform and Corporatism in the Netherlands.* Amsterdam: Amsterdam University Press.

Part II

Administering Health Insurance Programs and Reforms

8

Administering a Medicaid-plus-Tax-Credits Initiative

LYNN ETHEREDGE, JUDITH MOORE, SONYA SCHWARTZ, AND ALAN WEIL

For several years, there has been interest in proposals that would cover the uninsured through a combination of new federal health insurance tax credits and expansion of state Medicaid and the State Children's Health Insurance Program (SCHIP). Joining these two approaches may be the only way to reach compromise. This study was undertaken because implementing a nationwide initiative to cover 47 million uninsured persons, in more than fifty federal-state programs, would pose unprecedented, large, and complex administrative challenges for the public and private sectors. The project, supported by the Robert Wood Johnson Foundation, convened three working meetings with thirty federal, state, and private-sector experts likely to be involved in implementing a Medicaid-plus-tax-credits initiative. (A list of these experts is available in the appendixes to the full report on this study, at www.nashp. org/Files/Medicaid_TaxCredits.pdf.) This chapter provides an overview of the key administrative tasks and offers suggestions for efficiency.

A Medicaid-plus-Tax-Credits Scenario

If Congress and the presidential administration were to begin thinking about a Medicaid-plus-tax-credits program to improve access to health care coverage, some points of consensus, subject to negotiation, might include the following:

- A new federal health insurance tax-credit program will be created for individuals and families who meet the income requirements.
- Individuals and families could use the tax credit to buy health insurance in the health insurance market and coverage in purchasing pools and cooperatives, Medicaid, SCHIP, and other new and existing state programs.
- The federal tax credit will cover part but not all of the cost of comprehensive health insurance in the private market.
- The tax credit would be refundable, meaning that an individual would not need to owe taxes in order to claim it. It would also be available on an advanceable basis, meaning that it could be paid out on a monthly basis so an individual does not need to wait until the end of the tax year to receive it.

Table 8.1

Federal Government

Legislation	Design a federal-state Medicaid + Tax Credits initiative for covering 47 million persons, defining federal-state roles and state options and providing statutory authority, flexibility, and funding.
Tax credits	*For workers*: upgrade the W-4 and W-5 payroll deduction systems for payment of tax credits.
	For non-workers: upgrade the Health Coverage Tax Credit (HCTC) system for payment of tax credits.
Demonstrations	Support several state demonstrations to develop, test, and refine policies and systems before national implementation.
Advance funding for states	Invest in developing efficient, consumer-friendly state systems for: (1) application and enrollment; and (2) consumer choice.

- Medicaid, SCHIP, and other state programs exist as they do today but may be reformed to make it easier to align these programs with this new federal health insurance tax credit, so that they could provide the state supplements.
- States would be able to supplement this federal tax credit with additional state funding.

Overview of Major Administrative Tasks

A national initiative to cover the uninsured through new federal tax credits and expansion of state Medicaid and SCHIP programs would involve unprecedented, large, and complex challenges for the public and private sectors, with many new responsibilities falling on state governments.

The federal government's key role would be to write national legislation for the Medicaid-plus-tax-credits initiative (see Table 8.1). The Internal Revenue Service (IRS) would need to upgrade its W-4 and W-5 systems for paying workers' tax credits and its Health Coverage Tax Credit (HCTC) system for nonworkers' tax credits. The federal government, state governments, employers, and health plans would benefit from several state demonstrations of the Medicaid-plus-tax-credits model to develop, test, and refine new policies and systems before national implementation. Advance federal funding for new state administrative systems would be a critical investment.

An administrative challenge for states will be to upgrade or replace Medicaid's application and enrollment systems, a legacy of its history as a public welfare

Table 8.2

State Governments

Legislation	Enact legislation to cover the uninsured, using federal tax credit and possibly additional state supplements. Establish administrative systems that clearly define roles of state and local agencies, individuals, employers, and health plans. Provide authority and funding.
Eligibility rules	Establish income-based eligibility for state supplements (IRS's adjusted gross income).
Application and enrollment	Replace Medicaid's administrative complexity with a new consumer-friendly system offering one-page applications, multiple points of application (including on-line, worksite, and mail-in), and a one-stop service agency with excellent information technology systems.
Premiums	Use service agency for application/enrollment agency to notify applicants, health plans, IRS, Medicaid/SCHIP, and employers about enrollment, tax credits, state supplements, and individual premium shares, and payments: where, when, and how to send them.
Consumer choice	Provide a well-functioning market for affordable coverage, such as an FEHBP-type model.
Communications	Assure that eligible persons, employers, health plans, state and local agencies, health care providers and all others affected by the legislation know about the changes and their new roles and responsibilities.
Implementation	Assure that all policies and administrative systems are developed, coordinated, and operational on time, with high performance and consumer-friendly service.

program (see Table 8.2). Many states have moved toward simpler, consumer-friendly systems for Medicaid's parents and children, SCHIP, and state programs for uninsured workers that can be models. But other states still rely on paper applications and face-to-face interviews. By contrast, collection of taxes by the IRS simply requires mailing in 1040-series forms (with W-2s).

A second critical challenge for states will be to organize a well-functioning market that can ensure affordable coverage for recipients of federal tax credits and state supplements. Fortunately, there are good administrative models in the Federal Employees Health Benefits (FEHB) program and in a number of states, for example the California Public Employees' Retirement System (CalPERS), other states' public employee systems, and the new Massachusetts Health Insurance Connector.

Employers can contribute to efficient administration. Because 80 percent of the uninsured are workers (and their families), acceptance of work-site applications

Table 8.3

Employers

Application and enrollment	Facilitate workplace application by uninsured workers and families.
Premiums	Deduct workers' premiums and federal tax credits (W-4s and W-5s). Forward to health plans or FEHBP-type agency.

Table 8.4

Health Plans

Application and enrollment	Work with state-organized application and enrollment process.
Premium payment	Work with state-organized premium payment system.
Consumer choice	Work with state-organized market system.

(online, mail-in) would be an efficient method for enrolling uninsured workers (see Table 8.3). The payroll deduction system is efficient and is used for trillions of dollars of tax payments and health insurance premiums. We suggest a similar role for administering the new tax credits and premium shares for workers.

Many of the administrative tasks for a Medicaid-plus-tax-credits initiative arise from its intent to offer a competitive market of affordable health plans (see Table 8.4). Health plans have a huge stake in helping to make sure that all the administrative systems are first-rate in design and operations.

Envisioning a World-Class Administrative System

The health care financing system—and Medicaid, in particular—is an administrative morass. Many coverage initiatives have had large implementation problems, and new legislation could add more fragmentation and more complexity and could repeat past legislative mistakes. This chapter envisions a world-class administrative system focused on consumer service that has two key elements (see Table 8.5).

The following sections discuss key administrative areas: eligibility rules, application and enrollment processes, premium payments, consumer choice, and administrative costs.

Eligibility Rules

A fundamental challenge is to have eligibility rules developed and written so administrative systems can quickly and accurately determine eligibility for federal

Table 8.5

Toward a "World Class" Administrative System

- A one-page application/enrollment form. Eligible persons should do no more than fill out a one-page (or one Web-page) form to apply for benefits, select a health benefits option, and arrange for premium contributions.
- All other administrative functions would be handled by computerized information and financial exchanges among federal and state agencies, employers, and health plans. The administrative system's architecture should be designed to perform administrative functions "in the background" with outstanding efficiency, effectiveness, and customer service.

Table 8.6

Eligibility Rules

Basis of eligibility	Adjusted gross income (IRS)
Accounting period	Prior year's income, current year estimates
Verification	W-2s, 1099s, etc. filed by payers, in government computer files
Redetermination	Annual

tax credits and state supplements (see Table 8.6). The federal tax code and its administrative system are standardized nationally using adjusted gross income. However, Medicaid eligibility rules are an administrative jungle of fifty-six different systems and are incompatible with the tax code. Each state has its own rules about covering different categories of individuals for Medicaid (up to fifty categories in most states, with some states having many more), and other rules for SCHIP; each state counts income differently; and asset accounting is strikingly complex to administer.

The straightforward way to address eligibility is for the federal and state governments to standardize on *income-based eligibility,* using federal adjusted gross income. This would make possible a one-page application form; allow a joint federal-state application and eligibility-determination process; eliminate the need for large enrollment bureaucracies specializing in complex, categorical definitions, and income and asset accounting rules; and enable computer verification of income from tax forms, such as 1040s, W-2s, and 1099s.

A second approach is for states and the federal government to allow individuals to elect their *prior year's income* as a basis for establishing eligibility, facilitating use of computerized government records—1040s, W-2s, 1099s—rather than requiring applicants to submit additional, nonstandardized paper documents for caseworker review and verification. If there were major income changes during a year, individuals would be expected to adjust advance tax-credit payments via W-4 or W-5 deductions, rather than apply for a new eligibility determination.

A third measure is to require states to make tax-credit determinations and eligibility periods normal for a full year. Individuals would not be required, as is now the case in some states, to reapply, resubmit paperwork, and reestablish eligibility at less-than-yearly intervals. This would reduce the government's administrative tasks and recognize that individuals must contract for health insurance coverage on an annual basis.

Application and Enrollment

Application and enrollment are the first steps in the administrative process, and they are critical to the success of a coverage initiative. Many past federal and state coverage initiatives have run into implementation difficulties, including SCHIP in many states, which struggled to enroll even half of eligible uninsured children; Medicare's 1997 Medicare Choice initiative for private plan enrollment; and the recent addition of Medicare prescription drug options (Part D). Millions of low-income beneficiaries have not received intended benefits. The IRS has a straightforward application process for most tax credits. Individuals self-declare eligibility and apply for credits as part of their annual 1040 tax returns. Taxpayers can receive their estimated tax credits in advance, if they wish, by adjusting their income tax deductions from paychecks (via W-4 forms). For low-income individuals who owe few or no income taxes, the tax code provides a W-5 method for advance payment of the Earned Income Tax Credit. A worker submits the W-5 form to his or her employer, who adds the advance Earned Income Tax Credit to the worker's paycheck. The employer then (1) deducts this amount from the total tax withholding it forwards to the IRS and (2) reports the W-5 advance credits to the IRS. In addition, the worker files a 1040 tax return, verifying the advance tax-credit amounts paid and received.

In the future, the tax administrative system may become even more efficient. Since the substantial sources of income for most individuals (for example, wages, interest, and dividends) are now reported to the IRS by employers, banks, and other payers, it may be possible for the IRS to calculate income and income taxes without requiring lower-income taxpayers to submit paper forms and paper documents.

The state Medicaid application and enrollment systems are different and can be much less efficient (see Table 8.7). Although there has been progress for SCHIP and Medicaid parents and children, recent federal proof-of-citizenship requirements are a major reversal. In addition, there are still states where applicants are required to appear in person at county welfare offices; wait in line for individual face-to-face interviews; fill out applications that run twenty-five pages or more; navigate very complicated eligibility rules; provide paper documentation of paychecks, bank statements, citizenship, and the value of assets; and reapply at specified intervals. Applicants must often repeat this sort of process for other government low-income

Table 8.7

Multilevel Logit Models of Transitions from Private Insurance

	Private to Medicaid/SCHIP	
Variable	Estimated coefficient (.) Std Error	t-Value
Intercept	−10.1051*** (1.6107)	−6.2738
Contextual Factors		
Medicaid/SCHIP eligibility	−0.0982 (0.2613)	−0.3757
Old Medicaid eligibility	0.8638*** (0.2746)	3.1455
Medicaid/SCHIP*Pre-Post	0.3496 (0.3390)	1.0314
Old Medicaid Elig*Pre-Post	−0.3755 (0.3246)	−1.1567
Pre-Post	0.2407 (0.2026)	1.1877
Income disregards	−0.0527 (0.2511)	−0.2098
Medicaid expansion	0.2317 (0.3198)	0.7244
Mixed expansion	0.1134 (0.2868)	0.3956
Retail-service employment ratio	4.4961* (2.7697)	1.6234
Parent/Family Factors		
Mom works full time	−0.3172** (0.1425)	−2.2256
Mom works part time	−0.3000* (0.1731)	−1.7335
Mom works other	−0.1392 (0.3115)	−0.4471
Not a high school graduate	0.5178*** (0.1667)	3.1057
Some college	0.0661 (0.1312)	0.5042
College graduate	−0.5804** (0.2535)	−2.2894
Graduate education	−0.3619 (0.4935)	−0.7333
Family stability	−0.0148*** (0.0031)	−4.8197
Income-poverty ratio	−0.0032*** (0.0010)	−3.0809
AFDC receipts	1.6247*** (0.3195)	5.0852
Number of children under 18	0.0711*	1.7099

(continued)

Table 8.7 *(continued)*

Variable	Private to Medicaid/SCHIP	
	Estimated coefficient (.) Std Error	t-Value
	(0.0416)	
Resides in Northeast	0.9019***	2.6761
	(0.3370)	
Resides in Midwest	0.0327	0.1009
	(0.3239)	
Resides in West	−0.0315	−0.0909
	(0.3461)	
Individual (Child)		
Age 6–12 years	−0.1073	−0.7314
	(0.1466)	
Age 13–19 years	0.0322	0.2036
	(0.1581)	
Poor health status	0.5164	1.5069
	(0.3427)	
Black	0.4275***	2.7126
	(0.1576)	
Hispanic	0.9679**	2.2758
	(0.4253)	
Other minority	−0.0804	−0.2622
	(0.3066)	
Seam month	3.1000***	18.9531
	(0.1636)	
Duration 1–3months	−0.3307	−1.1463
	(0.2885)	
Duration 4–6months	1.8427***	12.7576
	(0.1444)	
Duration 7–9months	1.1414***	5.8903
	(0.1938)	
Duration 10–12months	0.1454	0.2812
	(0.5170)	
LLR	1,638,946	
AIC	1,638,954	
Person months (N)	153,626	

*   Significant at the 10 percent level.
** Significant at the 5 percent level.
*** Significant at the 1 percent level.

assistance programs, such as food stamps, low-income housing, school lunch, and the like, each having its own separate application process, eligibility rules, and eligibility specialists trained to understand and administer its complex rules and procedures. Multiple systems and their complexities need caseworkers to help beneficiaries understand and navigate the application and enrollment processes, and outreach efforts to encourage them to apply. Agencies now have little relationship to the IRS and tax administration or to employers. Sending tens of millions of uninsured persons to their county welfare offices to apply for health benefits through complex and non-user-friendly systems would not work.

Design and implementation of a new application and enrollment system for state-administered benefits, in collaboration with the IRS, employers, health plans, health care providers, and many application sites, should be a top priority. A Medicaid-plus-tax-credits initiative is not really practical without this approach. This system would make maximum use of computer systems. We suggest six elements.

The first three recommendations go together: a *one-page application, multiple points of application,* and *a single, one-stop service agency.* These are key elements for a consumer-friendly and efficient application and enrollment system for health benefits (and a possible prototype for all low-income assistance programs). With adoption of income-based eligibility, there could be a one-page (or one-Web-page) application form. This application would cover federal tax credits, state supplements, and health plan enrollment. Multiple points of application would make it as easy and as simple as possible for individuals to apply. For example, since 80 percent of uninsured persons are in working families, providing online applications from the worksite would be an efficient way to target and serve the uninsured. A single-stop state agency would make a common eligibility determination for both federal and state benefits; it would also advise federal and state governments, health plans, individuals, and employers about shares of premiums, payroll deduction amounts, and the identification codes to be used for making and proper crediting of automatic online payments. Several states have pioneered in developing prototypes of one-stop service agencies.

A well-designed application and enrollment system should achieve high participation rates at low administrative expense. Voluntary health insurance initiatives often have had distressingly poor sign-up rates. Far more efficient are *mandatory enrollment (with required proof of enrollment), automatic enrollment,* and *enrollment incentives.* The Massachusetts plan, for example, requires all individuals to sign up for basic health benefits, has proof-of-enrollment requirements, and has a financial penalty for failure to obtain coverage. Mandatory enrollment also makes clear to individuals that they need to take action, what action they need to take, and when they need to enroll. Automatic enrollment can also be effective; individuals are automatically enrolled unless they choose not to be covered. Medicare's beneficiaries are automatically enrolled in Medicare's Supplementary Medical Insurance (Part B), with premiums withheld from Social Security checks, unless a beneficiary specifically declines coverage. The Medicare take-up rate is about 95 percent. Automatic-enrollment features for employer-provided retirement and savings benefits have also proved effective.

Efficient administrative systems also need to prevent loss of coverage through a *focus on points of transition,* such as starting a new job, job loss, losing Medicaid or SCHIP coverage, or aging off a parental policy. Indeed, most of the uninsured population have had health insurance coverage but have lost benefits at one of these

Table 8.8

Premium Payment

Eligible group	Premium share	Payment method
Workers	Federal tax credits	W-4 payroll deductions
	Advance federal tax credits for low-wage workers	W-5 payroll deductions
	Individual premium share (Employer share, if any)	Payroll deductions
	State premium share	Medicaid/SCHIP
Nonworkers	Advance federal tax credits	IRS (HCTC or via Medicaid/SCHIP)
	Individual premium share	Individual payment
	State premium share	Medicaid/SCHIP

transition points. A Medicaid-plus-tax-credits gap-filling strategy would need to prevent lapses in coverage and keep individuals insured. It seems worthwhile to make sure people are informed of coverage options at these points of transition.

Finally, an enrollment system needs to set up new enrollees with insurance identification. This could be accomplished with the issuance of personal *health cards*. Cards would facilitate receipt of services, billing, and reporting of electronic health information to the individual's electronic health record. In Maine, such cards serve as debit cards; each month, the state electronically transfers its premium subsidy to the individual's card account so each person can pay his or her full premium.

Premium Payment

The second major step for an administrative system will be to assure timely and accurate payment of premiums and to coordinate premium payment shares from individuals, federal tax credits, state assistance, and perhaps employers (Table 8.8). As the advisory groups considered this problem, it proved useful to think of two different models. One would be for working populations and would make use of the highly efficient payroll-deduction system. The other would be for nonworking populations that are not able to use a payroll deduction system.

Workers

Employers are now required to make eight standard deductions: individual federal and state income taxes, employer Social Security and Medicare taxes, worker Social

Security and Medicare taxes, unemployment insurance, and workers' compensation. Employer payroll deductions forward to federal and state treasuries more than $3.5 trillion annually in tax revenues and more than $600 billion annually in employer and individual health insurance premiums. By extending this system, most workers would file a redesigned W-4 form that requests that employers (1) deduct from paychecks the worker's share of the premium; (2) reduce the worker's income tax deductions by the amount of the federal health insurance tax credit, as determined by the state's application and enrollment agency; and (3) forward the worker's premium share and the amount of the federal tax credit to the health plan selected by the worker (or an intermediary designated by the state). Low-income workers whose tax credits would be larger than their income taxes and who would thus need an advance tax credit would file a redesigned W-5 form that requests that employers (1) deduct from paychecks the worker's share of the premium; (2) advance the worker's health insurance tax credit, as determined by the state's application and enrollment agency, from amounts that the employer would otherwise pay to the IRS for income and Social Security taxes; and (3) forward the worker's premium share and the amount of the federal tax credit to the health plan selected by the worker (or the state-designated intermediary). If an employer chose to make a premium contribution, it could be forwarded as part of these payments. At the end of the year, employers' W-2 forms would show the amounts of the health insurance tax credits paid, for the IRS and for workers to include on their 1040s. State premium assistance would be paid by the Medicaid or SCHIP agency to the health plan or designated intermediary, in the amount determined by the application agency, using the identification and account numbers it assigned.

Nonworkers

For nonworkers, about 20 percent of the uninsured, the IRS would pay a monthly advance tax credit, using its HCTC system of electronic funds transfer to health plans, the Medicaid or SCHIP agency would forward the state assistance amount, and each individual would pay his or her premium share directly to the health plan. Amounts for each payer would be set by the state application and eligibility agency. Several variations on this arrangement are possible: The individual could send his or her premium share to the IRS, and the IRS could package it with the federal tax credit (today's HCTC system), or the IRS and the individual could send their premium shares to the Medicaid or SCHIP agency, which could send the full premium to the health plan or other appropriate entity.

Consumer Choice

Administrative systems for a Medicaid-plus-tax-credits initiative would be called on to facilitate consumer choice among competing health plans (and possibly state program options) (see Table 8.9). There are many controversial political and health policy

Table 8.9

Consumer Choice

Market structure and operation	Government-sponsored FEHBP-type competition, e.g., Massachusetts Health Insurance Connector
Health plan identification	Identification numbers
Information from health plans	Required as condition of participation

decisions to be made about how to structure markets and regulate health insurance products so they will be affordable. We offer three suggestions for efficiency.

A Medicaid-plus-tax-credits initiative could use government-sponsored FEHB-type competition to provide consumer choice. FEHB is the nation's largest system for employer-provided health benefits. The program offers eligible persons a competitive choice among leading health plans and handles many administrative functions, including qualifying plans, obtaining competitive premium bids, running an annual open season for consumers to make informed choices, collecting and distributing the employer and worker shares of premiums, ensuring open enrollment and portability of coverage, establishing common premium structures and rating policies, and overseeing a well-functioning market. CalPERS, the California public employees' health benefits system, is another large and proven model for the kind of administrative structure that would be needed. In another state, the Massachusetts health initiative has created the Massachusetts Health Connector to create a similar market-management structure for its Commonwealth Care Health Insurance Program enrollees. We suggest this approach to federal policy makers considering a combined Medicaid–tax-credit program for other states to (1) greatly simplify administrative tasks for states, the IRS, employers, and health plans; (2) improve administrative performance; (3) improve value for taxpayers; and (4) better serve consumers.

Two other suggestions address difficulties encountered in the HCTC initiative. The IRS, individuals, health insurance commissioners, and health plans have had difficulty communicating about which individual health plan options qualify for use of the HCTC. In part, this arises because health plans often have names that sound similar. We suggest that this could be addressed by a system of *health plan identification numbers* that provide a unique identifier. This would be similar to the CUSIP (Committee on Uniform Security Identification Procedures) system that now assigns a unique ID number to each security so that ownership and dividends can be accurately reported for tax purposes. With such a system, computers could accurately record and verify chosen health plan options, and payers could use electronic transmission for premium payments. Another suggestion, also from the HCTC experience, is a reminder to legislative drafters to include *authority for the*

IRS and other government agencies to be able to obtain information they need from health plans in a timely manner. Without such authority, it would be more difficult to run a high-performance administrative system.

Administrative Costs

Choices about administrative systems have implications for costs and performance. We found huge differences in administrative efficiencies and costs of ways to implement the Medicaid-plus-tax-credits initiative. *The IRS's tax administration and the payroll deduction system are models of administrative efficiency.* They operate with convenience and low cost (that is, it costs only a few dollars to adjust a W-4 withholding and create new deductions, fractions of a cent for electronic funds transmission) to collect and distribute trillions of dollars annually. They also automatically generate reports, such as W-2s, that provide a verification record from payers for the income, tax deductions, and advance tax credits claimed by individuals on 1040s. New administrative systems are not needed to duplicate what the IRS can do.

Traditional state- and county-run application and eligibility systems for Medicaid rank poorly in consumer service and administrative efficiency, with hundreds of dollars of government expense (and much hassle for applicants) to establish (and periodically reestablish) eligibility. These systems are also a hassle for enrollees. Some states, like Massachusetts, have redesigned their application and enrollment systems to work better for Medicaid parents and children, SCHIP, and health insurance programs for working populations. Our suggestions for a new state application and enrollment process, with income-based eligibility, one-page applications, multiple points for application, one-stop consumer centers, Web-based and mail-in applications, and excellent information technology systems continue and build on this progress.

The HCTC advance payment system appears to be today's most expensive administrative option. Calculated on a per-beneficiary basis, IRS administrative costs for HCTC are 88 percent higher than are state and federal administrative costs for Medicaid and SCHIP systems. The HCTC advance payment system would become even more expensive if it also needed to perform low-income testing for individuals who do not now file 1040 tax returns. (However, IRS processing of HCTC credits claimed through W-4s and 1040 filings seems to work well.) These suggestions would use the HCTC advance payment system for low-income nonworkers. State agencies would handle applications and eligibility, and the IRS would provide electronic transfer of advance tax credits, which it does with great efficiency.

Lessons Learned from Recent Coverage Expansions

Over the past decade, there have been major federal and state initiatives to expand coverage that offer important lessons for administrative planning for a Medicaid-plus-tax-credits initiative. These include the establishment of SCHIP, the enactment of the HCTC benefit as part of the Trade Act of 2002, and the implementation of the new Medicare Part D. Major lessons learned are as follows.

Implementation of a Federal-State Initiative Is a Joint Effort, and Every State Is Different

The federal-state Medicaid program now allows each state a lot of discretion in the structure and operation of its Medicaid and SCHIP programs. States also differ in policy preferences, political leadership, health insurance and medical delivery markets, regulatory approaches, health care costs, employer-based coverage, numbers of uninsured, and many other ways. With expanded use of Medicaid waivers over the past decade, the diversity has grown. There will be more than fifty different state or territorial programs for the federal government to partner with. At least two federal agencies, the Department of the Treasury and the Department of Health and Human Services, will need to be involved, and possibly the Department of Labor as well. There are successful examples, such as SCHIP and HCTC, where many aspects of federal-state partnership have gone well: Excellent federal leadership, well-developed consultative processes, lots of dialogue between federal and state governments, and professional commitment to first-rate public administration have been characteristics of successful aspects of these efforts. However, a Medicaid-plus-tax-credits initiative to cover 47 million uninsured would be a much larger and more complex undertaking.

Enrollment Is Critical to Success

All of the recent federal and state voluntary-coverage initiatives, whether federal (Medicare, tax credits) or federal-state (SCHIP), have struggled with the task of informing, enrolling, and serving new beneficiaries. Many millions of low-income children, senior citizens, and displaced workers did not receive benefits to which they were entitled, or were enrolled only after several years of marketing and outreach efforts. According to a recent article in *Health Affairs*, one-quarter of the nation's uninsured are already eligible for public coverage but not enrolled. Enrollment systems need to be a high priority, with consumer-friendly arrangements, such as workplace sign-up, payroll deductions, and marketing. In a voluntary market, attention must be paid to the price and value judgments made by potential enrollees as consumers about whether the financing and products available are desirable. As evidenced in the recent Massachusetts initiative, mandatory enrollment mechanisms and penalties for failures to enroll in coverage and automatic enrollment processes may need to be considered in order for the program to become really effective.

Eligibility Rules Rule

A critical administrative task for government programs and tax benefits is to make a clear, prompt determination of whether an individual is eligible and what the amount of the benefit is. This can be particularly complex for state Medicaid programs because federal law requires use of categorical eligibility; there are now more than fifty optional state categories. Each state has rules about how income is to be determined, for what period, how applications are made, the time period in which they must be processed, and so on. At the same time, the federal tax code now has its own—different—rules and procedures for applications and eligibility determinations for tax benefits. Uninsured persons need to be sorted out through administrative systems that direct each person to the federal tax credits, state supplements, Medicaid, SCHIP, and other state programs for which they or family members may be eligible and that determine their eligibility and benefits. Ambiguities about eligibility have many adverse implications for being able to inform and enroll beneficiaries, for expense and difficulty of administering the new programs, and for gaming, shifting of enrollment among programs, and fraud and abuse. The tasks of aligning state and federal eligibility rules and processes so they are clear and consistent is central to having a new Medicaid-plus-tax-credits system work well.

Large Initiatives Need Administrative Systems That Do Not Rely on Individual Casework

Administrative systems can have enormously wide variations in the effectiveness and costs of delivering health benefits. For enrollment, as an example, automatic enrollment procedures can produce take-up rates of 80 percent or more. In contrast, programs that require individuals to apply through a county welfare office often struggle to reach 50 percent enrollment. In addition, sign-up rates for health insurance (such as HCTC subsidies) and retirement tax benefits (such as self-organized IRAs) that individuals must seek out, arrange independently, and finance through voluntary contributions can be in the range of 10 to 15 percent or less. In terms of expense, the payroll deductions system that government uses for tax collection (and benefits) and employers use for fringe benefits can operate very efficiently (a few dollars to set up a new deduction, and fractions of a cent per electronic transaction). In contrast, an application for income-related benefits through a county welfare office for Medicaid typically costs several hundred dollars per family. Administrative processes that can be handled almost automatically and with computers are keys to standardization, accuracy, and efficiency. In contrast, processes that require individualized casework for millions of persons by large bureaucracies, need coordination among a number of public- and private-sector organizations, and confront customers with complicated, confusing, and difficult choices, limited assistance, and multistep procedural requirements are inherently much more expensive and time-consuming. At least six different kinds of administrative systems will potentially need some redesign in a Medicaid-plus-tax-credits initiative: the IRS, state Medicaid agencies, state tax agencies, county income eligibility-determination agencies, employers' payroll deductions systems, and health plans.

Simplify

A cross-cutting theme, endorsed and amplified by most who have been involved in large-scale implementation efforts, is that simple administrative systems are far easier to understand, explain, implement, and operate than complex systems. Coverage of 47 million persons in a new Medicaid-plus-tax-credits program will be a large challenge under the best of circumstances. For a consumer-oriented, voluntary initiative, it will be important that the consumer experience be simple, although there will be complex "wiring and plumbing" among the public- and private-sector administrative agencies that operate in the background.

Legislative Drafting and Advance Planning

The study's advisory panels offered several suggestions (and reminders) for those who may be involved in legislative drafting and early planning of new administrative systems. These suggestions reflect a wealth of experience from implementing health coverage initiatives in the public and private sectors.

- *Institute clear responsibilities.* For administrative systems to work well, everyone involved needs to know exactly what are they expected to do, when they are expected to do it, and how they are expected to work with others. All of this starts with legislative drafting.
- *Limit the number of state options, with waivers.* One of the reasons to enact a "federalism" initiative, like Medicaid-plus-tax-credits, is so that states have the flexibility to address problems in different ways. However, if fifty states adopt fifty different solutions to all the complex issues, the results could be too complex to understand or for the federal government to write regulations and assure accountability for public spending. The federal government balanced these considerations in the SCHIP statute, which spells out a limited number of state options but also allows states to propose modifications or seek waivers. Some states, for example, may want a state-run administrative system that uses state tax systems to pay the health insurance tax credits on behalf of the IRS. Others may prefer a stronger federal role.
- *Utilize demonstrations before full implementation.* It would be a valuable learning experience for several states to pioneer forms of a Medicaid-plus-tax-credits initiative before the nation fully implements a 47-million-person, nationwide initiative. The federal government, states, employers (and their payroll service firms), health plans, and future beneficiaries would all benefit. The current Massachusetts plan would be an excellent opportunity for a Medicaid-plus-tax-credits initiative; federal tax credits could easily be added to the Massachusetts reform plan.
- *Provide advance funding and advance planning.* A Medicaid-plus-tax-credits initiative cannot be implemented quickly without advance funding and ad-

vance planning. New state application and enrollment systems, for example, need many months or years in lead time and preparatory funds because of the need for state legislative review and approval of new budget requirements and changes. For systemwide planning, the federal government (the Department of Health and Human Services and the Department of the Treasury) could convene a work group of representatives from states, employers, payroll-system specialists, and health plans for detailed planning of administrative options and interoperable computer systems. There should be ongoing dialogue between congressional decision makers and those at states and in the private sector who would implement a Medicaid-plus-tax-credits design.

Although this project focused specifically on a Medicaid-plus-tax-credits initiative, most of the initiatives now being discussed for expanding health insurance coverage also involve new administrative roles for federal and state governments, employers, health plans, and individuals. The planners of these initiatives will need to consider use or redesign of tax administration, payroll deductions, state Medicaid and SCHIP application and enrollment processes, consumer choice, and other administrative issues discussed in this chapter. The third section of the full report, intended for technical experts and legislative drafters, offers an extensive discussion of the above issues and options. We hope that this chapter, as well as the full report, will be of broad use in the design of new initiatives for coverage of the 47 million uninsured.

Note

Support for this project was provided by a grant from the Robert Wood Johnson Foundation to the George Washington University.

9

Administering Health Insurance Mandates

C. Eugene Steuerle and Paul N. Van de Water

Many proposals to promote more universal health insurance coverage contain mandates requiring individuals to buy health insurance. Other proposals impose requirements on employers to provide or pay for coverage in addition to or instead of an individual mandate. "The general theoretical conclusion from economics," writes Mark Pauly, "is there is likely to be very little difference, in the long run, between an individual and an employer mandate" (Pauly 1994). This argument rests on the notion that if the same ultimate tax or mandate is imposed on the same activity, the ultimate economic incidence does not depend on who initially pays. People will eventually react to the same net incentives in the same way. In practice, however, significant differences arise between what can be implemented through charges on employers and what can be implemented through charges on employees, often guided by practical issues of administration and how people respond to alternative administrative structures.

While well-grounded in principle, mandates to pay for or purchase health insurance confront administrative challenges. Most important, for many people a mandate to purchase health insurance requires that they receive subsidies adequate to make the insurance affordable. Given the history of less-than-full participation in means-tested benefit programs, the administration of mandates and subsidies needs to be coordinated and thought out. In addition, since sizable penalties are hard to collect after the fact or at the end of the year, payments should be kept current and penalties modest. Among the available techniques are withholding, automatic enrollment, and relating the penalty to some other tax or transfer benefit that can be denied through administrative means.

This chapter identifies ways to structure health insurance mandates, if adopted at the federal level, so they are administered fairly and effectively. It draws on information about the administrative arrangements used in health insurance mandates in Hawaii, Massachusetts, the Netherlands, and Switzerland, as well as those proposed by California governor Arnold Schwarzenegger, the New America Foundation, and Senators Ron Wyden (D-OR) and Robert Bennett (R-UT). (The appendix to this chapter, available at www.nasi.org, provides detailed information about the administrative features of these existing and proposed mandates.)

Initial Considerations

Employer and individual mandates provide financing for expanded health coverage without being labeled as taxes. Unlike taxes, mandated premiums would not necessarily be recorded in the federal budget. Like taxes, mandates pose issues of equal justice for those equally situated (horizontal equity), not merely progressivity for people at different income levels (vertical equity). Progressivity can be achieved through redistributive means. Health insurance mandates require both universal participation in payment systems for health insurance *and* that money be spent on health insurance.

Mandates attempt to prevent people from being free riders, who depend on others to support the insurance, often implicit and insufficient, that they receive from society. If free or subsidized access to health care is provided to those without adequate resources at time of illness, then most people without private insurance can be considered to have a backup, if unstated, public health insurance policy. Without a mandate or more universal insurance, those who could have paid for insurance or saved to cover their costs, but did not, can shift their burdens onto others. Mandates require that at least some payment be made up front on a nearly universal basis—thus preventing people from shifting their health care burdens onto others who are no more capable of paying for insurance.

Mandates also aim to ensure that everyone who is in good health shares in helping those who face large health care costs, even when the health status of the individuals is known before the purchase of the insurance. Here, progressivity comes back into play. "Mandates greatly reduce insurers' legitimate fears that they may otherwise be forced to provide coverage for disproportionate numbers of individuals with high health costs," says Len Nichols. Mandates might also reduce administrative costs, depending on how they are designed. "Getting everybody into the market will lead to significant reductions in administrative and marketing costs that can be passed on to consumers and payers" (Nichols 2007, 20).

Any employer or individual mandate must specify the nature and size of the health insurance policy that must be purchased, either by listing benefits or by establishing a required actuarial value. At one extreme, the required insurance might cover a range of services with generous payment rates to providers and limited cost sharing by beneficiaries. At the other, if few restrictions are imposed, individuals might get by with a policy that covered only catastrophic events, and only up to a specified dollar limit. The more extensive the requirements, the greater will be the cost of the required insurance and the greater the burden of the mandate. Moreover, as the costs of health care rise, each year's cost increase of the mandated policy may increase the gap between the cost of insurance and the cost of paying a fine or penalty for not meeting the mandate. Thus, depending upon how the fine or penalty evolves, paying the fine may become easier than complying with the mandate.

Employer Mandates

Employers can be required to administer a mandate on individuals in their employ and to contribute to the purchase of health insurance for their employees. When we speak of an *employer mandate,* we are referring to the latter. When we turn to an individual mandate, later, we examine the potential role of employers in administering and enforcing that mandate.

Almost all states require health insurers to cover specific health care services, such as mammography screening and minimum maternity stays. The federal government also imposes requirements on health insurance plans, including self-insured employer-sponsored plans. Although often referred to as mandates, these requirements are not discussed here, since they apply only to employers that elect to provide health benefits to their employees.

An employer mandate alone cannot ensure universal health insurance coverage, since many uninsured people are not connected to the workforce, but it can strengthen the system of employer-sponsored insurance, the primary source of coverage for nonelderly Americans. Eighty percent or more of the uninsured are estimated to come from working families. Employer mandates may apply not only to current workers, but also to those who have left employment. For example, the Consolidated Omnibus Budget Reconciliation Act (COBRA) of 1985 requires that employers with twenty or more employees that provide employer-sponsored insurance offer access to continuing health insurance temporarily to some who have left employment or lost coverage.

Only Hawaii and Massachusetts impose mandates on employers to provide or pay for health insurance, although employer mandates have been proposed in other states and at the federal level. Limited use of employer mandates is partly a consequence of the federal Employee Retirement Income Security Act (ERISA) of 1974, which frees self-insured employment-based health plans from state regulation. ERISA prevents states from requiring employers to provide health coverage or to spend particular amounts on health coverage. Hawaii has a limited exemption from ERISA, but other states do not.

Types of Employer Mandates

Employer mandates can take one of two forms. In one, as in Hawaii, employers must provide most employees with health insurance and must make a prescribed contribution to that insurance. In another, often called play-or-pay, employers have the option of paying a tax instead of providing health insurance coverage. Massachusetts requires that employers make a "fair and reasonable" premium contribution toward a health insurance plan for their employees or pay the state a Fair Share Contribution of up to $295 annually per employee. The size of the contribution reflects the extent to which the government depends on employers to help achieve more universal insurance. Massachusetts kept the Fair Share Contribution modest to avoid an ERISA-based legal challenge, which remains a possible threat.

Employer mandates may, but need not, exempt small businesses. In Hawaii, the mandate applies to all nongovernmental employers except sole proprietors with no other employees. In Massachusetts, the mandates apply to firms with eleven or more full-time-equivalent employees. Some proposals set a cutoff at larger firm sizes. The extent of the required employer contribution may also vary by firm size or by a firm's average wage. Small business exceptions raise a variety of administrative issues. Closely held businesses might easily split into several different legal entities. Larger businesses might contract out more to smaller firms and independent contractors; indeed, this is already a way that employers can effectively avoid antidiscrimination rules that apply to retirement plans. This evolution does not have to be planned by the firm's owners or managers; firms with fewer mandates may be more competitive and grow faster than others—thereby gradually extending an exemption to more employers.

Proposals for employer mandates, at least so far in the states, often do not require covering dependents. The mandate in Hawaii does not apply to dependents, nor does the Fair Share Contribution requirement in Massachusetts. Nonetheless, firms that offer coverage for workers generally offer coverage for dependents as well, even if they do not contribute (or contribute less) to the cost of that coverage.

Whether or not dependents are included in an employer mandate, issues of coordinating public and private benefits arise. For instance, expansion of the State Children's Health Insurance Program (SCHIP) will displace some employer-sponsored coverage. Excluding dependents from a mandate might increase incentives for employers to drop insurance for dependents, since they could no longer drop insurance for everyone. Even if children are covered by mandates, they may be eligible for some benefits under SCHIP or Medicaid that are not provided under the employer plan.

While employers may be required to contribute toward health insurance, the size of the mandate may not be adequate to cover its cost. In Hawaii, for example, the employer must pay at least half of an individual health insurance premium, and the employee may be required to contribute up to 1.5 percent of wages. In Massachusetts, the individual mandate requires all adults to obtain insurance, whatever the employer's contribution to its cost. Other arrangements, of course, are also possible.

Experience with Employer Mandates

Although only Hawaii and Massachusetts offer any U.S. experience with health insurance mandates, employers are subject to mandates in other areas, such as paying a minimum wage, providing workers' compensation, and withholding and paying taxes. These examples provide some lessons about what to expect from an employer mandate and how to make it more effective.

Health Insurance Mandates

Since 1975, Hawaii's Prepaid Health Care Act has required nearly all employers to provide health insurance to employees who work twenty hours or more a week for four consecutive weeks. The Disability Compensation Division of the state's Department of Labor and Industrial Relations, which also administers workers' compensation, enforces the mandate by responding to complaints and conducting random compliance visits. The mandate appears to be effective in expanding health coverage. With the Prepaid Health Care Act, the rate of uninsurance in Hawaii dropped from 30 percent to as low as 5 percent (Hawaii Uninsured Project 2003). In 2004–6, according to the Census Bureau, it was 8.6 percent—the second-lowest rate in the nation. A 2004 analysis finds that the rate of insurance among workers in Hawaii is 10.9 percentage points above the level that would otherwise be expected (Kronick, Gilmer, and Rice 2004).

Massachusetts's employer mandates are less far-reaching than Hawaii's because Massachusetts—unlike Hawaii—does not have an exemption from ERISA. By the same token, Massachusetts relies more on other mechanisms, including an individual mandate. Under the reforms that became effective in 2007, Massachusetts firms with eleven or more employees must make a "fair and reasonable" premium contribution toward health insurance or pay the state a Fair Share Contribution. Firms must also offer a cafeteria plan meeting federal requirements (under Section 125) that allows employees to pay for health insurance coverage on a pretax basis. Firms that do not comply are subject to a Free Rider Surcharge—charging them for part of the care used by their employees or dependents that is financed by the state's Health Safety Net Fund.

Minimum Wage

The federal government and all but six states require that hourly employees in most industries be paid a minimum wage. Under the federal Fair Labor Standards Act, businesses must pay back wages if they fail to comply with the minimum wage, and are subject to fines for violations. Estimates of compliance with the minimum wage depend on the data and definitions employed. Using the 1973 Current Population Survey, Ashenfelter and Smith (1979) estimate an overall compliance rate of 69 percent, when compliance was measured by the fraction of covered workers earning minimum wage or less. In a 2006 survey, the Wage and Hour Division of the Department of Labor found that 92 percent of low-wage workers in low-wage industries were paid in compliance with the Fair Labor Standards Act (U.S. Department of Labor 2007). Whatever data and measures are used, however, the studies agree that compliance varies considerably among industries and locations, and that vigorous enforcement and higher penalties can increase compliance.

One economic objection to an employer mandate is that it operates like an increase in minimum wage, which can increase unemployment and off-the-books work among low-wage workers. The threat is much stronger the larger the increase in costs imposed. Enforcement and compliance problems are therefore likely to rise more than in proportion to any rise in the effective minimum wage. Introducing gradual increases in employer mandates in place of gradual increases in the minimum wage might alleviate economic and administrative concerns.

Unemployment Insurance and Workers' Compensation

Under the federal-state unemployment insurance program, employers must pay a payroll tax on the earnings of covered employees. In addition, every state except Texas mandates that private employers provide workers' compensation protection for nearly all of their employees. Coverage of the two programs is largely the same. As with the minimum wage, there are no consistent, comprehensive data on the rate of compliance with state workers' compensation laws. A study in New York State, however, offers evidence that employer noncompliance is a growing problem. The study cites findings that employers frequently misclassify employees as independent contractors, thereby avoiding responsibility for both unemployment insurance and workers' compensation. In addition, fewer workers in New York appear to be covered by workers' compensation than by the unemployment insurance system. The same study suggests that other states have been more effective in combating workers' compensation fraud through expanded enforcement efforts and increased penalties (Fiscal Policy Institute 2007).

A more thorough study in California finds that underreporting for workers' compensation increased from a range of 6 to 10 percent of total private industry payroll in 1997 to 19 to 23 percent of payroll in 2002—a period when premiums rose rapidly. Employers also misclassify workers in high-risk categories as earning wages in lower-risk occupations. The study estimates that, for very high-risk classes, as much as 65 to 75 percent of payroll is under- or misreported (Neuhauser and Donovan 2007).

Tax Compliance

In many cases the enforcement of an employer mandate rests with the tax authorities. Most employers are required to file returns regularly, turning over periodic tax payments, reporting on pensions and payments to retirement plans, and withholding taxes on employees' earnings. Not all of this is done seamlessly. Partnerships and self-employed individuals are estimated to underreport their net incomes on average by 30 percent or more. The tax authorities also get limited information on the provision of health insurance, but it is not currently compiled in ways conducive to a mandate. For example, the Internal Revenue Service (IRS) does not match up reports on general expenses and coverage with the participation of employees in health insurance in each payment period. Rules that attempt to limit transactions undertaken only for tax purposes are difficult to enforce, in part because the transactions are difficult to find. For instance, rules requiring employers to maintain current efforts when incentives encourage them to change the way they do things are almost impossible to enforce in the long run. As a simple example, it would be very hard to use tax penalties to restrict firms over time from splitting up into smaller entities if there are small-business exceptions to a mandate. Some of these issues arise, as well, with individual mandates enforced through employers.

Employers also face antidiscrimination rules regarding employer-provided benefits such as pensions and deposits to retirement accounts, as well as employee contributions to such plans. These rules add to compliance costs and threaten firms with lawsuits over whether certain actions are discriminatory. A requirement that any health insurance be provided equally among employees could raise similar issues of deciding what was discriminatory and what was not, as well as force further attention to exactly who is an independent contractor. Employers operating in more than one state also seek uniformity of treatment, which is a major reason for the provision in ERISA limiting state regulation of employee benefit plans.

Administrative Considerations

Whether or not to impose an employer mandate is likely to hinge as much on political as on administrative concerns. Generally speaking, an employer mandate encourages the notion that employees are getting something for nothing. While some minimum-wage employees might gain higher total compensation—imposing a mandate is like a requirement to raise the minimum wage, at least for those employees who maintain their employment—economists generally believe that employees bear the burden of the mandate in the form of lower cash wages, at least on average over time. Rapid increases in the cost of health insurance may prevent employers from shifting its entire burden to employees, although high profit rates cast doubt that this situation can hold for very long. In any case, hiding the true cost of a mandate may lead to mistakes in allocating burdens across society and in determining the amount of health insurance that is mandated.

One administrative complication with an employer mandate derives from its use as a way to prevent employees from being free riders on government systems. Not all employees who opt out of an employer's own plan are free riders. Some may acquire insurance from other sources, such as a spouse, parent, or other family member. Some older workers and persons with a disability may have access to Medicare or Medicaid. Children may have access to Medicaid or SCHIP. In addition, many workers hold more than one job at a time.

All these issues raise potential administrative complications about distributing the burden of an employer mandate fairly and efficiently among families with different work histories, sizes, labor force participants, and employers. Suppose, for instance, that employers are mandated to pay for the cost of a family policy for full-time workers. Policy makers might attempt to come up with formulas for allocating that requirement across several jobs held by several members of a family, but it is highly unlikely that its cost could be easily and precisely coordinated.

Therefore, rough-and-ready approaches to making an employer mandate administrable are inevitably employed, but at some cost in equity or efficiency. In Hawaii, an employee with two or more employers must designate a principal employer, responsible for providing health coverage, and employees may claim an exemption if they have other coverage. This could encourage employers to provide weaker plans (within the statutory requirement), so they can save costs by becoming less likely to be designated the principal employer. Because part-time jobs are excluded, a person with two fifteen-hours-per-week jobs will lack health insurance available to a person with one thirty-hours-per week job. In Massachusetts, the requirement that employers make a "fair and reasonable" premium contribution toward health insurance applies to the firm as a whole and not to individual employees.

With individual mandates (including those enforced by an employer) it is easier to reconcile payments at the end of the year when there are several employed family members and several employers. For example, reconciliation of employee Social Security taxes collected from multiple jobs is achieved with the employee's end-of-year income tax filing. In the case of the employer mandate to pay Social Security tax, however, no such reconciliation is attempted.

Any health reform plan that includes an employer mandate must make provision for noncompliance. Lack of compliance with a new mandate to provide health insurance is likely to be concentrated among firms that fail to comply with existing requirements. For example, agricultural businesses have a poor record of compliance with the requirement to report an employee's taxable earnings using the correct Social Security number, and garment makers have a low rate of compliance with the minimum wage. It is reasonable to surmise that some of these same firms would also fail to provide required health insurance to their workers.

If an employer fails to comply, what penalties will apply? Fines could be levied, and lawsuits could issue when they are not paid. The play-or-pay option adopted in Massachusetts was likely adopted not only as a matter of equity between employers with insurance and those without, but also for administrative simplification. In effect, it provides a fairly simple penalty structure: a flat penalty per employee not covered. Of course, once penalties are in law, other administrative mechanisms must be developed: reporting requirements, penalties for misreporting (not just failing to comply), judicial or administrative procedures to handle disputes, and collection agents to collect fines, penalties, and interest. Different enforcement mechanisms may be needed depending on whether the employer is a private taxable entity, a nonprofit organization, or a government. In Massachusetts, the Fair Share Contribution is collected by the Division of Unemployment Assistance, which also implements penalties for nonpayment.

Individual Mandates

Administering an individual mandate raises more issues than administering an employer mandate because it covers more people. A mandate on employees, administered by employers, may be no harder and sometimes easier for the employer to administer than an outright employer mandate. Moreover, an employer mandate is often backed up by an individual mandate to reach those outside the labor force. In the discussion below, we deal mainly with administrative issues that differ from those discussed previously for employer mandates.

When it comes to individual mandates, there are few existing models to follow. The federal government requires that draft-age men register with the Selective Service System. States require children to attend school up to a certain age and often require certain immunizations as a prerequisite. Since 2007, Massachusetts has required everyone over eighteen years of age to have health insurance, as long as it is defined as "affordable." Otherwise, governmental mandates "typically apply to people as parties to economic transactions, rather than as members of society" (Seiler 1994). Social Security taxes must be paid by individuals with wages or self-employment earnings, for example, but not by those without earnings from work.

Experience with Individual Health Insurance Mandates

Limited guidance may be found in individual health insurance mandates that have applied since 1996 in Switzerland and since 2006 in the Netherlands. Both countries have achieved coverage rates of 97 to 99 percent, but in both cases coverage was almost as high under the mixed public-private arrangements that existed before imposition of the mandate. In addition, their political and cultural institutions differ from those of the United States in some other major respects.

In Switzerland, for example, every resident must register his or presence with the local population-control office shortly after taking up a new place of residence. The enforcement of the health insurance mandate by Swiss cantons builds on this preexisting registration requirement, which is absent in the United States. If you do not sign up for insurance or pay your premium, an employee of your canton or commune is likely to knock on your door to obtain compliance.

In the Netherlands, several features hold down the level of premiums and thereby facilitate compliance with the mandate. The cost of health care is less than in the United States. Half the cost of insurance for adults is paid for by an income-related tax, and the government pays the entire cost for children. Moreover, 40 percent of the population is eligible for a premium subsidy. Even so, an estimated 1.5 percent of the legal population is estimated to be uninsured, and a similar number of people are delinquent in the payment of premiums. Since the architects of the Dutch mandate did not envision any problem with noncompliance, the initial legislation created few effective sanctions if a person does not take out insurance or pay premiums, and the government is currently developing enforcement mechanisms.

Massachusetts illustrates an attempt to administer an individual mandate in the context of comprehensive health-financing reform. In addition to the individual and employer mandates, the reform includes a restructuring of the individual and small-group market for health insurance, creation of an insurance-purchasing exchange (the Commonwealth Connector), and provision of subsidies for coverage to families with incomes up to 300 percent of the poverty level (Commonwealth Care). Massachusetts considered the administrative arrangements before enacting legislation, relied on existing state agencies to administer the new program (in addition to creating the Connector), left some discretion to program administrators, and provided assistance to individuals and employers on how to comply with new requirements. Although it is too early to determine the effectiveness of the mandate, almost all residents will be affected: An estimated 1 percent of the state's population will not be required to obtain insurance because it is still unaffordable.

Experience with Other Individual Mandates

Outside of the health insurance area, governments impose individual mandates for automobile owners to purchase liability insurance, for children to be immunized before attending school, and for recipients of income to pay taxes. Government experience in collecting benefit overpayments, student loans, and other debts also carries lessons for enforcement of individual mandates.

Automobile Insurance

Forty-six states (and the District of Columbia) have some form of compulsory automobile insurance, and all states hold motorists accountable for bodily injury and damage to other vehicles. The Insurance Research Council provides periodic estimates of the percentage of uninsured motorists in each state based on accident claims data. Nationwide, 15 percent of motorists in 2004 were estimated to lack coverage (Insurance Research Council 2006).

Both opponents and proponents of an individual health insurance mandate cite the experience with automobile insurance to bolster their cause. Opponents argue that requiring motorists to purchase insurance coverage and imposing penalties for violation have been ineffective at reducing the number of uninsured motorists (Kelly 2004). Proponents contend that efforts in California, Colorado, Georgia, and elsewhere show how data matching and information technology can be used to crack down on uninsured motorists—and, by extension, to enforce an individual health insurance mandate or to identify those to enroll in state health insurance coverage expansions. However, automobile insurance databases have sometimes proved costly, controversial, and error prone. In addition, for most households health insurance costs a lot more than automobile insurance.

Still, compulsory automobile insurance raises some of the same issues as a health insurance mandate. States may determine the extent of the required automobile liability insurance, but people may fail to purchase coverage because the cost is too high or their income is too low. Availability and cost of automobile insurance also depends on the driver's perceived risk. Most states that require automobile insurance have an assigned risk plan to assure that a driver can get coverage. The costs of insuring drivers under an assigned risk plan are high, but insurers must accept their share of those who cannot obtain insurance in the regular market. States generally do not provide subsidies for low-income drivers, although California in 2004 created the California Low Cost Automobile Insurance Program to offer insurance at subsidized rates to people meeting a "good-driver" standard.

Automobile insurance also illustrates the relationship between mandatory coverage and the pricing of insurance. Low-risk drivers often pay slightly higher premiums because their insurance companies are required to participate in the assigned risk pools; correspondingly, high-risk drivers pay lower rates than required to fully reflect their risk. However, automobile insurers still offer lower prices to individuals they perceive as belonging to lower-risk groups. In the case of health insurance, such pricing would favor younger people; with automobile insurance, the young are disfavored. The point here is simply that automobile insurance shows how an individual mandate is likely to be accompanied by requirements on insurers to accept high-risk policyholders—and these must be administered as well.

Federal Debt Collection

The federal government has faced difficulties in collecting nontax debts owed to it by the public. In fiscal year 2006, delinquent nontax debt totaled $65 billion, of which $44 billion had been delinquent for more than 180 days. Federal loan programs, primarily direct student loans, comprised 78 percent of total delinquencies (U.S. Department of the Treasury 2007).

Excluding loans, the largest amount of delinquent debt ($3.3 billion) is owed to the Social Security Administration (SSA). Debts to SSA arise when the agency pays an individual too much in benefits—for example, when someone receives excess Supplemental Security Income benefits because he or she fails to report an increase in income, or when a family member fails to report a Social Security recipient's death. The agency finds it relatively easy to collect overpayments when the debtor is still eligible for monthly benefits; in such cases, the overpayment is gradually recovered through the reduction of subsequent monthly payments. When the debtor is no longer on the benefit rolls, however, debt recovery is more difficult. Despite use of increasingly aggressive debt-collection tools, the amount of SSA's delinquent debt has increased by more than half in the last four years (U.S. Social Security Administration 2006).

Tax Compliance

Tax authorities often are the enforcing authority for mandates. As with the collection of excess benefits, however, tax officials rely, where possible, on receiving payments over the course of the year so that fewer liabilities are owed with year-end filing. Withholding on wages and periodic estimated taxes are examples of the methods used. Also, the IRS benefits from modest amounts of overwithholding during the year to help with enforcement, as those overwithheld tend to be more compliant than those underwithheld.

The IRS estimates that when there is withholding on wages, there is just under 99 percent compliance with the tax laws. With information reporting from third parties (for example, banks reporting to IRS the interest payments paid to individuals) but no withholding, compliance is on the order of 95 percent. Finally, where there is neither information reporting nor withholding, compliance is often less than 50 percent (Toder 2007).

The earned income tax credit (EITC) provides a variety of lessons for enforcement by tax authorities. Noncompliance with the EITC is fairly high, recently estimated to be between 27 and 32 percent (U.S. Department of the Treasury 2002). One major complication derives from determining in whose household or tax unit a child resides. Rules vary widely across welfare and tax programs, and children are often claimed for one tax unit when they fit into another, as in multigenerational households or when parents are present for only part of the year.

Although the EITC is technically available, at least in part, throughout the year, few employees take advantage of this option. One of the major problems is that the amount of subsidy is generally unknown at the start of the year because the amount varies widely with moderate changes in income. Also, many families gain or lose members throughout the year due to marriage, divorce, and births; these changes also affect considerably the size of subsidy.

Administrative Considerations

Individual mandates to obtain health insurance pose several administrative issues: how to encourage voluntary compliance with the mandate, what mechanisms to establish to enforce compliance, what agency or agencies should administer the mandate, and how extensive the mandate should be. Administration must also be coordinated with administration of subsidies to purchase insurance, as well as with other public insurance programs such as Medicaid and SCHIP.

Encouraging Voluntary Compliance

An individual mandate to purchase health insurance presumes that most of those affected can purchase insurance at an affordable price. Thus, proposals for individual mandates usually also provide for guaranteed issue of insurance, an insurance exchange or other arrangement to make insurance universally available, and some form of subsidies for low-income people. Clearly, in these cases achieving compliance with an individual mandate runs in parallel with efforts to make it easy for people to enroll for insurance and obtain available subsidies. A mandate also may apply more selectively, as when it is confined to those who pay income taxes, which excludes many lower-income individuals.

Although the term *play-or-pay* typically applies only to employer mandates, it can describe an individual mandate as well, to the extent that individuals face a choice between obtaining insurance and paying a penalty. Indeed, a subsidy contains an implicit play-or-pay mandate: The recipient must spend the subsidy on insurance (play) or lose it (pay).

Just like some play-or-pay provisions applying to employers, individual mandates may serve two purposes that fall short of universal health insurance. First, they can serve as a way of charging those without insurance for their implicit coverage under Medicaid or other public arrangements should they fall on hard times. Second, they can reduce the net difference in cost between buying and not buying insurance and thus serve as an inducement to buy.

Many individuals simply hate paying penalties, regardless of how mild they are; the incentive effect of a mandate may therefore be higher than the economic cost it imposes for not buying insurance. Thus, a mandate can be used as a tool toward achieving more universal insurance, even when administrative or equity issues prevent assessing a large penalty for not meeting the mandate and even when subsidies themselves may be inadequate for many people.

The cost of complying with the mandate will depend on the coverage of the required insurance policy, the rules governing the pricing of policies, other aspects of the health care financing system, and the overall cost of the health care delivery system. In the Netherlands, the average premium in 2007 was about $1,650 a year. In Switzerland, the premium varies by canton and averages about $3,100 a year for an adult. In Massachusetts, the cost of minimum creditable coverage can reach $4,920 for a person age fifty or over in the most expensive region of the state.

The lower the insurance premium, the easier it is to get people to comply with a mandate. Some proposals hold down premiums by providing for government reinsurance of high-cost cases. Of course, it is possible to shift rather than remove administrative problems by moving them from the mandate side to the subsidy side; in aggregate, they likely rise together with the cost of insurance.

Enforcement and Penalties

What penalties might apply with an individual mandate? In Massachusetts, where individuals are required to provide information about their health insurance status on their state income tax form, individuals could lose their personal income tax exemption for 2007. Massachusetts thus adopted the type of mandate first suggested by Steuerle (1994)—denial of certain tax preferences such as the personal exemption. However, this was for the federal level; at the state level, this exemption is of fairly limited value.

In 2008, Massachusetts began imposing monthly penalties for failure to comply with the individual mandate. The penalty is equal to half of the cost of the most affordable health plan available. Massachusetts also provides for waiving the penalty for certain people, such as those eligible for premium subsidies or those experiencing financial hardship.

Even at the federal level, year-end filing may not provide an adequate means of enforcing a mandate if the penalty is large. As noted, the tax authorities have significant problems collecting from those with liabilities that are large relative to their income. Many households have little or no savings from which to draw.

Pauly (1994) has proposed that an individual mandate be enforced through employers. In his plan, "[t]he employer would be required to ascertain whether or not the employee had obtained insurance (including as a member of an employment-related group) and, if not, to withhold from the employee's wages enough to pay for insurance from a government-contracted or government-run insurer of last resort." This idea has much to recommend it, since contemporaneous enforcement is likely to be more effective than retrospective enforcement. By the time a person has gone months without insurance, or has incurred uninsured medical bills, the prospect of recovering back premiums and charges, let alone penalties, is likely to be remote. Similarly, it seems infeasible, or unreasonable, to enforce a mandate by hitting uninsured people with large costs when they need care. However, as noted earlier, employers' compliance with mandates has also been less than complete, and not everyone is connected to an employer.

Administrative Agencies for Mandates and Subsidies

Administration of individual mandates is connected to the administration of premium subsidies. The attempt by states to use mandates and subsidies together reflects the high cost of even a modest health insurance policy. Subsidies by themselves could prove expensive for taxpayers, but mandates by themselves will heavily burden some individuals. Together, however, subsidies and mandates may succeed in creating a larger wedge between buying and not buying insurance, especially for many middle-income families. A crucial administrative issue, then, is whether subsidies and mandates can or should be handled by the same or a different agency.

Prime candidates for administering subsidies are the Internal Revenue Service (or comparable tax authorities, as in the Netherlands and Switzerland), the Social Security Administration (as in the Medicare low-income drug subsidy), state Medicaid agencies (as in Massachusetts), or a new federal or state agency. Whatever agency administers the subsidy, basing eligibility on assets as well as on income would complicate the process. Data on assets are not available, and asset tests have proved to be difficult to administer and to discourage program participation.

If the IRS is the administrative agency—at least for taxpayers—then a more complete reconciliation report might be filed once at the end of the year with the IRS. But if the cost of the mandate and the size of the subsidy is to be calculated by the employer and reflected in withholding with each paycheck, then more regular reports may be required. The great advantage of reflecting both the mandate and the subsidy in withholding (and effectively using the IRS as an enforcement agency) is twofold: People would see more immediately the consequence of not buying insurance, and regular calculations, reflected in withholding, reduce the likelihood that the government will have to collect much, if anything, at the end of the year.

An alternative approach that avoids an end-of-year reconciliation is to base eligibility for the subsidy, in most cases, on recent rather than current income. In the case of the low-income subsidy under Part D of Medicare, for example, the Social Security

Administration determines eligibility for the subsidy for the upcoming year using the most recent available data from the IRS. Thus, in late 2008, the SSA determines eligibility for the subsidy for 2009 using tax data for 2007. SSA generally reviews changes in income, resources, household composition, and other factors only once a year. In Switzerland, most eligible people receive their subsidy automatically based on their taxable income in the year before last. Under circumstances like these, of course, provision may need to be made to assist those who experience a major change in circumstances, such as the birth of a child or loss of a job.

Pauly (1994) suggests, "[T]he credit that would pay the subsidy need be no more difficult to administer than (and could even be merged with) the earned income credit. Finally, persons already receiving welfare payments could have their credit incorporated with their other government payment." Pauly may be too sanguine, especially about using a heavily income-related design for either a mandate or a subsidy. Although individuals may arrange for monthly payment of the earned income credit, most do not receive credits until they file their tax return. Also, government would still need a backup system to handle those who do not have sufficient earnings. (The EITC is based on earnings, so the IRS has some advantages in administering that provision, since it has good annual records on earnings. It is not the administrative agency for welfare programs that include many people with limited attachment to the labor force.)

Health mandates and subsidies administered by the IRS raise some but not all of the same types of problems that occur in the EITC. When mandates and subsidies vary widely with annual income, the employer has trouble knowing how much to reflect in withholding, and the individual has trouble knowing for how much he or she qualifies.

Ways are available to minimize this last set of administrative problems. For instance, if the subsidy is essentially flat or equal per person, then it is fairly easy to know what the subsidy is for each pay period. With a mandate, a flat amount would also be easy to reflect in withholding if the mandate is to apply at low- and moderate-income levels. Another route to simplicity is for the mandate simply to deny some tax benefits already reflected in withholding—the standard deduction, the child credit, and so on. Withholding tables are already set up to reflect the presence or absence of these items. If the penalty for lack of health insurance extended to denial of some of the EITC, it probably would be administrable as well, to the extent that the EITC is paid to most people only at the end of the year.

Steuerle (2003) has suggested that receiving the child credit, or at least increases in the child credit, could be made contingent on maintaining insurance for the child. Because the credit is a relatively flat amount throughout much of the income distribution, this type of approach would also be fairly easy to administer. The credit is only partially refundable, however, so that separate administration would be required if the child credit were extended much lower in the income distribution and made fully refundable. In all likelihood, a separate agency would be required for that population. Also, at that point, the credit would probably be integrated into Medicaid and SCHIP.

When the amount of the mandate and credit are known, insurance companies likely would get into the business of finding uninsured people, as they could more immediately sell them on making use of their subsidies and avoiding penalties associated with mandates. Indeed, with a flat or equal subsidy, it would be possible to let insurance companies file with an administrative agency, and skip individual filing for the subsidy almost altogether.

In 1990, Congress provided a limited individual health insurance tax credit for children as an addition to the EITC. A subsequent congressional investigation found that, in response to the credit, some insurance companies marketed policies with very limited benefits to unsuspecting low-income families. The credit came to be viewed as unwieldy and subject to abuse and was repealed in 1993. Although many problems were related to its limited scope, the experience warns us that issues of consumer protection can easily arise.

Family structure creates further complications for a mandate. A mandate on adults in a household raises issues of coverage for spouses, persons living together but not married, persons claiming to have common-law marriages, and multigenerational households such as parents living with adult children. Also, various programs employ various definitions of a household, so complications could arise if the health mandate chose a different definition than that used by the administrative agency or agencies enforcing a mandate or subsidy.

An added administrative issue is the interaction between new income-conditioned subsidies and existing means-tested programs. Instability of insurance coverage is a problem for public insurance programs, chiefly Medicaid and SCHIP. Coordination of old and new programs will obviously be required, and rules will be needed to determine what happens to a person who moves from one to another. In Massachusetts, for example, determinations of eligibility for the new subsidized Commonwealth Care program are made by the state Medicaid agency.

Another decision related to the choice of administrative agency is whether an individual mandate should be enforced through multiple channels. In the New America Foundation's proposal, for example, employers, tax authorities, health care providers, schools, and automobile insurers would all be required to ask for documented proof of health insurance coverage and to inform a new "insurance market administrator" of individuals who lacked coverage (Nichols 2007). More ways of enforcement would make a mandate more effective, but also more intrusive. At the same time, more immediate identification of the uninsured would allow for earlier efforts to overcome inertia, which can be a strong factor over and above economic incentives in determining why some fail to insure, and reduces the size of any penalties.

Extent of Mandates and Subsidies

These administrative issues pose greater challenges when the objective is to provide very large subsidies and mandates. Health insurance for a family often runs as much as $12,000 a year. The larger the subsidy, the more income conditioning is likely to save on costs. Depending on how it is structured, income conditioning of large subsidies and mandates can significantly increase marginal tax rates on additional earnings, as well as exacerbate marriage penalties. Similarly, the more costly the mandate, the more difficult it becomes to set penalties that would be large enough to ensure substantial compliance yet could be enforced or collected.

Graetz and Mashaw (1999) write, "Make no mistake: an individual mandate, whether to obtain automobile liability insurance, vaccinate your children before sending them to school, or pay your income taxes both encounters evasion and sometimes entails intrusive enforcement. This is a public 'bad' that must be weighed against the public 'goods' of universal health insurance protection and a fair distribution of the costs of coverage."

Automatic Enrollment

In recent years, behavioral economists have become increasingly aware of the power of inertia in individual behavior and have developed innovative approaches to harness that inertia in beneficial ways. They have found, for example, that more people contribute to retirement savings plans if they are enrolled automatically at work (but can opt out) than if they must take active steps to enroll. This finding has led to proposals that most firms be required to enroll new workers automatically in a retirement savings plan.

This same approach—termed *automatic enrollment* or *default enrollment*—could be employed as a backstop, or as an alternative, to a mandate to purchase health insurance. In Switzerland, for example, cantons (states) automatically enroll in a private health plan everyone who fails to comply with the individual mandate. In this case, the insured person does not have a choice of an insurer; he or she is billed by the insurance plan and is liable for payment of the premium. In the United States, enrollment in Medicare's Supplementary Medical Insurance is voluntary, but nearly universal, because applicants for hospital insurance are enrolled automatically in Supplementary Medical Insurance unless they opt out. At the start of Medicare Part D in 2006, beneficiaries dually eligible for Medicare and Medicaid were automatically enrolled in a low-cost prescription drug plan, although they could still select a plan of their own choosing. In addition, many low-income people were automatically enrolled in the low-income prescription drug subsidy.

As part of a plan for achieving near-universal health coverage, those without insurance could be automatically enrolled either in a private plan available through an insurance exchange (as in Switzerland or Medicare Part D) or in an existing or new public program (as in Supplementary Medical Insurance). Blumberg and Holahan (2008) propose that "the state deem all residents to be covered and that the tax penalty serve as a way of collecting unpaid premiums." Either way, enrolling people automatically in a health plan would encounter some of the same administrative issues as enforcing an individual mandate. Automatic enrollment might prove more successful if it were viewed as simpler and less punitive than an individual mandate.

Conclusion

Individual or employer mandates comprise part of the latest health care initiatives or laws in several states, as well as in countries such as the Netherlands and Switzerland. They also have been proposed by a number of elected officials and candidates for elective office. Strong equity and efficiency arguments can be made in favor of mandates in a world where the public provides some backup public insurance for almost any household that does not buy insurance on its own. To work effectively, however, mandates must be administered well.

Mandates can be administered effectively if not too much is demanded of them—that is, if the size of the insurance requirement is not too high and the size of the related penalty is not so large that compliance and enforcement are threatened. Among the more administrable types of penalties are denying tax benefits to individuals who do not buy insurance and engaging employers in a play-or-pay mandate that requires some contribution to government when they do not separately pay toward an employee's insurance.

A mandate can stand alone, but it generally forms part of a system of regulations and subsidies that aim to make health insurance more available and affordable. Even at a moderate level of penalty and mandate, however, many administrative issues arise: which household members to include, what constitutes qualified insurance, how to deal with multiple employers for the same family, and whether to extend a mandate below tax thresholds for individuals.

If these administrative considerations are given adequate weight, it is possible to set up effective incentives to buy at least a low-cost insurance policy through a combination of subsidies and mandates. This arrangement might go a long way toward encouraging people to buy insurance even when a subsidy and mandate do not together make it more expensive to be uninsured than insured. If administrative issues are only lightly considered, however, then more can be asked of mandates than they might be able to deliver.

References

Ashenfelter, Orley, and Robert S. Smith. 1979. "Compliance with the Minimum Wage Law." *Journal of Political Economy* 87 (2): 333–50.

Blumberg, Linda, and John Holahan. 2008. *Do Individual Mandates Matter?* Washington, DC: Urban Institute.

Fiscal Policy Institute. 2007. *New York State Workers' Compensation: How Big Is the Coverage Shortfall?* Washington, DC: Fiscal Policy Institute.

Graetz, Michael J. 1993. "Universal Coverage Without an Employer Mandate." *Domestic Affairs* 2 (Winter): 79–104.

Graetz, Michael J., and Jerry L. Mashaw. 1999. *True Security: Rethinking American Social Insurance.* New Haven, CT: Yale University Press.

Hawaii Uninsured Project. 2003. *Hawaii's Prepaid Health Care Act Ensures Health Coverage for Some Workers.* http://www.healthcoveragehawaii.org/pdf/PrepaidHealthCareAct.pdf.

Insurance Research Council. 2006. *IRC Estimates More Than 14 Percent of Drivers Are Uninsured.* News release, June 28.

Kelly, Greg. 2004. *Can Government Force People to Buy Insurance?* Alexandria, VA: Council for Affordable Health Insurance.

Kronick, Richard, Todd Gilmer, and Thomas Rice. 2004. "The Kindness of Strangers: Community Effects on the Rate of Employer Coverage." *Health Affairs,* 23: w328-w340. http://content.healthaffairs.org/cgi/search?andorexactfulltext=and&resourcetype=1& disp_type=&author1=kronick&fulltext=&pubdate_year=2004&volume=&firstpage= (Accessed 17 November 2008).

Neuhauser, Frank, and Colleen Donovan. 2007. *Fraud in Workers' Compensation Payroll Reporting.* Sacramento, CA: California Commission on Health and Safety and Workers' Compensation.

Nichols, Len M. 2007. *A Sustainable Health System for All Americans.* Washington, DC: New America Foundation.

Pauly, Mark. 1994. "Making a Case for Employer-Enforced Individual Mandates." *Health Affairs* 13 (2): 21–33.

Seiler, Robin. 1994. *The Budgetary Treatment of an Individual Mandate to Buy Health Insurance.* Washington, DC: Congressional Budget Office.

Steuerle, C. Eugene. 1994. "Implementing Employer and Individual Mandates." *Health Affairs* 13 (2): 54–68.

———. 2003. "A Workable Social Insurance Approach to Expanding Health Insurance Coverage." In *Covering America: Real Remedies for the Uninsured,* Vol. 3, ed. Elliot K. Wicks. Washington, DC: Economic and Social Research Institute, December.

Toder, Eric. 2007. *Reducing the Tax Gap—The Illusion of Pain-Free Deficit Reduction.* Washington, DC: Urban Institute.

U.S. Department of Labor. 2007. *FY2006 Performance Budget.* Washington, DC: Employment Standards Administration.

U.S. Department of the Treasury. 2002. *Compliance Estimates for Earned Income Tax Credit Claimed on 1999 Returns.* Washington, DC: Internal Revenue Service.

———. 2007. *U.S. Government Receivables and Debt Collection Activities of Federal Agencies, Fiscal Year 2006 Report to the Congress.* Washington, DC: Financial Management Service.

U.S. Social Security Administration. 2006. *Performance and Accountability Report for FY 2006.* Washington, DC: Social Security Administration.

10

Designing Administrative Organizations for Health Reform

PAUL N. VAN DE WATER

Any plan for expanding health coverage and containing the growth of health costs will necessarily create additional tasks for government, which may be assigned to existing or new governmental entities. Prompted by concerns over perceived political gridlock, the role of special interests, and inadequate or uncertain funding, several recent proposals would create new health-related entities or agencies with substantial independence from the usual political processes. Sometimes these proposed entities are referred to as a "Federal Reserve for Health."

This chapter describes proposals to create new entities or agencies as part of a reformed health coverage system, catalogs major federal executive agencies and nongovernmental entities, and considers issues involved in choosing an appropriate organizational design. (More detailed information about some specific proposals is provided in the appendix to this chapter, available at www. nasi.org.)

Proposals for New Health-Related Organizations

Proposals for new, independent, health-related agencies fall into four categories:

- An entity to conduct research on the comparative effectiveness of health care services,
- A commission or other entity to determine which health care items and services public and private insurers should cover,
- An agency to manage the marketplace where health insurance is sold, and
- An agency to offer health insurance services.

Under some proposals, a single entity would combine two or more of these functions. As the Congressional Budget Office has written, "The appropriate organizational form for any new or expanded federal entity, along with the mechanism and level of funding, may depend in large part on what activities it would carry out" (Congressional Budget Office 2007).

Producing Information on Comparative Effectiveness

In health care, comparative effectiveness analysis is a "rigorous evaluation of the impact of different options that are available for treating a given medical condition for a particular set of patients. Such a study may compare similar treatments, such as competing drugs, or it may analyze very different approaches, such as surgery and drug therapy. The analysis may focus only on the relative medical benefits and risks of each option, or it may also weigh both the costs and benefits of those options" (Congressional Budget Office 2007, 3).

Cost-effectiveness analysis is one category of comparative effectiveness analysis, where resources used in supporting an intervention are measured in monetary terms, but health outcomes or consequences are measured in natural units—number of lives saved, cases diagnosed, cases prevented, or increases in life expectancy or quality-adjusted life years. The strength of cost-effectiveness analysis is that no dollar value is placed on health outcomes or human lives, as in cost-benefit analysis, where costs and benefits are expressed in monetary terms. However, in cost-effectiveness analysis only interventions whose outcomes are measured in equivalent terms can be compared.

Comparative effectiveness analysis is advocated as a way of slowing the growth of health costs without incurring adverse health outcomes. Peter Orszag, since January 2007 the director of the Congressional Budget Office, writes, "The financial incentives for both providers and patients tend to encourage the adoption of more expensive treatments and procedures, even if evidence of their relative effectiveness is limited." He continues, "The expansion of research on comparative effectiveness could help to correct these problems, especially the addition of analyses that both examine the relative medical benefits and risks of each treatment option (for all patients or some subgroup thereof) and weight the benefits against the costs" (Orszag and Ellis 2007, 5).

The Medicare Payment Advisory Commission (MedPAC) (2007) has proposed one of the most detailed and carefully analyzed schemes for producing information on comparative effectiveness. It recommends creation of an independent entity to examine comparative effectiveness of alternative ways of diagnosing and treating health conditions, including drugs, medical devices, surgical procedures, and medical services.

The entity proposed by MedPAC would set research priorities, review existing evidence on comparative effectiveness, conduct or sponsor new studies, ensure that its findings are unbiased and not affected by the interests of researchers or funders, operate under a transparent process, obtain input from stakeholders, re-examine the effectiveness of services as new information and treatments become available, and disseminate its findings widely. Its mission would be "to sponsor studies that compare the clinical effectiveness of a service with its alternatives," but MedPAC "does not rule out" studies of cost-effectiveness as well. MedPAC "envisions that the entity would contract out most of the research to outside groups, including existing governmental agencies, with experience conducting comparative-effectiveness studies," although the entity would need experienced in-house staff to design proposals and monitor contracts. The entity "would have no role in making or recommending either coverage or payment decisions for public or private plans" (MedPAC 2007, 5).

The MedPAC report cites previous proposals by AcademyHealth, Joel Kupersmith and colleagues, Uwe Reinhardt, and Gail Wilensky (MedPAC 2007). As part of comprehensive plans to achieve universal health coverage, Ezekiel Emanuel and Victor Fuchs have proposed an Institute for Technology and Outcomes Assessment (Emanuel and Fuchs 2006, 2007), the Committee for Economic Development has proposed an Institute for Medical Outcomes and Technology Assessment (Committee for Economic Development 2007), and Len Nichols has proposed a Comparative Effectiveness Agency (Nichols 2007).

Some proposals would give the new entity a high degree of independence. The Committee for Economic Development institute would, "like the Federal Reserve Board," be "freestanding and semi-autonomous." It would have a "stable budget," independent of the annual appropriation process, "to provide thorough insulation from short-term political pressures" (Committee for Economic Development 2007). Such proposals are prompted by unhappy experience with prior efforts at technology assessment by government. The Office of Technology Assessment, a congressional agency, was abolished in 1995, and the predecessor to the Agency for Healthcare Research and Quality (AHRQ) faced a near-death experience in the same year after surgeons objected to its guidelines for back surgery (Lewis 1995; Institute of Medicine 2008). Proponents may also have in mind efforts by the Department of Health and Human Services to alter AHRQ's first annual report on racial and ethnic disparities in health care.

MedPAC has made no recommendation on how to structure or finance the proposed entity that would produce comparative-effectiveness information, except that the entity should be able to produce research that is viewed as objective and free of bias and conflict of interest, be independent of stakeholders and political pressures, and have stable financing and staffing. The commission's report considers the pros and cons of making the entity a government agency, a public-private partnership (e.g, a federally funded research and development center), or a private-sector organization (e.g., a congressionally chartered nonprofit).

The Children's Health and Medicare Protection Act of 2007 would establish a Center for Comparative Effectiveness Research within AHRQ (Section 904 of H.R. 3162). It would also establish an independent Comparative Effectiveness Research Commission to oversee, evaluate, and set priorities for the center's work. The commission would be comprised of two designated officials of the executive branch and fifteen additional members appointed by the comptroller general for four-year terms. The center and the commission would be supported by a permanent appropriation from a Comparative Effectiveness Research Trust Fund, which would be financed by fees on insured and self-insured health plans and transfers from Medicare.

A January 2008 report by the Institute of Medicine recommends that Congress direct the secretary of health and human services to establish "a single national clinical effectiveness assessment program . . . with the authority and resources to set priorities for and sponsor systematic reviews of clinical effectiveness, and to develop methodologic[al] and reporting standards for conducting systematic reviews and developing clinical guidelines. The Institute of Medicine panel also recommends that the secretary "appoint a broadly representative Clinical Effectiveness Advisory Board to oversee the Program" (Institute of Medicine 2008, 50). The panel, however, does not address the organizational issues of where to place the program and whether it should be public, private, or a public-private collaboration.

Making Coverage Decisions

Any government program to require or provide health insurance coverage requires determining the extent and nature of that coverage. While the law creating the program would most likely specify the scope of coverage to some degree (e.g., by category of service or actuarial value), the continual development of new medical services, drugs, and devices will always require an administrative agency to determine whether specific procedures or technologies should be covered. In the Medicare program, for example, coverage decisions are made by the Centers for Medicare and Medicaid Services (CMS) and its contractors, not only for traditional Medicare but also for participating private (Medicare Advantage) plans (Jost 2005).

Studies of coverage determinations typically find that proponents of new technologies are the most active participants in the process. In a recent international comparative study, for example, Jost concludes that economic and political pressure favors adoption of technology coverage, and that institutions are only partially insulated from this pressure (Jost 2005).

To reduce the influence of health care providers, drug companies, device manufacturers, single-disease organizations, and other interested parties, some have suggested that an independent entity should be created that would not only conduct comparative-effectiveness analyses but also make decisions about which items and services should be covered by public and private health insurance. Leif Haase (2005) has proposed the creation of an agency "to review the cost-effectiveness of medical procedures, therapies, and drugs" and to "fix the basis for coverage decisions for different plan benefit levels." Jost has proposed creation of a federal commission to determine which items and services insurers would cover. Jost makes explicit that his proposed commission would not only initiate and review assessments of comparative effectiveness but would also engage in policy making—for example, weighing costs and benefits of medical services and determining which items or services might prove particularly amenable to being used for risk selection. To shield the commission from political pressure, its members would be appointed by "someone reasonably apolitical" and serve for long terms (Jost 2007).

In Len Nichols's plan for universal coverage, a benefits board would establish a mandated benefits package, which would be the legally required minimum amount of health insurance coverage. The benefits board would also establish a structure of cost sharing, including cost-sharing subsidies for low-income individuals. The board would be "an independent entity" but "would be expected to work closely with Congress, more or less like the Federal Reserve chairman does" (Nichols 2007). Although Nichols suggests that the comptroller general of the United States appoint the members of the benefits board, this arrangement might well be unconstitutional, since the Supreme Court held in *Bowsher v. Synar* (1986) that the comptroller general may not perform an executive function (in that case, sequestration of spending authority under the Balanced Budget Act) because he is part of the legislative branch and subject to removal by Congress alone.

Managing the Marketplace for Health Insurance

Many proposals for expanding health coverage include a national system of health insurance exchanges, which would serve as a central marketplace in which much or all health insurance would be bought and sold. Although these plans differ in their details, the proposed exchanges would perform such functions as establishing a basic benefits package (if not determined by a separate benefits board or commission), creating and managing a market for health insurance, assuring that health insurance plans meet standards of financial soundness and customer service, providing educational material to potential applicants, enrolling people in plans individually or as members of a group, maintaining enrollment information as individual circumstances change, collecting individual premiums and government subsidies (if any), and distributing payments to plans on a risk-adjusted basis.

Nichols suggests that an insurance-purchasing exchange could be managed either by a government agency, like the Federal Employees Health Benefits (FEHB) Program, or by a nonprofit organization, like the Pacific Business Group on Health, which administers health insurance for large employers in California. Exchanges could be organized along state or regional lines (Nichols 2007). Emanuel and Fuchs and the Committee for Economic Development both model their proposed administrative structure—a central board with a network of regional exchanges—on the Federal Reserve System (Emanuel and Fuchs 2007; Committee for Economic Development 2007). In the Committee for Economic Development proposal, the governors of the "Health Fed" would be appointed for fourteen-year terms, and heads of regional exchanges would be selected by the board of governors. The Health Fed would be funded by fees, such as a levy on health insurance premiums, and not subject to annual appropriations. This model is designed to "convey impartiality, expertise, freedom from narrow political interests, stability, and a long-term perspective" (Committee for Economic Development 2007).

Former senate majority leader Tom Daschle (2008) has become an advocate of a Federal Reserve–like health board. Daschle argues that the failure to achieve universal coverage and contain health costs "is rooted in the complexity of the health-care issue, the limitations of our political system, and the power of interest groups . . . that have a direct stake in it." He goes on to say,

> I believe that the only way to solve the health-care crisis is to change the way that we approach the challenge. In this book, I propose a Federal Health Board, modeled loosely on the Federal Reserve System, to do so. It would create a public framework for a largely private health-care delivery system. Its main job would be to develop the standards and structure for a health system that ensures accessible, affordable, and high-quality care. . . . Like the Federal Reserve, the Federal Health Board would be composed of highly independent experts, insulated from politics. Congress and the White House would relinquish some of their health policy decisions to it.

The notion of a Federal Reserve–like board to manage a health insurance exchange appears to have originated in the early 1990s in the work of the Jackson Hole Group, an informal collection of health policy experts. In its original proposal in 1992, the group proposed a "new National Health Board as an independent agency, like the SEC [Securities and Exchange Commission]." In this way, it wrote, "The NHB will be free from day-to-day interference while still accountable to elected political officials." The group rejected "an autonomous Federal Reserve Board model," which "would have too little public accountability given the scale and public sensitivity of health care reforms" (Ellwood, Enthoven, and Etheredge 1992). Soon thereafter, however, one of the leaders of the group described the proposed board differently: "The board would have a status similar to the Federal Reserve Board, insulated from narrow interest-group pressure" (Enthoven and Singer 1994).

In 1999, Senator John Breaux and Representative Bill Thomas proposed an independent board to manage the Medicare program. Their proposal apparently stemmed from a desire to remove Congress from many of the details of administering Medicare and a belief that an inherent conflict exists in having a single agency administer a government-run fee-for-service plan and a system of private insurance plans. Breaux and Thomas proposed that the role of the Health Care Financing Administration, now renamed the Centers for Medicare and Medicaid Services (CMS), be limited to operating Medicare's fee-for-service program and that both the fee-for-service program and private plans be regulated by an independent "Medicare Board." They cited the Federal Reserve Board and the Federal Retirement Thrift Investment Board as possible models (National Bipartisan Commission on the Future of Medicare 1999).

Offering a Public Health Insurance Plan

In addition to serving as a clearinghouse for private insurance plans, a new agency might also offer a competing public health insurance plan. In Jacob Hacker's proposal, for example, "every legal resident of the United States who lacks access to Medicare or good workplace coverage would be able to buy into the 'Health Care for America Plan,' a new public insurance pool modeled after Medicare." Like Medicare, this plan would offer participants a choice of a public fee-for-service program and a range of private plans (Hacker 2007).

Hacker's proposal appears to combine the operation of the public insurance plan and supervision of the private plans in one administrative agency, as is now the case with Medicare, but these two functions could potentially be separated, as in the Breaux-Thomas proposal. In the Daschle proposal, the "Federal Health Board" "would work with Medicare to develop a public insurance option for the [national purchasing] pool, designing it to compete with private insurance plans on the FEHBP menu" (Daschle 2008). Daschle does not specify which agency would administer the public program.

Federal Agencies and Public-Private Entities

What types of organizational entities would best be tasked with carrying out the health-related functions just identified? "In organizational design," says Thomas Stanton, "the key is to fit the appropriate organizational form to the purposes to be achieved. . . . Once policy makers have identified the intended goals and purposes of an agency, they can look to existing organizations for possible models that they might adapt" (Stanton 2002). We therefore turn to identifying the menu of organizational options and the issues that arise in choosing among them (see Table 10.1).

For the most part, the federal government carries out its activities through agencies in the executive branch, of which the president is chief executive. However, the federal government has also created many public-private and private entities to help achieve public purposes. Governmental and quasi-governmental organizations exist in almost infinite variety, and the following taxonomy lists only the types that are relevant in the present context.

Federal Executive Agencies

The United States Government Manual identifies only two types of executive agencies—(1) departments and (2) independent establishments and government corporations (Federal Register 2007). A more refined taxonomy might distinguish independent regulatory commissions, government corporations, and other types of independent agencies, although the distinctions among these remaining categories are often blurred.

Executive Departments

The fifteen cabinet departments (State, Treasury, Defense, and so on) have been created as administrative agencies to assist the president in implementing laws enacted by Congress (Warren 1998). Executive agencies are therefore subject to many forms of presidential control (Garcia 1999):

Table 10.1

Types of Federal Agencies and Public-Private Entities and Their Characteristics

Type of Organization	Funding Authority	Operational Flexibilities	Political Independence and Accountability	Management Structure
Executive Departments	Annual appropriations; occasionally, permanent appropriations	Subject to general laws affecting personnel, contracting, disclosure, and due process; flexibility sometimes provided	Subject to presidential direction and control; agency head serves at the pleasure of the president	Headed by cabinet secretary
Independent Regulatory Commissions	Annual appropriations	Subject to general laws affecting personnel, contracting, disclosure, and due process	Regulations not subject to executive review; members appointed for staggered 5- to 7-year terms; some political balance required	Multi-member boards
Government Corporations	Income from business-type transactions; appropriations generally not required	Perform business-like functions; exempt from some or many legal limitations that apply to agencies funded by annual appropriations	May be independent entity with appointed board or part of an executive department	Executive appointed by the board manages operations
Other Independent Executive Agencies	Annual appropriations; occasionally, permanent appropriations	Subject to general laws affecting personnel, contracting, disclosure, and due process	Varies	Varies

Federal Reserve System	Income from U.S. securities acquired through open-market operations; charges for services	Exempt from many federal procedural requirements	Independent central bank; governors appointed for 14-year terms; chair appointed for 4-year term	7-member Board of Governors; 12 regional Federal Reserve Banks
Legislative Branch Agencies	Annual appropriations	Subject to most general laws affecting personnel, contracting, disclosure, and due process	Responsible to the Congress; serve in advisory capacity	Varies; may not carry out executive functions
Federally Funded Research and Development Centers	From the budget of the sponsoring agency and private sources	Generally exempt from federal procedural requirements	Under guidance and oversight of sponsoring federal agency	Managed by nongovernmental organizations
Agency-Related Nonprofits	From private sources	Generally exempt from federal procedural requirements	Legal relationship with a federal department or agency	Varies
Congressionally Chartered Organizations	From specific appropriations and private sources	Generally exempt from federal procedural requirements	Nongovernmental	Varies

- Each department is headed by a secretary, who is appointed by the president, confirmed by the Senate, and serves at the pleasure of the president. Noncareer appointees below the secretarial level are recruited and screened by the White House Office of Presidential Personnel, and many subcabinet positions require Senate confirmation.
- By statute or executive order, each department's budget request, staffing levels, congressional communications, and data-collection activities are subject to review or clearance by the Office of Management and Budget in the Executive Office of the President. The Office of Personnel Management determines how many senior executive service positions each agency will have.
- The Department of Justice serves as the central litigating authority for executive departments.
- The Office of Management and Budget reviews and clears newly developed regulations.

For the most part, funding for personnel costs and other day-to-day operating expenses of the cabinet departments depends on annual appropriations by Congress. Other governmental organizations may be exempt from some presidential or congressional controls.

Most federal health agencies—AHRQ, the Centers for Disease Control and Prevention, CMS, the Food and Drug Administration, the Health Resources and Services Administration, the Indian Health Service, and the National Institutes of Health—are part of the Department of Health and Human Services. Major health programs administered by other departments or independent agencies include military health care (Department of Defense), veterans' health care (Department of Veterans Affairs), the Federal Employee Health Benefits Program (Office of Personnel Management), and the Special Supplemental Nutrition Program for Women, Infants, and Children (Department of Agriculture).

Independent Regulatory Commissions

A number of commissions have been established outside the executive departments to make rules and orders to regulate specific activities or industries (Warren 1998). These so-called independent regulatory commissions include the Commodity Futures Trading Commission, Consumer Product Safety Commission, Federal Communications Commission, Federal Election Commission, Federal Mine Safety and Health Review Commission, Federal Trade Commission, National Labor Relations Board, National Transportation Safety Board, Nuclear Regulatory Commission, Occupational Safety and Health Review Commission, Postal Rate Commission, Securities and Exchange Commission, and United States International Trade Commission.

Several structural and procedural safeguards are designed to provide a substantial degree of independence for these commissions. They typically consist of three to five members, who are appointed by the president with the consent of the Senate. The members serve staggered five- to seven-year terms and cannot be removed except for cause. No more than a simple majority of a commission may consist of members of the same political party. Regulations issued by independent, multiheaded boards and commissions are not subject to review and clearance by the Office of Management and Budget (Garcia 1999). However, commissions generally remain subject to budgetary controls imposed by the president and Congress and to congressional oversight.

Government Corporations

Government corporations are agencies that perform a businesslike function and that are potentially self-sustaining through revenues generated by the sale of goods or services. For example, Amtrak is in the business of passenger rail transportation, the Federal Deposit Insurance Corporation charges for deposit insurance, the Tennessee Valley Authority sells power, and the U.S. Postal Service delivers mail. Other government corporations that are not part of cabinet departments include the Export-Import Bank, Overseas Private Investment Corporation, and Pension Benefit Guaranty Corporation. These corporations are governed by boards of directors appointed by the president and confirmed by the Senate. An executive appointed by the board typically manages the day-to-day operations of the corporation.

Some government corporations are part of executive departments and fall under the policy supervision and oversight of a cabinet secretary (Rivlin 1995). For example, Federal Prison Industries is overseen by the Bureau of Prisons in the Department of Justice, and the Federal Housing Administration is part of the Department of Housing and Urban Development.

Independent government corporations are generally included in the Budget of the U.S. Government, although they typically do not require annual appropriations, except when the government provides a subsidy. To that extent, wholly owned government corporations are exempt from many of the legal limitations that apply to agencies funded by annual appropriations (Stanton 2002). Ultimately, however, a government corporation will have as much or as little independence as Congress allows. Mark Merlis reports that different corporations were subject to as few as two and as many as fourteen out of fifteen laws imposing management requirements on federal agencies (Merlis 2000).

Other Types of Independent Executive Agencies

Several independent agencies—for example, the Environmental Protection Agency, Federal Retirement Thrift Investment Board, National Aeronautics and Space Administration, Office of Personnel Management, National Science Foundation, Peace Corps, Small Business Administration, and Social Security Administration—do not fit neatly into any of the previous categories. They are subject to most of the same laws and requirements as executive departments but, except for the Environmental Protection Agency, do not benefit from the prestige and presidential access that attach to cabinet status. (The administrator of the Environmental Protection Agency has been accorded cabinet-level rank.) Two of these independent agencies deserve special mention because they are sometimes cited as models for new health-related agencies.

The Social Security Administration manages the Social Security retirement, survivors, and disability insurance program and the Supplemental Security Income program for low-income aged and disabled persons and also performs many operational functions for Medicare. It has a staff of fifty-nine thousand and an administrative budget of some $9.5 billion (U.S. Office of Management and Budget 2007). The Social Security Administration was made an independent agency by the Social Security Independence and Program Improvements Act of 1994. "Proponents of SSA's [the Social Security Administration's] independence wanted to insulate it from everyday political, fiscal, and operational policy decisions of the Government" (DiSimone 1995), but that hope was unrealistic and has not been fulfilled. The 1994 act requires the commissioner of social security to prepare an annual budget for the Social Security Administration, which is to be submitted by the president to the Congress without revision along with the president's budget. This requirement is being satisfied only nominally through the inclusion of a paragraph in the budget's appendix, and appropriations for the agency's administrative expenses have been tight. Policy making for Social Security remains directed from the White House. The commissioner now has a six-year term, although the workability of this arrangement has yet to be tested when the presidency changes hands from one political party to another.

The Federal Retirement Thrift Investment Board manages the Thrift Savings Plan, a defined-contribution retirement savings program for participating employees of the federal government. The five members of the board are appointed by the president with the advice and consent of the Senate and serve on a part-time basis. The board appoints a full-time executive director, who is responsible for the day-to-day operation of the agency. The board and executive director serve as fiduciaries and manage the investments of the Thrift Savings Fund (now more than $230 billion) on behalf of participants. The board employs a staff of seventy-five and incurs annual administrative expenses of about $90 million. These administrative costs are financed from the Thrift Savings Fund and do not require annual appropriation (U.S. Office of Management and Budget 2007).

Federal Reserve System

From 1836, when the charter of the Second Bank of the United States expired, until 1913, when President Woodrow Wilson signed the law establishing the Federal Reserve, the United States had no central bank. During this long interregnum the concept of central banking remained controversial, and the Federal Reserve's unique structure reflects the historic circumstances of its birth—what one observer calls "the country's abiding fear of concentrated financial power" (Lowenstein 2008).

The Federal Reserve System comprises a board of governors and twelve regional Federal Reserve Banks. The seven members of the board of governors are appointed by the president and confirmed by the Senate for fourteen-year terms. The chairman and vice chairman of the board are named by the president from among the members and confirmed by the Senate for a term of four years. Each of the Federal Reserve Banks is supervised by a board of nine directors. Six directors are elected by member banks in the district, and three are appointed by the board. The directors appoint the Federal Reserve Bank presidents (the chief executive officers) to five-year terms, subject to approval by the board.

The Federal Reserve is responsible for conducting monetary policy in pursuit of stable prices and maximum employment. It is an independent central bank because its decisions do not need to be ratified by the president or anyone else in the executive branch. The Federal Open Market Committee oversees open market operations, the principal tool of monetary policy. The committee comprises the seven members of the board of governors, the president of the Federal Reserve Bank of New York, and presidents of four other Federal Reserve Banks, who serve as voting members on a rotating basis. One contemporary observer describes the Federal Open Market Committee as "an unwieldy and archaic body in the best of times" (Lowenstein 2008). The Federal Reserve also plays a major role in supervising and regulating the banking system and operating the payment system, including the distribution of cash and the clearance of checks and electronic payments (Board of Governors 2005).

The income of the Federal Reserve derives primarily from interest on the U.S. government securities that it acquires through open-market operations. The Federal Reserve also receives revenue from priced services, primarily check clearing. The system's income is available to pay its operating expenses (an estimated $3.3 billion in 2007) without congressional appropriation or review by the Office of Management and Budget (Board of Governors 2007). The rest of the system's income ($32 billion in 2007) is returned to the Treasury.

Legislative Branch Agencies

Several agencies, boards, and commissions—for example, the Government Accountability Office, the Congressional Budget Office, and MedPAC—are located in the legislative branch of the federal government. These organizations assist Congress in undertaking its legislative functions and serve Congress in a staff role or an advisory capacity. Any attempt to assign executive functions to a congressional agency would most likely "violate the Constitution's command that Congress play no direct role in the execution of the laws" (*Bowsher v. Synar*).

MedPAC, for example, is a seventeen-member commission that advises Congress on issues affecting the Medicare program, including payment rates, access to care, quality of care, and the interaction of Medicare policies with health care delivery generally. Commissioners are appointed to three-year terms by the comptroller general (who heads the Government Accountability Office) and serve part-time. The members include health care providers, payers, employers, consumers, biomedical and health services researchers, and health economists, but providers may not constitute a majority (Section 1805 of the Social Security Act).

Public-Private Entities

Sometimes the federal government carries out public purposes through nongovernmental organizations. Such entities are variously called public-private entities, quasi-governmental organizations, or private instrumentalities of government. Three types of public-private entities have been suggested as possible producers of information on comparative effectiveness: federally funded research and development centers, agency-related nonprofit organizations, and congressionally chartered nonprofit organizations. These entities have some legal connection to the federal government and may receive most or all of their funding from the federal government, but they are not federal government agencies. We do not consider government-sponsored enterprises, government-chartered and privately owned institutions created by Congress to help make credit more available to certain sectors of the economy (Kosar 2007).

Federally Funded Research and Development Centers

Federally funded research and development centers (FFRDCs) are nonprofit, private organizations that federal agencies sponsor to meet technical or research needs. FFRDCs are managed by nongovernmental organizations, including industrial firms, universities and colleges, and other nonprofit institutions, under the overall guidance and oversight of the sponsoring agency. Federal funding comes from the budget of the organization within the sponsoring agency that requests the work. An FFRDC may receive up to 30 percent of its funding from private sources (Institute of Medicine 2007).

Nine departments or agencies sponsor thirty-eight FFRDCs. The Department of Energy sponsors sixteen, and the Department of Defense sponsors ten (National Science Foundation 2007). For example, the National Cancer Institute at Frederick, operated by four firms for the National Institutes of Health, provides scientific and technical support services for programs of the National Cancer Institute. The Homeland Security Institute, administered by Analytic Services, Inc., evaluates systems and technologies and conducts risk analyses for the Department of Homeland Security (Institute of Medicine 2007). Fermi National Accelerator Laboratory, administered by a consortium of universities for the Department of Energy, conducts basic research in high-energy physics and related disciplines. If an FFRDC were established to conduct comparative-effectiveness analyses, it might be affiliated with AHRQ (Institute of Medicine 2007).

Establishment of an FFRDC does not absolve the sponsoring agency of responsibility if a problem arises. In 2003, for example, the Department of Energy put the management of Los Alamos National Laboratory up for competitive bidding after a series of security, safety, and financial lapses by its then operator, the University of California (Broad 2005). Nor do FFRDCs escape the uncertainties of the congressional appropriation process. Unanticipated reductions in spending for high-energy physics in the fiscal year 2008 appropriation required Fermi to lay off staff and furlough the rest for two days a month (Chang 2007).

Agency-Related Nonprofit Organizations

The term *agency-related nonprofit organization* covers several disparate types and an indeterminate number of organizations that have a legal relationship with a department or agency of the federal government. Sometimes agencies have found it useful to create such organizations to accept and administer gifts of money and property. The most prominent example is the National Park Foundation, established in 1967, which accepts and administers gifts given to the National Park Service. The secretary of the interior chairs the board and appoints its members. The foundation is viewed as an adjunct activity of the Department of the Interior and is controlled by the department, although the foundation is off budget, and its employees are not federal employees (Kosar 2007).

Another such organization is the Foundation for the National Institutes of Health (FNIH). Congress established the foundation as a nonprofit corporation in 1996 to support the research priorities of the National Institutes of Health by raising private-sector funds to stimulate and facilitate the formation of public-private partnerships (FNIH 2007a). The foundation is involved in nearly fifty public-private partnerships and has raised approximately $350 million since its inception, including $200 million from the Bill and Melinda Gates Foundation for the Grand Challenges in Global Health initiative (FNIH 2007b). Members of the foundation's board are appointed under the bylaws of the foundation, and the directors of the National Institutes of Health and the Food and Drug Administration are ex officio members (as clarified by Public Law 109–482, Section 107).

Congressionally Chartered Organizations

Congressionally chartered nonprofit organizations represent still another category of quasi-governmental organizations. Under Subtitle II of Title 36 of the U.S. Code, Congress has chartered ninety-two "patriotic and national organizations." The federal chartering process is largely honorific, and in recent years the congressional committees of jurisdiction have attempted to place a moratorium on new charters (Kosar 2007).

Congressionally chartered organizations do not receive direct federal appropriations. Charters of the National Academy of Public Administration and the National

Academy of Sciences, however, provide that the federal government may request that the academies prepare reports in their areas of expertise, and that the reports shall be paid for by the government from appropriations for that purpose (36 U.S.C. 1501, 1503). Although the academies also receive funding from private sources, the bulk of their funding comes from the federal government.

Issues in Choosing an Appropriate Organizational Structure

The choice of an appropriate organizational structure to carry out a particular public function raises several issues. These range from relatively mundane questions of funding sources and managerial flexibility to the highest one—whether the organization should be located in the public or private sector (Merlis 2000; Stanton 2002).

Funding Authority

The degree of control by the president and Congress over a government agency's funding—and the predictability of that funding—may vary, but it is not fully determined by an agency's organizational form. Most federal executive agencies, as previously noted, are subject to the executive budget process and rely on annual congressional appropriations to fund their personnel costs and other operating expenses. Even when administrative expenses are paid out of dedicated taxes or premiums (as for Medicare) or user fees (as with the review of drugs and medical devices by the Food and Drug Administration), annual appropriations action is usually required.

A permanent appropriation—authority to spend money without annual congressional action—can provide a substantial degree of stability in funding for an executive-branch agency. For example, the Office of the Comptroller of the Currency and the Office of Thrift Supervision, which regulate national banks and savings associations, respectively, are authorized to finance their administrative expenses through mandatory assessments on the institutions they regulate (U.S. Office of Management and Budget 2007). Despite this degree of financial independence, the two agencies remain responsible to the president (both are part of the Department of the Treasury) and Congress (through their authorizing statute and periodic oversight).

In contrast, entities that earn money from voluntary, business-type transactions with the public (such as the sale of power or postage) are subject more to market discipline than to the congressional power of the purse, yet even in those cases political and regulatory oversight is never entirely lacking. For example, the Postal Service (a government corporation) is regulated by the Postal Rate Commission (an independent regulatory commission), and Congress continues to name post offices, subsidize certain types of mail, and set the terms under which the Postal Service operates. No new agency can expect to obtain the financial independence of the Federal Reserve System, which can literally issue legal tender.

Operational Flexibilities

Government agencies are subject to various general laws affecting their operations, such as civil service and other personnel rules, contracting and other procurement requirements, and freedom-of-information or government-in-the-sunshine rules. These requirements were originally adopted to ensure organizational accountability, to prevent use of public positions and funds for political patronage or personal profit, and for other laudable purposes, but they are now sometimes seen as "barriers to efficient or responsive operations" (Merlis 2000).

Steps have been taken to provide additional flexibilities for government agencies. The Clinton administration established a new organizational type, the performance-based organization, which provides flexibilities in personnel, contracting, and other areas in exchange for a commitment to achieving performance goals. Only two performance-based organizations have been established—the Office of Federal Student Aid in the Department of Education and the Patent and Trademark Office in the Department of Commerce. "The PBO concept," writes Stanton, "is premised on the assumption that policy issues, which remain with the larger department, can be separated from operations, which are the province of the PBO" (Stanton 2002).

Stanton observes, however, that achievement of operational flexibilities does not necessarily require large-scale organizational redesign, and targeted solutions are often available and usually preferable (Stanton 2002). For example, the Office of Federal Housing Enterprise Oversight, an agency within the Department of Housing and Urban Development that regulates Fannie Mae and Freddie Mac (both government-sponsored enterprises), is exempt from many standard civil service personnel rules, including those for compensation. This exemption allows the office to compete for financial analysts and other skilled personnel. (In 2008, the Federal Housing Finance Agency replaced the Office of Federal Housing Enterprise Oversight.) Similarly, the National Institutes of Health and other agencies are provided special flexibilities for the hiring of physicians. Upon its creation in 2002, the Department of Homeland Security was exempted from many civil service requirements (Lee 2005). In the 2004 National Defense Authorization Act, Congress authorized the Department of Defense to design and implement a new personnel system for its civilian employees (Ballenstedt 2008).

Conversely, public-private organizations can also be made subject to some of the same procedural requirements as government agencies. In 1997, for example, Congress added certain requirements relating to the National Academy of Sciences and the National Academy of Public Administration to the Federal Advisory Committee Act (5 U.S.C. App. § 15).

Political Independence and Accountability

A public or public-private entity must maintain political accountability and avoid undue political interference. There is no clear line, however, separating accountability from interference, and two different observers may not view a situation in the same way.

The typical agency is subject to presidential direction, congressional oversight, and other outside influences, and the results are sometimes open to question. We have already recounted the story of AHRQ, which was almost abolished (Lewis 1995). AHRQ continues to conduct comparative-effectiveness reviews, although this is not the agency's main mission (Medicare Payment Advisory Commission 2007). In a study of selective Medicare coverage determinations, Jost (2005) found that the proponents of new technologies—such as providers, manufacturers, and single-disease advocates—were the only external participants in the decision-making process. Pharmaceutical companies continually attempt to speed up the the Food and Drug Administration's approval of new drugs.

How the form and locus of an organization affect its accountability and independence is not at all clear. If an agency is part of an executive department, the cabinet secretary can potentially assist the agency in the competition for resources and can defend the agency against outside pressures and narrow interests (Stanton 2002). As the previous examples show, however, this is not necessarily the result. Nor does making an agency independent necessarily solve the problem—as the Social Security Administration illustrates. Even (or especially) an independent agency is subject to what is called "regulatory capture"—domination by representatives of the industry that it oversees.

"The usual argument for removing a function from the political process," writes Merlis, "is that it is technical and better managed by experts. However, if an entity is freed from politics, if it does not answer to the President, just whom does it answer to? This is not just a question of accountability, but rather of the entity's own sense of its constituency and hence of its mission." In the case of a Medicare (or other health insurance) board, Merlis asks, who would be its constituency—beneficiaries, taxpayers, insurers, providers (Merlis 2000)?

Some contend that giving an agency more political independence will facilitate decisions that have long-term benefits but impose short-term costs. In the case of the Federal Reserve and other central banks, maintaining price stability or low inflation may require raising interest rates, which is likely to cause higher unemployment and lower plant utilization. An agency that conducts comparative-effectiveness analysis may issue findings that could cause economic losses for some providers (such as back surgeons) or producers (such as manufacturers of drugs or medical devices). An agency that makes coverage decisions will affect the livelihood of providers and manufacturers, the access of people to possibly lifesaving treatments, and the cost of health insurance to those who pay the taxes or premiums. Others would respond, however, that balancing such conflicting objectives is an inherently political responsibility that should not be assigned to an entity that is far removed from the normal political processes.

Management Structure

"As a general rule," writes Stanton, "a single administrator rather than multi-member board best governs a federal agency." Among the limitations of the board structure are the following:

- Members of a government board are likely to have divergent views on some major issues and little incentive to act in a collaborative fashion.
- The board structure can impede accountability, since no one person is fully responsible for decisions.
- Ex officio members of a board may be too busy to attend board meetings, and their alternates may not have the authority to act on their own.
- Boards are less capable than single administrators of timely decision making.

Conversely, Stanton notes, "there are some times when a board structure is appropriate or even necessary for a government agency":

- For regulatory agencies (but not operating agencies), a divergence of viewpoints may help ensure that a fair decision is reached.
- Multimember boards also help insulate agencies from possible political interference. In the case of both the Postal Service and the Federal Retirement Thrift Investment Board, the insertion of a board between the chief executive of the agency and the political process helps "insulate the agency's operations from the kind of untoward political intervention that characterized the Post Office Department" (Stanton 2002).

An advisory board can provide some of the advantages of a governing board without all the disadvantages. Federal agencies are advised by a vast number of boards and committees, whose operations are generally covered by the Federal Advisory Committee Act. Advisory boards provide an opportunity to involve a wide variety of stakeholders and points of view in a deliberative process. Their recommendations, even if only advisory, also provide some degree of political protection for an agency administrator. However, an agency that does not accept an advisory board's recommendation may invite political criticism.

The Commonwealth Health Insurance Connector Authority, which administers many elements of the health reforms in Massachusetts, is "an independent public entity" governed by a ten-member board. The Connector is assigned considerable discretion in important areas, for example, in establishing affordability standards and defining minimum creditable coverage for purposes of the individual mandate. Although described as independent, the Connector is closely tied to the political process. Four members of the board are state officials who serve ex officio, three are appointed by the governor, and three are appointed by the attorney general (who, like the governor, is directly elected). The appointed members are chosen from specified categories (actuaries, health economists, small business, consumer organizations, organized labor, and employee benefit specialists) and serve for three-year terms. The chair of the board, who is the governor's secretary of administration and finance, selects the executive director of the Connector (Commonwealth of Massachusetts 2007). In carrying out its functions, the Connector works closely with many other state agencies, including MassHealth (the state Medicaid agency), the Department of Revenue, the Division of Health Care Finance and Policy, the Division of Insurance, and the Division of Unemployment Assistance.

Public or Private

The ultimate issue in designing an organization to carry out a public purpose is whether it should be governmental or private. As a general principle, activities that are "inherently governmental" must be performed by a government agency and government personnel (U.S. Office of Management and Budget 2003). However, the scope of "inherently governmental" activities is contested and changeable. As part of its effort to put out more activities to private competition, the George W. Bush administration has narrowed the definition of "inherently governmental," though not without controversy. Some states and countries (notably, New Zealand) use private contractors to perform activities similar to those carried out by U.S. government personnel.

According to the current version of the Office of Management and Budget's *Circular A-76,* "An inherently governmental activity is an activity that is so intimately related to the public interest as to mandate performance by government personnel. These activities require the exercise of substantial discretion in applying government authority and/or in making decisions for the government. Inherently governmental activities normally fall into two categories: the exercise of sovereign government authority or the establishment of procedures and processes related to the oversight of monetary transactions or entitlements." The circular takes an additional page and a half to elaborate on this basic definition and to distinguish "inherently governmental" from "commercial activities," which may (but need not) be performed by the private sector.

An important difference between governmental and private entities is the extent of procedural and due process rights they must accord to individuals or businesses affected by their decisions (Merlis 2000; Stanton 2002). Medicare, for example, has formal appeal mechanisms both for health plans and for beneficiaries enrolled in both traditional Medicare and private Medicare Advantage plans. In contrast, most enrollees in employer-sponsored health insurance plans have "only a limited ability to contest plan benefit or coverage decisions" (Merlis 2000). The appropriate scope of appeal rights for those affected by cost-effectiveness studies, coverage decisions, health insurance exchanges, or a new public health insurance plan would doubtless be hotly debated. Although a governmental entity, the Federal Reserve System provides for no public input and no appeal by those affected by its decisions to raise or lower interest rates.

Stanton observes that governmental and private entities also perform differently because they have different incentives (Stanton 2002). Moreover, nonprofit private organizations differ from for-profit ones. None of the health reform proposals discussed here, however, involves creating a for-profit entity to carry out a public purpose.

Conclusion

A National Academy of Public Administration panel has identified several principles to guide the structure and organization of the federal government. One principle is that "organizational design should be tailored to reflect the distinct requirements of different types of government programs so as to facilitate effective performance and maintain accountability." In elaboration, the panel observes, "One size does not fit all types of governmental programs. . . . The distinction between agencies responsible [for] formulating basic policies and those responsible for operations is especially important." The panel expresses particular concern that mislabeling of governmental organizations as quasi- or nongovernmental entities "raise[s] serious constitutional questions" when they "use government powers and funds without being fully accountable either to the President or the Congress" (National Academy of Public Administration 1997).

This principle leads to the conclusion that a quasi-governmental organization might be suitable for producing advisory information on the comparative effectiveness of medical treatments and procedures but not for making coverage decisions or managing the marketplace for health insurance—activities that involve policy formulation. Proposals for a "Health Fed" to manage the health insurance marketplace also raise serious issues of accountability. One of the nation's foremost experts on administrative law and health policy, Jerry Mashaw (2007), observes:

> [A "Health Fed"] would quite clearly be the most powerful administrative agency ever created in the U.S. [The proposal] imagines that all the politically fraught decisions that this agency would be called upon to make (coverage, cost, payment rates, plan regulation, etc., etc.) could be taken out of politics. This seems to me to be "pie in the sky" thinking. There is a good reason that there is one and only one agency like the Fed—long painful experience in every industrialized country has demonstrated that you must have an independent central bank if you want any semblance of monetary stability. And the Fed does only one thing—regulate the money supply (sort of)—a thing that coerces no one and that affects ordinary Americans only indirectly and opaquely. Hence, the Fed's independence is acceptable—but only reluctantly. Maybe a similar case could be made for a health insurance czar, but I suspect that it could be only if one were thinking about a limited technical function—like setting risk adjustment formulae. The reason that no one has fleshed out the idea of a "Health Fed" that would administer a national health insurance system may be that it is simply too implausible to spend much time on.

In the end, as Stanton (2002) observes, "Many problems do not have solutions that involve organizational design. Elements such as leadership, quality of personnel and systems, level of funding, and freedom from unwise legal and regulatory constraints may be as important as organizational structure in the search for solutions to many problems that confront government agencies and programs."

References

AcademyHealth. 2005. *Placement, Coordination, and Funding of Health Services Research within the Federal Government.* Washington, DC: Academy Health.

Ballenstedt, Brittany. 2008. "Freedom to Manage." *Government Executive* (January 1).

Board of Governors of the Federal Reserve System. 2005. *The Federal Reserve System: Purposes and Functions.* Washington, DC: Federal Reserve System.

————. 2007. *Annual Report: Budget Review.* Washington, DC: Federal Reserve System.

Broad, William J. 2005. "California Is Surprise Winner in Bid to Run Los Alamos." *New York Times* (December 22).

Chang, Kenneth. 2007. "Budget Cuts Will Mean Layoffs at Fermilab." *New York Times* (December 22).

Committee for Economic Development. 2007. *Quality, Affordable Health Care for All: Moving Beyond the Employer-Based Health Insurance System.* Washington, DC: CED.

Commonwealth of Massachusetts. 2007. *General Laws, Chapter 176Q, Commonwealth Health Insurance Connector.*

Congressional Budget Office. 2007. *Research on the Comparative Effectiveness of Medical Treatments: Issues and Options for an Expanded Federal Role.* Washington, DC: CBO.

Daschle, Tom. 2008. *Critical: What We Can Do About the Health Care Crisis.* New York: St. Martin's Press.

DiSimone, Rita. 1995. "Social Security Administration Created as an Independent Agency: Public Law 103–296." *Social Security Bulletin,* 58 (1): 57–65.

Ellwood, Paul M., Alain C. Enthoven, and Lynn Etheredge. 1992. "The Jackson Hole Initiatives for a 21st Century American Health Care System." *Health Economics* 1 (3): 149–68.

Emanuel, Ezekiel J., and Victor R. Fuchs. 2006. "Health Care Vouchers—A Proposal for Universal Coverage." *New England Journal of Medicine* 352 (12): 1255–60.

————. 2007. *A Comprehensive Cure: Universal Health Vouchers.* Hamilton Project Discussion Paper 2007–11. Washington, DC: Brookings Institution.

Enthoven, Alain, and Sara J. Singer. 1994. "A Single-Payer System in Jackson Hole Clothing." *Health Affairs* 13 (1): 81–95.

Foundation for the National Institutes of Health (FNIH). 2007a. *2006 Annual Report.* Bethesda, MD: FNIH.

————. 2007b. "Fast Facts." http://www.fnih.org/index.php?option=com_content&task= view&id=419&Itemid=37 (Accessed 18 November 2008).

Garcia, Rogelio. 1999. "Organizational Factor Affecting Independence of Proposed Federal Medicare Board." Congressional Research Service Memorandum. February 23. thomas. loc.gov/medicare/medica-1.htm. (Accessed 1 July 2008).

Haase, Leif Wellington. 2005. *A New Deal for Health: How to Cover Everyone and Get Medical Costs Under Control.* New York: Century Foundation.

Hacker, Jacob. 2007. *Health Care for America: A Proposal for Guaranteed, Affordable Health Coverage for All Americans Building on Medicare and Employment-Based Insurance.* Washington, DC: Economic Policy Institute.

Institute of Medicine. 2007. *Learning What Works Best: The Nation's Need for Evidence on Comparative Effectiveness in Health Care.* Washington, DC: IOM.

————. 2008. *Knowing What Works in Health Care: A Roadmap for the Nation.* Washington, DC: IOM.

Jost, Timothy Stoltzfus, ed. 2005. *Health Care Coverage Determinations: An International Comparative Study.* Maidenhead, UK: Open University Press.

————. 2007. "Fresh Thinking—Legal and Regulatory Issues Presented by Health Care Reform." Unpublished paper.

Kosar, Kevin R. 2007. *The Quasi Government: Hybrid Organizations with Both Government and Private Sector Legal Characteristics.* Washington, DC: Congressional Research Service.

Lee, Christopher. 2005. "Civil Service System on Way Out at DHS." *Washington Post* (January 27).

Lewis, Neil A. 1995. "Agency's Report Provokes a Revolt." *New York Times* (September 14).

Lowenstein, Roger. 2008. "The Education of Ben Bernanke." *New York Times Magazine* (January 20).

Mashaw, Jerry. 2007. Personal communication with the author, December 7.

Medicare Payment Advisory Commission (MedPAC). 2007. "Chapter 2: Producing Comparative Effectiveness Information." In *Promoting Greater Efficiency in Medicare,* pp. 29–56. Washington, DC: MedPAC.

Merlis, Mark. 2000. "Administration of a Medicare Premium Support Program." In *Competition with Constraints: Challenges Facing Medicare Reform,* ed. Marilyn Moon, pp. 83–96. Washington, DC: Urban Institute.

National Academy of Public Administration, Standing Panel on Executive Organization and Management. 1997. *Principles of Federal Organization.* Washington, DC: NAPA.

National Bipartisan Commission on the Future of Medicare. 1999. "Medicare Board." thomas.loc.gov/medicare/3fmedbrd.htm. (Accessed 27 December 2007.)

National Science Foundation. 2007. *Master Government List of Federally Funded R&D Centers.* Special Report NSF 06–316, May. Washington, DC: NSF.

Nichols, Len M. 2007. *A Sustainable Health System for All Americans.* Washington, DC: New America Foundation.

Orszag, Peter R., and Philip Ellis. 2007. "Addressing Rising Health Care Costs—A View from the Congressional Budget Office." *New England Journal of Medicine* 357 (19): 1885–87.

Rivlin, Alice M. 1995. "Memorandum for Heads of Executive Departments and Agencies: Government Corporations." Office of Management and Budget, Washington, DC. www.napawash.org/aa_e_o_management/gov_corporation.pdf. (Accessed 27 December 2007.)

Stanton, Thomas H. 2002. *Moving Toward More Capable Government.* Arlington, VA: PricewaterhouseCoopers Endowment for the Business of Government.

———. 2003. "The Administration of Medicare: A Neglected Issue." *Washington and Lee Law Review* 60 (4): 1373–1416.

U.S. Office of Management and Budget. 2003. *Circular A-76 (Revised),* May 29. Washington, DC: OMB.

———. 2007. *Budget of the United States Government, Fiscal Year 2008—Appendix.* Washington, DC: OMB.

Warren, Kenneth F. 1998. "Agency." In *International Encyclopedia of Public Policy and Administration,* ed. Jay M. Shafritz, pp. 25–7. Boulder, CO: Westview Press.

11

Individual Health Insurance Plan Information

Too Much and Too Little

MICHAEL WROBLEWSKI

Recent state health care reforms and proposals to cover persons without health insurance have focused on subsidizing health insurance coverage that people buy directly from health insurers, usually referred to as individual (or nongroup) health insurance. In 2006, Massachusetts enacted comprehensive health insurance reform that, among other things, requires individuals to purchase health insurance coverage if they are not otherwise covered (referred to as the "individual mandate") by July 1, 2007. The success of this effort depends, in part, on the extent to which consumers can make informed purchase decisions.

In light of this attention to the individual health insurance market, Consumers Union, the nonprofit publisher of *Consumer Reports,* conducted research to determine how consumers shop for and purchase individual health insurance to determine the optimal time, content, and presentation of information to help consumers understand their purchase options.[1]

The starting point for this study was the existing literature on how consumers with employer-provided coverage choose their health plans. These studies generally assume that consumers act "rationally" when they purchase a health insurance plan (Scanlon, Chernew, and Lave 1997). In the health insurance market, this means that consumers have the information necessary to weigh health risks they face and the potential costs of medical care they may consume. Consumers seek to obtain the most appropriate level of insurance protection at the lowest price.

Qualitative research shows that consumers say that they would use information on how a plan works, what it costs, the covered benefits, the quality of care, and overall satisfaction with care if it were available (Edgman-Levitan and Cleary 1996). The empirical evidence supports this research, and it shows that price, quality, the degree of provider choice, the scope and breadth of benefits, and convenience help explain consumer health-plan choice. Indeed, one study of how consumers choose employer-provided health plans found that nineteen variables were statistically significant (Chakraborty, Ettenson, and Gaeth 1994). The most important attribute in consumers' choice of a plan was hospitalization coverage, followed, in order, by choice of doctors, policy premium, dental coverage, and choice of hospitals.

The question remains how consumers choose individual health insurance when they are required to assemble the information on the relevant attributes themselves, because they do not have an employer or union acting as an intermediary for this purpose. Unlike mortgage products, in which the market provides a variety of information for many standardized products (e.g., thirty-year mortgages), standardized individual insurance plans do not exist, and hence, comparative cost, coverage, and benefit data are much more difficult to obtain. Thus, consumers are often on their own to locate reliable information about their health insurance plans. This is a concern, because consumers will seek more information only if the search is expected to provide meaningful and useful results and outweigh the costs of the search.

Indeed, the nonprice barriers, such as the difficulty in obtaining relevant data, can have a real impact on how consumers even shop for insurance. A study by the RAND Corporation (RAND Health 2006) found that reducing the perceived difficulty of locating information about insurance products would spur purchases about as much as modest subsidies to help consumers purchase insurance.

Not only can information search costs create a purchase barrier, but economic research confirms the intuition that consumer confusion about terms and conditions of products and services can lead to suboptimal decision making. Recent field experiments in areas as diverse as consumer selection of mortgage products, public schools, and retirement savings and investment products have shown that confusing and complex information disclosures can cause consumers to make decisions that they would not have made had the relevant information been presented in a clear and timely manner.[2] The staff of the Federal Trade Commission recently concluded that when consumers do not understand the costs and terms of their mortgages, "they may pay more for their mortgage than necessary, obtain inappropriate loan terms, fall prey to deceptive lending practices, and experience unpleasant surprises and financial difficulties during the course of their loans."[3] Needless to say, these same outcomes can occur when purchasing individual health insurance. Indeed, consumer research in the insurance industry has showed that existing disclosures were often a mixed bag in terms of assisting consumer understanding of insurance products.

Another complicating factor is that although consumers know that their choices are important, the issues at stake are often not relevant to them at the immediate point of purchase. For example, young, single people typically anticipate little need for care and may, therefore, be relatively indifferent to distinctions among plans other than those related to cost. Moreover, consumers do not have a context in which to evaluate how a plan's coverage and benefit limitations may affect them at a future date for an unexpected illness, disease, or injury.

Finally, when the number of choices or features (or both) increases, consumers often seek to simplify their decision making and rely on a few key pieces of information (Hibbard and Peters 2003). In fact, for insurance products, consumers would like to have someone explain any disclosures to them, possibly their insurance agent.

I hypothesized that an easy-to-understand uniform disclosure delivered when consumers obtain a rate quote would assist consumers in both choosing among health plans and educating them about what questions to ask as they shop for individual health insurance.

Methodology

Consumers Union conducted qualitative market research in two phases, with more than fifty consumers, in Stamford, Connecticut, and Boston, Massachusetts. In the first phase, Consumers Union conducted focus groups among Connecticut residents who had purchased individual health insurance plans within the previous two years and who were ineligible for Medicare or Medicaid. The participants' ages ranged from twenty-two to fifty-nine. The purpose of this phase was to gain an understanding of why consumers purchase individual health insurance and the information that consumers want and actually used in making this purchase. The research was conducted in Connecticut because, like most states, it does not offer guaranteed-issue insurance and does not have community rating.

Based on the issues identified in the first phase, Consumers Union developed a plan-summary prototype disclosure to increase the understanding of the health insurance purchase decision. Using the principles of plain-English disclosures (Office of Investor Education and Assistance 1998), the two-page prototype uses a question-and-answer format to provide consumers with the information they want and need to use in language that they understand. In developing this prototype, Consumers Union worked with health policy experts, consumer groups, and providers to ensure its technical accuracy.

Through individual consumer interviews, we tested whether this prototype: (1) increased the consumer's understanding of the key elements of the insurer's health plan, (2) provided the consumer with essential information about the plan and where to get additional information, and (3) allowed the consumer to comparison shop among health plans. The participants in this phase were uninsured residents of Connecticut who were actively shopping for individual health insurance and were ineligible for Medicaid and Medicare. The plan-summary prototype summarizes the health plan's features and includes the plan's premium and deductible amounts. We translated the plans of two leading insurers operating in Connecticut into the prototype and we used cost information based on quotes obtained through eHealthInsurance.com. Thus, the prototype had the look and feel as if it were already in use.

In the third phase, we used focus groups of uninsured Massachusetts residents who would soon be faced with the decision of purchasing health insurance to do additional testing on the prototype plan summary to further refine the language and format of the prototype.

Summary Findings

Most of the participants purchased individual health plans to cover a major medical expense. The participants generally did not understand the different features or limitations of their recently purchased health plans' coverage. Coverage and benefit limitations such as whether there was a lifetime maximum, restrictions on the number and timing of emergency care, hospital stays, rehabilitation, and test expenses did not factor into their purchase decision. Few participants could recall even whether their policies contained these types of limitations.

To gain an understanding of how consumers shopped for and purchased health insurance, we conducted focus groups with individuals who had purchased an individual health policy within the previous two years. During this research we probed the reasons they purchased health insurance, the information sources they used to learn about the plans, and the factors that they considered when deciding whether to purchase one plan versus another.

Reasons for Purchasing Individual Health Insurance

Generally, most participants purchased insurance to cover a major medical expense either for themselves or for their children. Threat of financial ruin linked to a life-threatening illness or injury was the motivating factor in most cases. Numerous participants prefaced their explanation of why they purchased with the disclaimer, "God forbid that something should happen." One person's comment typified this thought: "As a self-employed person, you have to cover the big stuff first." A smaller number purchased their plan to cover current needs. For example, some anticipated a pregnancy or sought coverage to treat an existing chronic medical condition.

Although they purchased health insurance to cover a major medical expense, they did not have a context in which to evaluate what would be adequate coverage if they were to become seriously ill and incur a major medical expense. Even sophisticated consumers—long-time small-business owners and independent contractors—often knew only the basics of their policies, for example, monthly premium and deductible. Few were aware of their policy specifics: what kinds of expenses counted toward the deductible; which emergency, test, or other hospital costs would be covered; what type of plan they had (PPO or HMO); whether there was a lifetime maximum; or what the limits for preexisting conditions were, if any. One participant summed up their lack of knowledge and understanding, saying, "Its scary we are paying so much and don't understand what we are getting."

Information Sources Used to Purchase Individual Health Insurance

Participants performed little objective research and often relied heavily, if not exclusively, on word-of-mouth recommendations. For example, they obtained information about which insurer to use through friends and family members. They asked friends and family members who were in the same position as they were from whom they purchased health insurance. Participants compared different deductible and premium levels within a particular insurer's offers. They rarely compared different insurers' plans.

About half of the participants used an agent or broker to help them purchase their policy. Consumers who used an insurance broker had fewer complaints than others about the process of researching and purchasing a private health policy. However, they were just as uninformed about their policies as consumers who did not use intermediaries. A minority used the Internet to search and compare plans. Most online searches were limited to looking up the address or phone number of a particular company.

Consumers appeared unable to make an informed decision about how to purchase an individual health insurance plan that meets their needs. On the one hand, they were unaware of some valuable information resources (e.g., from state insurance departments) that could help them. On the other hand, participants indicated that information from insurance companies often is impenetrable. They expressed suspicion of everyone involved—insurance companies, hospitals, and physicians and other health care providers. This thought was expressed even by the attorneys and financial professionals who indicated that in their professional lives they were used to making decisions based on sophisticated information.

Nearly all believed that health insurance was more difficult to understand and purchase compared to auto, life, homeowners, and long-term disability insurance products. One man's colorful analogy summed this thought up when he said, "[T]he purchase of these other products is like rolling off a log."

Participants felt it was difficult to compare products and expressed confusion regarding which attributes they should compare. Others explained how it had been much more difficult to purchase individual health insurance than it had been to obtain a home mortgage. Moreover, they believed current disclosures were confusing and not written in a way that allowed them to understand what they had purchased. Indeed, they believed the language in policies was deliberately confusing and intended to cheat consumers.

Several mentioned that they would have liked to customize their purchase. For example, they mentioned they would like to answer a series of questions and then be presented with a set of options. Many expressed the concern, however, that they were not exactly sure which questions they should be asked and that they did not want to be asked questions for which they could not provide a reasonable answer. For example, one participant said she did not want to be asked, "What copay would you like for inpatient versus outpatient X-rays?"

Attributes That Mattered in Selection of an Individual Health Insurance Plan

With the major medical expense as the backdrop, participants weighed the deductible against the premium to determine which plan they purchased. The most important attributes when they selected their plans had been the monthly premium, deductible amount, and restrictions on doctor choice. Other factors that played into the purchase decision included prescription drug coverage, copay amounts, name-brand insurer, coverage of a specific condition, and scope of benefits.

Most participants could recall their premiums and their deductibles. Premiums ranged from approximately $150 a month for a barebones individual plan with a $5,000 deductible to more than $1,000 a month for a family plan with a lower deductible. Participants had more trouble recalling the type of plan they had, but most indicated that they could see any doctor they chose and that they did not need referrals from their primary care physician. A couple of participants had been turned down for a preexisting condition, but none of the participants believed they had a rider on their policy that excluded a certain condition based on medical history.

Although many stated why they had purchased their plan based on premium price or freedom to use any doctor, most were unsure whether they had gotten a "good deal." Typical of these comments was one by a participant who said, "I pay a thirty-dollar copay to visit the doctor, but I don't know if this is good." This finding is consistent with the participants' discussion that most had only examined one insurer's plans when they had purchased their plans.

Most tried not to use the coverage under their plans. They were unsure how usage of the benefits under the plan would affect their premium the following year. Many indicated that they wanted a refund or rebate for not using their plans. For example, a comment by a mother of three children typified this opinion when she said, "[T]here should be a rebate if you haven't gotten [reached] your deductible." Moreover, they were unclear how insurance worked altogether. For example, one participant summed up this confusion when she said, "I don't understand why existing customers [of an insurer] don't get as many choices [of plans] as new customers."

The item that consistently drew the most questions and discussion was the reasons for premium increases. Participants were confused about why premiums increase and what would happen to their premiums if they made a claim. Several comments summed this frustration up: "Mine [my premium] goes up every twelve months"; another participant added, "[A]nd they don't even tell you about it," other than sending the bill with the higher premium.

Women were more involved with the selection and use of a family's health insurance policy. Often they were primarily responsible for managing their family's health care and dealing with health care providers and insurers. They were, as a result, more critical of the frustrations that many complained were built into our health care system. Yet, like men, women often were unaware of the terms, conditions, and benefits of their own insurance plan.

Young adults without families, especially single men in their early twenties, do not want to be bothered with individual health insurance decisions at all. Some had responded to a sales pitch and purchased a policy, but until they had assets or family at risk, the threat of catastrophic illness was not real enough for them to worry about.

Very few participants choose a health plan based on service quality. In fact, they often equated a quality health plan with one that offered generous benefits. When probed about various service-quality measures, they expressed an interest in comparisons of complaint rates and trends in premiums of a particular company.

Policy Implications and Recommendations

Our research uncovered that consumers in the individual health insurance market were unable to make an informed decision about a plan that meets their needs. Consumers did not have knowledge about the components of a "good" plan to cover a major medical expense. The marketing materials that insurers provided them prior to the purchase (generally a quote sheet and a booklet) failed to educate them about the features of comprehensive insurance and frustrated consumers' ability to compare plans. Necessary information was not provided when it was most needed; in fact, the details consumers needed to fully evaluate plans were not provided until after the purchase of the plan had been made.

The lack of context and information was compounded by the timing of the purchase of health insurance. Although consumers knew that their choices were important, the issues at stake were not relevant to them at the immediate point of decision making. For example, young, single people anticipated little need for care and were indifferent to distinctions among plans other than those related to cost. Persons with special health concerns were more inclined to make efforts to match their anticipated need against specific plan benefits.

Added to this timing dilemma is the fact that consumer choice and competition assumes a careful examination and weighing of alternatives, but as the number of choices grows, this task becomes increasingly difficult and complex. Assumptions about informed choice work only if consumers have access to and can locate reliable information. If they do not have such access, they have no way of seeking an optimal solution. In our research, because of the large number of cost and coverage options and benefit limitations, consumers resorted to relatively simple preference criteria to direct their choice. They used friends and family to help them choose an insurer and they focused on cost and doctor restrictions because they often had limited information and no direct experience in this market.

Plan-Summary Prototype

Participants found the plan-summary prototype (see Table 11.1) easier to understand than the existing company documents about the plans' coverage and details. It provided them with the information they needed and wanted, and it allowed them to compare plans on the same basis prior to purchasing their plan.

Consumers liked the two-sided approach, in which the front side of the plan summary presented the most important consumer information. Many consumers indicated that they could make a purchase decision based on this information alone. This information provided a snapshot of the plan: current cost (premium

Table 11.1 *(front side)*

PLAN COST & COVERAGE

MODEL INSURANCE COMPANY
PPO 1500 PREMIUM PLAN

• The first column contains frequently asked questions about health plans.
• The second column explains new terms to answer the questions.
• The third column answers the questions for this plan.

Insured(s): _____

[State Name] requires each health plan to provide you a summary of their plan in this format. Use this form to compare plans on the same basis. The back of this form summarizes this plan's covered services (benefits).

Coverage Beginning: _____

FREQUENTLY ASKED QUESTIONS	EXPLANATION OF COMMONLY USED HEALTH PLAN TERMS	THIS PLAN'S COVERAGE
What are the different costs that I must pay for this health plan?	**Premium:** a flat monthly payment you make to buy and maintain a health plan. You pay this amount even if you do not receive medical services.	Premium: $_____
	Copayment: you pay this fee to the doctor, hospital, or pharmacy at the time you receive services.	Copayment: $_____
	Coinsurance: a percentage of the total cost of a service that you must pay for services you receive. A 20% coinsurance rate means you pay 20% of the cost of the service. The plan pays the remaining 80%.	Coinsurance: _____%
	Deductible: an amount you must pay for services you use before the plan begins to pay. This amount does not include your premium payments.	Deductible: $_____
Is there a cap on my total expenses each year?	The **out-of-pocket cap** is the most you will pay each year for covered services. Caps add your annual premium, deductible, and total coinsurance amounts. Caps do not include copayment you make.	Cap: $_____
Is this plan permanent or temporary?	Temporary policies are not **guaranteed renewable**. Renewability ensures you have no gaps in coverage.	_____
Are there dollar limits on this plan's overall health insurance coverage?	Plans limit the amount of money they will pay on a lifetime or illness basis, even if your own medical expenses are greater than this limit. These limits are called **maximums.**	$_____ lifetime maximum $_____ illness maximum
Do I need to choose a primary care doctor from the plan's list?	Plans may require you to choose a **primary care doctor** from a list of doctors in their **network**. If you do not use a network doctor, you pay higher coinsurance and copayments or you may pay the entire cost of the service received.	_____
Do I need a referral from my primary case doctor to see a specialist?	Plans may require you to get permission from you primary case doctor to see a specialist. This permission is called a **referral** or **pre-authorization.**	_____
Does this plan exclude conditions?	Plans may not cover treatment costs for medical conditions that you have prior to buying this plan. These conditions are called **preexisting conditions**.	_____
How long must I wait before I receive coverage under this plan?	Plans may require a **waiting period** before coverage begins for a preexisting condition.	_____

If You Have Questions, Call 1-800-555-1212 or Visit Our Website at www.modelinsurance.com.

(continued)

Table 11.1 *(back side)*

BENEFITS QUESTIONS		MODEL INSURANCE COMPANY PPO 1500 PREMIUM PLAN	
• The first column contains frequently asked benefits questions. • The second column lists the services you will typically use. • The third and fourth columns list you cost along with any limitation on the use of the benefits.			
COVERAGE QUESTION	EXPLANATION OF COMMONLY USED HEALTH PLAN TERMS	IN-NETWORK COSTS	OUT-OF-NET-WORK COSTS
If I am sick and go to the doctor's office	Primary Care Doctors Specialists X-Rays/Lab Testing/Imaging		
If I have surgery and stay overnight in the hospital	Surgeon Fees Fees for Anesthesiologists, Pathologists, and Radiologists Facility Fees X-Rays/Lab Testing/Imaging Services such as Radiation/Chemotherapy		
If I need emergency care	Emergency Room Fees		
If I need medicines to treat my illness or condition	Generic Drugs Preferred Brand Drugs Non-Preferred Brand Drugs Separate Prescription Drug Deductible		
If I have a long-term recovery	Home Health Services Hospice Skilled Nursing Physical/Occupational Therapy Durable Medical Equipment		
If I have mental health needs	Substance Abuse Treatment Mental Health Inpatient Admissions Mental Health Office Visits		
YOU MAY NEED THE FOLLOWING BENEFITS TO STAY HEALTHY			
If I go to the doctor's office for a check-up	Office Visits Annual OB/GYN Check-up Pap Smears/Mammograms Acupuncture Chiropractic Services Vaccinations/Immunizations		
If I have my eyes checked	Eye Exam Glasses Contact Lenses		
If I need maternity care	Outpatient Prenatal and Postnatal Care Delivery and All Inpatient Services Fertility Treatment		
If You Have Questions About Benefits Under This Plan, Call 1-800-555-1212 or Visit Our Website at www.modelinsurance.com.			

and deductibles), potential out-of-pocket costs and maximums should they face unexpected health issues, restrictions on doctor choice, and the extent of the coverage provided (exclusions and waiting periods).

If consumers sought additional information about specific benefits of the coverage provided, they could turn the prototype over to see the costs and limitations of benefits provided the plan. Further, the form provided specific instructions on where they could obtain additional information if they wanted it.

Cost and Coverage Questions (Front Side)

Most participants found the three-column format (frequently asked questions, explanations, and answers) easy to understand, clear, and self-explanatory. Typical of the participants' comments were "Everything I needed to know is there," "It is clear and straightforward," and "I could make a decision to buy based on this form."

The most important items on the form included the plan's cost (premium, deductible, copayments, coinsurance), restrictions on the choice of doctor, and whether referrals were necessary to see a specialist. To a lesser degree they focused on the out-of-pocket expense cap and the coverage maximums. Participants observed that they could use the out-of-pocket expense cap to determine whether they could afford a worst-case health scenario in which they were struck by an unexpected disease or illness. One participant noted that he could use the out-of-pocket cap to compare a plan that had copayments with a plan that had coinsurance because it would allow consumers to see, regardless of the individual cost, the most they would be expected to pay in any one year if they were hit with an unexpected illness. For those persons with chronic conditions or past illnesses, descriptions of exclusions and waiting periods were important.

During the course of the discussion and testing, we clarified the definitions of *coinsurance* and *copayment* because most consumers did not understand the difference between the two concepts. Moreover, we further refined the definition of a "maximum" because most consumers were unaware that their coverage could be limited.

Summary of Benefits (Back Side)

Consumers responded well to the three-column format that listed a basic health insurance coverage question, services you would likely need to answer the question, and the plan's coverage of these services. With a form structured in this fashion, consumers could determine the types of services they would use to answer one of their questions. It provided a way to educate them in a context in which they were receptive to understanding the information.

Within this format, participants wanted any limitation to the specific plan's benefit listed as well. They also wanted an affirmative statement on the form about where to look if the question they had was not listed on the back side.

*Issues Relating to Use of the Prototypes to Compare Different
Company Plans*

During this consumer testing, we found that existing marketing materials provided prior to purchasing a plan either contained too much detail, used terms or abbreviations for which no definitions were provided, or left the participants with too many questions. Another participant summed up the existing disclosures by saying, "I'm getting a lot of words, but not the information I need to make a decision."

Most participants found it very difficult to compare the existing company documents: "It is like comparing apples to oranges." They also could not find the same things on different companies' existing documents, and they were unsure whether the definitions were consistent across companies. It was painful to watch some of the participants wrestle with the existing company documents. They did not know where to begin to make the comparison. Use of the prototypes for this purpose made it much easier for the participants to compare plans on the features that mattered to them.

Comparison of the Plan-Summary Prototype to Other Health Plan Disclosures

The Massachusetts Commonwealth Health Insurance Connector Authority (the Connector) and the federal government (for Medicare Advantage and the Federal Employees Health Benefits [FEHB] Program) offer Web sites (www.mahealthconnector.org, www.medicare.gov/choices/advantage.asp and www.opm.gov/insure/health/, respectively) so that consumers can shop for and compare different features of health insurance plans. These Web sites are important because they can take the legwork out of searching for health plan information. The research showed that because most consumers examined only the plans offered by one insurer, online tools that allow for a broader comparison can help consumers shop for and compare different health plan offerings.

All three Web sites allow consumers to input basic information about themselves to obtain a list of plans that match their profile information (the "first comparison"). This list also provides basic features of each of the plans, comparable to the front side of the plan summary. All three Web sites then allow the consumer to seek more detailed information about a limited number of plans (the "second comparison"). At this point, all three Web sites present all of the plans' features and benefits, which is comparable to the back side of the plan summary. Of course, the consumer can redo the second comparison any number of times by selecting a different set of plans to compare to get more detailed information about each plan.

We compared the plan features listed on the front side of the plan summary to the information that the Connector and the federal government presented in the first comparison. We concentrated on the information presented at this stage for two reasons. First, the research showed that a limited amount of relevant information

Table 11.2

Plan Summary and Other Information Compared

Information category\sponsor	Plan summary prototype	Massachusetts	Medicare Advantage	FEHB
Premium	Yes	Yes	Yes	Yes
Deductible	Yes	Yes		Yes
Copayments for various services	Yes	Yes		Yes
Coinsurance for various services	Yes	Yes		Yes
Out-of-pocket cap	Yes			Yes
Temporary policy	Yes			
Maximums	Yes			
Doctor restrictions and referrals	Yes	Yes	Yes	
Exclusions	Yes			
Waiting periods	Yes			
Quality ratings				Yes
Prescription drug costs		Yes	Yes	Yes
Vision			Yes	
Typical estimated costs			Yes	

Source: The author.

about the plan was sufficient for some consumers to make a purchase decision. Thus, it is important to provide the most important cost and coverage features. Second, the research showed that the amount and presentation of information matter. Additional information at this stage would turn into information overload, in which the information that matters is lost to the consumer. In sum, the information presented at this stage can inform consumers about those cost and coverage features they value highly. Table 11.2 summarizes the different information provided. The plan summary emphasizes plan features different from those on the three existing government-provided health insurance Internet sites.

The Massachusetts Connector is a direct comparison to the plan summary because it provides information on individual, not group, plans. Medicare Advantage and FEHB are group plans that the federal government has subsidized and have limited use of certain features found in individual insurance plans—maximums, exclusions, and waiting periods. These features can have a significant impact on the coverage provided by the plan.

Massachusetts residents can use the Connector's Web site to shop among plans offered. As of 2007, the Connector had approved six insurers to offer plans with different levels of cost sharing (e.g., different combinations of premium and deductible amounts). The Web site allows residents to input basic information (age, gender, zip code, industry code) to obtain a comprehensive list of plans offered.

The first comparison list of information includes premium and deductible amounts; doctor, prescription drug, and emergency room copayment amounts; hospital stay costs; and a link to doctors available in the plan. This information is similar to the information presented by the federal government for FEHB plans. This list of information does not include out-of-pocket cap, maximums, information on referrals, whether the plan is temporary, and exclusions and waiting periods, which are included on the front side of the plan summary.

Further consumer testing could examine whether the Connector's listing of the three copayment amounts and hospital-stay cost information is necessary, or whether consumers would benefit from the listing of the out-of-pocket cap and maximums (which are significantly more important to a consumer's overall budget than the copayment amount for a doctor's visit) or the information on referrals. FEHB plans highlight the out-of-pocket cap in their first comparison information; indeed, it is the feature listed right after the premium amount on their first comparison displays.

The FEHB Program also lists quality data as part of its first comparison. The plan summary and Connector disclosures do not contain such information. Additional consumer testing may be warranted to determine the importance of quality information when presented in conjunction with plan cost and coverage features.

Notes

1. It is beyond the scope of this research to examine whether the individual health insurance market is the ideal solution for health care reform. For an overview of the non-group health insurance market, see Kaiser Family Foundation/eHealthInsurance, Update on Individual Health Insurance, Revised (August 2004), Washington, DC: Kaiser Family Foundation. For an overview of problems with the individual health insurance market, see Karen Pollitz, Richard Sorian, and Kathy Thomas, "How Accessible Is Individual Health Insurance for People in Less-Than-Perfect Health?" Report for the Kaiser Family Foundation, Menlo Park, CA, June 2001.

2. Federal Trade Commission Bureau of Economics, *Improving Consumer Mortgage Disclosures,* June 2007, Washington, DC: author; Justine Hastings, Richard Van Weelden, Jeffrey Weinstein, National Bureau of Economic Research, "Preferences, Information, and Parental Choice Behavior in Public School Choice" (NBER Working Paper 12995, March 2007); James J. Choi, David Laibson, and Brigitte C. Madrian, National Bureau of Economic Research, "Reducing the Complexity Costs of 401(k) Participation Through Quick Enrollment" (NBER Working Paper 11979, January 2006).

3. Federal Trade Commission Bureau of Economics, *Improving Consumer Mortgage Disclosures,* ES-12.

References

Chakraborty, Goutam, Richard Ettenson, and Gary Gaeth. 1994. "How Consumers Choose Health Insurance." *Journal of Health Care Marketing* 14 (1): 21–33.

Edgman-Levitan, Susan, and Paul D. Cleary. 1996. "What Information Do Consumers Want and Need?" *Health Affairs* 15 (4): 42–56.

Hibbard, Judith H., and Ellen Peters. 2003. "Supporting Informed Consumer Health Care Decisions." *Annual Review of Public Health* 24 (January): 413–33.

Office of Investor Education and Assistance. 1998. *A Plain English Handbook: How to Create Clear SEC Disclosure Documents.* Washington, DC: U.S. Securities and Exchange Commission, August.

RAND Health. 2006. "Consumer Decision-Making in the Insurance Market." *Research Highlights.* RAND Corporation, Santa Monica, CA.

Scanlon, Dennis P., Michael Chernew, and Judith R. Lave. 1997. "Consumer Health Plan Choice: Current Knowledge and Future Directions." *Annual Review of Public Health* 18: 507–28.

Part III

Controlling Costs Under Health Care Reform

12

Controlling Health Care Costs

Mark Merlis

Proposals to expand health insurance coverage are almost always accompanied by proposals to control growth in health spending. Some say that universal coverage cannot be achieved without cost containment, others that real cost savings will not be feasible without universal coverage. These arguments are considered below. Whether or not coverage expansion and cost controls are inseparable, it is likely that how society goes about covering the uninsured may have implications for the feasibility of different approaches for controlling costs, and vice versa.

People who favor a particular approach to covering the uninsured may also tend to favor certain cost-containment approaches. For example, people who believe that consumers would be more cost-conscious if they were enrolled in high-deductible health plans are also likely to believe that coverage expansion should include tax subsidies to purchase health insurance in a largely unregulated individual market. However, it is possible to conceive of a single-payer plan whose benefit package included a high initial deductible. The two pieces are not inherently contradictory or even ideologically inconsistent, particularly if the deductible were progressively income based. It just happens that, in the current political environment, the intersection between consumer-directed health care advocates and single-payer advocates is practically a null set.

This chapter treats coverage-expansion approaches and cost-containment approaches as two distinct columns in the menu of health-reform options: Any choice from column A could theoretically be combined with any choice from column B. In practice, some combinations may work better than others, and the interplay of approaches to coverage and savings is the focus here. There is no attempt here to diagnose the sources of rapid health spending growth or to evaluate the likelihood that different proposed solutions can actually slow that growth. There is no shortage of analyses addressing these questions. Instead, the assumption is that every solution may offer at least some promise of savings—whether small or large, onetime or continuous. What kind of insurance arrangements may make a preferred solution more or less workable?

The chapter begins with a brief review of the question posed at the outset: whether coverage expansion and cost controls must go hand in hand. It then lays out the menus of commonly proposed coverage approaches and available savings measures before considering how the two might go together. Because the number of combinations is large, discussion focuses on just a few of the savings measures that have received the greatest attention from policy makers. This chapter does not address measures intended to reduce the administrative costs of health insurance, as opposed to direct medical expenditures. (Options for administrative simplification and their cost implications for insurers and providers are in Chapter 13.) However, evaluating different coverage-expansion approaches may require balancing their potential for medical spending restraint against their likely impact on administrative costs.

Coverage Expansion and Health Spending

It is a commonplace that the United States cannot afford to provide universal coverage without first or simultaneously getting a handle on the cost problem. As one recent analysis has argued, this truism has been in circulation for at least forty years and may have been a major barrier to proposals to cover the uninsured (Feder and Moran 2007).

In fact, the aggregate increase in national health expenditures (NHE) that could be expected to result from universal coverage might be relatively small. Recent estimates by the Lewin Group of the costs of some proposals that would reach near-universal coverage suggested a net increase in NHE of 2.1 percent to 3.4 percent (Sheils and Haught 2003).[1] Estimates in the early 1990s were in the same range; for example, a RAND Corporation study in 1994 projected a 1.8 percent to 3.2 percent increase in NHE, with a "best estimate" of 2.2 percent (Long and Marquis 1994).

There are two reasons that increases in health spending might not be proportionate to increases in the insured population. First, the uninsured might be healthier than the insured. The data used in the RAND estimates indicated that insured nonelderly adults were about 50 percent more likely than the uninsured to report that they were in fair or poor health. However, this difference may have diminished over time. Nonelderly adults with and without health insurance in 2005 were about equally likely to report fair or poor health.[2]

Second, the uninsured are already obtaining considerable amounts of care—paid for out of pocket, provided through public programs (such as the Veterans Administration or community health centers), or subsidized through cost shifting, as in the case of uncompensated hospital care. The RAND study found that uninsured adults had 61 percent as many ambulatory care contacts, and 67 percent as many inpatient hospital days, as comparable insured adults. The size of the "access gap," too, may have changed over time; for example, competition may have made providers less willing or able to cross-subsidize care for the uninsured. Despite these trends, much of the effect of universal coverage would be to shift existing spending from one set of pockets to another. (Some components of health spending, such as nursing home care, would not be affected at all.)

Whatever the size of any onetime increase in spending, the cost would be compounded if spending for the newly insured rose in tandem with those for the already insured. Suppose, for example, that universal coverage in 2008 would raise NHE by as much as 5 percent, from the projected $2.4 trillion to $2.5 trillion (Keehan et al. 2008). If spending growth for both the currently and newly insured rose at the projected annual rate of 6.7 percent, NHE would reach 20.5 percent of GDP by 2017, compared to an estimated 19.5 percent without universal coverage. Of course, 1 percent of GDP is a lot of money, but perhaps not enough to affect people's judgments about the level of health spending that society could sustain.

Some people claim that universal coverage would actually produce savings because the newly insured would stop using emergency rooms and some serious conditions might be caught earlier, when they were less costly to treat. While this might be true, any such savings are already implicitly accounted for in the estimates. The basic method is, first, to estimate current annual spending by or on behalf of the uninsured, then to estimate their spending if their utilization resembled that of comparable currently insured people; the difference is the estimated aggregate spending increase. A newly insured person might substitute a physician office visit for a more costly emergency room visit, but this person might also add three office visits, because he or she would not have to wait twelve hours to be seen at each encounter. The net effect is an aggregate increase. In addition to the increase in direct medical spending, there would also be the new administrative costs of insurance, which would be only partially offset by providers' savings on billing and collection expenses for self-pay patients.

If the cost of covering the uninsured is comparatively small, why has it been such a concern? One problem is that any measure to cover the uninsured will almost certainly also affect coverage and expenses for people who already have insurance. A small increase in total spending could entail large shifts in spending from some payers to other payers. For example, a new tax credit for individual health insurance could help not only the uninsured but also people who are already buying coverage without assistance; private spending would be replaced by a federal tax expenditure. Politicians deal with specific programs, not with abstractions like the national health accounts, and the effect of coverage expansions on federal or state budgets could be much larger than the effect on aggregate spending. A second consequence, less frequently discussed, is that currently insured people with very poor coverage might gain better coverage and incur higher costs. In particular, it is hard to imagine how Medicaid programs could continue sometimes draconian benefit limits and low payment rates while categorically ineligible low-income people received more generous subsidized private coverage.

Whatever the effects of health-coverage expansion on national health spending, it is certainly the case that high health care costs have contributed to the erosion of health insurance coverage, leading some employers to curtail health benefits and making nongroup coverage less affordable for people without access to employer or public plans. Continued unchecked growth in health costs could make the goal of universal coverage a moving target. While coverage-expansion measures might be designed to reach people who do not have access to employer coverage today, rising premiums could mean that people who already have employer coverage might lose it in the future. Unless private-sector costs can be brought under control, universal coverage through tax subsidies or public programs would mean not just a onetime increase in public spending, but a steady shift from private to public spending.

Conversely, some argue that cost containment even for those who are already insured may not be achievable without universal coverage, for two reasons. First, certain approaches that some (by no means all) observers think could produce savings—such as health promotion and disease prevention—may not be workable if people are continually moving in and out of health coverage. Second, measures to reduce excess spending by the insured could squeeze out the fat in the system that currently subsidizes essential services for the uninsured. This could mean that access problems for the uninsured could become too glaring for society to continue to ignore (Aaron 2005).

Whatever the practical arguments for linking cost containment and coverage expansion, there has also been a political linkage. Offering the prospect of ultimate cost savings could be a way of garnering support for the temporarily disruptive system or market changes needed to achieve universal coverage. Alternatively, the offer of universal coverage could be used to overcome resistance to potentially painful cost-containment measures. The political calculus involved is beyond the scope of this chapter, but polling data suggest that different Americans have very different ideas about what should be the major focus of health reform (see Figure 12.1).

Views of Republicans and Democrats about the key goal for health reform are almost mirror images, while independents are about equally divided: 50 percent for universal coverage and 48 percent for affordability. In this environment, it is hard to say which of the two goals is the sugar coating and which the pill. It should be noted, however, that the survey asks about making insurance "affordable." Results might be quite different if voters were asked about measures to reduce the quantity and price of the services they themselves consume.

Defining a Matrix of Coverage-Expansion and Cost-Containment Options

In order to clarify the interplay of coverage expansion and cost containment, this section describes a simple matrix of basic coverage models and cost-containment approaches.

Coverage-Expansion Models

The five models considered here suggest a basic typology of the options currently receiving the most discussion. Some of the models are often combined (e.g., play-or-pay for workers and a public program expansion for nonworkers). One key variable that is not considered here is whether a proposal includes an individual mandate. The

Figure 12.1 **Registered Voters' View of the Main Goal for Improving the Health Care System in the United States, April 2008**

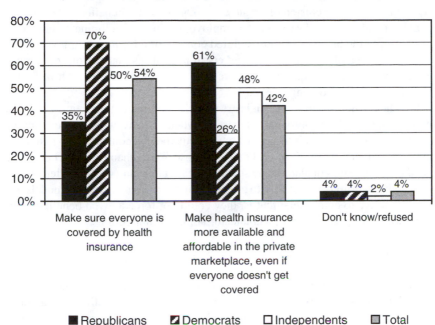

■ Republicans ▨ Democrats ▢ Independents ▢ Total

Source: Henry J. Kaiser Family Foundation, *Kaiser Health Tracking Poll, Election 2008.* Available at http://www.kff.org/kaiserpolls/upload/7771.pdf.

presence or absence of a mandate obviously has implications for the size of the population that would be covered and for the workability of such possible program features as guaranteed issue or community rating. Cost implications are less clear. Presumably, without a mandate, the average risk level of the insured population would be higher than under full universal coverage. This would change the baseline against which insurers' or other actors' cost-containment efforts would be measured but would not necessarily affect the relative success of those efforts *for the covered population.*

In considering how different models might affect cost-containment options, the key issue is what kind of market would emerge under each model. Who would have the leverage to push for system change: consumers, insurers, employers, a connector administrator, or regulators? The answers given here are frankly speculative, and should be taken not as predictions but as illustrations of some of the possible dynamics.

1. Subsidized Nongroup Coverage

Consumers receive financial assistance—a tax credit or deduction or a voucher—to help cover the cost of health insurance premiums. The consumer may purchase coverage from any insurer, but benefits may be required to meet some minimum standards. Such proposals are often accompanied by a proposal to eliminate or place a dollar cap on the exclusion of employer-provided health benefits from workers' taxable income. In some variants, the employer exclusion is eliminated but workers can apply the tax credit to any required contribution for their employer coverage. Assuming a plan of this kind, workers in large firms that can offer favorable premiums might retain their current coverage, while those in smaller firms might shift to the subsidized nongroup market.

It is unclear how the insurance industry would evolve under this option—whether there would still be many small players or whether there would be continuing consolidation. It seems fair to say that there would be less consolidation under this option than under options 2 and 3. For the purpose of this chapter, it will be posited that the option leaves in place many small commercial insurers with limited market power. These insurers would have to offer benefit packages and delivery models that were attractive to consumers; that is, they could not force a given benefit change in the way a large employer or a connector administrator could.

2. Connector

Consumers receive financial assistance, as in option 1, but may or must buy coverage through insurers participating in some form of connector or pooling arrangement. Some connector proposals would effectively eliminate the nongroup and perhaps the small-group market by providing that subsidies could be used only for connector coverage. Others—such as the proposals by several of the 2008 Democratic presidential candidates—would allow outside insurers to compete with the connector but would subject them to guaranteed-issue and community-rating requirements. Some insurers would exit the market under these conditions, while others might find it difficult to compete with the connector plans—particularly if the connector plans could achieve significant administrative cost savings (also see Chapter 13). It seems likely that, in this environment, the connector would capture the lion's share of its target market. In the absence of the employer mandate provided in option 3, many small and medium-sized employers might offer their workers increased wages or other compensation in place of health benefits, shifting them into the subsidized connector market.

A key issue is whether the connector would resemble the current Federal Employees Health Benefits (FEHB) Program or whether it would come closer to the "pure" managed competition model represented, for example, by the health alliances in the 1993 Clinton plan. In a pure managed competition system, all insurers offer the same benefit package (although they may impose different levels of network restriction), consumers pay the entire difference between the cost of their selected plan and the least costly plan (or some other bid-based benchmark), and payments to plans are risk adjusted. Plans compete solely on price and quality. FEHB, on the contrary, has no standard benefit and no risk adjustment; there is price competition, but the formula for computing the federal contribution limits the reward for joining a low-cost plan or the penalty for joining a high-cost one. This chapter assumes a middle option, under which benefits are not fully standardized but the connector can issue occasional fiats in the form of statements such as "All plans must cover procedure x," or "All plans must have a pay-for-performance system that rewards achievement of objective y." The connector thus has some power to guide the system, but without the direct market power of a single-payer plan. (This power would be enhanced if the connector could select a limited number of plans through some form of bidding or competitive negotiation process, rather than accepting all qualified carriers.)

The market power of individual plans within the connector might also depend on how closely it resembled FEHB. FEHB has a few national preferred provider plans (PPO) plans, with uniform national premiums, competing with local health maintenance organizations (HMOs) that charge local market prices. The national plans are more costly than the HMOs in some areas and less costly in others. While this oddity has been tolerated in FEHB, it seems less tenable in a connector that would serve tens of millions of people. This chapter assumes some geographic contribution adjustment, meaning that competition would probably tilt toward national plans and regional plans with sizable market power. (In practice, finding a fair way of compensating for geographic differences in medical care spending has long been a difficult—and highly politicized—problem for the Medicare Advantage program and its precursor health plan contracting programs.)

Note that some connector proposals include a public insurance plan that would be offered as an alternative to the available private plans. This variant is considered in Chapters 1, 2 and 9 of this book; this chapter will assume that all connector coverage is through private plans.

3. Play-or-Pay

Employers may be required either to offer health coverage to employees and contribute some share of the premium or to pay into a public fund. If an employer chooses to offer coverage, it may self-insure or buy insurance; again, benefits may be required to meet some minimum standards, and a pooling arrangement may be made available for employers below some size threshold. If instead the employer contributes to a public fund, the proceeds may be used to finance option 2 or may be used to fund a public program expansion.

In terms of changes in the insurance market, this option might not play out very differently from option 2. It is included here simply to have one model in the matrix that emphasizes the employer's role as a purchaser of services, a designer of benefit packages, and possibly an influence on workers' health-related behaviors. There are differing views about whether large employers should continue to play a significant role in shaping health insurance options. Some people argue that employers have responded to cost pressures simply by shifting costs to workers, and that even some employers' attempts to address costs directly—for example, through wellness programs or value-based purchasing—are too fragmented and therefore unlikely to lead to fundamental changes in health care delivery (Committee for Economic Development 2007). Others contend that employers have been the major source of innovation in plan design in recent years, and that shifting workers out of employer-sponsored plans and into some form of connector arrangement might actually reduce the potential for innovation (Ginsburg 2008).

4. Public Program Expansion

A public program such as Medicaid or the State Children's Health Insurance Program (SCHIP) would be expanded to reach a larger population. Some proposals would allow people at all income levels to buy into public coverage by paying a premium. This would make the public program option very much like the connector approach, particularly as many Medicaid and SCHIP programs are already offering coverage through competing managed care plans. To distinguish this option from option 2, this chapter assumes a fee-for-service program with some form of means testing but without the categorical eligibility restrictions (such as exclusion of single adults and childless couples) still imposed in most Medicaid and SCHIP programs. The expanded program might have greater purchasing power than the public programs do now. One trade-off, suggested earlier, is that it might be less able to impose arbitrary benefit limits and low payment rates that arguably shift costs for program participants to other payers. (Of course, one cost problem facing Medicaid programs is the growing burden of financing long-term care and Medicare wraparound benefits for the elderly and disabled. These issues are beyond the scope of this chapter.)

5. Single-Payer

Everyone is enrolled in a public program. In a Medicare-for-all plan, enrollees could choose between the public program and competing Medicare Advantage plans; the result might look very much like a connector option that included a public program component. In a "pure" single-payer plan, all enrollees would be in the public program, and supplemental coverage could be offered only for noncovered services (rather than, as under Medigap, for deductibles and coinsurance). This chapter assumes a pure plan—able to exercise more market power than Medicare but, like Medicare, subject to political and due-process constraints that might not affect very large employers or private insurers. A second question is whether the program would operate nationally or at the state or regional level.[3] A localized program would have considerable buying power, but variations in coverage rules, performance standards for providers, or other policies might influence the effectiveness of cost-containment efforts. (If the goal is to change in some way the culture of medical practice, it is not clear whether national or local signaling would be more powerful.) This chapter assumes a national program.

Cost-Containment Options

Health care spending for a given population might be roughly defined as a function of five basic factors: (1) population needs or morbidity; (2) access to services; (3) propensity to seek services; (4) volume, nature, or intensity of services supplied or ordered; and (5) unit cost or price of services.

Cost containment here is defined as any set of policies or measures intended to affect any one or more of these factors. Measures designed only to shift costs for a given population from one payer to another, such as raising the eligibility age for Medicare or reducing an employer's percentage contribution to premiums, are not considered here. (Note, however, that there are some measures that both shift and reduce costs, and therefore warrant inclusion; for example, increasing a health plan deductible both deters utilization and shifts some costs to the policyholder.) Again, measures to reduce the administrative costs of insurance are considered in Chapter 13.

Table 12.1 shows a variety of measures that have been suggested as possible ways of reducing health spending or slowing spending growth. For each measure, the table indicates whether it is highly compatible (↑), less compatible (↔) or incompatible (↓) with each of the five coverage models. Because the focus of this chapter is on the interaction of coverage models and cost-containment options, the matrix omits some options that are entirely regulatory and whose implementation could be independent of the coverage system. Among these are malpractice reform, revived certificate-of-need programs for new facilities or major capital investments, stricter criteria for FDA approval of new drugs and devices, restrictions on direct-to-consumer advertising of drugs, and stronger (or, as some would prefer, weaker) enforcement in such areas as physician self-referral and antitrust. Some of these approaches might make one or another expansion model more workable, but none of them requires direct action by payers. Some other measures, identified (√) in the last column, might be advanced by both purchasers and regulators.

Each cost containment measure has been grouped according to the health spending factor at which the measure is chiefly targeted. This grouping is necessarily arbitrary, because some measures affect more than one factor. In addition, some measures directly targeted at one factor are also intended to have indirect effects on another. For example, high-deductible plans are meant to modify consumers' care-seeking behavior but might also, according to their proponents, induce price competition among providers.

The last set of options, labeled *instrumental measures* in the table, includes comparative-effectiveness research, greater use of electronic health records and other health information technology, and measures to promote greater price and quality transparency. These are not in themselves cost-containment measures but may instead be prerequisites for the success of other approaches. For example, knowing what medical practices are most effective is not the same as getting providers to adopt them, but may be essential for developing defensible coverage

Table 12.1

Matrix of Coverage Expansion Models and Cost Containment Options

Cost containment options	Coverage expansion models					
	Subsidized nongroup coverage	Connector or exchange	Play-or-pay (employer mandate)	Medicaid or other public coverage expansion	Single payer	Regulatory or public health component
Reducing Need for Services						
Primary and secondary prevention	↓	↑	↔	↑	↑	
Health promotion and education	↓	↑	↔	↑	↑	
Health behavior-based premiums	↔	↔	↑	↓	↓	√
Patient safety and reduced medical errors	↓	↑	↑	↑	↑	√
Modifying Consumer Demand						
High-deductible plans	↑	↔	↑	↓	↔	
Progressive cost sharing	↓	↔	↓	↓	↑	
Tiered cost sharing	↔	↑	↑	↓	↔	
Differential cost sharing by service/procedure	↔	↑	↑	↓	↔	
Modifying Provider Behavior						
Pay-for-performance	↓	↑	↔	↔	↑	
Bundled payment and capitation	↓	↑	↔	↑	↑	
Coverage rules and preauthorization	↑	↑	↑	↔	↔	
Controlling Prices						
Uniform pricing	↑	↔	↔	NA	NA	√
All-payer systems	↓	↔	↓	NA	NA	√
Instrumental Measures						
Electronic health records and other IT	↔	↑	↑	↓	↑	
Clinical effectiveness and cost-effectiveness research	↔	↔	↓	↔	↔	
Price transparency	↑	↔		NA	NA	√

Key: Model and option are: ↑ = highly compatible; ↔ = compatible; ↓ = incompatible; NA = option not applicable under expansion model.

and payment rules. An electronic health record might alert a provider that a patient has already received a particular diagnostic test but will not necessarily preclude a duplicate test if the provider will be rewarded for conducting it.

Interplay of Cost and Coverage Options

Reducing Need for Services

Preventive Services

The familiar problem with preventive services in an insurance context is that the services cost money now but may produce savings only much later—if ever. If many people change insurers from year to year, Insurer A might be making an investment that produces savings for Insurer B. Possibly under the connector option, if it has a limited number of insurers and relatively stable enrollment, insurers would be willing to invest voluntarily in efforts to promote use of preventive services. (This is a question for game theorists.) In the play-or-pay environment, some employers with a stable workforce might have similar incentives.

Under the nongroup option, basic policy standards to qualify for a subsidy could include coverage of specified preventive services and reduced cost sharing for these services. Similar standards could be imposed under the other options, but they might also afford opportunities to promote greater use of the services. These could be consumer focused. For example, some Medicaid programs are experimenting with contracts with beneficiaries, under which full benefits are contingent on the beneficiaries' compliance with specified utilization rules. An employer might require employees to obtain some preventive services as part of a behavior-based premium scheme, discussed later in this section. (Providers could be given incentives to promote use of preventive services through a pay-for-performance system, discussed below.)

Health-promotion activities, such as smoking cessation or weight-reduction programs, are commonly public health efforts or are conducted by employers. Because employers who offer these programs are often concerned as much with productivity as with potential health-benefit savings, it seems unlikely that play-or-pay would induce many additional employers to undertake these activities. At least some insurers are also working on individualized health-promotion programs, such as multidisciplinary efforts to combat childhood obesity (Dietz et al. 2007). From the insurer perspective, the incentive problems are similar to those for preventive services. One way of furthering health-promotion activities would be through an outcomes-based pay-for-performance program. Because outcomes for health promotion may be extremely long term, this approach might work best under the single-payer option.

One analyst has argued that current financing mechanisms are unlikely ever to place adequate emphasis on prevention and health promotion, and has suggested the establishment of a Wellness Trust (Lambrew 2007). This would be an agency within the Department of Health and Human Services, funded by assessments on insurers, that would pay directly for preventive services for all consumers as well as fund health-promotion programs. Possible concerns are that such a program would add complexity and inhibit coordination of preventive and curative services.

Behavior-Based Premiums

Insurers may offer different premiums, or employers may offer different premium contributions, to enrollees displaying approved or avoiding disapproved behaviors. At this time, insurers are offering smoking and nonsmoking rates, but some employers are considering other factors, such as participation in wellness programs. It is possible to conceive of programs that would reward participants for bringing their blood pressure under control or losing an appropriate amount of weight. But it is hard to imagine how such programs would be conducted by a nongroup carrier, with limited monitoring ability, and they may not be politically feasible in a connector or single-payer arrangement. For this reason, the option is chiefly available to large employers (although it may raise concerns about hiring discrimination based on health behaviors). Again, Medicaid programs might achieve similar results through beneficiary contracts.

Patient Safety and Reduced Medical Errors

Improvements in patient safety are included in the category of need reduction because the victims of medical errors require additional services they would not otherwise need. Medicare has announced that it will not pay hospitals for services required as a result of certain preventable conditions or injuries that should never occur, and some other purchasers are adopting similar policies. More broadly, patient safety could be considered in pay-for-performance systems. Both types of payment measures may be most effective under the connector and public program options; see the discussion of pay-for-performance systems, below. Regulators can also promote patient safety through licensure procedures.

Modifying Consumer Demand

High-Deductible Plans

High-deductible health plans (HDHPs) are intended to deter unnecessary utilization of services, lead consumers to consider costs and benefits in considering alternative treatment, and encourage price shopping—which, in turn, it is hoped, will promote price competition among providers. The plans may be combined with a tax-favored health savings account or, in employer plans, with a health reimbursement arrangement. As suggested earlier, a high-deductible plan design is hypothetically compatible with all of the coverage options except Medicaid expansion. If incorporated in a single-payer approach, it would need to be accompanied by some protection for low-income participants. It seems unlikely that an HDHP would be the sole option under a connector model. However, the connector could offer such plans among a range of other options, as FEHB has done.

A nongroup model could specify a minimum deductible for qualified plans. However, this would conflict with the consumer-choice orientation of these proposals. Notably, President Bush's most recent tax-credit proposal specified a maximum out-of-pocket limit, but not a minimum deductible. Although the HDHP concept seems to fit best with the subsidized nongroup option and has been incorporated in several proposals, it might be of greater interest to employers than to consumers. Although HDHP plans had high initial penetration in the nongroup market, recent growth in HDHP enrollment has been larger in employer plans (America's Health Insurance Plans [AHIP]). If a play-or-pay model specifies a minimum set of benefits to be offered by employers wishing to avoid the tax or assessment, the package is unlikely to be a high-deductible plan. However, employers could be allowed to offer an HDHP as a low-cost alternative for employees. In addition, it might be possible to develop rules under which a combination of the HDHP and employer contributions to a health savings account or health reimbursement arrangement could be determined to be actuarially equivalent to the required minimum benefit.

Progressive Cost Sharing

One issue raised by HDHP plans is that they are likely to have limited effects on the behavior of higher-income participants. At least one analyst has suggested a progressive cost-sharing system, under which the family deductible would be a fixed percentage of family income (Furman 2007). This is probably most workable retrospectively, through the tax system. (The author suggests a 7.5 percent threshold, making the option conceptually equivalent to replacing the current medical-expense deduction for itemizers with a refundable medical-expense credit.) This option is most compatible with a single-payer system, because everyone would have the same benefit package and the information needed could be readily assembled. The potential trade-off would be loss of political support for the system among middle- and high-income taxpayers.

Tiered Cost Sharing

Tiered cost sharing offers enrollees in network plans reduced cost sharing if they use a preferred subset of network providers, selected by the plan on the basis of efficiency, quality, or other criteria. Small insurers under the nongroup option would have too little data to make the selection but might use this option if there were a public database on provider costs and quality (see the discussion of price transparency later in this chapter). It is not clear, however, whether this benefit feature would be attractive to nongroup purchasers. Identifying the preferred providers would be politically very difficult under the single-payer option, and tiering would not be workable under a Medicaid expansion. This option is thus most compatible with the connector and play-or-pay options.

Differential Cost Sharing

Payers could require higher cost sharing when a consumer obtains a treatment deemed to be less effective or less cost-effective than alternative treatments (Orszag and Ellis 2007; Schoen et al. 2007). This approach is less harsh than actual denial of payment (discussed under coverage policies, below); providers would still be paid for the service, but patients would have an incentive to consider other treatment options. This approach is compatible with all the coverage models except Medicaid expansion but may be politically difficult under a single-payer model. This is especially true for procedures that offer slight improvements in outcomes but only at a much higher cost than some other treatment. Private insurers may be in a better position than a public program to make patients take cost into account. However, marketability of this approach depends on effectiveness research that can quantify cost-outcome trade-offs.

Modifying Provider Behavior

Pay-for-performance (P4P) programs reward providers either for achieving some target level of performance on selected process or outcome measures or for improving performance relative to some baseline measurement. P4P has received so much attention that this chapter could easily be devoted solely to this option. The following discussion considers how just a few key implementation issues might play out under the different coverage models.

Uniform or Varying Systems

P4P may have a greater effect on provider behavior if all, or at least many, major payers adopt comparable systems. Otherwise providers would be expected to collect different data and meet different objectives for different payers, making it difficult to prioritize or make necessary investments or organizational changes. Uniformity can emerge from insurer or provider initiatives, as in the case of California Integrated Healthcare—although even this program has not been able to establish uniform payment incentives across insurers, partly because of antitrust concerns (Integrated Healthcare Association 2007). Clearly a single payer or a connector administrator would be best positioned to develop uniform systems.

However, some people say that, because P4P is still in its infancy, it would be better to have continued experimentation with a variety of systems (Wilensky 2007). This could be allowed by the connector and might occur naturally under the play-or-pay option. However, considerable resources may be needed to develop measures (including appropriate risk adjusters for outcome measures), test incentives, and monitor results. It is not clear how many individual insurers would make the investment to develop programs that could be adopted by others. The single-payer model might be in a better position to experiment with different approaches through a demonstration authority comparable to Medicare's.

Form and Amount of the Incentive

P4P can just involve rewards for good performance or can also include penalties for poor performance. The proposal by the Centers for Medicare and Medicaid Services for a value-based purchasing system for Medicare inpatient services would fund incentive payments for high performers through an across-the-board reduction in base diagnostic-related-group payments (Centers for Medicare and Medicaid Services 2007).[4] This budget-neutral system effectively transfers funds from poor to high performers. Because it is hard to see how individual insurers could negotiate such an arrangement with providers, it is probably workable only in the single-payer and possibly the connector models. (Possibly some Medicaid programs could adopt this option, but not if their baseline payments to providers are already below cost.) A second issue is how big the incentives should be. A provider may not make system changes unless the amount of money in play for meeting a given objective is greater than the cost (Miller 2007). Again, uniformity across payers may play a role here. A single insurer might have to pay a great deal to steer performance on a measure of its own devising, while multiple insurers using a common system might achieve results with smaller incentive payments.

Whose Performance Is Measured and Who Is Paid

P4P for process measures can be implemented at the level of individual providers. However, rewarding (or penalizing) outcomes is more difficult, because patients with chronic conditions or complex problems may be seen by multiple providers. One suggested option, that the payer somehow allocate bonuses among the treating providers—Physician A gets x percent, Hospital B gets y percent—seems impossibly complex (Schoen et al. 2007). One alternative is simply to reward a single provider for the outcome. However, providers are unlikely to be willing to enter into P4P arrangements that depend on the performance of others over whom they have no control.

P4P for outcomes may be most practical if performance on a given measure is assessed and incentives provided for integrated groups of providers—such as for a hospital and its affiliated physicians, or for a primary care physician and some set of specialists he or she commonly works with. This in turn requires that providers come together and contract jointly to accept responsibility for care of certain kinds of patients: an ad hoc or formal network would contract with Acme Health Plan to guarantee some level of performance for the care of diabetics, for example. Or—because some of the patients included in the diabetic P4P measure are also included in the cardiac P4P measure—an entire integrated delivery system would accept responsibility for overall care of a defined population. This fundamental reorganization of health care delivery is the ultimate direction in which P4P, as well as some of the other options discussed below, seems to point. Providers are not likely to form integrated systems just to deal with Acme Health Plan. They might do so in order to deal with a single payer and, possibly, in some communities, to contract with an expanded Medicaid program. How delivery system reorganization would fit under any of the options that retain multiple competing insurers is considered below.

Bundled Payments and Capitation

Payers could make a single payment for an entire episode of care—for example, combining inpatient and physician payments into a comprehensive diagnostic-related-group payment for a hospital admission, or broadening this payment to include postdischarge care for some period, thus covering follow-up visits, home health, and so on (Schoen et al. 2007; Pham and Ginsburg 2007). This approach, meant to encourage hospitals and their affiliated physicians to work together to improve efficiency, would clearly be possible under a single payer or an expanded Medicaid program. But either might face political concerns about the possibility of underservice. Large insurers under the connector or play-for-pay options might have greater leeway to adopt bundled payments—if they have sufficient market power. But one observer notes that insurers have not tended to be very innovative in their payment methods; few have even reached the point of adopting diagnostic-related-group systems, instead paying hospitals a per diem rate or negotiating a fixed discount from billed charges (Ginsburg 2007).

Providers could also be capitated for providing the full range of services (or some subset, such as all ambulatory care or all care related to a specific condition) to a defined population for a fixed period. It is a little startling to see this option advanced by some analysts as a new concept. Capitation was widespread twenty years ago but has become less common, partly because of patient and regulator concerns, and perhaps partly because provider groups big enough to accept significant financial risk have enough market power to refuse it. One analysis has suggested that similar effects might be achieved through P4P systems that used overall spending for patients with a given condition as one of the measures considered in calculating bonuses (Pham and Ginsburg 2007). This would provide incentives for efficiency without placing providers at excessive risk. These schemes, too, have been tried before. They raise the same questions already discussed in the context of P4P: For which providers is efficiency measured, and who gets the payment? Again, the option may imply the emergence of integrated systems.

Coverage Policies

Under any of the coverage models, payers would continue to make decisions about what services will not be covered or will be covered only under specified circumstances or with prior authorization. Of course, coverage decisions have been a source of friction among health plans, consumers, employers, and regulators for many years. Some of this contention would be eased if research broadens the knowledge base about effective clinical practices. However, as discussed below, research may just shift the field of debate from effectiveness to cost-effectiveness, leading to even more painful disputes about the value of different treatments. It is not at all clear which model would promote more aggressive use of cost-effectiveness information. A single payer or connector might face more frequent political intervention in coverage decisions, while carriers under the nongroup or play-or-pay models might have greater freedom to restrict access to services deemed ineffective. Over the long term, however, coverage denials might lead once again to the backlash in the 1990s that produced patient bill of rights legislation and employer pressure to loosen managed care restrictions.

One alternative is to allow health plans to compete explicitly on the basis of the overall stringency of their evaluations and their price (Pauly 2005). That is, Plan A might have a high premium but cover every new treatment that shows up in the newspapers, while Plan B might have a lower premium but more rigorous review of new services. Consumers could then sort themselves out on the basis of their price sensitivity and their willingness to accept the plan rather than the physician as the arbiter of their care. There is a possible risk-selection problem that would need to be addressed, and it is not clear that this consumer-choice model would take all the politics out of coverage decision making: Consumers who accept a hypothetically limited plan when they are well might not be stoical about the plan's limits once they become sick. Still, plan competition on this basis is not inherently less reasonable than competition on the basis of the tightness of network restrictions. It seems more likely that such a market would emerge under the nongroup and play-or-pay options than under the connector model.

Controlling Prices

In the current system, health plans negotiate prices with providers, with the size of discounts theoretically dependent on the relative power of insurers and providers in a particular market. A single payer, of course, can ratchet down prices until quality and access problems (or predictions of these problems) create political counterpressure. The reverse might be true under a large Medicaid or public program expansion; programs might have to bring their payment rates closer to market prices or at least to marginal costs. Among the private insurance options, assuming that the connector model is more likely to promote consolidation than the nongroup model, participating plans would have enhanced market power and might be able squeeze down prices (possibly at the expense of whatever payers, such as self-insured employers, might be left out of the system). However, concentration in the insurance industry may be offset by consolidation of hospitals and other providers. Also, insurers' leverage in price negotiations may be affected, not only by their market share, but also by enrollees' demands for access to a wide selection of community providers (Ginsburg 2005). Advocates of a nongroup model with high-deductible plans contend that these plans would lead consumers to shop for better values and thus drive down prices. In practice, most of these plans give enrollees access to negotiated network prices before the deductible is met, dampening any incentive for shopping, and a plan that exposed enrollees to full provider charges would have difficulty competing.

Some people have suggested that the current pricing system is inherently inefficient and inhibits real competition among providers. At least two solutions have been suggested: uniform pricing by each provider and a return to the all-payer systems that proliferated in the early 1980s but have now largely vanished. Both of these are basically regulatory options but are discussed here because they may have different effects under different coverage models.

Under *uniform pricing,* each provider would set its own rates but would be required to charge the same rates to all payers (Porter and Teisberg 2004). (An open question is whether individual payers' P4P programs would still be permitted under this option.) Under an *all-payer system,* rates for institutional services might vary by provider, but each provider's rates would be approved by a regulatory entity; rates for physicians would be set on some uniform basis.

Uniform pricing would reduce the competitive advantage of large insurers under all private insurance models, although they would still have economies of scale and a greater ability than smaller competitors to use other cost-control techniques. All insurers would be able to steer their enrollees to lower-priced providers, but there might be no rationale for formal insurer-provider network contracts. One risk, possibly greater under the nongroup model, is that insurance market segmentation would emerge, with some plans offering affluent enrollees access to costly providers who were (or were perceived to be) of higher quality, while cut-rate plans offered only the lower-priced providers. Another concern, that safety-net providers would be disadvantaged, would depend in part on the extent to which a coverage model achieved universal coverage.

All-payer systems, at least for the hospital sector, are effectively the same as the global budgets established, for example, by Canada's provincial health plans. The regulator determines the hospital's total revenue needs for its projected volume and mix of cases, and rates are set at the level needed to achieve this total. In the physician sector, rate setting might be designed to limit total growth in physician expenditures, using some target comparable to Medicare's sustainable growth, which is meant to link physician fee increases to growth in GDP.

While this kind of general health care budgeting is common in single-payer systems, it is not clear how well it can be made to fit with approaches that retain competing private health plans. In the 1993 Clinton plan, regional alliances (more or less comparable to connectors, but with control over all except the self-insured employer market) would have set the rates to be paid by fee-for-service health plans, leaving managed care plans the option of trying to negotiate lower rates. This set up a conundrum: providers granting discounts to the managed care plans would have sought to shift costs to fee-for-service plans. If an alliance allowed the cost shift in its rate setting, the fee-for-service option would have become steadily less affordable, creating political problems. If it did not allow the cost shift, managed care plans—especially in rural areas or other areas with limited provider competition—would have had difficulty obtaining discounts and would have had to compete solely on their ability actually to control utilization, also leading to potential political backlash. (Some of the trade-offs involved were discussed—before the Clinton proposal—by Ginsburg and Thorpe [1992].) In Germany, all competing insurers (sickness funds) pay the same rates, negotiated jointly by plans and providers, without discounting. This has left plans to compete largely on the basis of risk selection; a new risk-adjustment system in 2009 aims to force plans to compete instead on the basis of disease management and gatekeeping (Cheng and Reinhardt 2008).

In both these cases, price controls and insurer competition are made to work together through an arrangement that oversees coverage for nearly the entire patient population and that uses risk adjustment to ensure that competition is on the basis of care management. This suggests that price controls would be compatible with a near-monopsony connector scheme and less so under the subsidized nongroup or play-or-pay options.

Instrumental Measures

Health Information Technology

Health information technology can be said to consist of three main components: electronic health records, maintained at the provider level; exchange of clinical data among providers using interoperable systems; and a personal health record (PHR) that ideally would include comprehensive information on an individual consumer's health conditions, medications, and past medical services and test results. A key difference between an electronic health record and a PHR is that the electronic health record includes only information entered by one provider or network of providers and is "owned" by those providers, while a PHR is theoretically owned by the consumer and includes information about services received from all the providers the consumer has used.

The role of payers in promoting the use of electronic health records and clinical data exchange is probably limited. The strategy for addressing the barriers to universal implementation of these components—standardization, capital, and technical assistance—has so far relied chiefly on providers and government as regulators and facilitators rather than purchasers. Public and private payers may play an indirect role to the extent that their information requirements for P4P and other purposes may spur smaller providers to invest in technology or consolidate into larger groups.

Payers might play a larger role in the development of PHR systems, which offer the potential for savings by reducing duplicative services, drug interactions, and so on. There are currently a number of PHR models (California HealthCare Foundation 2007). Consumers can simply enter their own data—such as medication lists, known health conditions, records of recent visits, perhaps test results that the patient knows about—using software such as Microsoft's new HealthVault. "Tethered" PHRs are maintained for patients by providers and can thus contain much more information, but only on services and findings at that provider or network of providers. Finally, insurers and employers are designing PHRs that can include data drawn from claims as well as data entered by the consumer. This information would be broader but less detailed than that in provider-developed PHRs and could be portable—allowing a lifelong record, regardless of whether the consumer changed providers, employers, or insurers. To address consumer confidentiality concerns, several major employers are funding an independent system called Dossia that would maintain the record for the consumer without making it available to employers and insurers.[5]

An insurer- or employer-based PHR might have the greatest long-range savings (and quality) potential, because it could give providers access to a patient's entire medical history. However, it might then raise the same issue as funding preventive services: Why make the investment in something whose savings potential might be long term and might benefit the patient's next insurer? The investment seems to make more sense if enrollment is fairly stable, perhaps under the connector model. A single-payer plan, of course, could access data needed to assemble a comprehensive PHR but for this reason may raise greater concerns about protection of patient privacy.

Effectiveness Research

Sound information about the comparative effectiveness of different treatment options is essential if public and private insurers are going to use coverage and payment policies to drive system performance. Although some insurers have conducted or sponsored studies of specific treatments or of multiple treatments for a specific condition, it seems unlikely that individual insurers would make a large investment in research whose results would benefit their competitors (Congressional Budget Office 2007). A single payer or connector administrator might fund effectiveness research, but there is an emerging consensus that findings are more likely to be credible if the research is conducted by an entity independent of payers (e.g., Medicare Payment Advisory Commission 2007).

Payers might play a larger role in assessing *cost*-effectiveness, as opposed to effectiveness per se. While an independent effectiveness research program might conclude that treatment A provides one more additional quality-adjusted life year than treatment B at a cost of $100,000, it might not be in a position to say whether treatment A should therefore be approved or disapproved (Congressional Budget Office 2007). Someone has to decide what a quality-adjusted life year, or whatever the outcome is, is worth. In the near term, this is likely to be difficult for a single-payer or Medicaid program, because of political pressure to pay an infinite sum for a quality-adjusted life year.[6] There might be somewhat more leeway under the connector and play-or-pay models, and considerably more under the nongroup model, for payers to deny services of small marginal value. Again, in all the models except Medicaid expansion, differential cost sharing for cost-ineffective services might be more palatable than outright denial.

In a world of perfect knowledge by all parties, competition among insurers might depend in part on how much different consumers were willing to pay in premiums for slightly improved outcomes (Pauly 2005). This would mean a shift from the implicit income-based rationing in the current system to explicit income-based rationing, and could lead to greater pressure for a single-payer system. (Even then, there would remain the question of whether a parallel private system, as in England, would be permitted.)

Price Transparency

Improving information about provider prices is key to the high-deductible plan concept and is important even for enrollees in conventional network plans, who are seldom able to ascertain whether they would pay more at one network provider than at another or what additional cost they would incur for an out-of-network service.

Many insurers are now providing at least some kind of price information to their enrollees, but few have reached the point of full transparency, including disclosure of negotiated network prices. A connector administrator or a large employer under the play-or-pay option might compel this disclosure. There is some debate about the possible effects of full transparency on competition among providers, or health plans, or both. Suppose that all hospitals and health plans in an area knew all the prices paid for a given procedure. If a hospital learned that a given insurer was paying other hospitals more for the procedure than it was receiving, it might demand the higher price. Conversely, if a health plan learned that a hospital had granted steeper discounts to competing insurers, it might ask for the same discount. Whether providers or health plans would prevail in this scenario would depend on which had the greater bargaining power.

Simply knowing prices would be insufficient for consumers to make fully informed choices, for two reasons. First, patients rarely know exactly what services they will receive during a given encounter. Second, Physician A will often order tests from Lab B and refer the patient to Specialist C. What the patient really needs to know is how the total out-of-pocket cost for an episode of care for a given condition will vary according to the patient's entry point into the system—and, ideally, how this total might change under alternative treatment options. Some insurers are now making estimates of this kind for internal purposes—for example, to select the preferred providers in a tiered cost-sharing system—but none are disclosing the results to enrollees. This is partly because providers would protest that the results were distorted by inadequate risk adjustment or other problems. At least one analyst has suggested that a fair system of cost transparency might require rules set by an independent arbiter, much as the Financial Accounting Standards Board sets rules for corporate financial statements (Galvin 2007).

Conclusion

Many of the cost-containment approaches described in this chapter are intended to induce changes in the health delivery system or will be more effective if these changes occur. Some people believe that steps should be taken to encourage the development of new kinds of providers. For example, Regina Herzlinger favors "focused factories," which would be centers for the comprehensive treatment of a single condition such as diabetes or AIDS. This approach has a large regulatory component—or perhaps, more properly, *de*regulatory component—as it may involve relaxing various restrictions that might inhibit innovation. These might include licensure and scope of practice laws, which some people characterize as perpetuating a "guild system" in health care; laws against the corporate practice of medicine; and perhaps antitrust laws (Galvin 2007).

While regulators may have a role in eliminating barriers to new types of care, payers will decide which are financially possible. Practitioners or entities (such as retail clinics) that can provide individual services at low cost may thrive under high-deductible plans. New types of facilities, on the other hand, can operate only if insurers are willing to pay for them. (The biggest insurer, Medicare, can bring new categories into being, as in the case of medical assistance facilities—quasi hospitals in isolated areas. The principle might be, "If you pay for it, they will build it.") Innovation could be hastened if a connector or other regulator required insurers to cover new provider types, although this would be equivalent to the much-derided state-mandated benefit laws.

Whatever new types of specific providers may emerge, many possible measures to improve incentives for efficiency seem to point in the direction of integrated delivery systems that cross provider boundaries and that are able to bear bundled or capitated payment risk and can be held accountable for high performance, however defined. The systems that might be expected to emerge might closely resemble the integrated systems contemplated in classic managed-competition proposals, with one critical difference. In the Enthoven model, the integrated system *was* the insurer, the "accountable health plan" competing for enrollment with other systems under the eye of the cooperative or alliance or connector that organized the competition (Enthoven 1988). Under the models currently under discussion, the integrated system would be *paid* by the insurer, possibly with a transfer of some amount of the insurance risk.

Why should the providers who have invested in the development of an integrated system sell their services on a risk basis to Acme Health Plan instead of offering themselves directly as Provider Health Plan? One answer is that past attempts to form Provider Health Plans have not been successful, because of limited access to capital, conflicts of interest between the plan and its constituent providers, and other factors. Entry barriers would be greater if consolidation in the insurance industry continues at its recent pace or is accelerated—as might occur under a connector model. So what could emerge is what some observers have called a two-market model: provider systems competing for insurers and insurers competing for enrollees (Chernichovsky 2002).

If the provider systems are competing on dimensions of cost-effectiveness, quality, patient satisfaction, or whatever other metrics are thought to be desirable, what is the basis of insurer competition? In the subsidized nongroup model, unless it included strict regulation of underwriting and rating practices, insurers might continue to compete through risk selection, perhaps rendering the relative efficiency of their provider networks moot. In an FEHB-like connector arrangement, risk adjustment could deal with this problem, but insurers might still offer varying benefit packages—making it difficult for participating consumers or employer groups to assess whether price differences reflected benefits or efficiency. This problem, too, could be addressed through benefit standardization. There might be a little bit of competition on the basis of customer service or "amenities," but essentially plans would be differentiated by the relative quality and (passed-through) prices of the provider systems with which they contracted.

This chapter began with the premise that coverage-expansion models and cost-containment options were more or less independent, although some combinations might work better than others. However, increasing numbers of analysts contend that cost containment will require sweeping changes in the way health services are delivered. If it is expected that these changes will be driven by the way providers are paid, then the basis of competition among payers becomes central. Different coverage-expansion models are debated in terms of a preference for public or private funding sources, relative equity, ease of administration, degree of disruption of current arrangements, and so on. But different models also imply differences in the kind of insurance market created and the incentives that exist for insurers to drive change in the delivery system.

As was suggested at the outset, this chapter's assumptions about the kind of market that would emerge under each expansion model amount to speculation and not prediction. But each model will affect the market *somehow*. The point to be emphasized is that choices among models are not just about the simplest (or most readily enacted) way of getting some kind of health insurance card into every American's hands, but about what those cards will buy and how they might be leveraged to improve the performance and value of the health system.

Notes

1. These were the estimates for the two proposals most nearly achieving universal coverage, reaching 40.3 million of a baseline 41.9 million uninsured; the remaining 1.6 million were undocumented or "hard to reach" people.

2. Author's analysis of *2006 Annual Social and Economic Supplement* (ASEC) to the Current Population Survey, U.S. Bureau of Census.

3. One example of a state-level single-payer proposal is Representative Charles Dingell's national health insurance plan, H.R. 15 in the 110th Congress.

4. Medicare has long prohibited hospitals from sharing savings even on the base diagnostic-related-group payment with physicians. The Centers for Medicare and Medicaid Services is now conducting a "gainsharing" demonstration, under which incentive payments are permitted at selected sites (Centers for Medicare and Medicaid Services 2006).

5. The Dossia initiative was delayed by contract problems and has not yet been implemented (Smerd 2007).

6. The Oregon Health Plan in the 1990s adopted a prioritization system for Medicaid benefits, ranking diagnosis-treatment pairs by probability of preventing death or disability and excluding low-ranking services. The threshold was set low enough that only clearly ineffective services were excluded, and the rules were not binding on the private health plans that served most Medicaid beneficiaries (Bodenheimer 1997).

References

Aaron, Henry J. 2005. *Treatment of Coronary Artery Disease: What Does Rationing Do?* Policy brief 148. Washington, DC: Brookings Institution, December. www.brookings. edu/papers/2005/12useconomics_aaron02.aspx. (Accessed 8 July 2008.)

Bodenheimer, Thomas. 1997. "The Oregon Health Plan—Lessons for the Nation." *New England Journal of Medicine* 337 (9): 651–56.

California HealthCare Foundation. 2007. *Perspectives on the Future of Personal Health Records.* Oakland, CA, June. www.chcf.org/documents/chronicdisease/PHRPerspectives. pdf. (Accessed 8 July 2008.)

Centers for Medicare and Medicaid Services. 2006. "DRA 5007 Medicare Hospital Gainsharing Demonstration Solicitation." www.cms.hhs.gov/DemoProjectsEvalRpts/ downloads/DRA5007_Solicitation.pdf. (Accessed 8 July 2008.)

———. 2007. *Report to Congress: Plan to Implement a Medicare Hospital Value-Based Purchasing Program.* Baltimore. www.cms.hhs.gov/AcuteInpatientPPS/downloads/ HospitalVBPPlanRTCFINALSUBMITTED2007.pdf. (Accessed 8 July 2008.)

Cheng, Tsung-Mei, and Uwe E. Reinhardt. 2008. "Shepherding Major Health System Reforms: A Conversation with German Health Minister Ulla Schmidt." *Health Affairs* Web exclusive (April 8): W204–W213. http://content.healthaffairs.org/cgi/search?and orexactfulltext=and&resourcetype=1&disp_type=&author1=cheng&fulltext=&pubdate _year=2008&volume=&firstpage= (Accessed 18 November 2008).

Chernichovsky, Dov. 2002. "Pluralism, Public Choice, and the State in the Emerging Paradigm in Health Systems." *Milbank Quarterly* 80 (1): 5–39.

Committee for Economic Development. 2007. *Quality, Affordable Health Care for All: Moving Beyond the Employer-Based Health-Insurance System.* Washington, DC: Committee for Economic Development. www.ced.org/docs/report/report_healthcare200710.pdf. (Accessed 8 July 2008.)

Congressional Budget Office. 2007. *Research on the Comparative Effectiveness of Medical Treatments.* Washington, DC: Congressional Budget Office. www.cbo.gov/ftpdocs/88xx/ doc8891/12–18-ComparativeEffectiveness.pdf. (Accessed 8 July 2008.)

Dietz, William, Jason Lee, Howell Wechsler, Sarath Malepati, and Bettylou Sherry. 2007. "Health Plans' Role in Preventing Overweight in Children and Adolescents." *Health Affairs* 26 (2): 430–40.

Enthoven, Alain C. 1988. "Managed Competition: An Agenda for Action." *Health Affairs* 7 (3): 25–47.

Feder, Judith, and Donald W. Moran. 2007. "Cost Containment and the Politics of Health Care Reform." In *Restoring Fiscal Sanity 2007: The Health Spending Challenge,* ed. Alice M. Rivlin and Joseph R. Antos, chapter 7. Washington, DC: Brookings Institution.

Furman, Jason. 2007. *The Promise of Progressive Cost Consciousness in Health-Care Reform.* Washington, DC: Hamilton Project (Brookings Institution), April.

Galvin, Robert S. 2007. "Consumerism and Controversy: A Conversation with Regina Herzlinger." *Health Affairs* Web exclusive (July 24): W552–W559. content.healthaffairs. org/cgi/content/full/hlthaff.26.5.w552v1/DC1. (Accessed 8 July 2008.)

Ginsburg, Paul B. 2005. "Competition in Health Care: Its Evolution Over the Past Decade." *Health Affairs* 24 (6): 1512–22.

———. 2007. "Private Payer Roles in Moving to More Efficient Health Spending." In *Restoring Fiscal Sanity 2007,* ed. Alice M. Rivlin and Joseph R. Antos, chapter 6. Washington, DC: Brookings Institution.

———. 2008. "Employment-Based Health Benefits Under Universal Coverage." *Health Affairs* 27 (3): 675–85.

Ginsburg, Paul B., and Kenneth E. Thorpe. 1992. "Can All-Payer Rate Setting and the Competitive Strategy Coexist?" *Health Affairs* 11 (2): 73–86.

Integrated Healthcare Association. 2007. *Advancing Quality Through Collaboration: The California Pay for Performance Program.* Oakland, CA. www.iha.org/wp020606.pdf. (Accessed 8 July 2008.)

Keehan, Sean, John A. Poisal, Christopher Truffer, Sheila Smith, Andrea Sisko, Cathy Cowan, and, Bridget Dickensheets. 2008. "Health Spending Projections Through 2017: The Baby-Boom Generation Is Coming to Medicare." *Health Affairs* Web exclusive (February 26): W145–W155. http://content.healthaffairs.org/cgi/search?an dorexactfulltext=and&resourcetype=1&disp_type=&author1=keehan&fulltext=&pub date_year=2007&volume=&firstpage= (Accessed 18 November 2008).

Lambrew, Jeanne M. 2007. *A Wellness Trust to Prioritize Disease Prevention.* Washington, DC: Hamilton Project (Brookings Institution).

Long, Steven H., and M. Susan Marquis. 1994. "Universal Health Insurance and Uninsured People." CRS Report 94–689 EPW. Report prepared by the RAND Corporation for the U.S. Office of Technology Assessment / U.S. Congressional Research Service, August 5.

Medicare Payment Advisory Commission. 2007. *Report to the Congress: Promoting Greater Efficiency in Medicare.* Washington, DC. June. www.medpac.gov/documents/ Jun07_EntireReport.pdf. (Accessed 8 July 2008.)

Miller, Harold D. 2007. *Creating Payment Systems to Accelerate Value-Driven Health Care: Issues and Options for Policy Reform.* New York: Commonwealth Fund, September.

Orszag, Peter R., and Philip Ellis. 2007. "Addressing Rising Health Care Costs: A View from the Congressional Budget Office." *New England Journal of Medicine* 357 (19): 1885–87.

Pauly, Mark V. 2005. "Competition and New Technology." *Health Affairs* 24 (6): 1523–35.

Pham, Hoangmai, and Paul B. Ginsburg. 2007. "Unhealthy Trends: The Future of Physician Services." *Health Affairs* 26 (6): 1586–98.

Porter, Michael E., and Elizabeth Olmsted Teisberg. 2004. "Redefining Competition in Health Care." *Harvard Business Review* (June), reprint R0406D.

Schoen, Cathy, Stuart Guterman, Anthony Shih, Jennifer Lau, Sophie Kasimow, Anne Gauthier, and Karen Davis. 2007. *Bending the Curve: Options for Achieving Savings and Improving Value in U.S. Health Spending.* New York: Commonwealth Fund, December.

Sheils, John, and Randall Haught. 2003. *Cost and Coverage Analysis of Ten Proposals to Expand Health Insurance Coverage.* Report by the Lewin Group for the Robert Wood Johnson Foundation Covering America project, October. www.esresearch.org/publications/SheilsLewinall/Sheils%20Report%20Final.pdf. (Accessed 8 July 2008.)

Smerd, Jeremy. 2007. "Year-Old Dossia Hits Restart Amidst Legal Spat." *Workforce Management* (October). www.workforce.com/section/00/article/25/15/16.html. (Accessed 8 July 2008.)

Wilensky, Gail R. 2007. "The Challenge of Medicare." In *Restoring Fiscal Sanity 2007: The Health Spending Challenge,* ed. Alice M. Rivlin and Joseph R. Antos, Chapter 3. Washington, DC: Brookings Institution.

13

Simplifying Administration of Health Insurance

MARK MERLIS

The high administrative costs of America's health insurance system, with its thousands of insuring entities and more than a million providers and practitioners, have been a focus of policy discussion for decades. Advocates of single-payer options have often pointed to the lower costs in other countries' systems or in our own Medicare program and have suggested that savings on administrative spending from adoption of universal public insurance could finance much of the cost of care for the uninsured. Conversely, those who favor a reduced role for insurance in medical care financing—for example, through the promotion of high-deductible insurance plans—contend that this approach would save money because a third party would not be interposed in many routine consumer-provider transactions.

In effect, both those views point toward a utopia of simplicity in which there would be no insurance-related costs. At one extreme might be, not universal insurance, but a claims-free system of budgets and salaries—such as the pre-Thatcher British National Health Service. At the other extreme, all costs of health care would be paid by the consumer. Some individual practitioners and entire sectors—for example, hearing aids and related care—still operate in this prelapsarian way.

This chapter assumes that, whatever shape health reform might take, there will still be at least one insurer, doing some of the things insurers currently do. It begins with a review of some ways of defining or classifying administrative costs, both of insurers and of other participants in the system, and the fragmentary estimates of how large these costs are. This is followed by a discussion of current efforts to reduce administrative costs, many of which have focused on standardizing and simplifying transactions among insurers, providers, and employers. It then considers how various health care reform proposals, whether or not directly targeted at administrative costs, might reduce—or add to—the complexity of the current system.

Defining and Classifying Administrative Costs

Administrative costs of the health insurance system include (1) spending by public and private health insurers other than actual payments to providers and (2) costs incurred by other system participants, including providers, employers, and consum-

267

ers, in dealing with insurers. Identifying and estimating the second class of costs has proved elusive, but even the first is less clear-cut than it appears.

In an influential article, Kenneth Thorpe (1992) suggested that administrative costs could be classified in terms of four functions—transaction related, benefits management, selling and marketing, and regulatory and compliance—and then showed how these categories apply in several sectors—health insurance, hospitals, nursing homes, physicians, firms, and consumers. Some of the costs Thorpe cites—for example, hospital waste management—might be classified as patient care rather than administration. Others, while clearly administrative—for example, strategic planning or advertising—are not related to the health insurance system. For example, providers would advertise to attract patients even in an insurance-free, cash-on-the-table system. (Indeed, they might advertise more, because they could not rely on insurers to steer patients to them through network arrangements.) Still, the formulation is useful in emphasizing that health insurance imposes costs on different actors and that some of these are intangible opportunity costs—such as time spent by consumers in finding a health insurer and choosing among available benefits.

Perhaps a simpler way of thinking about insurance-related administrative costs is to enumerate all the activities that people or organizations must perform that they would not perform in a cash-only universe. Many of these can be characterized as transactions or as exchanges of information between two different parties in the system (see Table 13.1). Other columns or rows could be added—for example, for transactions with government, as regulator or tax collector, and for the brand-new world of transactions with the financial institutions that hold health savings account deposits. And there certainly might be more items in each cell.

In an insurance-free world, there would be only one sector—provider-consumer—and there would only be one kind of transaction, billing and collection. Even this would be dramatically simplified: The bill might just read, "Saw Mrs. Jones, $150." In a world with just one insurer, such as a Canadian provincial health plan, the employer column would disappear (unless private supplementary coverage was permitted, an important qualification discussed later). In a multi-insurer world with employer-based coverage, all the cells remain. The goal of simplification in this context is to eliminate some of the transactions in a given cell or make it possible to complete them more easily or expeditiously.

Estimates of Administrative Costs

There are numerous estimates of the administrative costs of health plans and public insurance programs, as well as a few attempts to estimate costs borne by providers and employers. This section begins with the most commonly cited figures, those in the national health expenditures (NHE) series developed by the Centers for Medicare and Medicaid Services (CMS n.d.). It then briefly summarizes some of the other estimates of private insurance and provider costs. (More details of individual results are furnished in an appendix at www.nasi.org.)

Table 13.1

Insurance-related Transactions or Information Exchanges

	Employer	Insurer or ASO[a]	Provider
Consumer	Plan selection, enrollment, status changes. Payroll deduction. Complaint resolution. COBRA.	Marketing, nongroup plan selection and enrollment. Underwriting. Process, reimburse nonassigned claims. EOBs. Info about covered dependents. Grievances, appeals.	Obtain insurance information. Collect copays, balance billing. Provide/obtain required referrals. Provide info needed by consumer for nonassigned claim.
Employer[b]		Select, contract with insurer(s). Provide enrollment, status change info. Pay premiums. May require quality, P4P, or other reporting.	[Some possible contacts in the context of worker's compensation claims, which will not be considered here.]
Insurer[c]		Insurer-to-insurer: coordination of benefits.	Contracting, price negotiation. Verify insurance enrollment, service coverage. Credentialing. Claims. Pre-authorization, UR, and disease management. Quality and P4P reporting.

[a] Agents/brokers may be involved in some functions. ASO = Administration Services Only
[b] Other than employer acting as insurer.
[c] Includes self-insured employer or its administrative service organization, ASO.

Figure 13.1 **Administrative Costs and Net Cost of Private Insurance as Percent of Total Cost, 1966–2005**

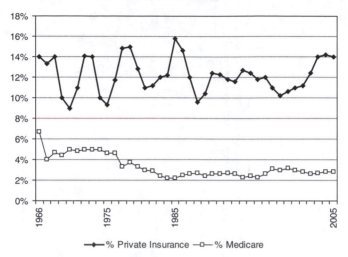

National Health Expenditures

The NHE has a category denoted as "administrative costs and net costs of private insurance." For public programs, such as Medicare and Medicaid, the figure is derived from Treasury documents, additional CMS data, and state reports. The private insurance figure, constructed from a variety of sources, is meant to equal total premium revenue minus benefit payments; it thus includes administrative costs, other expenses such as taxes, and surplus or profit. Nonpremium revenues, such as investment income, are omitted (CMS 2006).

Figure 13.1 shows the NHE estimates for private insurance and Medicare from 1966 through 2005. The numbers are administrative costs and profit as a percentage of total costs. Note that the NHE does not include estimates of provider administrative costs.

As America's Health Insurance Plans (2006b) have pointed out, the private insurance number varies considerably, ranging from 9 to 15 percent over the years (Lemieux 2005). This may reflect fluctuations in profitability. Health insurance was long thought to be subject to a six-year "underwriting cycle," with years of higher profits followed by years of lower ones. This cycle has clearly moderated in recent years, and some analysts contend that it no longer exists. One possible factor is increasing consolidation in the health insurance industry, an issue considered below. Declining competition in many markets may make it easier for insurers to pass rising benefit costs to purchasers instead of accepting reduced profit margins.

The total Medicare estimate includes payments to Medicare Advantage plans, and the Medicare administrative costs include the administrative component of Medicare Advantage plan bids—on average, about 8 percent of the bid.

If Medicare Advantage costs are excluded, administrative costs for original Medicare in 2005 drop from the 3 percent shown in the figure to about 2 percent. Implementation of the new Part D prescription drug program in 2006 has probably increased Medicare's administrative cost percentage, but estimates are not yet available.

Some believe Medicare figures are understated, or comparisons between Medicare and private insurance are inappropriate (e.g., Litow 2006; Zycher 2007; Lemieux 2005):

- The NHE estimates fail to allocate to Medicare some program-related costs incurred by other federal agencies (such as prosecution of Medicare fraud by the Justice Department or policy making by Congress, equivalent to private insurance management). While this is true, analysts' attempts to allocate these outside costs are not very persuasive.
- Medicare has lower claims-processing costs relative to benefit costs than private insurance, because the average Medicare claim is larger. This is definitely not true of inpatient care—beneficiaries have more discharges at a lower cost per discharge—and probably not for other services. However, it is the case that Medicare's fixed costs are being compared to a larger amount of aggregate benefit spending, resulting in a lower percentage.
- Medicare spends too little on valuable administrative activities such as disease management, member education, and customer service.

Whatever the merit of these objections, it is clear that private insurers incur some costs—such as for marketing and underwriting—not incurred by public programs. And of course even nonprofit health plans seek to achieve some surplus, as a cushion against future losses or to fund capital spending. Whether profits should be included in estimates of administrative cost is debatable. Some of the estimates described in the next section include profit, and others do not.

Private Insurance Administrative Costs

Estimates of insurance costs are derived from surveys of insurers or from insurer filings with state insurance departments. Total costs for Blue Cross plans and commercial insurers across all lines of business, not including profit or surplus, tend to be about 12 percent of premiums. (One lower estimate in the appendix excludes some sales costs.) Although there is a long-standing perception that health maintenance organizations (HMOs) have higher costs because of their more intensive care-management activities, one study of the Blues' commercial business found that HMOs' costs were actually slightly below those for indemnity or preferred-provider-organization plans and higher than those for point-of-service plans. This may be because all types of plans have now adopted some HMO-like management practices.

Breaking down insurers' costs is quite difficult because each of the available studies has a different way of categorizing functional components. Very roughly, claims processing and customer service account for 2 to 4 percent of premiums. Direct sales and marketing expenses, including underwriting costs, are 3 to 4 percent of premiums, although one study that tries to estimate the share of non-marketing cost centers that might be considered as marketing related gives an indirect marketing cost estimate of 8 percent. State premium tax rates range from 0 to 4.3 percent but are commonly in the 2 to 3 percent range (Actuarial Research Corporation 2003). These taxes are sometimes waived for the Blues and are never paid by self-insured employers.

Administrative costs are much higher for small employer groups—often in the range of 20 to 30 percent of premiums—than for larger ones, for several reasons. First, marketing costs are higher. While larger groups commonly deal directly with the insurer, small groups are enrolled by agents and brokers who are paid on commission. Second, because expenses for small groups are difficult to predict, insurers often demand higher risk reserves. Third, small-group carriers in states still engage in underwriting, with its attendant costs, to set group premium rates. For these reasons, costs in the nongroup market may be even higher, although there are no reliable data.

Larger employers who self-insure generally contract with insurers or other third-party administrators on an administrative-services-only basis. Blue Cross administrative-services-only charges range from 8 to 9 percent of total health benefit spending; noninsurer third-party administrators may charge less. In either case, costs are lower than for insured groups of the same size because marketing expenses are negligible, the plan pays no premium taxes, and the contractor establishes no risk reserves. In addition, the employers themselves usually perform some functions—such as processing enrollments and collecting premiums—that would otherwise be performed by an insurer.

Provider Costs

Overall administrative costs for physicians range from 25 to 30 percent of practice revenues. Hospital administrative costs appear to be lower, although the distinction between patient care and administrative costs may be fuzzy. Separating out insurance-related costs is difficult—especially for physician offices, where the same employee may be scheduling appointments (noninsurance), obtaining coverage information from patients (insurance), and so on.

For physicians, one study found costs related to claims and utilization management amounting to 10 percent of practice revenues. Another study, which estimated insurance-related costs in more cost centers and included an estimate of physicians' time spent on insurance matters, estimated costs for a primary care office of 15 percent of revenues.

For hospitals, insurance-related costs may be in the range of 7 to 11 percent of total patient revenues. It should be noted, however, that the available studies are all based on costs in California. Total hospital spending in California, per capita, was $1,613 in 2004, compared to a national average of $1,931 (Author's calculation from CMS estimates; available at www.cms.hhs.gov/NationalHealthExpendData/downloads/res-us.pdf). If fixed costs are being spread across smaller total revenues in California than elsewhere, they might be higher as a percentage of revenues than national averages.

Employer Costs

Larger employers—those with two hundred or more workers—often perform enrollment and premium-collection functions that would otherwise be performed by an insurer or administrative-services-only contractor. A study in 2000 estimated that these employers were spending $250 per covered worker to administer health benefits (Kaiser Family Foundation and Health Research and Educational Trust 2000). This would have been about 10 percent of health benefit costs for single coverage and 4 percent of costs for family coverage in that year. (This assumes that the employer's administrative costs are about the same for both coverage types.) As compensation of human resources personnel has probably not kept pace with rising health care costs, these percentages are likely to have dropped in more recent years.

Simplifying Insurance-Related Transactions

There has been substantial progress toward standardization of provider-insurer and employer-insurer information exchanges, partly spurred by the 1996 enactment of the Health Insurance Portability and Accountability Act (HIPAA). While HIPAA has been largely implemented, there remain many complications and some areas in which uniformity remains a distant goal. Less has been done to simplify transactions between consumers and the other actors, partly because most efforts have focused on electronic exchanges to which consumers are rarely a party. (This could well change, as it is easy to imagine that some consumers will expect to be able to perform some functions online, such as adding a dependent to their coverage or filing a nonassigned claim.)

It is important to distinguish the information exchanges discussed in this chapter, which involve insurance-related transactions, from electronic health information exchange among different providers. There is interest in the development of computerized medical records and interoperability standards that would allow exchange of these records among providers, to improve coordination, reduce medical errors, and so on. While insurance-related exchange and electronic health information are not unrelated—for example, information needed to file a claim could be derived from a medical record entry—electronic health information is a grander and more difficult undertaking than measures considered here.

Pre-HIPAA initiatives

Standardization began with the development of uniform claims forms. Work in this area began in 1968, just after the implementation of Medicare and Medicaid. The first standard form, the UB-82, for institutional services, was finally approved by the National Uniform Billing Committee in 1982; its successor, the UB-92, is now in more or less universal use. The parallel form for practitioner services was the HCFA-1500 (now the NUCC-1500, for the National Uniform Claim Committee).

While many payers and providers adopted these paper forms, their use was by no means universal, and the transition to electronic billing and payment was hindered by the existence of numerous different processing systems, each with its own expectations about what fields needed to be completed and how data were to be coded. Private and sometimes public clearinghouses emerged—in effect, translation services that converted data submitted by one party to the form preferred by the other and, as necessary, requested additional needed information. The American National Standards Institute and other organizations began to develop uniform data standards, but their adoption was voluntary. A 1995 survey of insurers found that, while 55 percent of insurers could accept some claims electronically, they were using data sets from different standard-setting organizations or proprietary systems of their own (Health Insurance Association of America 1997). Meanwhile, there were still many payers, and many more providers, who continued to use only paper forms.

Some states encouraged or imposed standardization. In New York, the state health department, with funding from the Robert Wood Johnson Foundation, established Universal New York Health Care in 1990 (Beauchamp and Rouse 1990). Under UNY-Care, all hospitals in one region of the state were to submit their claims to a single entity (actually two contracting clearinghouses), which would pay the claims and then obtain reimbursement from insurers. The initiative was voluntary and ended with the expiration of the grant in 1993. The following year, New York passed a law phasing in a requirement that all providers submit claims electronically and developed its own standard forms. (Maryland passed a similar law in 1993 but repealed it after realizing that providers were incapable of complying; cited in Maine Task Force 1998.)

The Utah Health Information Network was established in 1993 as a voluntary coalition of government, payers, and providers. Initial participants contributed start-up funding, and data standards were developed by consensus. The network functions as the clearinghouse for eligibility, claims, and other transactions between more than 450 payers (including Medicare and Medicaid) and 100 percent of Utah hospitals and 90 percent of Utah physicians. Providers pay an annual membership fee, while payers pay a transaction fee. The program is now working toward clinical data interchange (Sundwall 2006).

Under a 1994 law, Minnesota required insurers, providers, and employers who used electronic data interchange to conform to a set of state-developed specifications based on standards of the American National Standards Institute. No one was required to submit claims or other transactions electronically; only parties that chose to do so were subject to the standards (Maine Task Force 1998). A 2007 law requires electronic filing by 2009 (see Minnesota Statutes 2007, Chap. 62J.536).

HIPAA and the Administrative Simplification Compliance Act

HIPAA, enacted in 1996, required the secretary of the Department of Health and Human Services to develop standard forms and uniform data elements for electronic transmission of nine common transactions:

- Health claims or equivalent encounter information;
- Health claims attachments (i.e., detailed information on conditions or procedures needed for adjudication of a claim);
- Enrollment and disenrollment in a health plan;
- Eligibility for a health plan;
- Health care payment and remittance advice;
- Health plan premium payments;
- First report of injury (for workers' compensation cases);
- Health claim status; and
- Referral certification and authorization.

All health plans and health care clearinghouses would have to accept electronic transactions in standard format from any employer or provider. Note that the rule was one-way. Plans had to accept standardized transactions; that is, they could not refuse electronic submissions or impose alternate formats. But the standards applied to employers and providers only if they chose to submit transactions electronically. Providers could still choose to do all their business on paper.

Standards have been finalized for all the transactions except first report of injury and health claims attachments; the latter raise difficult issues, considered below. After a complicated phase-in, compliance with published standards is mandatory for all covered entities.

The secretary was also required to develop unique health identifiers for individuals, employers, health plans, and health care providers. Identifiers for health plans and providers have been adopted, and are fully mandatory since mid–2008. A proposed rule on health plan identifiers has been postponed, and Congress has since 1998 repeatedly specified that Department of Health and Human Services appropriations may not be used to develop individual identifiers, because of privacy concerns and also because some people viewed an individual ID as providing "a key element needed for a government takeover of health care" (Armey 2001).

In 2001, the Administrative Simplification Compliance Act required all Medicare providers and suppliers to submit Medicare claims electronically and in compliance with HIPAA standards by October 2003. While the rule applies only to Medicare, possibly providers shifting to electronic filing for one payer would be more prone to do so for others. However, providers with fewer than twenty-five employees and practitioners or other suppliers with fewer than ten employees are exempt. This exception exempts an estimated 71 percent of physician offices and 69 percent of home health agencies (CMS 2003).

Progress and Barriers

Even before HIPAA, large payers and providers had made progress in electronic claims processing. Surveys by America's Health Insurance Plans and its predecessor Health Insurance Association of America have found that the percentage of claims submitted electronically went from 2 percent in 1990 to 40 percent in 1999 and 44 percent in 2002 (America's Health Insurance Plans 2006b). Of the 1 billion claims submitted to Medicare in fiscal year 2002, before the effective date of the Administrative Simplification Compliance Act, all but 13.9 percent were submitted electronically (CMS 2003). As of 2006, the America's Health Insurance Plans survey found that 75 percent of claims to private insurers were submitted electronically. This might indicate that HIPAA and the Administrative Simplification Compliance Act accelerated the move to electronic claims, but it also suggests that there is limited take-up by small providers and practices. There are no equivalent data for other key HIPAA transactions, such as transmission of enrollment data by employers and eligibility verification.

Payers and providers are also working outside the HIPAA framework to further expedite common transactions. The Council on Affordable Quality Healthcare has developed standards for real-time verification of eligibility and benefits and certifies vendors whose systems meet those standards. Providers who use one of the certified vendors can obtain coverage information from any of the health plans participating in the program.

Some individual insurers have developed systems, available to their network providers only at this point, that move beyond verification toward something resembling real-time claims adjudication. In CIGNA's HealthePass program, for example, the provider swipes a member ID card, enters the procedures performed, and learns immediately what will be paid and the amount of the patient's liability. (Humana has a similar system.) As with a credit card charge, the transaction is processed for payment without a further claim from the provider. The service is promoted as especially useful for patients with health savings accounts; the insurer ID card can function as a debit card that draws the required patient contribution from the patient's account. More controversially, for patients who do not have health savings accounts the ID can function as a credit card, with patient liability added to a running debt balance.

There are also efforts to address transactions not yet subject to HIPAA standardization. For example, the Council on Affordable Quality Healthcare has developed a universal credentialing database. Providers anywhere in the United States can enter credentialing information on a single standard form, and participating plans and hospitals can use this information for initial applications, recredentialing, and other functions. At least one state is reportedly working on its own to develop a unique patient identifier, the original HIPAA goal blocked by congressional action.

Whatever further progress may be made by private groups or state governments, the HIPAA process has revealed at least two key barriers to simplification.

First, the HIPAA standards do not establish absolute uniformity in payers' systems. Standards for a particular transaction specify a set of fields, formats, and a range of possible entries for the field. But a health plan may require that certain fields be completed, forbid the completion of others, and specify that only certain codes are valid within a given field. These requirements are spelled out in "companion documents" issued by individual payers. (The Claredi organization, for example, has compiled more than one thousand of these documents.) Even Medicare carriers in different regions issue separate companion documents. This means that, despite HIPAA, even the largest providers are continuing to rely on clearinghouses to format and transmit their data to multiple payers.

Second, there may be some amount of irreducible complexity in insurance-related transactions. Some kinds of transactions are comparatively straightforward. In the case of pharmacy services, the claim is for a particular quantity of a drug with a specific National Drug Code (NDC), and the payer can write simple decision rules for each code. (This is why real-time adjudication is already a reality for drug benefits.) For other kinds of services, preauthorization or claims processing may require more extensive communications between provider and payer. Payers may require detailed information on patient medical history, diagnostic test results, or past treatment to make coverage decisions. These information exchanges are the subject of the key HIPAA-specified transaction for which final standards have not yet been issued, claims attachments. Part of the problem is that much of the information needed cannot be readily reduced to a few codes on a standard form, and few providers would be capable of coding the information even if such a form could be devised. (The CMS draft rules would have required insurers to accept scanned documents, natural language text, or coded information, whichever the provider chose; CMS 2005.)

Even if forms and coding could be standardized, these transactions are likely to continue to require staff or professional time at both ends. Payers have to be able to say exactly what they need, the provider has to figure out what to send and extract the specific information needed, and the payer has to manually review what was sent and determine if further information is needed. It is not certain how many claims can be processed simply and routinely and how many require further information. In its proposed rule, CMS cited a 1993 estimate by the Workgroup for Electronic Data Interchange that 25 percent of all health care claims require additional documentation; CMS guessed that half these documentation requests might be met by the standard formats it was proposing. Some commenters on the rule contended that these estimates were too high.

Policy Options

Policy makers could take a number of steps to simplify or expedite insurance-related transactions.

National Clearinghouse

There is an entire industry of private clearinghouses that function as intermediaries between payers and providers, and some states are following Utah in developing a statewide clearinghouse system. However, no single clearinghouse can yet undertake to match every provider with every payer. Even Utah's system, which includes every in-state insurer, can process transactions for people covered by some out-of-state insurers but not others. Wicks, Meyer, and Silow-Carroll (undated) have suggested that there should be a single national clearinghouse. All insurers and health plans would have to participate, and ongoing operations would be funded by contributions from insurers and self-insured employer plans. Health plans would issue enrollees a standardized card, resembling the CIGNA HealthePass, which could be read by any provider.

This would fill some holes in the current ad hoc system, and might be especially helpful in streamlining coordination-of-benefit transactions involving more than one insurer. To be fully effective, however, it would need to resolve some of the HIPAA problems discussed earlier, and there might still be many small providers operating outside the electronic universe. In addition, insurers might question why they should bear the entire funding burden. (Currently providers pay clearinghouses; anecdotally, the charge is somewhere in the range of 15 to 20 cents a claim, or more if the provider submits paper documents or its submissions need extensive massaging. Providers must also pay the clearinghouse to receive a remittance advice back from the insurer.)

Require Electronic Filing

As noted earlier, the Administrative Simplification Compliance Act applies only to Medicare transactions, and a large number of small providers and suppliers are exempt. Minnesota's new universal electronic transaction law has no such exemption, and federal law could similarly apply to all providers and all payers. (Possibly the law could be limited to some subset of common transactions, such as eligibility inquiries—perhaps the easiest—and claims not requiring attachments.) Such a rule would place an initial investment burden on small providers, but they would save money over time. Ultimately, if the larger goal of electronic health interchange is ever to be achieved, all providers are going to have to enter the computer age sooner or later.

Fully Standardize Transactions

One drawback to a universal filing requirement is the continuing nonuniformity of payers' implementation of HIPAA. It may seem unduly burdensome to compel small providers to pay a clearinghouse to deal with complexities that were created by payers. Minnesota's law requires everyone to conform to a set of standard coding rules developed by the state and explicitly forbids payers to issue companion documents or other supplemental instructions. Why could HIPAA standards not go further, so that all providers and payers used identical coding and no intermediary translator was necessary? One reason is cost: It is less expensive for both sides to pay a clearinghouse than to modify existing systems. In addition, shifting to a new, uniform system could require redesign of internal processes, not just external transactions, and possibly render institutions' pre-redesign data unusable. Another factor may be that payers' coding rules can embody policies, rather than just data formats—for example, rules about coverage of assistant surgeons or physician extenders, or about which services may be billed separately and which may be bundled (Vermont Commission on Health Care Reform 2007).

Some people would argue that consolidation in the health insurance industry could gradually make any of these large government initiatives less necessary or urgent. One recent study found that the Blue Cross and Blue Shield plans (including the large multistate plans) and three major non-Blues carriers (Aetna, CIGNA, and UnitedHealth) control more than 60 percent of the market in thirty-four states and more than 70 percent in twenty-three states (Robinson 2004). This means that, for many providers, a substantial majority of their claims are going to just a few payers (including the local Medicare carrier and Medicaid agency or intermediary). Robinson contends that consolidation is likely to continue, as the big plans swallow little ones, as new plans face barriers to market entry, and for other reasons. Whatever the overall advantages or disadvantages of industry concentration, it is clearly easier for providers and clearinghouses to deal with a few plans, rather than many.

Reform Proposals with Implications for Administrative Complexity or Costs

So far this chapter has focused on measures intended to streamline insurance-related transactions. Generally, these measures do not actually eliminate any transactions, but merely make them easier and (perhaps) less costly to conduct. However, there are also proposals that would change the way the insurance market operates and that have implications for administrative costs of insurers, employers, or consumers. Some of these proposals target administrative costs directly. Others are offered in the context of general health care reform plans but incidentally might have some effect, whether or not intended, on insurance-related administrative costs.

This section considers the possible administrative effects of seven proposals or components of proposals that might affect administrative costs and complexity. The list is meant to include only ideas that have received widespread discussion or support, or both: Each of the ideas was endorsed by one or more of the original field of 2008 Democratic and Republican presidential contenders.

(Two elements of many plans that would obviously affect administrative costs and complexity—premium subsidies and employer or individual mandates—are omitted here because they are the subject of Chapter 9 in this book.) The discussion here considers only the proposals' administrative implications and not their likely effects on improving access to coverage, control of health care spending, or other goals.

Open Federal Employees Health Benefits Program or Similar Exchange to General Public

Some proposals would either open the Federal Employees Health Benefits (FEHB) Program to individuals or small groups or would create a similar national or regional program. While these proposals are intended to ensure access to insurance and provide a range of coverage choices, their proponents also tend to assume they would reduce administrative costs.

The Office of Personnel Management spent $27 million—less than one-tenth of 1 percent of total FEHB spending—to administer the program in 2007 (Office of Management and Budget 2008). However, the Office of Personnel Management only negotiates and oversees carrier contracts and directly processes enrollment transactions for federal annuitants. The other functions of a large employer, such as processing new enrollments and enrollment changes and collecting and transmitting employee and employer premium contributions, are performed by the employing agencies. Costs are in each agency's budget for personnel operations. In addition, administrative costs for each participating carrier are included in premiums. The Office of Personnel Management estimated in 2003 that Blue Cross and the other national plans spent about 7 percent of premiums on administration (Block 2003). The figure for HMOs is probably comparable to their administrative loading for their other large-group business. Based on the estimates supplied earlier, combined total FEHB administrative costs might be in the range of 15 percent, roughly the same as those for other very large groups.

Costs would certainly be higher if FEHB or a similar exchange had to deal with a great many small groups or individual enrollees. Whether they would approach the 25 percent range typical of small-group coverage depends on several factors. Marketing costs would be lower if most applicants dealt directly with the exchange. However, most state-level exchanges have wound up paying commissions to agents and brokers. All the proposals assume guaranteed issue and at least adjusted community rating, so underwriting costs would be reduced or disappear (at the price of possible adverse selection, unless similar rules were imposed in the nonexchange market). At least at the outset, however, carriers would likely demand much higher risk reserves, as they faced hordes of new enrollees for whom no experience data were available. Overall, the expectation that an exchange could reduce administrative costs may depend on an assumption of some economies of scale that might or might not materialize.

Guaranteed Issue and Community Rating

Some proposals would establish a form of federal standards governing the under-writing and rating practices of all insurers, rather than just those participating in an exchange arrangement. Whatever their effects on general costs and availability, these options could be expected to reduce insurers' administrative costs to the extent that they eliminate the practice of examining applicants' health status or claims history.

While underwriting costs cannot be isolated in any of the available studies, they might be 2 percent or more of total premiums for small-group and nongroup carriers. In addition, agents and brokers may sometimes function as the first line in underwriting, screening out some applicants and obtaining health information about others. These functions are implicitly included in commissions—and sometimes explicitly, if an insurer rewards agents for sending on only insurable applicants.

Savings on underwriting costs would materialize only if insurers were required to use full community rating (no premium variation for any reason) or adjusted community rating (premium variation based on geographic or demographic factors, but not health status). If instead the federal or state rules involve rating bands—allowing some specified percentage variation in rates based on health status or a combination of factors including health status—then insurers would continue to evaluate individuals, and there might be no underwriting savings.

Minimum Loss Ratio

Some have proposed establishing a fixed minimum loss ratio, perhaps 85 percent, for health insurance plans. That is, 85 cents of every premium dollar would have to be paid out in benefits, meaning administrative costs and profits could not exceed 15 percent of premiums. Many states have set minimum loss ratios for small-group or nongroup coverage or for specific classes of plans, such as HMOs, but usually at much lower levels, such as 55 to 65 percent. In some states, there is no absolute rule, but plans meeting a specified limit are deemed to have "reasonable" rates, while plans not meeting it will be subject to greater scrutiny. Federal law requires that Medicare supplemental policies, or Medigap, have a minimum loss ratio of 65 percent for individual policies and 75 percent for group policies.

The available estimates of insurer costs would suggest that an 85 percent loss ratio in the individual and small-group markets is simply unattainable, even if insurers were to forgo any profit at all. Possibly some major insurers could meet the target if they were allowed to average their losses across all lines of business, including large group. But large employers would simply be driven to self-insure if they were expected to cross-subsidize administrative costs in the other market sectors. Conceivably a national minimum loss ratio set at some lower level could squeeze out excess administrative costs and profits in states that that have not already imposed these requirements. However, while loss ratios may be useful to regulators and buyers as general guidelines for assessing the reasonableness of insurers' premium rates, there are several arguments against fixed loss ratio rules.

First, a minimum loss ratio potentially penalizes an insurer that is controlling health benefit costs through added administrative activities, such as utilization review, case management, or value-based selection of network providers. If Insurer A spends $850 on benefits and $150 on administration, while Insurer B spends $750 on benefits and $200 on administration, it is the more "efficient" Insurer B that fails an 85 percent test. (Of course, Insurer B could also fail the test if it wrongly denied valid claims.) Second, there are numerous problems of accounting and of comparison across carriers. Which activities are clearly administrative as opposed to patient-care related? What if some administrative costs borne by insurers in the small-group market are shifted to employers in the large-group market? How should reinsurance and claims reserves be treated? Finally, loss ratios can fluctuate over time because of unpredictable changes in utilization or provider charges; a minimum ratio is especially problematic if it is applied over a limited time period to every block of business an insurer sells.

Single Payer

A single-payer plan would produce savings in both health-plan administrative costs and provider transaction costs, with the possible trade-offs in access or care management cited by critics of this approach. Whatever the overall pros and cons of single-payer proposals, there are several single-payer models with different potential effects on administrative complexity.

Some plans, such as the one introduced by Representative John Conyers (H.R. 676, 110th Congress), would be based on the Canadian model, with global budgets for hospitals and fee-for-service payment to practitioners; there would be no patient cost sharing for covered services. Staff-model HMOs could contract to provide care on a capitated basis, but no other insurers could participate, and they would be permitted to offer supplemental policies only for noncovered services such as cosmetic surgery. In contrast, Representative Fourtney Stark's plan (H.R. 1841, 107th, First Session) would provide Medicare for all. Providers would be paid under current systems, with modifications, and beneficiaries would be required to pay cost sharing, again with some changes from current rules. Insurers could sell the equivalent of Medigap supplemental plans; employers could provide supplemental coverage; and private health plans could contract to provide covered benefits in the same way as Medicare Advantage plans (except program payments would be limited to average fee-for-service costs).

The Conyers plan would eliminate billing by hospitals; other providers would still have to bill for services but would not have to collect patient cost sharing or deal with supplemental insurers. Under the Stark approach, providers would still have to deal with contracting private health plans, incurring costs for eligibility verification, credentialing, claims filing, and so on, as well as with supplemental carriers and employer groups. Consumers—including those now in employer groups, frequently offered no choice of health plans—would have to perform the complicated tasks that now sometimes baffle Medicare beneficiaries, such as choosing from an array of coverage options and (for those selecting supplemental coverage) deciphering explanations of benefits from two payers for the same service. The plan would thus retain some of the complexity of the current system.

Reinsurance

Several proposals seek to hold down premiums by providing federal reinsurance for all insurers or for some subset, such as retiree health plans. All of these plans involve reimbursement of catastrophic losses on specific cases, rather than aggregate stop-loss coverage, and thus entail at least administrative costs for the review of individual claims. In addition, reinsurance is difficult to administer fairly if participating plans have different benefit packages. Suppose, for example, that the catastrophic threshold is $25,000 and a patient incurs $35,000 in total costs. If the patient is in a plan with a $1,000 deductible, the insurer will spend $34,000 and the reinsurance will pay out $9,000. If the patient is in a plan with no deductible, the insurer will spend $35,000 and the reinsurance will pay out $10,000. This problem could arise under any proposal that does not combine reinsurance with benefit standardization.

There are some options for addressing this problem, but at the expense of greater complexity. One would be for the reinsurance program to apply its catastrophic threshold to total spending, by both the insurer and the enrollee; this would provide equal subsidies for people with equal costs, regardless of the specifics of their benefit package. A second option would be to recalculate the insurer's costs using a sort of virtual standard benefit: What would the insurer have paid out if the deductible were x and the coinsurance were y? Either of these approaches might effectively require the reinsurer (or the claiming primary insurer) to recalculate every single claim, doubling the claims-processing costs for high-cost enrollees.

Interstate Sale of Insurance and Association Plans

Proposals for interstate sale would allow a health plan licensed in any one state to sell coverage in all other states under the rules of the licensing state. Proposals for association plans would exempt insurers selling coverage to groups of multiple employers or other affinity groups from state rules governing the small-group market—such as benefit mandates or restrictions on premium variation. Both proposals are focused on reducing benefit costs for all buyers (by eliminating mandates or by allowing multiple groups to bargain jointly) or for low-risk groups (by eliminating rating restrictions). However, there are also claims that these approaches would reduce administrative complexity and costs.

Interstate sale would reduce insurers' administrative costs by eliminating the need to deal with multiple state regulators. Underwriting costs would probably rise, assuming insurers would make their home in states with the least-restrictive enrollment and rating requirements. Supporters of this approach contend that it would also have more general effects on insurers' administrative costs and profits by promoting national competition. However, it is uncertain how creation of a national market would play out. It might accelerate consolidation of the insurance market, perhaps leading to smaller administrative costs but higher profit margins.

The effects of allowing association plans are unclear. The association must have substantial enrollment to achieve any economies of scale in administrative options. However, a large association would also have a heterogeneous population—especially if, as in some proposals, an association could not exclude a high-risk applicant who otherwise qualified for membership. As one of the underlying points of the association plan approach is to allow formation of homogeneously low-risk pools that would benefit from an association-specific premium, the associations that would emerge might be quite small, perhaps focusing on one or more lower-risk occupational groups. While they might realize savings on benefit costs, savings on administration might be negligible.

Encourage Health Savings Accounts or Higher-Deductible Plans

In theory, if everyone had only some form of catastrophic coverage, the volume of insurance-related transactions would drop dramatically. If the coverage threshold were high enough, many people would never meet it and would receive all their care on a cash basis. Ultimately, however, providers would need to submit and payers would need to adjudicate all the subthreshold claims for the minority of patients who met the threshold. Conceivably this could be done retrospectively and only for those patients whose spending was approaching the deductible. However, this would create situations in which consumers who were spending their way up to, say, a $5,000 deductible would learn only after the fact that the insurer was going to disallow $3,000 of what the consumer had already paid. In the old indemnity world, people could keep their receipts in the proverbial shoebox and be confident that they would be compensated when the deductible was reached. In a world of utilization management, high-deductible plans are likely to be tolerated only if predeductible spending has already been cleared by the insurer. This means filing of all claims for all participants, negating any supposed savings from reduced transaction volume.

Once a high-deductible plan is combined with a health savings account, administrative costs are likely to rise. Most current high-deductible / health savings account plans offer enrollees some assistance in tracking expenses; often the plan is linked to an associated financial institution that manages the account and pays out the enrollee's liability as it is incurred. All of this makes eligibility and claims processing transactions more, rather than less, complex. This is one of the reasons for initiatives like CIGNA's HealthePass. If, however, consumers are left to manage their own finances, they will incur nonquantifiable administrative costs of their own, as well as possible actual financial losses from failure to claim appropriate reimbursement.

Conclusion

Despite years of effort to simplify the administration of insurance, little is known about whether any of the actors—insurers, providers, or employers—have seen any savings. What Thorpe called the "black box" of administrative costs is still quite opaque. Any efficiencies that have been achieved may be offset in future years by new complications, such as pay-for-performance systems (with associated reporting) or health savings accounts. Meanwhile, little has been done to make things simpler for the fourth set of actors, consumers, although some insurers have been working to provide clearer explanations of benefits and other improved communications.

Policy makers will need to determine what role government should play in pursuing simplification. Government as regulator can mandate change, as in the case of HIPAA, but this built on years of private efforts, and can be seen to some extent as codifying rather than innovating. Government as the largest purchaser of health services—through Medicare, Medicaid, FEHB, and other programs—can promote change by deciding what it wants to buy. It has the greatest leverage with providers, but the growth of Medicare Advantage and Medicaid managed care gives it considerable influence over health plans as well. Finally, government may need to finance change, to provide the capital and training needed to move hundreds of thousands of smaller providers beyond the realm of paper and typewriters.

Meanwhile, one person's complexity is another person's income. In 2004, health plans employed 470,000 people, not counting independent agents and brokers (America's Health Insurance Plans 2006a). In addition, there has arisen an entire industry of intermediaries between insurers and providers—not just clearinghouses, but also consultants who help providers maximize, and insurers minimize, claims. None of these players are likely to wish to be simplified out of a job.

Ultimately, complexity is not just a by-product of the insurance system: It is what insurers are selling. The value added of the managed care industry consists of the very features that make insurance complicated: different coverage rules and formularies, authorization requirements and careful scrutiny of claims, and so on. The variations are what differentiate one plan from another, and competition and uniformity may be conflicting goals.

References

Actuarial Research Corporation. 2003. *Study of the Administrative Costs and Actuarial Values of Small Health Plans.* Annandale, VA: Actuarial Research Corporation. www.sba.gov/advo/research/rs224tot.pdf. (Accessed 1 July 2008.)

America's Health Insurance Plans. 2006a. *Health Insurance: Overview and Economic Impact in the States.* Washington, DC: America's Health Insurance Plans. www.ahipresearch.org/PDFs/StateData/StateDataFullReport.pdf. (Accessed 1 July 2008.)

———. 2006b. *An Updated Survey of Health Care Claims Receipt and Processing Times, May 2006.* Washington, DC: America's Health Insurance Plans. www.ahipresearch.org/pdfs/PromptPayFinalDraft.pdf. (Accessed 1 July 2008.)

Armey, Dick. 2001. Letter to Tommy G. Thompson, Secretary of Department of Health and Human Services, May 15. www.techlawjournal.com/cong107/privacy/idnumbers/20010515armey.asp. (Accessed 1 July 2008.)

Beauchamp, D.E., and R.L. Rouse. 1990. "Universal New York Health Care: A Single-Payer Strategy Linking Cost Control and Universal Access." *New England Journal of Medicine* 323 (10): 640–44.

Block, Abby. 2003. Senior Advisor for Employee and Family Policy, Office of Personnel Management. Testimony Before the Senate Finance Committee. April 3.

Centers for Medicare and Medicaid Services (CMS). N.d. *National Health Expenditures Accounts: Definitions, Sources, and Methods Used in the NHEA 2004.* Baltimore: CMS.

———. 2003. "Medicare Program; Electronic Submission of Medicare Claims" (interim final rule). *Federal Register* 68 (158): 48805–13.

———. 2005. "HIPAA Administrative Simplification: Standards for Electronic Health Care Claims Attachments" (proposed rule). *Federal Register* 70 (184): 55990–56025.

———. 2006. *National Health Expenditures Accounts: Definitions, Sources, and Methods, 2006.* Baltimore: CMS. www.cms.hhs.gov/NationalHealthExpendData/downloads/dsm-06.pdf. (Accessed 1 July 2008.)

Health Insurance Association of America. 1997. Testimony presented to National Committee on Vital and Health Statistics (NCVHS), Subcommittee on Health Data Needs, Standards and Security. April 15–16.

Kaiser Family Foundation and Health Research and Educational Trust. 2000. *Employer Health Benefits: 2000 Annual Survey.* Menlo Park, CA, and Chicago. www.kff.org/insurance/20000907a-index.cfm. (Accessed 1 July 2008.)

Lemieux, Jeff. 2005. *Perspective: Administrative Costs of Private Health Insurance Plans.* Washington, DC: America's Health Insurance Plans. www.ahipresearch.org/pdfs/Administrative_Costs_030705.pdf. (Accessed 1 July 2008.)

Litow, Mark. 2006. *Medicare Versus Private Health Insurance: The Cost of Administration.* n.p. www.cahi.org/cahi_contents/resources/pdf/CAHIMedicareTechnicalPaper.pdf. (Accessed 1 July 2008.)

Maine Task Force to Study the Feasibility of a Single Claims Processing System for 3rd-Party Payors of Health Care Benefits. 1998. *Final Report.* Augusta: Maine Task Force to Study the Feasibility of a Single Claims Processing System for 3rd-Party Payors of Health Care Benefits.

Minnesota Statutes 2007, Chap. 62J.536.

Office of Management and Budget. 2008. *Budget of the United States, 2008: Budget Appendix.* Washington, DC: Office of Management and Budget, 999–1011.

Robinson, James. 2004. "Consolidation and the Transformation of Competition in Health Insurance." *Health Affairs* 23 (6): 11–24.

Sundwall, David N. 2006. "eHealth in Utah: Medicaid, Health IT and RHIO." Presentation to HHS Medicaid Commission, Washington, DC, July 12. aspe.hhs.gov/medicaid/july06/sDavid%20Sundwall.pdf. (Accessed 1 July 2008.)

Thorpe, Kenneth. 1992. "Inside the Black Box of Administrative Costs." *Health Affairs* 11 (2): 41–55. content.healthaffairs.org/cgi/reprint/11/2/41?ck=nck. (Accessed 1 July 2008.)

Vermont Commission on Health Care Reform, Common Claims Work Group. 2007. *Interim Report.* Concord: Vermont Commission on Health Care Reform.

Wicks, Elliot, Jack Meyer and Sharon Silow-Carroll. Undated. *A Plan for Achieving Universal Health Coverage.* http://www.esresearch.org/RWJ11PDF/wicks.pdf. (Accessed 17 November 2008.)

Zycher, Benjamin. 2007. *Comparing Public and Private Health Insurance: Would a Single-Payer System Save Enough to Cover the Uninsured?* New York: Manhattan Institute for Policy Research. www.manhattan-institute.org/html/mpr_05.htm. (Accessed 1 July 2008.)

Part IV

Using Performance Management to Enhance Health Care Reform

14

Management and Performance of Federal Health Care Programs

F. Stevens Redburn and Terry F. Buss

Since 2002, the Office of Management and Budget (OMB) has systematically rated the management and performance of federal programs using a standard assessment instrument. Assessments, along with accompanying explanation and evidence, are publicly available. This analysis draws on that information for insights into management challenges facing the largest federal health care programs and identifies opportunities for improving their performance. The exercise is, in turn, a test of the OMB assessments' value in guiding management-improvement strategies for federal health care programs. When a new administration takes office in January 2009, this overview might provide valuable guidance in building management and performance capacity into reformed or new health care programs.

OMB's PART Process

The Bush administration developed the Program Assessment Rating Tool (PART) process in 2002 to provide a uniform instrument and procedures for assessing the management, performance, and results of all major federal programs.[1] The PART process was intended to complement and expand federal agencies' efforts to plan strategically and develop performance measures and reports in response to requirements of the Government Performance and Results Act of 1993. The act pushed agencies to greater consideration of the outcomes they intended to achieve and to measure their programs' contributions to those outcomes. Agencies, in response, invested substantially in new strategic plans focusing on measurable goals, on the development of arrays of new performance indicators and supporting information collection, and on incorporating performance information into their annual reporting. The PART process was intended to exploit this investment and, as some have said, to "put teeth" into the act by linking the planning and performance measurement and reporting systems built over the preceding eight years with assessments of programs that focused attention on their contributions to intended outcomes and on ways to improve results.

In 2007, at the end of a five-year full cycle, just over one thousand federal programs have been rated using PART. This asks approximately twenty-five important, yet commonsense, questions about a program's performance and management.[2] For each question, there is a short answer and a detailed explanation with supporting evidence. Answers, prepared by OMB career program examiners with input from the agency's program staff, determine a program's overall rating. Once each assessment is completed, OMB works with the agency to develop a management-improvement plan, including specific recommendations to address identified weaknesses. The ratings, supporting explanation and evidence, and management-improvement plan are published and Web accessible (see www.whitehouse.gov/omb/expectmore/index.html).

PART's value for decision making and as a platform for program improvement is yet to be fully established. However, it has at a minimum provided citizens, program stakeholders, Congress, and policy analysts with a window into OMB's institutional perspective on the performance of federal programs. Moreover, by standardizing the analytical framework and rating process, it facilitates aggregate and cross-program analyses that may identify patterns of weakness or opportunities for broad strategies to improve performance. For example, PART processes may show that some program designs are less likely than others to yield expected benefits. PART analyses of programs with overlapping or complementary objectives may identify opportunities for consolidation or improved coordination. And, most relevant perhaps to analysis of health programs, PART may highlight mismatches between formal authority and the ability to manage determinants of program cost and effectiveness or misalignment of incentives that encourages wasteful or inappropriate use of program resources.

What can PART tell us about management and performance of federal health services? PART can help identify barriers to improving the performance of federal programs individually or as a system. PART is a rough-and-ready-diagnostic tool that can pinpoint symptoms and—when it is used as it is here to look across the full set of programs—possibly identify a pattern of symptoms or a syndrome indicative of an underlying condition affecting the system's ability to function and deliver services as intended. It gives heaviest weight to evidence that the program plans strategically, measures its contribution and progress toward well-defined outcome goals, and achieves the intended results.

PART analyses also may serve as a springboard for treatment to improve the management and performance of individual programs, ranging from management strategies to investments in technology and human capital to organizational reform or even program redesign. PART results provide a high-level portrait of management and performance of federally supported health services delivery and financing programs, looked at from a chief executive's (presidential) perspective. They do not provide detailed diagnoses or a road map for management improvement. Nevertheless, OMB and agencies use results as a basis for negotiated commitments to program improvement. A program-improvement plan committing the program to specific reforms is included with the published PART results and updated annually. Published PART analyses also present annual performance measures that the program wishes to highlight as indicative of how it measures its effectiveness and efficiency.

Ten Largest Federal Health Care Programs

In this chapter, we use PART processes for the largest ten federal health programs, which when combined accounted for approximately $665 billion or 24 percent of all fiscal year 2007 federal spending, to assess the management and performance of federal programs (see Table 14.1).

Program Management and Performance Assessed

Analysis below illuminates the value and limits of PART assessments as a source of insight into federal health care program management and performance. Our analysis focuses on using PARTs to identify *barriers* to improved management and performance of federally supported health services. Improving performance in the health care system requires planning and executing system-level change. Success depends on:

1. Setting clear outcome goals and developing/tracking appropriate measures over time of key outcomes: access to care; quality of health care provided; relevant health outcomes; and cost-effectiveness or efficiency. The latter can be expressed as a ratio of any of the outcome measures to program spending (preferably including allocated indirect expenses whether budgeted as part of the program account or not).
2. Giving administrators and others both authority and means to improve performance—including necessary resources and useful, timely information about performance and its relationship to their actions, that is, aligning authority and means with responsibility; and
3. Providing administrators and others with incentives that include rewards for support of the changes necessary to improve performance.

Next we look at the latest program PART assessment reports. It should be noted that programs have been rated over a five-year cycle, so some of the assessments and the information on which they are based may be less timely than others. PART regulations allow agencies and their OMB examiners to update performance measures and provide an opportunity to revisit all or portions of the assessment of a given program as often as annually. Nevertheless, given the emphasis on developing improved performance information and the fact that PARTs are not always fully updated, some of the descriptions and explanations provided are not current.

In any case, what can PART results tell us about each of these three sets of necessary conditions for program improvement? The ratings of the ten programs on each of the four PART sections and each program's summary rating are presented in Table 14.2.

Table 14.1

Ten Largest Federal Health Programs

Program	Estimated 2007 spending ($ millions)
Medicare: Medicare finances health insurance for eligible elderly and disabled individuals. As of January 1, 2006, the Medicare benefit includes outpatient prescription drug coverage.	367,474
Medicaid: Medicaid is a means-tested, federal-state funded entitlement program that provides medical assistance, including acute and long-term care, to families with dependent children as well as aged, blind, or disabled individuals. The Centers for Medicare and Medicaid Services (CMS) provides federal oversight of this program.	191,876
Veterans Medical Care: This medical care system provides health care services to eligible veterans. The program provides most services through a nationwide network of medical centers and clinics.	32,262
Federal Employee Health Benefits: The program provides federal employees and retirees with health insurance benefits to meet their individual and family health needs. Because it is an important component of the federal government's compensation package, it also supports the federal government's ability to recruit and retain quality employees.	32,126
Defense Health Care: The Defense Health Program trains military medical personnel and provides health care in peace and war to active duty members, retirees, and their families around the globe.	24,287
State Children's Health Insurance: The State Children's Health Insurance Program provides funds to states to expand health insurance coverage to low-income, uninsured children under age 19.	5,647
Women, Infants, and Children: The program safeguards the health of low-income women, infants, and children up to age 5 who are at nutritional risk by providing nutritious foods to supplement diets, information on healthy eating, and referrals to health care and social services.	5,168
Ryan White HIV/AIDS: The Ryan White HIV/AIDS Program addresses the unmet care and treatment needs of persons living with HIV/AIDS who are uninsured or underinsured and unable to pay for HIV/AIDS health care and vital health-related support services. Funding goes to states, metropolitan areas, and other public, private, and nonprofit entities.	2,063
Indian Health Service Federally Administered: The purpose of the Indian Health Service is to raise the physical, mental, social, and spiritual health of American Indians and Alaska Natives. Through its federally administered activities, the Indian Health Service provides clinical and preventive health services directly and through purchasing from the private sector.	2,005
Health Centers: This program provides grants to health centers to provide medical care to uninsured, underserved, and vulnerable populations to rural and urban areas. In 2005, 3,745 heath centers provided care to over 13 million people.	1,943

Source: Office of Management and Budget, ExpectMore.gov. Available at http://www. whitehouse.gov/omb/expectmore/.

Table 14.2

Summary of PART Scores for Ten Health Programs

Program Name	Agency	Rating	Program Purpose and Design (%)	Strategic Planning (%)	Program Management (%)	Program Results/ Accountability (%)
Medicare	HHS	Moderately effective	80	100	72	67
Medicaid	HHS	Adequate	80	86	56	33
Veterans Medical Care	VA	Adequate	55	75	70	60
Federal Employee Health Benefits	OPM	Adequate	80	75	86	20
Defense Health Care	DoD	Adequate	100	80	65	40
State Children's Health Insurance	HHS	Adequate	80	84	43	67
Women, Infants, and Children	DA	Effective	100	100	100	74
Ryan White HIV/AIDS	HHS	Effective	100	86	91	100
Indian Health Service Federally Administered	HHS	Moderately effective	100	72	57	74
Health Centers	HHS	Effective	100	88	90	87

Source: Office of Management and Budget, ExpectMore.gov. Available at http://www.whitehouse.gov/omb/expectmore/.

1. Outcomes and Measures

We look first at whether programs have set clear outcome goals and are using an appropriate array of measures to track key outcomes. The average score for these ten programs on the section of the PART dealing with strategic planning is 85 points (out of a possible 100).

Further insights can be gained by examining the array of performance measures reported as part of the PART summary for each program. These can be categorized by whether they measure outputs, outcomes, or efficiency. Output measures can track either services or benefits received or various administrative actions. Outcomes, for health programs, can be categorized as measures of access to care, quality of care, health, or other changes expected to result. Efficiency measures can be ratios of outputs or outcomes to budgeted expenditures, although efficiency gains can sometimes be inferred from other measures such as reduced administrative error rates. (All of the performance measures reported in the PART summaries for these programs are listed and categorized in an appendix at www.nasi.org.)

OMB and the PART process put special emphasis on the development of outcome and efficiency measures. Guidance for assessments and surrounding rhetoric stress the importance placed on measuring and demonstrating "results." The measures reported with PART for a given program are intended to support answers given in PART and do not represent the full range of measures used or reported by the program. Agencies typically report a much larger array of performance measures in their annual performance and accountability reports and in their annual budget submissions to Congress, although these are not in all cases linked to specific programs. Many programs use a variety of internal measures for management purposes. Some take a balanced scorecard approach that combines output and outcome measures related to the program goals with other perspectives on the program, including measures related to financial management, public views of the program's operation and services, and measures of clinical activity or interim product.

Given that the measures reported in PART summaries are an incomplete subset of all measures used for a given program and not necessarily selected in a consistent fashion from one program to the next, care must be taken in interpreting them as representative of the measurement efforts of each program. Nevertheless, it is important to see what measures are highlighted in PART for each of the ten largest health programs. The overall picture is of a robust but scattered set of meaningful output, outcome, and efficiency measures, but there seems to be a remaining need to ensure that these are balanced to reflect all dimensions of performance, as in the balanced scorecard concept. The array of measures for the ten largest health programs also suggests an opportunity for further work to develop a standard set of common measures of outcomes for multiple health programs and for the health care system as a whole. Program-level measures are part of a natural hierarchy of performance measures, with national indicators at the top that are used for strategic planning at the level of the national health care system or the agency level and with measures for individual providers or networks of providers toward the bottom. In an ideal, neatly integrated world the lower-level measures would be aggregated in many cases to yield corresponding higher-level indicators used for program management, strategic planning, and broader national policy guidance. At the highest level a common set of international health indexes would facilitate meaningful cross-country comparative analyses and foster international standards of care. However, at the present time efforts at bottom-up aggregation are hampered by the incomplete development of and sharp disagreements over the utility and proper use of provider-level measures of health care quality as well as a lack of standardized "episodes of care" packages that can be compared across providers, patients, and settings.

There is little evidence, taking the array of measures presented here at face value, of any organized effort within the U.S. government to develop a common set of standard measures that might be used, for instance, to judge the relative or combined effects of different programs on the health of a given population. Instead, we see inconsistency and missed opportunities. Although improved health is obviously central to the rationale and mission of each program, the six largest programs list no health-outcome measures. For example, both Health Centers and Medicaid are targeted to low-income communities where access to high-quality health care is one factor affecting health. While the Health Centers program sets goals for reduction in low-birth-weight births and control of hypertension and diabetes, Medicaid does not.

Part of the explanation for the apparent lack of attention to health outcomes by the largest programs may be that they provide financing for care rather than treatment and for clinical services in government-funded facilities and are therefore more focused on intermediate outcomes such as access to care and quality of care. However, this does not explain the lack of measures for Veterans Health Administration or Defense Health Care, both of which directly support administration of hospitals and clinical services.

Strong health-outcome measures are found in programs that have a narrower mission or population focus. For example, Ryan White measures reductions in the national death rate from AIDS. The Indian Health Service estimates years of potential life lost in the American Indian / Alaska native populations. Health Centers, which targets low-income communities, measures low-weight birth rates and percentages of adult patients controlling their diagnosed hypertension and diabetes. Women, Infants, and Children employs multiple health-outcome measures including an index of healthy diet and measures of low birth weight, breastfeeding, anemia, and overweight condition among children two to four years of age.

Other outcome measures focus on access to care or quality of care. The Medicare program tracks an array of access measures, including vaccination rates for flu and pneumonia and rates of testing and examinations for age-related conditions. On the contrary, the Medicaid program appears not to employ similar measures of access for persons. Each program reports only a single, narrowly focused quality-of-care measure: for Medicare, optimization of timing of antibiotic administration following surgery and, for Medicaid, prevalence of restraints in nursing homes. The Veterans Medical Care program reports comprehensive index scores for both access to care and quality of care. The quality of care index "follows national clinical guidelines of care for patients with specific diagnoses." The State Children's Health Insurance Program uses its own index combining seven measures of care quality reported at the state level. PART narratives for both Medicaid and the State Children's Health Insurance Program suggest that joint efforts in cooperation with the states are under way to develop and report a variety of quality measures and to establish baselines and long-term targets for these measures, so the quality-measurement picture may soon improve for these programs. Oddly, Women, Infants, and Children; Indian Health Service; and Health Centers list no access-to-care or care-quality measures.

Efficiency measures may estimate the ratio of either outputs or outcomes to cost. Although OMB encourages such measures, which obviously can aid in budget decisions as well as program management, PART summaries include only a scattering of these. Some measures—such as reductions in the percentage of improper payments—are only indirect measures of efficiency. Perhaps most surprising, not a single program lists a measure showing the cost of achieving an important outcome. For example, there is no measure showing the average or marginal cost of achieving a given increase in vaccination or exam coverage, much less a reduction in the incidence of a specified disease or specified improvement in health. The evidence of PART summaries strongly suggests that a step crucial to rational allocation and effective management of program resources has not yet been taken.

How much of the observed pattern is a function of selective listing of measures in PART and how much reflects genuine variation in the types and coverage of performance measures used by these ten programs is unclear and worthy of follow-up investigation. Nevertheless, the evidence is sufficient to conclude that each program has been working more or less in isolation to define and present performance information across the largest federal health programs. Even for programs administered by the Department of Health and Human Services, which might have been expected to promote adoption of a common core of measures for its programs, there is no evidence of coordinated performance measurement.

2. Organizational Responsibility and Authority

A second set of factors likely to determine success of efforts to improve performance concerns the match between assignments of organizational responsibility, on the one hand, with authority and means to carry out responsibilities, on the other. The ability of administrators and others (including consumers) to improve health and health care outcomes is hampered by program design and obstacles to coordinated delivery, for example, fragmentation of administrative responsibility, lack of interoperable or shared information systems and data, and confused or uncertain role assignments. The health care system is notorious for its disorganization and fragmentation of roles and responsibilities. For example, most consumers lack the ability to identify and select the optimal mix of care and cost, doctors often have difficulty accessing complete medical histories for their patients, and providers have insufficient means or authority to control costs.

These questions may be insufficiently pointed to get at design flaws that limit the ability of those operating within the program to carry out their responsibilities. Nevertheless, their open-ended nature provides PART analysts with an opportunity to diagnose and cite studies or other evidence suggesting that the program's organization is a factor limiting performance.

Six of the ten programs received a "no" answer to the question about whether the program was free of design flaws or optimally designed for its purpose. One program, Defense Health Care, was given a "not applicable" because of redesign efforts (under the label "TRICARE") that were under way in 2003, when the program was last rated.

The accompanying explanations give an indication of the kinds of design problems noted by the raters. For example, Medicare is observed to have design problems in that the program's benefits and payments structure is modeled on the typical private-sector health insurance of 1965 and is "no longer state of the art"— while taking note of recent enactment of prescription drug coverage. In addition, the rater noted that unlike most private health insurance, Medicare does not provide catastrophic protection. Moreover, it "sets reimbursement through administratively determined prices that do not always keep pace with advances in medical practice or changes in the health care market," and the program "cannot [by statute] use modern acquisition practices . . . commonly used by other government agencies." Within the limits of its statutory framework, Medicare is credited with meaningful management improvements, including controls to protect against waste and fraud, efforts to reduce erroneous payments, and many information technology improvements contributing to greater cost-effectiveness.

Medicaid is seen as flawed in its design because its open-ended financing structure encourages states to maximize federal matching, thereby shifting costs to the federal government. This statutory design flaw is seen as making the program vulnerable to waste, fraud, abuse, and mismanagement, leading to explosive federal spending growth and threatening the program's financial stability. The program receives credit for financial management reviews that have curtailed payments for fraudulent or incorrect claims.

Veterans Health Care is viewed as flawed because it has a system of hospitals that is "not right-sized or in appropriate locations." However, this report was written in 2003, noting that a pending study and decisions to be finalized by December 2003 could alter the picture.

Programs perceived as free of major design flaws limiting their effectiveness are Women, Infants, and Children Indian Health Service federally administered programs and Health Centers.

3. Effectiveness and Incentives

A third set of PART questions that should help diagnose problems limiting program effectiveness are those dealing with the incentives for managers, providers, funders, and consumers. Many have argued forcefully that incentives for efficient use of resources are mixed or weak in the health sector, particularly for large financing programs through which third parties finance the cost of decisions about treatment made by doctors and hospitals with limited impact on the patient's finances or where delivery is a government or tribal monopoly.

The Federal Employee Health Benefits (FEHB) Program is sometimes cited as a model of consumer-driven decision making, offering federal employees a choice of competing private insurance packages varying in their mix of charges and benefits. FEHB is credited with reporting systems that hold managers accountable and set out performance standards for carrier contracts and that are the basis for extra service payments based on surpassing contract criteria.

For Medicaid, by contrast, analysts concluded that "neither Federal managers nor States are held accountable for Medicaid cost or performance results." In the Medicare program, "statutory requirements make it hard to hold key partners accountable. Most reimbursement is based on estimates of procedure cost; high quality providers receive the same reimbursement as low-quality providers. On the administrative side, outdated statutory requirements prevent use of modern procurement practices . . . to process claims." This criticism appears dated in light of the competitive contracting procedures enacted in 2003, suggesting that greater efforts are needed to update PART analyses for such major changes and to revise their scoring accordingly. Medicare is criticized for lacking efficiency measures "for some key areas."

Veterans Health Services is sometimes recognized for reforms that provided regional network managers with performance-based contracts and greater discretion and incentives for using resources to optimize patient outcomes. In contrast to the three largest programs discussed above, the Veterans Health Administration often delivers medical care directly through its network of hospitals and other facilities. For Veterans Health Administration, the analyst found that "network directors have performance criteria in contracts, [but] they do not capture all of the key cost, schedule, and performance results." Nevertheless, "performance evaluations are linked to critical issue areas, and program partners are held to performance standards."

The State Children's Health Insurance Program is viewed as having weak accountability for managers and program partners. The explanation notes that "without more extensive GPRA [Government Performance and Results Act] and annual performance measures, the Center for Medicare and Medicaid Services (CMS) cannot hold either its managers or the States accountable for cost, schedule, and performance results."

Implied Strategies for Program Improvement

What do the PART analyses of these ten programs suggest about an overall approach or strategy to improve the management and performance of federally supported health services?

Not surprisingly, great emphasis is given to the development and use of appropriate performance measures. Fundamental design problems are seen as limiting the opportunities or incentives for managers and partners to improve performance in most programs, most notably in the huge financing programs for the elderly and the poor. In particular, the structural and incentive flaws at the heart of Medicare and Medicaid are noted if not highlighted. The limits of PART are most evident when one looks for a road map to structural reform or to other changes that go beyond the design or management of individual programs.

Final Observations

What are the limitations of the PART process itself as a diagnostic tool and as a springboard for improving the performance of federally supported health care? Is it better at identifying specific symptoms than at diagnosing underlying systemic conditions? Do the improvement plans for individual programs have the potential to address fundamental management problems, or do these require broader, systemic solutions?

It is important, in addressing these questions, to recognize that PART is not intended as a detailed diagnostic tool. Given that it must be applied to all major federal programs and employs a standard set of general questions meant to apply to most or all programs, it should be seen as a preliminary screen for more detailed testing and analysis of the specific design flaws and management deficiencies it identifies.

Within its limitations, the performance-improvement plans accompanying the PART analyses are a direct indication of its utility. These tend to focus on important short-term tasks that can yield performance improvements quickly within the current statutory framework. That is, their utility is limited by the program's statutory design. Examples include efforts to develop improved contract specifications, establish baselines for improved outcome and efficiency measures, and demonstrations of pay-for-performance schemes. These are likely to yield useful knowledge, including in some cases information that could inform larger decisions about the limits of current program design and the need for broader restructuring.

The potential of PART to inform and encourage improved program management and performance has not been fully realized. A review of these ten PART analyses highlights the need to update the assessments frequently to reflect and reward program improvements. A more serious analytical gap is the absence of a crosscutting or systemic view of the limits on performance arising from the overall design of the federal government's contributions to health care financing and delivery. The scale of the largest federal health programs makes their management and performance central to that of the health care system, especially as it affects the poor and the elderly. PART analyses, while pointed with respect to the weaknesses of individual programs, do not convey—even when read as a set—an overall sense of the directions that those interested in improved performance should take. For example, they do not explicitly suggest the importance of developing a common, integrated set of performance measures applicable to all programs and useful at various levels of management and policy direction. This is surprising given the weight given by PART assessments to development and use of performance information. It is difficult to determine, based on PART alone, whether identified performance shortfalls in a particular program are largely attributable to design flaws or are susceptible to treatment and improvement through better administration. Nor do PARTs, taking one program at a time, specify broader systemic changes that might be needed to drive down costs and achieve better outcomes for those served by federal programs. This suggests a need, perhaps, for supplementary analyses of federal health programs that could foster management- and performance-improvement strategies addressing several programs simultaneously and in an integrated fashion.

Finally, the value of the PART process as an impetus to reform depends on its ability to engage not only government analysts and managers but also the many others interested in improving the performance of the health care system. Its format and mode of presentation, including the more-accessible but very general PART summaries available on the Web, are not engaging or persuasive even to those most interested in and familiar with the health care system and its intricacies. Therefore, more thought should be given to analytical and presentation approaches that could convey clearly the most important reasons why programs sometimes fall short of their goals and where the design or logic of a program seems to break down in practice.

Notes

1. See www.whitehouse.gov/omb/part/index.html (Accessed 10 December 2007). For a comprehensive review of PART and other performance initiatives, see F. Stevens Redburn, Robert J. Shea, and Terry F. Buss, eds., *Performance Management and Budgeting: How Governments Can Learn from Experience* (Armonk, NY: M.E. Sharpe, 2008).

2. For example, the Women, Infants, and Children's program PART is found at www.whitehouse.gov/omb/expectmore/summary/10003027.2006.html (Accessed 10 December 2007).

15

Performance-Based Management Under Ryan White

The BPHC Initiative

Nicole Rivers, Sandy Matava, and Terry F. Buss

Over the past two decades or so beginning with David Osborne's book *Reinventing Government* (1993), public managers have increasingly been held accountable for the performance of their programs, especially in an era of competition, scarce resources, privatization, and performance-based management. Federally funded health care programs are no exception. With a new national administration taking office in 2009, regardless of the party or candidate in office, performance is likely to continue to be an important goal, especially in health care. In this chapter, we look closely at an innovative performance-based management initiative in the delivery of HIV/AIDs services in the Boston area. The Boston initiative provides valuable insights into the design and implementation of a performance system at the local level, something often not given much attention in national debates about health care reform. We discuss challenges and successes—political and technical—encountered during the ten-year evolution of the performance-measurement system. We present data to illustrate the complexity of service delivery to a chronically ill population, clarify the struggle in identifying and serving diverse needs of individual clients, and stress the importance of continuously assessing and modifying the system. The chapter concludes with lessons learned and prospects for the future.

Ryan White Programs

Through 2005, the Centers for Disease Control and Prevention reported that 550,394 people in the United States had died from AIDS. The HIV/AIDS epidemic from 1991 to 1995 produced 45,352 deaths annually on average. With the introduction of antiretroviral medications, average annual deaths declined to 17,288 from 2000 to 2005. Even so, the epidemic remains a major public health issue.

In 1990, recognizing the need to address the HIV/AIDS epidemic, Congress enacted the Ryan White Comprehensive AIDS Resources Emergency (CARE) Act. The CARE Act, named for Ryan White, a teenager who died in 1990 after a six-year struggle with the disease, was a direct response to the demands of urban public hospitals overwhelmed by increased numbers of uninsured patients dying in their care from AIDS. Amended in 1996 and 2000, the CARE Act improved the quality and availability of care for low-income, uninsured, and underinsured individuals and families affected by HIV/AIDS.

The Health Resources and Services Administration of the Department of Health and Human Services administers the CARE Act, funding services not covered by Medicare or Medicaid (hab.hrsa.gov/programs/CareActOverview/). Four program grants comprise the CARE Act. This chapter looks only at Title I services, around which Boston's performance-system initiative was developed.

Ryan White programs fund a veritable patchwork of services delivered by numerous providers. According to the Health Resources and Services Administration, in 2004, 45 percent of CARE Act providers were community-based organizations. Other providers included hospitals (14 percent), publicly funded community health and mental health centers (10 percent), health departments (13 percent), and other agencies such as the Veterans Administration (18 percent). Of the 2,569 providers, 56 percent received funding from Title I. Although some providers received funding from several CARE sources, 70 percent of providers were funded from a single source.

Ryan White funding has become more flexible over time. The CARE Act was replaced in 2006 by the Ryan White HIV/AIDS Treatment Modernization Act (Kaiser Family Foundation 2006). The Treatment Modernization Act allows more discretion in directing funds to the areas of greatest need by offering new supplemental grants to states that show an increasing need for HIV/AIDS-related services. The legislation expands services for women, infants, and children and supports family-centered care. It recognizes the disproportionate impact of HIV/AIDS on African Americans (49 percent of all HIV/AIDS cases in 2005 were African Americans), allocating separate funding for minorities through the Minority AIDS Initiative.

The new act advocates a medical model of service delivery, stipulating that grantees spend at least 75 percent of funds on core medical services, including outpatient and ambulatory health services, pharmaceutical assistance, substance abuse outpatient services, oral health, medical nutritional therapy, health insurance premium assistance, home health care, hospice services, mental health services, early-intervention services, and medical case management (including treatment-adherence services). Remaining funds support outreach, medical transportation, language services, respite care, and referrals for health care and support services.

In addition to new spending directives, the Treatment Modernization Act modified funding formulas to include HIV as well as AIDS cases. Along with funding modifications, the new legislation calls for more aggressive program evaluation, in keeping with the positive trend in public accountability. The Treatment Modernization Act also includes development of a core list of medications states must provide (at minimum) to manage symptoms associated with HIV infection through the AIDS Drug Assistance Program.

Table 15.1

FY07 Planning Council Priorities

Service	Budget	Service	Budget
Primary medical care	$308,559	Food services	$1,626,735
Drug reimbursement	$1,710,815	Peer support	$669,655
Housing	$2,000,447	Transportation	$419,723
Case management	$2,382,360	Client advocacy	$437,764
Substance abuse	$977,737	Evaluation	$102,560
Mental health	$449,199	Support services	$292,271
Dental	$566,355	Quality management	$250,000

Source: Boston Public Health Commission.

Boston Eligible Metropolitan Area

The Boston Eligible Metropolitan Area (EMA) has been a nationally recognized exemplar over the past decade in performance-based management in continuously improving service delivery in a region.

The Boston EMA spans most of central and eastern Massachusetts and southern New Hampshire and encompasses 350 cities and towns in ten counties. Representing 6,451 square miles, the Boston EMA includes both urban and rural areas. The Boston EMA does not include western Massachusetts, Cape Cod, or the islands.

Since 1991 the Boston EMA has received a total of $173,846,870 in Title I funds. In 2005, there were more than 16,000 people living with HIV/AIDS in the Boston EMA. The annual incidence rate is 22.3 cases per 100,000 population. The Boston EMA made up 84 percent of the total AIDS cases in Massachusetts. In New Hampshire, the three Boston EMA counties account for 66 percent of reported AIDS cases in the state (Boston AIDS Consortium 2006). The Boston EMA ranks thirteenth among the fifty-one EMAs in number of AIDS cases.

In the Boston EMA, the mayor of Boston is responsible for the Ryan White program, and the Boston Public Health Commission is the designated grantee to receive CARE funding. The mayor appoints a planning council. At least 30 percent of the planning council members must be people who receive HIV-related services. Members representing groups, organizations, and consumers cannot have a conflict of interest with the financial or governing interest in Title I–funded agencies. The planning council assigns funding priorities, assesses service quality, and monitors other sources of funding to ensure that CARE is the payer of last resort.

Based on the planning council's fiscal year 2007 funding priorities, the Boston Public Health Commission, as the designated grantee, awarded $12,861,137 in Part A (formerly Title I) funds to 103 programs within fifty-five agencies, as shown in Table 15.1.

Since fiscal year 2003, Title I funding for the Boston EMA has declined from

$15.4 million funding nineteen services and 142 programs to $13 million in fiscal year 2007, eliminating thirty-nine programs and three support services—adoption, day care, and complementary therapies. Recent funding cuts provided local decision makers with strong motivation to improve performance.

Challenges to Performance Management

Local Ryan White programs, the Boston EMA being no exception, pose management challenges in maintaining and improving performance.

- Funding covers numerous disparate programs, agencies, and vendors; is geographically dispersed; and addresses different needs and client bases.
- Funding levels vary, and over recent years continuously declined, forcing tough choices about what gets funded and what gets dropped.
- Funding decisions are sometimes politicized and contentious, with competing voices contending for scarce resources.
- Some programs are large, well staffed, and adequately resourced; while others have few resources, small staffs, and little management capacity.

Clients in the health care delivery system pose performance-management challenges as well.

- Ryan White–eligible clients can access care not only from Ryan White programs, but also from charitable organizations, public and private hospitals, and numerous other organizations delivering HIV/AIDs services. Clients are difficult to track or monitor when they move from one system to another, and sometimes within the system as well.
- Clients often drop into and out of care, and many are noncompliant. It becomes difficult to assess the impact of care received when it is so sporadic.
- Clients access the Ryan White system presenting with different needs, different coping abilities, and hence different prospects for successful treatment or service impact. Clients are difficult to classify into easily manageable categories.

We now turn to the Boston Public Health Commission's initiative seeking continuous improvement in performance over the past decade or so.

Boston Public Health Commission Performance Initiative

Recognizing the disparate funding components of the CARE Act and potential overlap or gap in services within the Boston EMA, the Boston Public Health Commission frequently collaborates with stakeholders in accessing service needs, allocating funding against priorities, and evaluating Title I service impacts.

One of the longest and most successful collaborations is with Suffolk University's Center for Public Management. In 1996, the Boston Public Health Commission partnered with Suffolk to develop an Outcomes Measurement System for its Title I programs. Three factors contributed to the need for the Outcomes Measurement System. First, in 1993, Congress enacted the Government Performance and Results Act, requiring that the results or outcomes from federally appropriated dollars be measured and reported. Second, the Health Resources and Services Administration, through its Title I mandates, required that the quality of outcomes and cost-effectiveness of services be measured and reported. Third, the Boston Public Health Commission and the planning council sought assurance that HIV/AIDS clients in the Boston EMA were receiving services that improved their quality of life and health status, *regardless* of federal mandates.

The Boston Public Health Commission initiative progressed through three phases as it matured. (All forms created under this project are available at www.nasi.org.)

Phase I: System Design and Initial Implementation

After considering numerous options, Suffolk designed the Outcomes Measurement System based on the United Way model, developed in the mid-nineties as a process-based outcomes-measurement system for its member agencies (www.unitedway.org). Importantly, the ultimate goal of the United Way model was not only to quantify outputs (i.e., number of service units delivered or dollars spent) as was common in past performance efforts, but also to gauge the impact each service had on clients. Because successful outcomes could not be defined as the elimination of the disease, client outcomes focused on maintaining or improving health, slowing down the progression of the disease, minimizing the impact of the disease, and increasing consumer support for and access to available resources.

The Boston Public Health Commission and Suffolk University implemented Phase I over a three-year period for each contracted Title I service. The Boston Public Health Commission and Suffolk felt strongly that the system should utilize the knowledge and insight of the people delivering the services, rather than imposing an accountability system from above. Although gathering performance data was not new to Title I providers (at least in terms of producing outputs), it took numerous discussions to finally convince providers that measuring and assessing impacts was important. In addition, providers resisted the need to measure the impacts of program goals of other services. As a result, Suffolk University reluctantly—at least in Phase I—allowed each service area to develop its own set of outcomes. Although uncertain about the number of outcomes this methodology would produce, Suffolk University felt that trading efficiency (i.e., the number of outcome measures) for provider buy-in was crucial to successfully implementing the system.

Thus, following extensive, long-term negotiations with providers, Suffolk University began conducting on-site interviews with each of the contracted service providers to learn more about the services themselves, better understand the desired outcomes for each service area, and formally assess the evaluation tools currently in use. Interviews also built rapport, trust, and buy-in with service providers, Suffolk University, and the Boston Public Health Commission.

Based on provider feedback, Suffolk University developed quality and effectiveness measures for each service area. Measurement tools were distributed to participating providers at formal working sessions in which implementation instructions and other support training were provided. Protocols established early on (1) allowed flexibility among providers to choose from a list of outcome measures, (2) did not require a uniform tool or instrument for reporting on outcomes measures (this allowed agencies to use their existing tools), (3) encouraged agencies to integrate outcomes measures into their existing evaluation process, and (4) did not assume that agencies would utilize outside sources of information, such as physicians or other clinicians, but rather would rely primarily on their internal staff.

Early engagement of direct service staff in the system's development yielded both support and further buy-in for the outcomes-measurement initiative. However, it took considerably longer for senior staff to recognize that the Outcomes Measurement System was a management tool and not a direct evaluation of their performance. Providers expressed concern that the Outcomes Measurement System would be used to determine future funding awards for their individual agencies. (As it turned out, some programs were eventually defunded for poor performance when funding declined.) Over time, though, providers eventually acknowledged that collection of the outcomes data was beneficial in both assessing the changing needs of their clients and advocating for additional state and federal funding.

As mentioned, each of the first three years focused on a different set of service areas. During the first year (March 1997–February 1998), Suffolk University developed outcome measures through interviews with providers of the following services: adult and pediatric day care, peer support, drug reimbursement, and alternative therapies providers. The Boston Public Health Commission and Suffolk University compiled outcome measures for providers. Suffolk instructed providers to report on those measures they felt best reflected their program's goals. Importantly, Suffolk University collected information on level of functioning and outcomes for new clients (measured at intake) and ongoing clients over two six-month periods to determine whether or not outcomes were positive, negative, or unchanged.

During the second year (March 1998–February 1999), Suffolk University piloted outcome measures for six additional services: primary medical care, ob-gyn, mental health, transportation, dental, and respite care services, yielding a total of fifty-six outcome measures.

Following the research protocol established in the first year, Suffolk University based all outcome measures on on-site interviews with providers in each service area, and flexibility was afforded to providers in selecting the outcomes reported. Suffolk tested outcomes measures for the remaining services in the third year (March 1999–February 2000): adoption and foster care, case management, client advocacy, housing, meals, and substance abuse.

Provider interviews yielded data for eighty-five different outcomes and measures. Notably, some services areas were highly problematic when defining successful outcomes. For example, it proved difficult for providers to envision successful outcome goals for hospice care, whose purpose was to mitigate the dying process.

One limitation of the system was that providers produced data for only those clients receiving services a one point in time. Providers were not required to track client outcomes through time. Clients entering and exiting a service potentially affected caseload data at any given time. Data, by necessity, captured only snapshots in time of an ever-changing population. To compensate for this shortcoming, analysts placed each new incoming cohort into a program in a group, then analyzed and compared them to other cohorts. Although this was not an optimal solution, analysis nonetheless allowed policy makers to see how client cohorts faired over time.

Suffolk University achieved a number of important objectives in Phase I. The Outcomes Measurement System stimulated discussions on how to improve program quality, perpetuated the sharing of best practices, and produced outcomes data that helped increase funding for HIV/AIDS in the Boston EMA. However, as with any new system, there were some problems. Providers noted that the reporting tool itself was confusing. In addition, providers reported difficulties in establishing a baseline of measurement for new clients and measuring change in performance or need for clients from one reporting period to the next. Suffolk employed on-site technical training to remove provider confusion. The goal of the training was twofold: (1) to provide staff with technical assistance for completing the assessment tool and (2) to directly convey to providers the importance of their participation in the performance-measurement system. Suffolk also believed it was important for providers to see results of their efforts. Thus, Suffolk University began offering agency-specific reports. Reports gave agencies benchmark performance data they could use to apply for other grants and private foundation monies. Through on-site support and outcome data sharing, Suffolk kept providers engaged in the process.

In addition to agency-specific reports, researchers began to generate overall outcomes data for the Boston EMA. In June 2001, Suffolk University prepared a six-month snapshot of the March 2000–August 2000 reporting period comparing the needs and outcomes for primary care, peer support, alternative therapies, day care, respite care, mental health, transportation, ob-gyn, and dental services. The report suggested that a full array of medical and support services was needed to promote client well-being. Support services actually facilitated access to primary care and other medical services while meeting important needs in their own right. The report also highlighted the changing need for services over time and the varying levels of outcome changes across service areas. Differences across services raised multiple questions among service providers. For the first time, many providers began to think critically about what modes, timing, units, and combination of services would be most helpful to clients. In the past, providers tended to offer services carte blanche.

Phase II: Refining the System

Based on the initial three-year success of the Outcomes Measurement System, the Boston Public Health Commission continued its partnership with Suffolk University and entered into Phase II of the Outcomes Measurement System Development Project in 2001. In doing so, both stakeholders acknowledged that the utilization of eighty-five outcomes measures was not an efficient and effective way to collect data. Specifically, the multitude of outcome choices yielded limited client data per outcome, making it difficult for providers to make meaningful comparisons across outcomes and among services. Further, having so many choices made it a confusing and tedious process for providers (particularly among agencies providing multiple services). Suffolk addressed the issue by interviewing providers to gain their input on condensing related but somewhat different outcomes into a shorter list of options. Additionally, Suffolk discussed mandatory reporting in the interviews. Subsequently, Suffolk and the Boston Public Health Commission reduced the number of outcomes from eighty-five to between fifteen and twenty outcomes yielding six health and eight quality-of-life measures. Health outcomes included CD-4 counts, HIV progression–viral load, knowledge about HIV/AIDS, ability to access medical care and other support services, ability to maintain medical care, and ability to adhere to medical therapies. Quality-of-life outcomes included ability to advocate, ability to maintain housing, network of support, coping skills and levels of stress, level of depression, level of crisis-intervention services, level of side effects, and level of criminal behavior.

Resistance to reducing the number of outcomes was minimal among providers because they recognized the importance of assessing client health and quality of life across the Boston EMA, not just within individual programs.

In addition to the reduction in numbers of outcome measures, another important aspect in Phase II was the development of a data-collection system that utilized unique client code identifiers. (The methodology around developing the unique client code identifiers in the Boston EMA is explained in subsequent sections of this chapter.) This innovation allowed providers and the Boston Public Health Commission to track clients within the system over time, looking at units of services consumed, costs, and timing. The Boston EMA, we believe, was the first to track clients using unique identifiers. Other EMAs have not used unique identifiers out of concerns for privacy and confidentiality.

Suffolk University adopted a uniform scale, with outcomes measured on four levels. The levels evaluated outcomes based on service need ranging from a state of "crisis" to "no need" (see Table 15.2). A client in crisis was considered to be in need of substantial services, whereas a client with no need had achieved the optimal outcome goal and was utilizing services to maintain his or her status.

The updated system continued to allow choice for each provider but required that the providers, at a minimum, report on five outcomes for each client served (three of which must be health outcomes, including CD-4 counts and/or viral

Table 15.2

Outcomes Measurement Scale

Client's Level of Need

Outcomes:	Crisis	High Need	Moderate/Low Need	No Need
To improve and/or stabilize . . .	In crisis and in need of substantial additional services.	Making some progress toward reaching the outcome goal. There is a significant need for additional services.	Making significant progress towards outcome goal. Needs some additional services to reach the goal.	Achieved outcome goal. May need continued services to maintain goal achievement.
CD-4 counts	☐ Less than 50	☐ 50–199	☐ 200–500	☐ >500

loads). The mandatory reporting of CD-4 count / viral loads policy stemmed directly from Boston EMA managers and federal funders concerned that support service providers were not routinely collecting medical indicators from their clients. Even so, because providers could choose which outcomes to track, data gaps continued to exist across the system as a trade-off for provider compliance and cooperation.

Suffolk now requires that providers submit outcome reports every six months on all clients receiving Title I services. From an analyst's viewpoint, condensing outcomes increased data validity and reliability, so Suffolk archived data collected and used 2001 data as a baseline.

Two variations on the basic process should be noted. First, providers who served large numbers of clients during each reporting period were allowed to submit plans for sampling their client load. Each plan needed Boston Public Health Commission approval. Second, providers who provided pass-through or vouchers for services such as housing, transportation, and dental services were permitted to select a random sample of one hundred clients rather than assessing their entire caseload. Again, such trade-offs were necessary to gain provider cooperation.

Phase II of the Outcomes Measurement System recognized high turnover rates among providers. Yearly provider training was instituted, which included both verbal and written instructions. Suffolk University inserted all documentation and instructions for completing and submitting outcome measurement forms into the Boston Public Health Commission's providers' manual. The Boston Public Health Commission coordinated technical assistance for agencies related to outcomes submission and Suffolk University provided on-site training.

In fiscal year 2003, providers submitted more than fourteen thousand outcome-measurement reports to Suffolk University for analysis. Suffolk spent approximately 750 hours each reporting period sorting through, organizing, and checking the paper submissions for errors. To improve the integrity of these data and increase efficiency, Suffolk created an electronic spreadsheet. The electronic outcomes form allowed providers to track clients from period to period. Recognizing that some providers lacked the staff support and skills to utilize spreadsheets, Suffolk reluctantly allowed providers the option of continuing with paper submissions.

Increased electronic submissions over three fiscal years—2003 to 2006 (over 60 percent in fiscal year 2006) have improved the accuracy and consistency of outcomes reports by reducing missing, duplicate, or incomplete data historically inherent with the paper surveys. Notably, the time to manage and enter the outcome-measurement reports per reporting period decreased substantially from 750 to 150 hours. However, even in the current system, a 3–5 percent measurement error still exists. This is due in part to data-entry errors inherent in the electronic files submitted by providers.

In January 2005, Suffolk University used the merged demographic-outcomes database to conduct a regional analysis. The Boston, Metro West, Northeast, Southeast Central, and New Hampshire regions were included in the study. Suffolk University assessed differences in health and quality-of-life outcomes across the region for 1,903 new clients and 4,655 ongoing clients. While it was the case that Suffolk observed a number of statistically significant differences among regions on a variety of health and quality-of-life outcomes for new and ongoing clients, management and policy implications were problematic: Results did not suggest any common themes across regions and in some cases seemed counterintuitive; thus, Suffolk recommended that additional analysis was warranted to sort out relationships in the data.

Phase III: Reassessing Performance Measures

In 2006, the Boston Public Health Commission and Suffolk University reexamined the fifteen outcomes assessed by service providers. The need for reassessment emerged from Suffolk University, the planning council, and service providers each offering a different point of view. Stakeholders agreed that limitations raised in the *FY06 Annual Report* needed to be addressed to improve data reliability. One concern was that comparisons of average health and quality-of-life outcome-measurement scores across fiscal years were not reliable since individual outcomes selected by an agency may be inconsistent from one reporting period to another. Another concern was that some of the measures might no longer be accurate. For example, the success of antiretroviral therapies had raised the bar of what was deemed excellent health in terms of medical indicators (i.e., CD-4 counts and viral loads).

In October 2006, Suffolk University asked providers once again to participate in the assessment and improvement of the Outcomes Measurement System. Suffolk University and the Boston Public Health Commission facilitated provider focus groups. Suffolk divided seventy-two participants into medical providers, case managers, and support-service providers. Suffolk asked providers to assess the accuracy of the outcomes, whether or not certain outcomes should be eliminated, and whether there were new measures that should be added.

Some concerns raised by providers included losing the current value of historical data, subjectivity of the current outcomes, and lack of definition for assessing each outcome. In terms of the Outcomes Measurement System, participants recommended providing automatic agency reports that detailed individual outcomes over time, benchmarking data to compare individual agency data and sharing of best practices across agencies.

Upon completion of the provider discussion, the Boston Public Health Commission and Suffolk University launched the newest iteration of the Outcomes Measurement System tool in March 2007. These data continue to be collected every six months, and the new system will require agencies to report on all nine outcomes for every client who receives services under Title I funding. The new outcomes include CD-4 counts, viral load, maintenance of primary medical care, adherence to prescribed HIV-related medical therapies, impact of side effects from HIV-related medications, mental health status, access to psychosocial support, level of self-sufficiency, and housing status.

The 2007 Outcomes Measurement System further improves data quality. Upon receipt, Suffolk University reviews each outcome-measurement report for missing or inconsistent information. After data entry, Suffolk University randomly selects surveys and cross-references them with the database for data-input errors. Reports detailing clients entered into the database continue to be distributed to providers submitting paper outcome-measurement reports. These reports continue to be helpful to larger providers or for agencies with high staff turnover. These reports are used as a reference to ensure that the same clients receive reports in the next reporting period. In addition, upon request, client history reports are generated showing not only unique client identifiers, but also client outcomes.

Unique Client Identifiers

As Phase III evolved, stakeholders in the Boston EMA became more interested in looking at Title I services' impact on individual clients rather than in the aggregate. Working with the Massachusetts Department of Mental Health, the Boston Public Health Commission adopted unique client identifiers, as noted. To ensure confidentiality, the unique client code consisted of a thirteen-digit client code, which was comprised of the first three letters of the client's mother's first name, the client's six-digit date of birth, and the last four digits of the client's Social Security number. Although providers were initially concerned about the resources required to utilize the thirteen-digit code, the benefit of being able to assess the impact of their services on individual clients outweighed the initial cost in time and training.

Adoption of unique client identifiers allowed Suffolk University to conduct more in-depth analysis of the outcomes data. For example, in 2004, analysts integrated the Boston Public Health Commission demographic database into the Outcomes Measurement System. Suffolk generated a demographic analysis of a cohort of 2,295 clients under Title I. This cohort included clients who had received an outcomes-measurement report (at least once in each fiscal year) over a three-year period (March 2001–February 2004).

Phase III Sample Findings

In 2006, Suffolk University examined the relationship between utilization of services and the change in health and quality of life of a client cohort in the Boston EMA. Managers wanted to predict how much and what combination of services would produce the greatest level of improvement among their clients. However, because Suffolk University was only able to measure the utilization of Title I services and could not account for services from other funding sources, accurate predictions could not be made.

Using the unique client code identifiers, Suffolk merged the Boston Public Health Commission's utilization database with the outcomes databases. The preliminary look at service utilization within a cohort of the Boston EMA presented several interesting findings. Overall, analysis suggested that more services, both volume and type, positively impact outcomes. Clients were more likely to have improved health outcomes if they were receiving one or more health-related support services rather than just medical services only. Also, in general, both health and quality-of-life outcomes scores were positively impacted by receipt of a combination of support service types rather than one service type alone. Notably, supplementing medical or support services with case-management services substantially increased the likelihood (by 400–600 percent) that clients had stable or improved health outcome scores. Finally, while volume of service units received appears to impact health and quality-of-life outcome scores within only a few service categories, there was a positive relationship between high utilization and stable or improved outcomes in all service categories (see Table 15.3).

Suffolk University reported data collected through the Outcomes Measurement System reports to the Boston Public Health Commission annually. The annual report compares health and quality-of-life outcomes data for all clients receiving Title I services during each fiscal year. The annual report evaluates health status and quality of life of clients who are new to Title I services as well as clients who are continuing to receive services on an ongoing basis.

From fiscal year 2002 to fiscal year 2006, the number of outcome reports collected ranged from 7,329 to 9,293. These outcome-measurement reports represented four thousand–plus unique clients. In fiscal year 2002, sixty-eight providers were funded for service. In fiscal year 2006, only fifty-three providers received funding. Findings from the most recent annual report, for fiscal year 2006, suggest a number of trends since fiscal year 2002. Specifically, medical outcomes (CD-4 counts and HIV viral loads) showed that both clients new to Ryan White Title I Services and those continuing to receive services were in good to excellent health. However, a review of the three-year cohort (clients who consistently received an outcomes-measurement report at least once in each fiscal year over a three-year period, March 2004–February 2007) highlighted a slight decline in the overall quality of life for clients in the Boston EMA and a widening gap between health and quality of life.

In addition, an examination of individual quality-of-life outcomes showed that only four of eight outcomes indicated good or excellent outcome scores for ongoing clients. The other four indicators showed a fair quality-of-life status for ability to advocate, coping skills and level of stress, level of depression, and level of crisis intervention. A potential area for future investigation includes reviewing the delivery of services to assess ways of assisting clients to achieve optimal outcomes. Thinking about the indicators used to measure quality of life, it is important to note that the housing outcome has been one of the more difficult outcomes to analyze over time: Clients tend to fall at either the crisis (not permanently housed) or optimal (permanently housed) end of the measurement scale.

A comparison of clients by status (new vs. ongoing) in fiscal year 2006 suggested that Title I services had a positive impact on clients. For the September 2006–February

Table 15.3

The Relationship Between High Service Utilization and Health and Quality of Life Outcome Scores

	High Levels of Service Utilization							
Level of Change	Drug Reimbursement (n = 73)	Food (n = 596)	Housing (n = 344)	Mental Health (n = 253)	Peer Support (n = 70)	Primary Care (n = 124)	Substance Abuse (n = 99)	Transportation (n = 425)
Health Outcome Score								
Stable/Improved	82.2% (60)	78.0% (465)	79.4% (273)	67.6% (171)	68.6% (48)	67.7% (84)	75.8% (75)	75.8% (322)
Declined	17.8% (13)	22.0% (131)	20.6% (71)	32.4% (82)	31.4% (22)	32.3% (40)	24.2% (24)	24.2% (103)
Quality of Life Outcome Score								
Stable/Improved	82.2% (60)	71.8% (428)	70.9% (244)	66.4% (168)	85.7% (60)	84.7% (105)	72.7% (72)	70.6% (300)
Declined	17.8% (13)	28.2% (168)	29.1% (100)	33.6% (85)	14.3% (10)	15.3% (19)	27.3% (27)	29.4% (125)

2007 reporting period, ongoing clients had higher scores than new clients for the following indicators: knowledge about HIV/AIDS (12 points higher for ongoing clients), access to medical care (31 points higher for ongoing clients), ability to maintain housing (41 points higher for ongoing clients), and network of support (15 points higher for ongoing clients). Researchers limited analysis to client status (new vs. ongoing) and did not reflect individual client progress from new to ongoing status.

The most significant change in individual outcome scores was for new clients and their ability to access medical care (20-point drop over the previous two fiscal years). This finding could be further investigated to determine whether or not this is a reporting anomaly or whether access to medical care is more limited for people who are not part of the Title I service delivery system.

Voices of Experience

Aside from outcomes reporting and the evaluation studies, stakeholders acknowledged the importance of evaluating service delivery from a client perspective. During the past ten years, the Boston Public Health Commission and Suffolk University collaborated on three consumer-based research studies, *Voices of Experience* (1996; 2000; 2003), designed to gauge consumer experiences accessing and using Ryan White and other HIV/AIDS services. All three studies recruited consumers to participate in peer-to-peer personal and telephone interviews. The consumer research associates were culturally diverse, spoke multiple languages, and received specialized training in interview techniques.

Some 351 consumers participated in the first *Voices* study. Initially, Suffolk University talked primarily to providers, although interviews were conducted with consumers on consumer advisory boards and the planning council. Through these discussions and earlier evaluations, key themes emerged. First, consumers reported considerable difficulty initially accessing services and in coordination and linkage with other Ryan White and social service providers. They also reported confusion about overlapping services and unclear understanding about what services were offered by providers. Three data-collection methods were utilized in order to reach a broad sample of people living with HIV/AIDS. Methods included individual face-to-face or phone interviews of a systematic sample of 176 clients of providers using a long survey form, two interviews of groups of four to eight consumers (group surveys), and short surveys completed by consumers from surveys distributed to a wide variety of sites where clients might either be given them or pick them up. The study showed that the average clients had been living with HIV/AIDS for approximately five years; were just as likely to get test results from a doctor, hospital, or testing center; and learned about available HIV services through a doctor or friend. On average, participants waited two years to use services following a positive diagnosis. At this time, the greatest areas of need were getting help with family placement or adoption, getting money to pay for living expenses, getting money management or financial advice, getting help with child care, and getting help in caring for family.

Voices 2000 focused on experiences of persons underserved and culturally diverse, as well as persons using combination or cocktail drug therapies.

Some 528 surveys were completed through multiple methods: face-to-face interviews, telephone surveys, and paper surveys. There were many important findings from the 2000 study, which included: (1) the vast majority of clients relied on their primary care provider to be their main source of HIV/AIDS information and intervention; (2) despite the medical model of care and improved longevity, the quality of life for most clients was significantly diminished as result of side effects from medications; (3) basic needs for housing, transportation, food, and financial and health entitlements were becoming significantly more important; (4) a significant portion of the population acknowledged participating in high-risk behaviors; and (5) clients living outside of Boston found it more difficult to access services.

Suffolk University designed the *Voices 2003* study to better understand consumer views on their needs for services in Massachusetts and the Boston EMA. Some 466 people living with HIV/AIDS who received services for their HIV disease in Massachusetts and southern New Hampshire participated in the study. *Voices 2003* differed from the previous two studies in that it involved additional stakeholders. Many consumers who participated in the study lived alone, were on Medicaid, and had complicated health problems including high rates of hepatitis C and other acute illnesses. Most received appropriate levels of medical care and case management. However, participants reported a need for dental care and mental health counseling services, but they experienced barriers in accessing care. Reasons for not accessing services included not knowing where to go for services in the area or having difficulty accessing service providers. Many reported that providers did not talk to them about other critical, related issues, such as domestic violence, counseling at-risk partners, safer drug use, or substance abuse treatment. Consumers opined that their service needs would change in the future, and they were worried about how that would affect their health and quality of life.

Other Performance Partnerships

In addition to outcomes data, evaluation reports, and consumer studies reported on by Suffolk University, the Boston Public Health Commission also contracted with JSI Research and Training to provide in-depth clinical quality assurance chart reviews at Title I–funded primary care sites. JSI also provided technical assistance to individual sites for performance improvement. In a comparative study conducted by the Boston Public Health Commission in 2004, medical indicators collected through the Outcomes Measurement System tool (CD-4 counts and viral loads) and *Voices 2003* were statistically similar to the data collected by JSI during the medical chart reviews, seemingly validating both studies.

A comparison of data collected through case reviews and through the Outcomes Measurement System continues to be an important part of the Title I evaluation process in the Boston EMA. In January 2007, Suffolk worked with JSI to match other outcomes data collected through the medical records review process with the Outcomes Measurement System database for more than nine hundred clients receiving outcomes measures from March 2003 to February 2006.

Suffolk University presented all findings from the quality assurance projects, evaluation reports, and consumer studies to the planning council and consumer committee biennially. Additionally, other stakeholders such as the Boston AIDS Consortium and the Massachusetts Department of Public Health present findings from their research throughout the year.

Conclusions

The capacity to systematically collect and report performance-measurement data for individuals receiving Title I services in the Boston EMA proved a useful tool for the administrators of Title I funds. For example, the Boston EMA uses outcomes and utilization data to test combinations of services and determine which services have the greatest impact on outcomes. Recognizing that resources are scare, the Boston Public Health Commission, with the guidance of the planning council, justifies the continuation of certain services based on the data collected through the performance-measurement system. In addition, the ability to merge demographic data with outcomes data allowed researchers to determine whether or not there are disparities in care across demographic groups.

From a policy perspective, although medical outcomes remained steady, quality of life declined and the gap between health and quality of life for clients in the Boston EMA widened. This quantitative evidence allowed the Boston Public Health Commission to advocate at the federal level for the importance of continuing and perhaps increasing support services for clients.

Providers also benefited from the outcomes measurement system. First, the performance data allow providers to measure their success internally and against the Boston EMA in improving clients' health and quality of life. Second, it equips providers with the quantitative data needed to support their achievements when applying for other funding sources. Last, it encourages accountability and focuses providers on meeting a common goal—delivering quality services that will help all in need in the Boston EMA achieve and maintain optimal health and quality of life.

The Outcomes Measurement System also opened the door to consumer-based studies such as *Voices of Experience,* which not only helped decision makers in the Boston EMA better understand needs and unmet needs of clients, but also engaged consumers in research, which in turn increased consumer understanding and acceptance of the outcomes measurement system.

Lesson Learned

Over the past decade many important lessons have been learned in the development of the Title I Outcomes Measurement System. First is the need to engage all stakeholders, not only in the initial stages of development, but throughout implementation, as circumstances change and stakeholders become more sophisticated in using outcomes data. Second is the importance of continuously assessing and reassessing the performance measures being used and collected. Measures used early on, even with wide consensus, may not be appropriate for stakeholders later. Third is the willingness to go beyond the performance-measurement system and utilize both inferential statistics (e.g., utilization and demographic studies) and qualitative research (e.g., *Voices of Experience*) to better understand the impact of Title I services on clients in the Boston EMA to continuously improve performance. Outcome reports are of no use unless they improve the system. Last is the need to continuously advocate for and educate consumers, policy makers, and decision makers about the importance of performance-measurement data and its role in stakeholders making rational, evidence-based, policy decisions. This is important because stakeholders, especially over a decade, change over, and their replacements often lack a sense for how the performance system evolved and where it is headed.

Future Outlook

In the future, the Boston EMA will continue to face obstacles in working toward an ideal measurement system. According to the Boston Public Health Commission's client services director, Michael Goldrosen, one consistent barrier is the inability to access outcomes data on clients who receive services other than Part A (Title I). In other words, there is no universal system to assess the impact of services provided through other funders (e.g., MassHealth, Medicaid, and private insurance companies). Goldrosen suggests that a case management model, where all clients receiving HIV/AIDS-related services would be assigned a single case manager, might be one method of centralizing data collection and in turn allow for a uniform measurement tool across the Boston EMA. However, evaluators recognize that an ideal system may never be achieved. Demographic changes (i.e., the aging client population), shrinking funds, the turnover of key decision makers and stakeholders, and the changing service needs of clients in the Boston EMA will continue to perpetuate the need to assess and modify the performance-measurement system.

References

Boston AIDS Consortium. 2006. "Assessment of Need Among People Living with HIV/ AIDS in the Boston EMA." February.
Kaiser Family Foundation. 2006. *Ryan White Comprehensive AIDS Resources Emergency Act.* Washington, DC: Kaiser, June.
U.S. Government Accountability Office. 2007. *Ryan White Care Act.* GAO-08–137R. Washington, DC: U.S. Government Accountability Office, October.
Osborne, David. 1993. *Reinventing Government: The Five Strategies for Reinventing Government.* New York: Penguin.

Part V

Empirical Studies

16

Expanding Access to Health Care for Hispanic Construction Workers and Their Children

Xiuwen Dong, Knut Ringen, and Alissa Fujimoto

Millions of Americans and their children lack health insurance. In 2006, more than 46 million (16 percent) of Americans were uninsured and more than 9 million of those uninsured were children (Appleby 2006). In the same year, only 59.5 percent of people received health insurance through their jobs. While the proportion of workers with job-based health insurance is falling, insurance premiums are increasing (Kaiser Family Foundation 2006). Moreover, research has found disparities in health status and access to health care among different racial and ethnic groups and socioeconomic circumstances (e.g., Egede 2006). This is especially true for Hispanics—the fastest-growing population in the United States, and the core of the debate over immigration policy.

The construction industry has the highest percentage of Hispanic workers. From 1990 to 2005, the proportion of workers who identified themselves as Hispanic increased by 86 percent for all industries, while it jumped by 156 percent for construction. In 2006, construction employed 2.9 million Hispanic workers, which accounted for 25 percent of the industry's employment and 66.5 percent of the increase in employment for that year. Recent Hispanic arrivals employed in construction increased by about 255,000 in 2006 and comprised 45.6 percent of the total increase in the construction industry (Pew Hispanic Center 2007). Moreover, many undocumented Hispanic workers may not be included in this figure. Construction is the largest employer of short-term illegal workers, with some 550,000 unauthorized migrants arriving between 2000 and 2005. Overall, more than 1.4 million (12 percent) unauthorized workers are employed in the construction industry—the largest amount in any major industry. Unfortunately, health insurance coverage and access to health care have not increased as the number of Hispanic immigrants has grown.

Disparities in health care coverage between Hispanics and other racial and ethnic groups have been well documented (Callahan, Hickson, and Cooper 2006; DeNavas-Walt et al. 2005; Documét and Sharma 2004; Hargraves, Cunningham, and Hughes 2001; Waidmann and Rajan 2000). Such disparities not only are found for adults, but also exist for Hispanic children (Ojeda and Brown 2005; Byck 2000). Despite the increased awareness of health care disparities, few studies have analyzed relationships between health insurance and patterns of health expenditures and sources of payment, and even less research has been conducted on Hispanic construction workers and their children.

Although frequently neglected in the health policy debate, work-related health risks account for significant morbidity and mortality in many occupations, especially construction. Despite much effort made to reduce occupational injuries and illnesses, the construction industry continues to account for a disproportionate share of work-related injuries and illnesses. Work-related death rates for Hispanic construction workers were consistently higher than those of their non-Hispanic counterparts, especially for workers in some high-risk occupations (Dong and Platner 2004). Historically, Hispanics experience a higher amount of accidents and fatalities than workers from other backgrounds in jobs high in physical labor (Acosta-Leon et al. 2006). Between 1996 and 2002, in comparison to white, non-Hispanic construction workers, Hispanic construction workers were 53 percent more likely to have work-related medical conditions, but 48 percent less likely to receive payment for medical costs from workers' compensation (Dong et al. 2007).

Given the rapidly increasing Hispanic workforce in construction and the dangers associated with the work, information on health services for this important worker group and their dependents is needed to guide health policies and interventions. This chapter examines health services issues for Hispanic construction workers and their dependents, including health insurance coverage, health status, patterns of health services and expenditures, and sources of payment for medical care. Consequences of the lack of health services and possible remedies to increase access to health care for the uninsured are also discussed.

Research Methods and Data

A large national population-based survey, the Medical Expenditure Panel Survey 2004, was used for this study. It provides nationally representative estimates of insurance coverage, health care use, medical expenditures, and sources of payment for the civilian noninstitutionalized population (Agency for Healthcare Research and Quality 2007). The survey includes household, insurance, and medical provider components. The household component collects data from households and their members who participated in the prior year's National Health Interview Survey, supplemented by data from their medical providers. The insurance component collects data on employment-based health insurance from employers.

Construction workers are those who were employed in the construction industry during at least one of the three waves of data collection during 2004. *Hispanic* refers to any person or individual whose origin is Mexican, Puerto Rican, Cuban, South or Central American, Chicano, or other Latin American, regardless of racial background and country of origin. *Dependents of construction workers* were identified by linking family IDs between children (age zero to sixteen years) and their parents. *White, non-Hispanic workers* were used as the comparison group in this study. Using the above methods, 1,513 construction workers and 1,644 children of these workers were identified. Among them, 544 workers and 831 children were of Hispanic origin, representing 2.6 million Hispanic construction workers and 2.9 million of their children.

Findings

Profile of Hispanic Construction Workers

In 2004, one in five construction workers were of Hispanic origin (Table 16.1). Hispanic workers were more likely to be male, younger, and less educated. On average, Hispanic workers were nearly five years younger than white, non-Hispanic workers. Nearly one in three Hispanics had less than nine years of education compared with only 3 percent for whites. The family size of Hispanic workers was larger, but family incomes tended to be lower than those of white non-Hispanics. About 30 percent of Hispanic construction workers had family incomes at or below 124 percent of the federal poverty level, more than three times that for non-Hispanic counterparts. More than 74 percent of Hispanic workers were foreign-born, and 70 percent of immigrant workers reported that they felt uncomfortable speaking English. Also, nearly 90 percent of Hispanic construction workers were concentrated in the South and West. Hispanic construction workers were likely to work in blue-collar occupations (e.g., construction laborers, carpenters, crane and tow truck operators), but less likely to have been self-employed and unionized when compared with white non-Hispanics. In addition, many construction workers were employed with small employers (fewer than twenty employees), and the proportion was slightly higher for Hispanics than for their white, non-Hispanic counterparts.

Access to Health Services Among Hispanic Workers

Three-fifths of Hispanic construction workers had no health insurance, nearly three times more than white, non-Hispanic workers (21 percent; Table 16.2). Compared with whites, Hispanics were less likely to have health insurance offered by their employer, and were even less likely to accept such an offer. About 32 percent of Hispanic workers reported that they had health insurance from their employer for some of the year, and only 20 percent had such insurance for the entire year. A small proportion of construction workers had health insurance from public sources. Hispanic workers received more assistance from Medicaid and the State Children's Health Insurance Program (SCHIP) than white, non-Hispanic workers. In addition, 30 percent of Hispanics reported they had a usual source of care (USC) provider—less than half of that for white workers. When uninsurance status was examined, more than 6 percent of Hispanic union members did not have insurance compared with more than 66 percent of Hispanic non-union workers.

Disparities in health insurance were also observed among children of construction workers (Table 16.3, p. 328). The percentage of uninsurance among children of Hispanic workers was more than double that for children of white workers (22.7 percent

Table 16.1

Profile of Construction Workers

Characteristics	All (N = 1,513)[1] Percent	Hispanic (N = 544) Percent	Lower 95% CI	Upper 95% CI	White, Non-Hispanic (N = 840) Percent	Lower 95% CI	Upper 95% CI
Age*							
16 to 21	7.0	8.3	5.5	12.5	6.6	4.8	8.8
22 to 35	35.4	47.0	41.7	52.3	33.5	30.0	37.2
36 to 45	25.9	26.9	21.5	33.1	25.4	21.8	29.4
46 to 64	29.1	17.4	13.0	22.7	31.2	27.8	34.8
65 and up	2.7	0.4	0.1	1.4	3.3	2.1	5.1
Average age*	39.2	35.1	34.2	36.0	39.6	38.7	40.5
Female worker*	9.0	2.8	1.6	5.1	11.0	9.0	13.2
Education*							
< 9 grade	8.3	31.0	26.1	36.4	3.2	2.0	5.0
9–11 grade	20.2	25.7	21.1	30.8	17.6	14.8	21.0
12 grade	39.8	30.0	24.8	35.7	42.8	38.7	47.0
Some college	21.3	10.9	7.0	16.5	23.8	20.4	27.6
College and up	10.5	2.5	1.2	5.0	12.6	10.1	15.7
Poverty level*							
Under 100%	9.5	20.1	16.0	24.9	6.6	4.9	8.8
100% to 124%	4.1	9.1	6.4	12.8	2.8	1.8	4.2
125% to 200%	13.1	19.6	15.9	23.9	11.1	9.1	13.5
201% to 399%	38.8	36.9	31.8	42.2	39.1	35.1	43.2
400% or more	34.5	14.4	10.4	19.6	40.5	36.1	45.1
Foreign-born[2]*	19.9	74.1	66.7	80.3	5.9	4.2	8.2
Spanish at home*	13.8	73.0	65.8	79.1	0.1	.03	0.4

Uncomfortable to speak English	.	69.5	62.1	76.1	2.8	2.7	2.9
Family size average*	3.0	3.7	3.6	3.9	.	.	.
Marital status*							
Married	57.8	58.8	52.7	64.6	59.5	55.0	64.0
Was married	15.8	10.0	6.5	15.3	16.7	13.7	20.1
Never married	26.4	31.2	26.0	36.9	23.8	20.6	27.4
Region*							
Northeast	17.0	3.7	2.1	6.7	20.2	16.7	24.3
Midwest	20.8	6.7	4.0	11.1	25.3	21.5	29.5
South	37.2	42.6	35.3	50.3	33.6	29.5	38.0
West	25.0	47.0	39.8	54.2	20.9	17.2	25.0
Blue-collar worker*	78.9	92.3	88.3	95.0	74.5	71.1	77.7
Self-employed*	28.8	17.7	14.1	22.0	31.4	27.6	35.5
Union member[3]*	14.9	8.2	5.4	12.3	16.5	13.4	20.1
Establishment size							
Less than 20	68.4	71.5	64.5	77.6	68.6	63.6	73.3
20 to 49	12.4	10.8	7.2	15.8	12.6	9.6	16.3
50 to 99	9.0	8.6	6.1	12.0	9.2	6.8	12.2
100 or more	10.1	9.2	5.4	15.2	9.6	7.2	12.8
Total	100%		100%			100%	
Weighted Number	13.5 M		2.6 M			10.0 M	

Source: 2004 Medical Expenditure Panel Survey (MEPS).
[1] Includes workers in other races and ethnicities (e.g., African-American).
[2] 2003 data.
[3] Self-employed workers were excluded from this calculation.
*p < .05.

Table 16.2

Health Insurance Coverage and Access to Health Care: Construction Workers

Health Insurance	All (N = 1,513)[1] Percent	Hispanic (N = 544) Percent	Lower 95% CI	Upper 95% CI	White, Non-Hispanic (N = 840) Percent	Lower 95% CI	Upper 95% CI
Health insurance coverage*							
Any private	63.6	32.8	27.9	38.2	72.9	69.1	76.4
Public only	5.7	5.3	3.6	7.7	5.9	4.1	8.3
Uninsured	30.7	61.9	56.8	66.8	21.2	18.1	24.7
Employer provided insurance coverage*[2]							
Offered	73.6	52.9	44.0	61.7	78.3	72.9	82.9
Covered some months	58.1	32.2	26.7	38.1	65.9	62.0	69.7
Covered entire year	50.9	20.4	15.7	26.0	51.9	47.8	56.0
Unable to receive medical care							
Could not afford	77.2	100.0	.	.	68.9	43.6	86.4
Insurance company would not cover	17.9	0.0	.	.	24.4	9.8	49.0
Doctor refused insurance plan	4.9	0.0	.	.	6.7	0.9	36.8
Ever have Medicaid/SCHIP during year	4.3	5.9	3.9	8.6	4.0	2.5	6.3
Ever have Medicare during year*	2.7	0.4	0.1	1.4	3.3	2.1	5.1
Have USC provider*	60.1	30.2	25.6	35.3	68.6	64.9	72.1
Total	100%	100%			100%		
Weighted Number	13.5 M	2.6 M			10.0 M		

Source: Medical Expenditure Panel Survey (MEPS). From *Justification for Budget Estimates for Appropriations Committees, Fiscal Year 2004,* February 2003. Agency for Healthcare Research and Quality, Rockville, MD. Available at http://www.ahrq.gov/about/cj2004/meps04.htm.

[1]Includes workers in other races and ethnicities (e.g., African-American).

[2]Not mutually exclusive and may overlap. Some respondents might be represented in more than once in the categories of offered, covered some months, and covered entire year.

*$p < .05$.

for Hispanic children versus 9.8 percent for white children). Source of insurance also differed between Hispanic and white, non-Hispanic children. Hispanic children were more likely to receive insurance from public sources (55 percent) while the majority (64.8 percent) of white children had private insurance coverage. The gap in having a USC provider between these children is as large as that in insurance coverage: About 20 percent of Hispanic children lacked USC providers compared with 7 percent of children of white workers.

Impact of Health Insurance on Medical Expenditures and Types of Services

The impact of insurance coverage on medical expenditures is remarkable when insurance status is stratified. On average, the insured spent much more on health care than the uninsured. For example, a Hispanic worker with insurance spent an annual average of $1,540 on health care, more than five times the average expenditure ($300) for a Hispanic worker without insurance. A similar difference was observed among white, non-Hispanic workers: The average medical expenditure for the insured is more than six times that of the uninsured ($2,650 versus $403). Ethnic disparities in medical expenditures existed for both the insured and the uninsured, with Hispanic workers without insurance being left far behind others in this comparison (Table 16.4). However, the impact of insurance status on use of health services overtook the impact of ethnicity.

Patterns of health services usage differ between insurance status and ethnic groups. The uninsured Hispanics, on average, spent more on inpatient services (47.5 percent) and emergency room services (12.5 percent), but less on office-based services (15.9 percent) and prescription drugs (10.7 percent) than other groups in this comparison. Health-seeking behaviors were largely affected by insurance status and ethnicity. However, this estimate did not take age, health status, and other possible confounders into account. Most likely, medical urgency was a more significant determinant of health care use in the Hispanic population.

Disparities among children of construction workers tended to follow the same trends as did disparities among their parents, although the average amount of medical expenditures per child was much lower than that per worker (Table 16.5). Overall, children who had insurance spent much more on health services than children without insurance. Hispanic children without insurance spent about one-quarter of the average amount Hispanic children with insurance had. Ethnic disparities existed within the uninsured children as well. Uninsured Hispanic children spent half the amount that uninsured white children did, both in total and on average. Types of health services used by those children are different from those used by construction workers, or adult counterparts. Children from all ethnicities spent less on inpatient services and prescription drugs, but more on dental care when compared with adults across the board (Tables 16.4 and 16.5).

Table 16.3

Health Insurance Coverage and Access to Health Care: Children of Construction Workers

Health Insurance	All (N = 1,644)[1] Percent	Hispanic (N = 831) Percent	Hispanic Lower 95% CI	Hispanic Upper 95% CI	White, Non-Hispanic (N = 665) Percent	White Lower 95% CI	White Upper 95% CI
Health insurance coverage*							
Any private	51.1	22.3	17.1	28.5	64.8	58.4	70.7
Public only	35.7	55.0	48.7	61.1	25.5	20.2	31.6
Uninsured	13.2	22.7	17.8	28.5	9.8	6.7	14.0
Employer-provided insurance coverage through parent(s)*[2]							
Covered some months	44.2	20.3	15.2	26.6	55.4	48.6	62.1
Covered entire year	35.4	15.2	10.9	20.7	45.0	38.4	51.8
Ever have Medicaid/SCHIP during year*	40.1	59.1	52.8	65.0	29.8	23.9	36.5
Ever have Medicare during year	1.4	1.9	.9	4.1	.8	.4	1.7
Have USC provider*	88.9	79.8	74.0	84.6	93.0	89.4	95.4
Total	100%	100%			100%		
Weighted Number	10.8 M	2.9 M			7.0 M		

Source: Medical Expenditure Panel Survey (MEPS). From *Justification for Budget Estimates for Appropriations Committees, Fiscal Year 2004,* February 2003. Agency for Healthcare Research and Quality, Rockville, MD. Available at http://www.ahrq.gov/about/cj2004/meps04.htm.

[1] Includes workers in other races and ethnicities (e.g., African-American).

[2] Not mutually exclusive and may overlap. Some respondents might be represented in more than once in the categories of covered some months and covered entire year.

*p < .05.

Table 16.4

Types of Service by Insurance Status and Hispanic Ethnicity: Construction Workers

Sources	All (N = 1,513)[1]			Insured Hispanic (N = 194)		
	Mean[2]	Percent	Sum[3]	Mean[2]	Percent	Sum[3]
Outpatient[4]	209.79	11.53	2,835.24	121.70	7.90	118.29
Office-based	384.35	21.13	5,194.35	264.86	17.20	257.43
Emergency room	126.89	6.98	1,714.97	107.31	6.97	104.30
Inpatient[5]	571.99	31.45	7,730.27	683.94	44.42	664.75
Dental care	174.75	9.61	2,361.71	126.17	8.19	122.63
Prescription	348.30	19.15	4,707.12	210.71	13.68	204.80
Total expenditures[6]	1,819.19	100.00	24,585.70	1,539.72	100.00	1,496.53

(continued)

Table 16.4 *(continued)*

Sources	Insured White, Non-Hispanic (N = 623)			Uninsured Hispanic (N = 350)			Uninsured White, Non-Hispanic (N = 217)		
	Mean²	Percent	Sum³	Mean²	Percent	Sum³	Mean²	Percent	Sum³
Outpatient⁴	306.14	11.55	2,408.10	12.03	4.02	19.00	24.54	6.08	52.02
Office-based	570.66	21.54	4,488.75	47.74	15.93	75.39	113.1	28.05	239.74
Emergency room	183.69	6.93	1,444.89	37.52	12.52	59.26	10.12	2.51	21.46
Inpatient⁵	832.20	31.41	6,546.08	142.49	47.54	225.03	26.71	6.63	56.63
Dental care	245.26	9.26	1,929.19	21.51	7.18	33.98	115.78	28.71	245.43
Prescription	509.84	19.24	4,010.37	31.96	10.66	50.47	113.36	28.11	240.29
Total expenditures⁶	2,649.51	100.00	20,840.85	299.71	100.00	473.34	403.23	100.00	854.73

Source: Medical Expenditure Panel Survey (MEPS). From *Justification for Budget Estimates for Appropriations Committees, Fiscal Year 2004, February 2003.* Agency for Healthcare Research and Quality, Rockville, MD. Available at http://www.ahrq.gov/about/cj2004/meps04.htm.

[1] Includes workers in other races and ethnicities (e.g., African-American).
[2] In 2004 dollars, per person per year, on average.
[3] Number in millions of dollars.
[4] Includes ambulatory services and home health services.
[5] Includes hospital inpatient services.
[6] Totals may not add to detail due to rounding and "Other equipment" data not included.

Table 16.5

Types of Service by Insurance Status and Hispanic Ethnicity: Children of Construction Workers

Sources	All (N = 1,644)[1]			Insured Hispanic (N = 631)		
	Mean[2]	Percent	Sum[3]	Mean[2]	Percent	Sum[3]
Outpatient[4]	77.18	7.62	835.88	137.09	18.29	308.01
Office-based	244.19	24.12	2,644.55	192.81	25.73	433.21
Emergency room	88.93	8.78	963.18	77.92	10.40	175.06
Inpatient[5]	264.95	26.17	2,869.41	155.23	20.71	348.76
Dental care	225.94	22.32	2,446.88	98.03	13.08	220.26
Prescription	100.49	9.93	1,088.26	81.78	10.91	183.74
Total expenditures[6]	1,012.19	100.00	10,962.02	749.46	100.00	1,683.91

(continued)

Table 16.5 (continued)

Sources	Insured White, Non-Hispanic (N = 593)			Uninsured Hispanic (N = 200)			Uninsured White, Non-Hispanic (N = 72)		
	Mean²	Percent	Sum³	Mean²	Percent	Sum³	Mean²	Percent	Sum³
Outpatient⁴	47.62	4.21	301.41	1.98	1.10	1.30	0.00	0.00	0.00
Office-based	301.21	26.65	1,906.57	54.77	30.38	36.12	129.13	36.29	88.56
Emergency room	102.85	9.10	651.06	6.32	3.50	4.17	70.69	19.87	48.48
Inpatient⁵	242.32	21.44	1,533.80	50.19	27.84	33.10	1.74	.49	1.19
Dental care	303.51	26.86	1,921.18	47.03	26.08	31.02	111.22	31.26	76.28
Prescription	120.44	10.66	762.36	11.84	6.57	7.81	25.93	7.29	17.78
Total expenditures⁶	1,130.10	100.00	7,153.33	180.31	100.00	118.93	355.80	100.00	244.02

Source: Medical Expenditure Panel Survey (MEPS). From *Justification for Budget Estimates for Appropriations Committees, Fiscal Year 2004,* February 2003. Agency for Healthcare Research and Quality, Rockville, MD. Available at http://www.ahrq.gov/about/cj2004/meps04.htm.

[1]Includes workers in other races and ethnicities (e.g., African-American).

[2]In 2004 dollars, per person per year, on average.

[3]Number in millions of dollars.

[4]Includes ambulatory services and home health services.

[5]Includes hospital inpatient services.

[6]Totals may not add to detail due to rounding and "Other equipment" data not included.

Impact of Health Insurance on Sources of Payment

Sources of payment for medical expenditures were largely affected by health insurance status (Table 16.6). Workers without insurance self-paid most of their expenditures—82 percent among Hispanics and 72 percent among whites—while insured Hispanics and whites self-paid 24 percent and 21 percent, respectively. The ethnic disparities in sources of payment are sizable for all insurance statuses. Among workers having insurance, only 24.5 percent of the payment for insured Hispanics was paid by private insurance compared with 60.7 percent for insured whites. About 48 percent of the payment for insured Hispanics was from public sources (such as Medicaid, Medicare, and other federal, state, and local public sources; excluding workers' compensation and Veterans Administration benefits), while only 4 percent for the insured whites was paid by these public sources. Within the uninsured workers, Hispanics were more likely to self-pay than whites, but less likely to have had payments from other private and public sources. For example, the Veterans Administration paid about 9 percent of medical expenditures for the uninsured white non-Hispanics, but nothing for the uninsured Hispanics.

Insured white workers received more payment (in amount and proportion) from workers' compensation than any other group in this comparison. However, this does not mean these workers had more work-related conditions than others. On average, uninsured workers received a smaller amount of workers' compensation than their insured counterparts even though the proportion of workers' compensation for the uninsured Hispanics was relatively higher. Combined with workers' compensation, the estimated amount paid by private and public sources for the uninsured totaled $83.4 million for Hispanics and $240.4 million for whites in 2004. Obviously, in addition to the payment from the uninsured workers and their families, the financial burden of the uninsured is split among society and taxpayers.

The patterns of payment follow the types of insurance coverage among children (Table 16.7). Among the insured children, the largest medical payments for Hispanic children were paid by Medicaid (68 percent), while about half (50.5 percent) of the expenses for insured white, non-Hispanic children were paid by private insurance. In 2004, the payment from Medicaid alone accounted for $1,143.8 million for the insured Hispanic children.

Hispanic families are about four times more likely to self-pay for their children's health care if they do not have insurance compared with Hispanics with insurance (50.4 percent versus 11.1 percent, respectively). In addition to the payment from families, other public sources (including state and local, other public, and other unknown sources, but excluding Medicaid and Medicare) paid $57.7 million for the uninsured Hispanic children, accounting for 48.5 percent of the total medical expenditures by these children. The financial burden of health care for Hispanic children, either insured or uninsured, is shared by the public and society.

Table 16.6

Sources of Payment by Insurance Status and Hispanic Ethnicity: Construction Workers

Sources	All (N = 1,513)[1]			Insured Hispanic (N = 194)	
	Mean[2]	Percent	Sum[3]	Mean[2]	Percent	Sum[3]
Workers' compensation	115.35	6.34	1,558.88	26.24	1.70	25.51
Private insurance	1,005.91	55.29	13,594.51	376.92	24.48	366.35
Medicaid	29.09	1.60	393.13	135.60	8.81	131.80
Medicare	59.93	3.29	809.91	337.64	21.93	328.16
Tricare	11.99	.66	162.07	0.00	0.00	0.00
VA	66.86	3.68	903.52	7.86	.51	7.64
Other federal	.75	.04	10.11	0.00	0.00	0.00
Other private	23.99	1.32	324.28	6.30	.41	6.13
Other public	1.30	.07	17.55	5.51	.36	5.36
Other state/local	30.02	1.65	405.75	261.67	16.99	254.33
Other sources	40.18	2.21	542.99	13.28	.86	12.91
Self/family	433.83	23.85	5,863.11	368.68	23.94	358.34
Total expenditures[4]	1,819.19	100.00	24,585.70	1,539.72	100.00	1,496.53

Sources	Insured White, Non-Hispanic (N = 623)			Uninsured Hispanic (N = 350)			Uninsured White, Non-Hispanic (N = 217)		
	Mean[2]	Percent	Sum[3]	Mean[2]	Percent	Sum[3]	Mean[2]	Percent	Sum[3]
Workers' compensation	176.25	6.65	1,386.36	15.53	5.18	24.53	13.50	3.35	28.62
Private insurance	1,608.22	60.70	12,650.19	0.00	0.00	0.00	0.00	0.00	0.00
Medicaid	31.49	1.19	247.73	0.00	0.00	0.00	0.00	0.00	0.00
Medicare	58.39	2.20	459.32	0.00	0.00	0.00	0.00	0.00	0.00
Tricare	20.60	.78	162.07	0.00	0.00	0.00	0.00	0.00	0.00
VA	102.44	3.87	805.78	0.00	0.00	0.00	35.05	8.69	74.30
Other federal	1.28	.05	10.06	.03	.01	.05	0.00	0.00	0.00
Other private	28.32	1.07	222.75	20.16	6.73	31.84	28.50	7.07	60.41
Other public	.03	0.00	.21	1.48	.49	2.34	.02	0.00	.04
Other state/local	18.83	.71	148.09	1.94	.65	3.06	.13	.03	.27
Other sources	53.30	2.01	419.24	13.69	4.57	21.62	36.24	8.99	76.82
Self/family	550.37	20.77	4,329.16	246.87	82.37	389.89	289.80	71.87	614.29
Total expenditures[4]	2,649.51	100.00	20,840.85	299.71	100.00	473.34	403.23	100.00	854.73

Source: Medical Expenditure Panel Survey (MEPS). From *Justification for Budget Estimates for Appropriations Committees, Fiscal Year 2004,* February 2003. Agency for Healthcare Research and Quality, Rockville, MD. Available at http://www.ahrq.gov/about/cj2004/meps04.htm.

[1]Includes workers in other races and ethnicities (e.g., African-American).

[2]In 2004 dollars, per person per year, on average.

[3]Number in millions of dollars.

[4]Totals may not add to detail due to rounding.

Table 16.7

Sources of Payment by Insurance Status and Hispanic Ethnicity: Children of Construction Workers

Sources	All (N = 1,644)[1]			Insured Hispanic (N = 631)		
	Mean[2]	Percent	Sum[3]	Mean[2]	Percent	Sum[3]
Workers' compensation	.12	.01	1.32	0.00	0.00	0.00
Private insurance	378.50	37.39	4,099.17	124.79	16.65	280.39
Medicaid	280.91	27.75	3,042.24	509.08	67.93	1,143.82
Medicare	95.22	9.41	1,031.26	1.85	.25	4.16
Tricare	.03	0.00	.28	0.00	0.00	0.00
VA	11.75	1.16	127.27	.68	.09	1.53
Other federal	.30	.03	3.27	0.00	0.00	0.00
Other private	28.22	2.79	305.59	25.08	3.35	56.35
Other public	4.32	.43	46.79	0.00	0.00	0.00
Other state/local	4.93	.49	53.34	3.05	.41	6.86
Other sources	6.70	.66	72.53	2.09	.28	4.70
Self/family	201.20	19.88	2,178.96	82.81	11.05	186.07
Total expenditures[4]	1,012.19	100.00	10,962.02	749.46	100.00	1,683.91

Sources	Insured White, Non-Hispanic (N = 593)			Uninsured Hispanic (N = 200)			Uninsured White, Non-Hispanic (N = 72)		
	Mean[2]	Percent	Sum[3]	Mean[2]	Percent	Sum[3]	Mean[2]	Percent	Sum[3]
Workers' compensation	.21	.02	1.32	0.00	0.00	0.00	0.00	0.00	0.00
Private insurance	571.03	50.53	3,614.50	0.00	0.00	0.00	0.00	0.00	0.00
Medicaid	191.94	16.98	1,214.96	0.00	0.00	0.00	0.00	0.00	0.00
Medicare	52.62	4.66	333.08	0.00	0.00	0.00	0.00	0.00	0.00
Tricare	.04	0.00	.28	0.00	0.00	0.00	0.00	0.00	0.00
VA	18.89	1.67	119.60	0.00	0.00	0.00	8.96	2.52	6.14
Other federal	.05	0.00	.31	0.00	0.00	0.00	4.31	1.21	2.96
Other private	21.39	1.89	135.38	5.54	3.07	3.65	158.31	44.49	108.58
Other public	0.00	0.00	0.00	67.16	37.25	44.29	3.64	1.02	2.50
Other state/local	7.09	.63	44.90	.21	.12	.14	.69	.19	.47
Other sources	8.41	.74	53.26	20.12	11.16	13.27	.53	.15	.37
Self/family	258.42	22.87	1,635.75	87.29	48.41	57.57	179.35	50.41	123.00
Total expenditures[4]	1,130.10	100.00	7,153.33	180.31	100.00	118.93	355.80	100.00	244.02

Source: Medical Expenditure Panel Survey (MEPS). From *Justification for Budget Estimates for Appropriations Committees, Fiscal Year 2004,* February 2003. Agency for Healthcare Research and Quality, Rockville, MD. Available at http://www.ahrq.gov/about/cj2004/meps04.htm.

[1]Includes workers in other races and ethnicities (e.g., African-American).

[2]In 2004 dollars, per person per year, on average.

[3]Number in millions of dollars.

[4]Totals may not add to detail due to rounding.

Impact of Health Insurance on Perceived Health Status

When construction workers were asked to assess their health, perceived health status varied by ethnicity. Hispanics' perceived health leaned more toward the negative end of the distribution, whereas white counterparts fell at the positive side of the health status spectrum. When health status was stratified by health insurance status, for either Hispanics or whites, the uninsured workers were more likely to report fair and poor health compared with the insured workers, and the Hispanic uninsured workers ranked the highest in fair or poor health reporting (Table 16.8). This measurement of perceived health status by insurance status could reflect the consequences of lacking access to health care, but could also be affected by cultural perceptions and perspectives.

Although the children of workers rated their health as "excellent" more frequently than their parents, the trends and disparities were similar to those of construction workers. Hispanic children had not perceived their health as favorably as their white counterparts overall. Among Hispanic children, the uninsured children were more likely to have poor health status than children with insurance (Table 16.9). As with construction workers, the data from perceived health statuses for children could reflect actual health needs in addition to cultural differences.

Conclusion

This chapter documents ethnic disparities in insurance coverage, health status, health services, and sources of payment among construction workers and their children. The insurance issue is no longer simply an altruistic concern on behalf of those without insurance coverage, but a matter of self-interest for everyone. If we are to learn from this study, we need to critically review the current health care system in order to identify a possible remedy. Since employer-sponsored insurance is still the cornerstone of the U.S. health care system and the predominant source of coverage for nonelderly adults, extending coverage through a worker's job would help alleviate and reduce uninsurance. Other chapters in this book provide several blueprints for achieving this goal.

Table 16.8

Distribution of Perceived Health Status Among Construction Workers

Perceived Health	Uninsured Hispanic (N = 350)			Uninsured White, Non-Hispanic (N = 217)		
	Percent	Lower 95% CI	Upper 95% CI	Percent	Lower 95% CI	Upper 95% CI
Health status						
Excellent	26.4	22.7	30.4	31.9	28.4	35.7
Very good	29.9	26.7	33.5	35.6	32.1	39.3
Good	33.1	29.1	37.4	25.8	22.3	29.6
Fair/Poor	10.6	8.2	13.7	6.7	5.0	9.0
Total (Weighted)	100% (1.6 M)			100% (2.1 M)		

(continued)

Table 16.8 *(continued)*

Perceived Health	Uninsured Hispanic (N = 350)			Uninsured White, Non-Hispanic (N = 217)		
	Percent	Lower 95% CI	Upper 95% CI	Percent	Lower 95% CI	Upper 95% CI
Health status						
Excellent	26.4	22.7	30.4	31.9	28.4	35.7
Very good	29.9	26.7	33.5	35.6	32.1	39.3
Good	33.1	29.1	37.4	25.8	22.3	29.6
Fair/Poor	10.6	8.2	13.7	6.7	5.0	9.0
Total (Weighted)	100% (1.6 M)			100% (2.1 M)		

Source: Medical Expenditure Panel Survey, in Agency for Healthcare Research and Quality, *Justification for Budget Estimates for Appropriations Committees, Fiscal Year 2004* (Rockville, MD: Agency for Healthcare Research and Quality, February 2003), http://www.ahrq.gov/about/cj2004/meps04.htm.

Table 16.9

Distribution of Perceived Health Status Among Children of Construction Workers

Perceived Health	All (N = 1,644)[1] Percent	Insured Hispanic (N = 631)			Insured White, Non-Hispanic (N = 593)		
		Percent	Lower 95% CI	Upper 95% CI	Percent	Lower 95% CI	Upper 95% CI
Health status*							
Excellent	48.8	38.9	33.2	45.0	53.0	47.4	58.5
Very good	30.7	28.4	23.3	34.0	31.9	27.3	36.9
Good	17.6	27.7	22.7	33.3	13.2	9.8	17.6
Fair/Poor	3.0	5.0	3.1	8.0	1.9	1.0	3.8
Total (Weighted)	100% (10.8M)	100% (2.2 M)			100% (6.3 M)		

(continued)

Table 16.9 *(continued)*

Perceived Health	Uninsured Hispanic (N = 200)			Uninsured White, Non-Hispanic (N = 72)		
	Percent	Lower 95% CI	Upper 95% CI	Percent	Lower 95% CI	Upper 95% CI
Health status						
Excellent	32.3	23.8	42.1	58.3	39.8	74.8
Very good	32.4	21.9	45.1	25.0	12.8	43.1
Good	29.7	19.5	42.5	12.5	5.9	24.5
Fair/Poor	5.6	3.0	10.2	4.2	0.6	25.2
Total (Weighted)	100% (0.7 M)			100% (0.7 M)		

Source: Medical Expenditure Panel Survey (MEPS). From *Justification for Budget Estimates for Appropriations Committees, Fiscal Year 2004,* February 2003. Agency for Healthcare Research and Quality, Rockville, MD. Available at http://www.ahrq.gov/about/cj2004/meps04.htm.
[1]Includes workers in other races and ethnicities (e.g., African-American).
*$p < 0.05$.

References

Acosta-Leon, Adiana L., Brandon P. Grote, Sam Salem, et al. 2006. "Risk Factors Associated with Adverse Health and Safety Outcomes in the U.S. Hispanic Workforce." *Theoretical Issues in Ergonomics Science* 7 (3): 299–310.

Agency for Healthcare Research and Quality. 2007. "Survey Background of the Medical Expenditure Panel Survey." www.meps.ahrq.gov/mepsweb/about_meps/survey_back.jsp. (Accessed 1 June 2007.)

Appleby, Julie. 2006. "Consumer Unease with U.S. Health Care Grows." *USA Today* (October 16).

Byck, Gayle R. 2000. "A Comparison of the Socioeconomic and Health Status Characteristics of Uninsured, SCHIP-Eligible Children in the US with Those of Other Groups of Insured Children: Implications for Policy." *Pediatrics* 106 (1): 14–21.

Callahan, Todd, Gerald B. Hickson, and William O. Cooper. 2006. "Health Care Access of Hispanic Young Adults in the US." *Journal of Adolescent Health* 39 (5): 627–33.

DeNavas-Walt, Berndatte Proctor, and Cheryl Lee. 2005. *Income, Poverty and Health Insurance—2004.* Washington: Bureau of Census, Current Population Reports, P60–229, August.

Documét, Patricia I., and Ravi K. Sharma. 2004. "Latinos' Health Care Access: Financial and Cultural Barriers." *Journal of Immigrant Health* 6 (1): 5–13.

Dong, Xiuwen, and James W. Platner. 2004. "Occupational Fatalities of Hispanic Construction Workers from 1992 to 2000." *American Journal of Industrial Medicine* 45: 45–54.

Dong, Xiuwen, Knut Ringen, Yurong Men, and Alissa Fujimoto. 2007. "Medical Costs and Sources of Payment for Work-Related Injuries Among Hispanic Construction Workers." *Journal of Occupational and Environmental Medicine* 49 (12): 1367–75.

Egede, Leonard. 2006. "Race, Ethnicity, Culture, and Disparities in Health Care." *Journal of General Internal Medicine* 21 (6): 667–69.

Hargraves, Lee, Peter J. Cunningham, and Robert G. Hughes. 2001. "Racial and Ethnic Differences in Access to Medical Care in Managed Care Plans." *Health Services Research* 36 (5): 853–68.

Kaiser Family Foundation. 2006. "Kaiser/HRET Survey of Employer-Sponsored Health Benefits, 1999–2006." www.kff.org/insurance/7527/index.cfm. (Accessed 1 July 2007.)

Ojeda, Victoria D., and Richard Brown. 2005. "Mind the Gap: Parents' Citizenship as Predictor of Latino Children's Health Insurance." *Journal of Health Care for the Poor and Underserved* 16: 555–75.

Pew Hispanic Center. 2007. "Construction Jobs Expand for Latinos Despite Slump in Housing Market." Fact Sheet: March 7. pewhispanic.org/files/factsheets/28.pdf. (Accessed 1 July 2007.)

Waidmann, Timothy A., and Shruti Rajan. 2000. "Race and Ethnic Disparities in Health Care Access and Utilization: An Examination of State Variation." *Medical Care Research and Review* 57 (1): 55–84.

17

Expanding Access to Health Insurance for Children

The State Children's Health Insurance Program, 1997–2007

CHRISTEN HOLLY AND DANIEL P. GITTERMAN

States' initial choices, under the State Children's Health Insurance Program (SCHIP), of Medicaid expansion (M-SCHIP), separate state plan (S-SCHIP), or combination program (C-SCHIP) have received attention in the public administration literature. Attempts have been made to establish statistically significant links between choice of administrative model and program enrollment and retention (Kronebusch and Elbel 2004; Wolfe, Scrivner, and Snyder 2005; Sommers 2005, 2007), but results have been inconsistent (Nicholson-Crotty 2007). A more nuanced interpretation of this key administrative choice will reestablish its relevance to the expansion of coverage for children.

We propose a conceptual framework in which *expansion of coverage for children* is the dependent variable. Acknowledging the scope of potential explanatory variables, we confine our analysis to states' administrative choices and explore the relevance of federal parameters and state contextual characteristics in influencing those choices. Likewise cognizant of the number and complexity of methodologies for measuring expansion, we adopt a simple state-centered concept of expansion that refers to changes versus a state's baseline SCHIP enrollment.

Scrutiny of administrative choices under SCHIP endorses the claim that "[s]tructural choices have important consequences for the content and direction of policy, and political actors know it. When they make choices about structure, they are implicitly making choices about policy. And precisely because this is so, issues of structure are inevitably caught up in the larger political struggle" (Moe 1989, 268).

Background

Following the demise of broader health care reform in 1994, the growing ranks of uninsured children attracted attention. Medicaid guidelines required states to provide coverage only to children under age six up to 133 percent of the federal poverty level (FPL), and to children age six to fourteen up to 100 percent FPL, with children over 14 covered only under residual provisions of the Aid to Families with Dependent Children program.

As part of the 1997 Balanced Budget Act, Congress approved SCHIP, or Title XXI of the Social Security Act, to encourage states to provide health insurance to low- and moderate-income children under age nineteen who were ineligible for Medicaid and did not have access to employer-sponsored health insurance coverage. SCHIP was created as a block grant program and funded for a ten-year period.

Congress considered a number of proposals for expanding health care programs for children. The broader political debate centered on the appropriate degree of autonomy the states should be granted in designing their programs (Brandon, Chaudry, and Sardell 2001). The bipartisan compromise agreement between a Republican Congress and a Democratic president allowed states to use SCHIP funding to expand their Medicaid programs (M-SCHIP), establish separate or stand-alone programs (S-SCHIP), or structure a combination of the two (C-SCHIP).

States manage their SCHIP programs subject to federal guidelines and receive matching federal funds, at a rate that exceeds the Medicaid match, to cover as much as 85 percent of program costs. The total federal outlay is capped. State allocations are determined by a formula based on the state's number of low-income children and low-income, uninsured children, and annual wages in the state's health care industry. States have three years in which to use their allotments, after which remaining funds are diverted to a pool for redistribution.

Authority granted to the states was described as a "new form of cooperative federalism" in which the states retained more autonomy to make policy (Rich, Deye, and Mazur 2004, 109). In choosing an administrative model, states endorsed a specific type of federalism that accommodated their vision of expanding health care for children. Despite SCHIP's success in expanding coverage for children, President George W. Bush authorized funding only through March 2009.

Analytical Approach and Selection of States

As of 1999, twenty-four states and the District of Columbia had expanded Medicaid, fourteen had developed separate plans, and twelve had chosen a combination of the two approaches. By 2006, states were operating fourteen Medicaid expansions, seventeen separate programs, and nineteen combination programs, indicating that dynamic conditions were governing their initial and later choices.

To understand the implications of states' administrative choices and their influence on program expansion, we look at the experience of four states—Ohio, Texas, California, and North Carolina—selected to represent a sample of the key administrative models. State demographics related to children in poverty, insurance, and SCHIP enrollment were also considered, as well as the magnitude of SCHIP expenditures (see Table 17.1).

Table 17.1

Current Descriptive Statistics for Case Study States, FY2006

State	Current Program Structure	Enrollment[a]	Kids in Poverty[a]	Uninsured Kids[a]	SCHIP Expenditures[b]	Federal Funds as % Allotment FY2007
CA	Combo	861 (1st)	2,561 (1st)	1,338 (2nd)	$1,771 (1st)	137
NC	Combo[c]	144 (7th)	556 (10th)	261 (8th)	$239 (10th)	195[d]
OH	Med Exp	143 (9th)	615 (8th)	236 (11th)	$236 (11th)	117
TX	Separate[c]	293 (3rd)	1,946 (2nd)	1,340 (1st)	$372 (5th)	69

Source: The Henry J. Kaiser Family Foundation, available at http://www.kff.org for FY2006 unless otherwise noted.

[a]Numbers in thousands (rank nationwide).

[b]Numbers in millions (rank nationwide).

[c]Program type has changed since original implementation. NC transitioned from Separate to Combo and TX switched from Expansion to Separate.

[d]Projected to incur an overall federal funding shortfall for FY2007.

California, Texas, and Ohio were selected because they operate the largest (based on number of enrollees) examples of combination, separate, and Medicaid expansion programs, respectively. North Carolina was identified as an additional case because ongoing changes to its program illustrate that ten years in, SCHIP administrative choices have continued relevance in expanding care for children.

Structuring Administrative Choices

We propose a conceptual model of SCHIP administrative choices that categorizes the explanatory variables as federal parameters or state contextual characteristics. Federal parameters determine the degree of discretion granted to the states in making administrative choices. We describe states' political, fiscal-economic, and structural features as the formative elements of states' commitment to expanding health care for children.

Federal Parameters: Granting Discretion to the States

Achieving significant expansion of health insurance coverage involves important policy and administrative trade-offs, many of which are defined by federal parameters. Our framework considers three categories of federal parameters that influence state administrative choices. The first is the federal SCHIP legislation that defined the initial trade-offs in discretion and financial risk states faced in the M-SCHIP versus S-SCHIP choice. The second category includes mechanisms for modifying those trade-offs that exist in the form of secondary administrative choices and waivers. The third category is Medicaid legislation.

SCHIP Legislation

Federal legislation allowed states to establish separate programs (S-SCHIP), expand their existing Medicaid programs (M-SCHIP), or combine the two approaches (C-SCHIP). Following the example of other analyses, our framework focuses on M-SCHIP and S-SCHIP as the two discrete initial alternatives. These models varied in the level of discretion retained and the financial risk incurred by the states.

For M-SCHIPs, some limits were imposed on state authority to define benefits, set eligibility levels, manage enrollment, and structure administrative procedures. All benefits available under Medicaid must be offered to the Medicaid expansion group. Medicaid is required to provide coverage to meet the needs of each child as defined in the Early and Periodic Screening, Diagnosis, and Treatment standards, and is more extensive than coverage required by SCHIP, which does not include a comparable entitlement to treatment for all medical needs.

M-SCHIPs were authorized to extend eligibility up to 50 points above the FPL threshold then in effect for their state Medicaid plan. The state must enroll all eligible applicants—it could not close enrollment or take other measures to reduce enrollment. Cost sharing was generally prohibited (until changes were enacted as part of the 2005 Deficit Reduction Act).

In exchange for limits on state discretion, Medicaid expansions received the funding guarantee conveyed by a traditional entitlement program. If a state depleted its SCHIP allotment, state expenditures for M-SCHIP participants would continue to qualify for federal matching payments, though at the lower Medicaid matching rate.

S-SCHIP programs retained more authority to manipulate enrollment, expand eligibility thresholds, and limit benefits. S-SCHIPs can define benefits to be included in the package; manage enrollment via freezes, waitlists, or closure; enforce waiting periods and impose cost-sharing requirements to reduce "crowd out" of private insurance; and manipulate other program details to achieve enrollment and expenditure objectives. S-SCHIP programs do not receive federal matching funds after a state's allotment is depleted. Thus, for an increased level of state discretion, S-SCHIPs incur greater financial risks if expenditures exceed allotments.

In our conceptual model, we position the M-SCHIP/S-SCHIP choice as a significant indicator of state preferences for discretion and financial risk. Discretion, or autonomy, can be exercised in two directions—to expand coverage beyond mandated minimums or to retrench coverage through enrollment or benefit reductions or both. Likewise, financial risk has two dimensions. Depending on the number of anticipated enrollees, M-SCHIP benefit requirements and federal funding guarantees can exacerbate or mitigate financial risk.

We propose that the significance of the M-SCHIP/S-SCHIP administrative choice, as it relates to expanding coverage, resides not simply in *which* model states selected, but in *why* they selected it and *how* they used the discretion it bestowed.

Mechanisms for Change

Beyond the choice of administrative model, many secondary administrative choices were left up to the states under both M-SCHIP and S-SCHIP provisions. Secondary administrative choices include definition of income in eligibility determinations, outreach approaches, documentation requirements, and other application requirements and enrollment procedures. State autonomy in these areas transformed the discrete M-SCHIP/S-SCHIP dichotomy into a more sophisticated array of administrative choices.

Though these bureaucratic arrangements may be less visible to the average citizen, a number of cross-state studies suggest that they are important determinants of state success in expanding coverage. For example, enrollment and recertification procedures have been shown to play a role in take-up and dropout rates (Sommers 2005), and treatment of asset tests, income disregards, and other criteria have been linked to enrollment growth (Kronebusch and Elbel 2004). Representative program details are listed in Table 17.2.

Section 1115 waivers and Health Insurance Flexibility and Accountability demonstration initiatives (henceforth generalized as "waivers") are two addi-

Table 17.2

Effects of Secondary Administrative Choices on Enrollment

Program details	Predicted enrollment effects
Presumptive eligibility*	+
Self-declaration of income*	+
Continuous eligibility*	+
Passive renewal**	+
Premiums*	−
Waiting period*	−
Asset test*	−
Procedural complexity***	−

*Kronenbusch and Elbel 2004.
**Dick et al. 2002.
***Hill and Lutzky 2003.

tional mechanisms by which states can request federal approval to implement features of Medicaid or SCHIP or both not permitted by the original legislation. The significance of waivers in expanding coverage for children has been considerable, allowing for increases in eligibility thresholds, expansions of target populations, and experimentation with service provision and cost-sharing alternatives (Ryan 2002).

In our framework, waivers and secondary choices are critical mechanisms for effecting nonstatutory change in the basic administrative models. They transformed the initial M-SCHIP/S-SCHIP dichotomy into a broad spectrum of administrative models. We hypothesize that this variation has eroded the explanatory power of a simple dichotomous M-SCHIP/S-SCHIP variable in a range of existing models and equations.

Medicaid Regulations

Federal regulations on Medicaid eligibility levels, benefit packages, and documentation requirements have spillover effects on SCHIP that affect state autonomy. Under the Omnibus Budget Reconciliation Acts of 1989 and 1990, Congress increased mandated eligibility levels for children's Medicaid. All children under the age of six whose family income was below 133 percent of the FPL were to be covered, and coverage for those born after September 30, 1983, whose family income was under 100 percent FPL was to be phased in until everyone under nineteen years of age was covered. When SCHIP legislation reached states' policy agendas in fiscal year 1998, states were in the process of extending coverage to children turning fifteen years old whose family income was under 100 percent FPL. Many states leveraged the enhanced SCHIP matching rate to accelerate compliance with the higher eligibility levels, though these populations reverted to the lower Medicaid matching rate in September 2002.

Under the 2005 Deficit Reduction Act, Congress imposed citizenship documentation requirements and expanded cost-sharing allowances in state Medicaid programs. These requirements have spillover effects for states operating M-SCHIPs. Documentation requirements affect S-SCHIPs as well, since many states had developed a single screening and application process for Medicaid and SCHIP. The Medicaid mandate of the Omnibus Budget Reconciliation Acts influenced initial SCHIP choices, and ongoing changes in Medicaid legislation, such as the Deficit Reduction Act, continue to influence the nature of M-SCHIP/S-SCHIP trade-offs.

State Contextual Characteristics: Shaping States' Commitment to Expanding Care

State contextual features can be grouped into political, fiscal-economic, and pre-existing structural considerations that shape a state's commitment to expanding care and help explain variations in the administrative choices made in response to uniform federal parameters.

Political Context

In studies of enrollment determinants, political variables center on partisan control of the legislature and party affiliation of the governor (Kousser 2002; Sommers 2005). Beyond these indicators, the strength of insurance, health care provider, and child advocacy lobbies is mentioned in accounts of SCHIP implementations (Brandon, Chaudry, and Sardell 2001).

Fiscal-Economic Context

Fiscal and economic variables are the purview of health economists, and this model does not attempt to thoroughly catalog those as they pertain to state fiscal health, health expenditure needs, federal funding, and state revenue-generating capacity. Following a decade punctuated by state budget crises and characterized by constantly climbing health care costs, the significance of fiscal considerations is uncontested. For this framework we emphasize that fiscal and economic characteristics place constraints on states' capacity to fund their share of SCHIP expenditures and ability to tolerate the financial risks of expanding care.

Preexisting Program Structure and Status

The initial M-SCHIP/S-SCHIP choice was influenced by the states' preexisting policy choices and the status of their public health insurance programs. The condition of a state's Medicaid program would determine whether Medicaid was a viable foundation for expanding care or a broken system that should be discarded. The abbreviated lead time between SCHIP authorization and availability of federal funds would have encouraged states to consider leveraging the existing Medicaid infrastructure. Title XXI was enacted in August 1997, only two months before the beginning of fiscal year 1998, when funds were available for drawdown by the states.

Commitment to Expanding Coverage

Often omitted among traditional explanatory variables is the level of state commitment to health care. Commitment, as originally formulated, "refers to the degree to which processes of policy formulation and implementation in a state manifest greater effort to [ensure] that all of its residents have access to health care of good quality" (Thompson 2001, 48). Thompson notes the difficulties in measuring this concept but proposes an insightful list of indicators that include state health expenditures per capita, generosity of eligibility criteria and benefit packages, and program beneficiaries as a percentage of population below a certain percentage of the FPL. Track records of state public health insurance initiatives prior to SCHIP are additional indicators.

Commitment offers a more textured view of state inclinations to expand care than can be inferred from political and economic-fiscal conditions alone. Measures of partisan control fail to account for ideological convergence of expanding care for children. Likewise, basic economic-fiscal measures do not capture the states' prioritization of spending on health care for children relative to other state fiscal obligations. Political, economic-fiscal, and structural characteristics shape states' commitment and capacity to expand care. Understanding this relationship is fundamental in gauging *how* states will exercise discretion.

Discretion and Commitment: Choosing a Path for Expanding SCHIP

For illustrative purposes, we juxtapose two explanatory variables mentioned above, discretion and commitment, on a two-dimensional grid. Figure 17.1 shows state commitment to expanding care relative to state preferences for discretion. The result is a typology of SCHIP administrative models that offers a rationale for the circumstances that produce a given state choice.

Imagining SCHIP enrollment as the third dimension of this graph, we suggest that a state's SCHIP expansion can be described as a function of its commitment to provide coverage for children (bound by political, fiscal-economic, and structural contexts) and the level of discretion it was granted to accomplish this (constrained by the initial M-SCHIP/S-SCHIP choice and adjusted by waivers, secondary administrative choices, and changes in Medicaid legislation).

Figure 17.1 **Influence of Discretion and Commitment on Initial Administrative Choices**

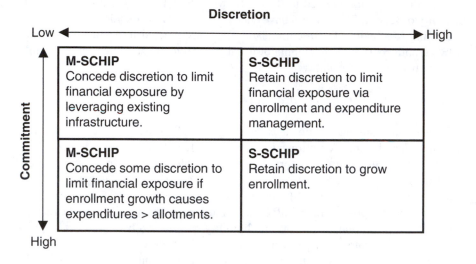

Discretion

Low ◄─────────────────────────────► High

M-SCHIP Concede discretion to limit financial exposure by leveraging existing infrastructure.	**S-SCHIP** Retain discretion to limit financial exposure via enrollment and expenditure management.
M-SCHIP Concede some discretion to limit financial exposure if enrollment growth causes expenditures > allotments.	**S-SCHIP** Retain discretion to grow enrollment.

Commitment (vertical axis, Low at top to High at bottom)

Choosing an Initial Administrative Model

Figure 17.2 positions the four case study states within this typology, based on their initial choice of administrative model and an interpretation of their commitment to expanding SCHIP. (Descriptive information about the selected states' contextual characteristics at the time of the SCHIP legislation are available at www.nasi. org.)

Ohio: Remodeling Medicaid

When Governor George Voinovich took office in 1991, he cited health and education of the state's children among his top priorities (Brandon, Chaudry, and Sardell 2001). Legislation to expand Ohio's Medicaid program, Healthy Start, predated federal SCHIP provisions, demonstrating the state's initiative to expand care without federal incentives. Timing of SCHIP legislation enabled the state to subsidize that expansion at the higher matching rate. In January 1998, Ohio's SCHIP Phase I leveraged federal funds to bring Healthy Start into compliance with the federal Medicaid mandate (covering all children below 100 percent FPL) and further expanded coverage to 150 percent FPL.

Early work on SCHIP implementations suggested that Republican administrations were more likely to design a separate SCHIP (Beamer 1999). Ohio fit this profile of preferring discretion and devolution, as later indicated by its assignment of SCHIP outreach and enrollment to the counties, but chose instead to

Figure 17.2   **States' Initial Administrative Model, Time 1**

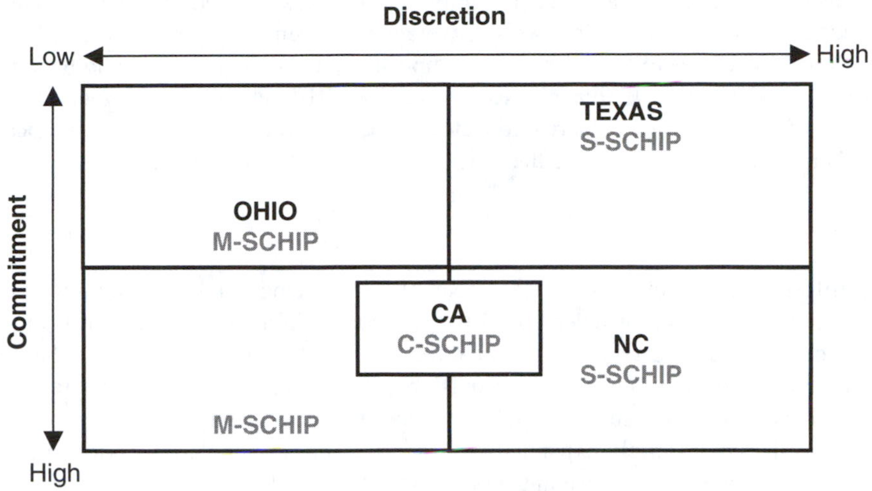

Discretion

Low ◄──► High

```
         ┌─────────────────────────────┬─────────────────────────┐
    ▲    │                             │      TEXAS              │
    │    │                             │     S-SCHIP             │
    │    │         OHIO                │                         │
         │        M-SCHIP              │                         │
Commitment├───────────────┬─────────────┴─────────────────────────┤
    │    │               │   CA                                  │
    │    │               │ C-SCHIP        NC                     │
    │    │               │              S-SCHIP                  │
    ▼    │        M-SCHIP└─────┘                                 │
         └─────────────────────────────────────────────────────┘
High
```

implement an M-SCHIP. The concessions on autonomy were prompted by two considerations. First, the decision to build on the existing Medicaid infrastructure at least partly substantiates the continued influence of established institutions on subsequent structural choices. Second, the M-SCHIP concession mitigated the state's immediate and long-term financial exposure in reducing implementation costs and ensuring long-term federal funding if future SCHIP expenditures were to exceed allotments.

Texas: Limiting Liability

Prior to the SCHIP legislation, Texas had one of the highest rates of uninsured children in the country. Despite the potential of SCHIP funds to alleviate this, then governor George W. Bush was reluctant to commit to an SCHIP program (Dunkelberg 2007). State fiscal capacity in Texas was perceived by the administration as insufficient to cover the large number of children estimated to be eligible for SCHIP coverage. SCHIP expenditures would strain state funds, especially in the context of the governor's antitax rhetoric (Wiener and Brennan 2002). The thrust of the debate in Texas was primarily about retaining authority to manage the state's fiscal exposure.

Texas submitted a placeholder M-SCHIP plan to use SCHIP funds to meet the 100 percent FPL Medicaid mandate. Though the plan was labeled CHIP Phase I, its transient nature (mandated increases forfeited SCHIP matching rates after 2002) and minimalist effort caused us to focus instead on CHIP Phase II as more indicative of Texas's preferences for discretion and commitment to expanding coverage.

Texas was reluctant to grant entitlement status to SCHIP beneficiaries. CHIP Phase II was designed as a separate program and was enacted after an ongoing debate concerning eligibility levels. Coverage was eventually granted to children below 200 percent FPL, with the state imposing various cost-sharing and benefit restrictions to limit its financial exposure. The CHIP Phase II implementation was a deliberate vote for increased state discretion in the public health insurance sphere—discretion to manage the state's liability for the uninsured.

California: Building Capacity

California health policy serves the needs of a staggering number of low-income children. Even before the federal SCHIP legislation, California grappled with a number of strategies to extend health care coverage. Since 1995, employer mandates, single-payer systems, play-or-pay provisions, and universal access for children all languished for want of sufficient public support. In lieu of major health care reform, California incrementally expanded coverage for certain populations prior to the SCHIP legislation through a number of public programs, demonstrating California's commitment and fiscal capacity to expand health care coverage.

After passage of the SCHIP legislation, California was quick to capitalize on enhanced federal matching rates to extend coverage to low-income children. Like many other states, it was already in the process of complying with federal Medicaid mandates. In March 1998, California implemented the Medicaid expansion portion of its SCHIP plan to bring Medi-Cal eligibility into compliance. It also extended Medi-Cal coverage to children of participants in the Access for Infants and Mothers program from birth to one year up to 250 percent FPL.

The Healthy Families Program, a stand-alone component of the California CHIP implementation, was launched shortly after the Medi-Cal expansion, in July 1998. It was presented as a mechanism for introducing the uninsured to the private insurance market, and cost sharing based on sliding-scale premiums was a key component of the original program design. The initiative established a purchasing pool for individuals in the 100 to 200 percent FPL range and offered a variety of plan options to enrollees.

California's combination program reflects preferences for discretion and financial risk mitigation. Like Texas, it favored the administrative discretion of the S-SCHIP structure. However, California's commitment to expanding care places it in a different category than the reluctant Texas.

North Carolina: Keeping Commitments (and Discretion)

North Carolina had expanded its Medicaid program in accordance with the federal mandate prior to 1997. When SCHIP was enacted, North Carolina responded with a special legislative session in February 1998 (Lewin Group 2007).

Governor James Hunt, a Democrat, and the Democratic Senate proposed a Medicaid expansion for children at 100 percent to 200 percent FPL. The Republi-

Figure 17.3   **States' Evolution of Administrative Models, Time 2**

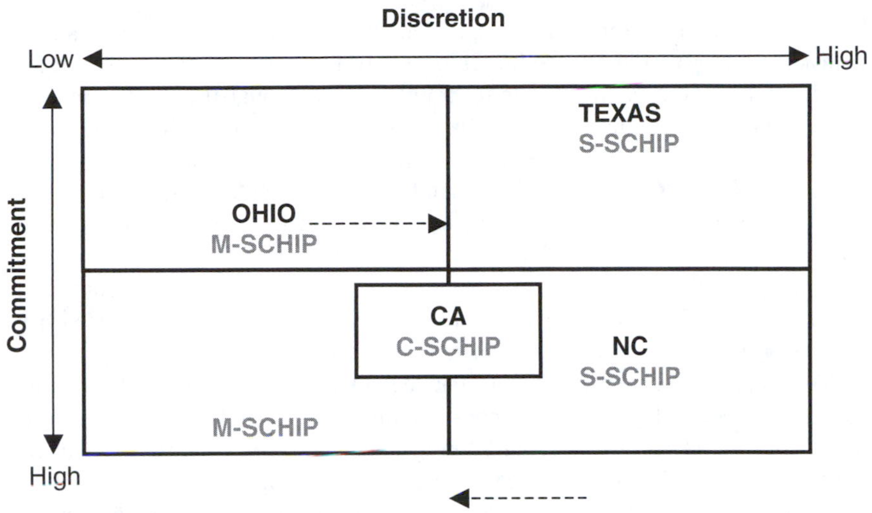

can House resisted the M-SCHIP's lack of discretion in managing enrollment and instead proposed a stand-alone SCHIP implementation to cover children up to 185 percent FPL. The compromise legislation created Health Choice North Carolina as a separate program that covered children up to 200 percent FPL, with low annual premiums for children between 150 and 200 percent FPL.

Health Choice North Carolina was implemented on October 1, 1998, assuming responsibility for the eight thousand enrollees of Caring for Children, a privately funded Blue Cross and Blue Shield initiative to cover low-income children in the state. Our framework characterizes North Carolina's administrative choice as a function of high preference for discretion and high commitment to expansion.

Manipulating Initial Administrative Choices

The initial administrative choices place our four case studies in distinct positions on the grid in Figure 17.2. Over time, programs evolved in important ways. States could initiate changes in the administrative models via waivers and secondary administrative choices, as outlined above. These changes reflect the results of their own experience, policy diffusion, or best practices, from other states and responses to changing state contextual features, notably the budget crises of the early 2000s. These changes transformed the M-SCHIP/S-SCHIP dichotomy and repositioned the states (see Figure 17.3). The new positions show a tendency toward convergence in which states seek to exploit the discretion and financial benefits of both models, with Texas as the notable exception. The following narrative describes the evolution of the states' administrative models.

Ohio: Expanding Incrementally

The second phase of Ohio's CHIP implementation was also a Medicaid expansion. A task force considered options for Ohio's CHIP Phase II, and debate centered on entitlement status and choice of administrative model. Though the task force recommended a separate program with cost sharing, legislators deemed infrastructure costs of operating two programs excessive and chose a Medicaid expansion instead.

In 2000, Ohio's CHIP Phase II extended coverage to children up to 200 percent FPL. The state pursued other incremental but successful expansions—extending wraparound coverage to Healthy Start enrollees up to 150 percent FPL, covering parents up to 100 percent FPL, and lengthening the renewal period from six to twelve months. Consequently, Ohio's SCHIP enrollment steadily increased from just under 90,000 in 1999 to about 210,000 in 2006.

Three features effected substantial change in Ohio's second Medicaid expansion. First, Ohio received a waiver to impose sliding-scale cost-sharing provisions for enrollees in the 150 to 200 percent FPL range. Second, lessons learned from the first expansion triggered revisions in the second effort that remodeled Ohio's Medicaid enrollment process to resemble the streamlined procedures of other states' separate programs. Third, CHIP Phase II was not granted entitlement status but was made subject to available state funding. These changes transfigured Ohio's Medicaid expansion to share many of the characteristics more typical of separate SCHIPs. Evolution of Ohio's M-SCHIP program is trending toward more discretion (see Figure 17.3).

Texas: Retrenching

From the beginning, Texas struggled to manage enrollment. The original estimate of CHIP eligibles was 478,000, but enrollment had already surpassed 516,000 by February 2002, less than two years after the separate CHIP program opened (Texas Health and Human Services Commission 2007, 7–2). Rising program costs coincided with an economic downturn, during which time the governor's administration maintained a steadfast commitment to tax relief (Wiener and Brennan 2002).

Beginning in 2003, the legislature exercised its authority to manipulate secondary administrative features to achieve desired budget reductions in the CHIP program. Changes included a ninety-day waiting period, shortened (from twelve to six months) continuous eligibility, elimination of income disregards, imposition of asset tests, and increased cost sharing and premiums. Despite the high matching rate for its CHIP expenditures, "local stakeholders indicate[d] that . . . the dollar amount of state spending and not the federal allocation or the matching rate [drove] state decisions about SCHIP funding" (Bergman, Williams, and Pernice 2004, 4).

Enrollment fell precipitously from more than 507,000 in September 2003 to less than 327,000 in January 2005 (Texas Health and Human Services Commission 2007, 7–4), even though eligibility levels were maintained at 200 percent FPL. After hovering for a year, enrollment dropped again after additional modifications

Figure 17.4   **Texas SCHIP Enrollment**

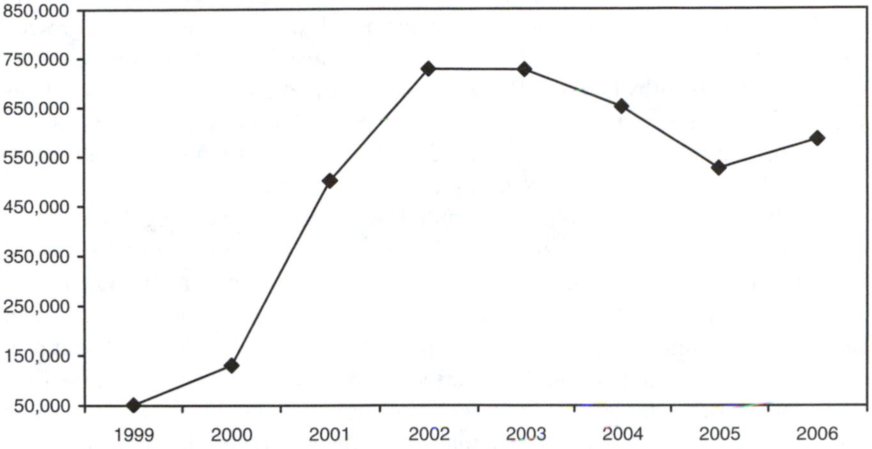

to renewal requirements, to 291,530. Alarmed by the magnitude of these effects, the state attempted to improve enrollment statistics throughout 2006.

A chronological display of the impact of changes in SCHIP administrative choices on enrollment reveals how expansion was undermined by more subtle changes in program features (see Figure 17.4). It is a sobering lesson in the precedence that state fiscal considerations take over federal legislative intent and the potential use of state discretion to retrench public programs.

CHIP evolution in Texas reveals the continued relevance of administrative choices in state approaches to expanding, or in this case retrenching, care for children. The initial choice of a separate implementation plan protected the state's authority to manage enrollment and expenditures. In 2003, changes in the state's fiscal health prompted actions to reduce the operating budgets of many public programs. Unchecked, Texas adjusted administrative choices to cause huge changes in enrollment, systematically dismantling a large portion of the gains made in expanding coverage.

Texas has a large population of low-income, uninsured children that threatens to deplete state and federal SCHIP funding in the face of high enrollment. Yet there has never been momentum to limit financial exposure by leveraging the federal financing guarantee of an M-SCHIP entitlement structure (Dunkelberg 2007), which indicates the state's preference to maintain discretion over its future CHIP liabilities. Texas remains stationary (see Figure 17.3), with high preferences for discretion and low commitment for extending care.

California: Experimenting and Expanding

A chronological summary of changes in the Healthy Families Program demonstrates a trend of expansion in service provision and target population. Amendments to increase eligibility levels from 200 to 250 percent FPL, provide coverage for Medi-Cal / Healthy Families Program transitional periods, and offer presumptive eligibility for certain income segments contributed to steady enrollment growth. Concurrent improvements in enrollment procedures also fueled program expansion. Consequently, Healthy Families Program enrollment reached 73,314 children in its first year of operation and grew steadily to exceed 800,000 by fiscal year 2006.

Facing state budget shortages in 2003–4, California responded proactively to manage the impact on public programs and sustain slow growth in SCHIP enrollment. These efforts were eventually limited by funding, illustrating that political willingness to expand coverage is subject to state and federal fiscal capacity. However, the nature of California's response reveals its commitment to maintaining enrollment. Though outreach efforts were virtually eliminated and provider reimbursement rates were frozen, the state continued to simplify enrollment procedures and regulations during this period. Budget shortages also prompted the development of the innovative County Health Initiative Matching Program, which allowed counties to provide the state match in order to raise eligibility from 250 to 300 percent FPL. California's policy demonstrates the role that commitment can play in determining responses to budget crises.

From the beginning, California operated a dual SCHIP implementation. Framed in terms of risk management, it could be interpreted as a diversified portfolio that protected the programs and the state in times of fiscal crisis. In Figure 17.3, California remains in equilibrium, dynamically balancing administrative choices to expand its programs.

North Carolina: Exploiting Administrative Choices

Similar to Ohio, North Carolina relied on local efforts for outreach and enrollment, which met with success. The unfortunate consequence was a funding crisis that precipitated an enrollment freeze in February 2001. A waiting list grew to thirty-four thousand children before the state appropriated enough funds to reopen enrollment in October 2001. As the state continued to overspend its federal SCHIP allotment and rely on redistributed funds, legislators sought programmatic changes to maintain gains in coverage for children with sustainable federal funding.

The North Carolina Assembly passed legislation that transitioned children up to age five from Health Choice to Medicaid, effective January 2006. Medicaid eligibility thresholds were increased to 200 percent FPL to accommodate children up to age five in Health Choice North Carolina, with older children remaining in the separate Health Choice program. This strategic reorganization bestowed entitlement status on the younger group, guaranteeing federal funds above the SCHIP allotment, and maintained state discretion in coverage for the older age group. The Health Choice–to–Medicaid transition is an excellent example of a state exercising discretion to respond strategically to changing fiscal conditions.

On July 31, 2007, Governor Michael Easley, a Democrat, signed a budget that allocated $7 million, starting in July 2008, to establish NC Kids Care, which will cover thirty-eight thousand children in the 200 to 300 percent FPL range with affordable, state-subsidized health insurance. NC Kids Care was framed against a growing loss of employer-based insurance in the state. Crafted by a children's advocacy group to build on the existing tiers of children's health care programs in North Carolina, the legislation demonstrates that commitment to expanding coverage does not have to be confined to traditionally defined "low-income" children. Building on the experience and infrastructure of SCHIP, many other states have taken similar steps. By 2007, eighteen other states had already provided coverage to children over 200 percent FPL.

The prospect of chronic funding shortages resulting from pressure to continue expanding coverage for children produces strategic responses to maximize federal funds and limit state fiscal exposure. In North Carolina, initial ideological preferences for the more autonomous S-SCHIP structure were set aside when fiscal conditions became dire. The North Carolina example shows how administrative choices can respond to changing state contextual characteristics. In Figure 17.3, the North Carolina experience is characterized by a move toward the center on the discretion axis, representing the Health Choice–to–Medicaid transition and the state's shift toward a combination SCHIP implementation.

Reauthorizing SCHIP

The SCHIP program entered its reauthorization phase in the summer of 2007 with bipartisan support for additional program funding and expansion. Cushioned by budget surpluses from the early years of the program when states did not draw down all the available funds, SCHIP's popularity survived the first ten years of the program's charter unblemished. It was only during the reauthorization proceedings that funding negotiations underscored the degree of federal control and state dependence implicit in the SCHIP structure.

Despite estimates from the Congressional Budget Office that SCHIP would require an additional $14 billion over a five-year period to maintain coverage, the president's 2008 budget provided $5 billion and reduced the length of funding availability. During the summer of 2007, two bills were introduced in the House and Senate providing for major increases in funding ($50 billion and $35 billion, respectively) with offsetting revenues from tobacco taxes. Though these bills were revised at several points to address opponents' concerns about eligibility levels, crowd-out provisions, and documentation requirements, the president vetoed all SCHIP legislation except the continuance bill, which allowed for emergency provisions to keep the program up and running through March 2009.

In the midst of the reauthorization debate, the Centers for Medicare and Medicaid Services issued a policy directive that imposed substantial changes to SCHIP's administrative rules to limit access for children in families with incomes over 250 percent of the poverty level. In a directive released in August 2007, the Centers for Medicare and Medicaid Services conditioned SCHIP funding for this group on a 95 percent participation rate for children under 200 percent FPL; imposed additional provisions to minimize the crowd-out of private coverage; instituted a minimum one-year waiting period; required copays and premiums comparable to private insurance; and required states to adopt laws preventing employers from reducing their coverage policies and document that private coverage does not fall by 2 percent over a five-year period. New policies were immediately subject to these rules and old policies had a year to comply.

The sudden and sweeping nature of the directive took many by surprise. It was the first conspicuous instance in SCHIP history where the discretion dimension had been narrowed. The sequence of events surrounding reauthorization reinforces the importance of both dimensions of our conceptual model, discretion and commitment.

Conclusion

SCHIP allowed states to choose a model of federalism that accommodated their vision of health care for children. The result was a series of administrative choices, beginning with the initial selection of the M-SCHIP or S-SCHIP model. Within federal parameters and compensating for their unique contextual characteristics, states balanced preferences for discretion with needs to mitigate financial risks as they sought to expand care for children.

Our framework has demonstrated the evolution of the initial M-SCHIP/S-SCHIP dichotomy into a spectrum of secondary administrative choices that affect expansion of care. Many states chose to implement S-SCHIPs, but their common preference for discretion was motivated by different objectives. Selection of the S-SCHIP is, in isolation, an endorsement of discretion. However, the importance of discretion in expanding health care for children depends on states' commitment to exercise it in a certain direction.

References

Beamer, Glenn D. 1999. "Ideology, Partisan Control, and the Politics of the Children's Health Insurance Program." Paper presented at the Annual Meeting of the American Political Science Association, Atlanta, GA, September 2–5.

Bergman, David, Claudia Williams, and Cynthia Pernice. 2004. "SCHIP Changes in a Difficult Budget Climate: A Three-State Site Visit Report." Portland, ME: National Academy for State Health Policy, April.

Brandon, William P., Rosemary V. Chaudry, and Alice Sardell. 2001. "Launching SCHIP: The States and Children's Health Insurance." In *The New Politics of State Health Policy*, ed. Robert B. Hackey and David A. Rochefort, 142–85. Lawrence: University Press of Kansas.

Dunkelberg, Anne, Associate Director of the Center for Public Policy Priorities. 2007. Telephone interview with Christen Holly. University of North Carolina at Chapel Hill, July 24.

Hill, I. and A. Westpfahl Lutzky. 2003. *Is There a Hole in the Bucket?* Washington, DC: Urban Institute.

Kousser, Thad. 2002. "The Politics of Discretionary Medicaid Spending, 1980–1993." *Journal of Health Politics, Policy and Law* 27 (4): 20–31.

Kronebusch, Karl, and Brian Elbel. 2004. "Simplifying Children's Medicaid and SCHIP." *Health Affairs* 23 (3): 233–46.

Lewin Group. 2007. "SCHIP in North Carolina: Evolution and Reauthorization, Challenges and Opportunities." www.healthwellnc.com/LewinSCHIP07report.pdf. (Accessed 11 August 2008.)

Moe, Terry. 1989. "The Politics of Bureaucratic Structure." In *Can the Government Govern?* ed. John E. Chubb and Paul E. Peterson, 267–329. Washington, DC: Brookings Institution.

Nicholson-Crotty, Sean. 2007. "The Impact of Program Design on Enrollment in State Children's Health Insurance Programs." *Policy Studies Journal* 35 (1): 23–35.

Rich, Robert, and Cinthia Deye, with Elizabeth Mazur. 2004. "The State Children's Health Insurance Program: An Administrative Experiment in Federalism." *University of Illinois Law Review* 2004 (1): 107–36.

Ryan, Jennifer. 2002. "1115 Ways to Waive Medicaid and SCHIP Rules." Issue brief 777. Washington, DC: National Health Policy Forum, June 13.

Sommers, Benjamin. 2005. "From Medicaid to Uninsured: Drop-Out Among Children in Public Insurance Programs." *Health Services Research* 40 (1): 59–78.

———. 2007. "Why Millions of Children Eligible for Medicaid and SCHIP Are Uninsured: Poor Retention Versus Poor Take-Up." *Heath Affairs* Web exclusive. content.healthaffairs.org/cgi/content/abstract/hlthaff.26.5.w560. (Accessed 8 August 2008.)

Texas Health and Human Services Commission. 2007. *Texas Medicaid in Perspective.* 6th ed. January. www.hhsc.state.tx.us/Medicaid/reports/PB6/PinkBookTOC.html. (Accessed 22 July 2007.)

Thompson, Frank J. 2001. "Federalism and Health Care Policy: Toward Redefinition?" In *The New Politics of State Health Policy,* ed. Robert B. Hackey and David A. Rochefort, 142–85. Lawrence: University Press of Kansas.

Weil, Alan R. 2007. Testimony on SCHIP Before the Subcommittee on Health, Committee on Energy and Commerce, U.S. House of Representatives, March 1. www.nashp.org/Files/SCHIP_Testimony_Weil.pdf. (Accessed 11 August 2008.)

Wiener, Joshua M., and Niall Brennan. 2002. "Recent Changes in Health Policy for Low-Income People in Texas." Washington, DC: Urban Institute, March.

Wolfe, Barbara, Scott Scrivner, and Andrew Snyder. 2005. "The Devil May Be in the Details: How the Characteristics of SCHIP Affect Take-Up." *Journal of Policy Analysis and Management* 24 (3): 499–522.

18

Did Medicaid/SCHIP Crowd Out Private Insurance Among Low-Income Children?

ADETOKUNBO B. OLUWOLE AND DENNIS G. SHEA

Prior to the mid-1980s, Medicaid eligibility for children had largely been restricted to children in one-parent families participating in welfare programs such as Aid to Families with Dependent Children. From the mid-1980s through 1991, Congress expanded Medicaid to cover families not in the Aid to Families with Dependent Children program, targeting near-poor pregnant women as well as children in two-parent families with low incomes (Blumberg, Dubay, and Norton 2000; Yazici and Kaestner 2000; Shore-Sheppard 2005).

Public insurance for children was further expanded in August 1997 when Congress enacted the State Children's Health Insurance Program (SCHIP) as Title XXI of the Social Security Act, which makes provision for children living in families with income up to 200 percent of the federal poverty line (FPL) to be eligible for subsidized health insurance coverage. SCHIP further gives states the option to expand income eligibility limits for subsidized health insurance coverage beyond 200 percent of FPL.

Efforts at expanding public health insurance coverage for children succeeded as the proportion of children with Medicaid coverage increased; for example, the proportion of uninsured children living in families whose incomes were between 100 and 200 percent of the FPL declined.

However, increases in public insurance coverage were accompanied by decreases in private insurance coverage (U.S. General Accounting Office 1997; Cunningham, Hadley, and Reschovsky 2002). The substitution of public insurance for private coverage, also known as crowd-out, represents a potential unintended effect of Medicaid/SCHIP eligibility expansion. Crowd-out occurs when (1) individuals move from private to public coverage as a result of gaining eligibility through expansions; (2) uninsured individuals choose to enroll in public insurance programs instead of obtaining private coverage; or (3) individuals choose to remain in publicly supported insurance instead of making a transition to private insurance. Different pathways render measurement and analysis difficult.

Crowd-out attracted increased attention during the past decade as research efforts developed various measures and hypothesized a variety of factors influencing health insurance transitions (Cutler and Gruber 1996, 1997; Blumberg, Dubay, and Norton

2000; Kronick and Gilmer 2002; Long and Marquis 2003; Yazici and Kaestner 2000; Shore-Sheppard 2005). Very few of these studies cover the post-1996 Medicaid/ SCHIP expansion only (LoSasso and Buchmueller 2002; Cunningham, Hadley, and Reschovsky 2002). In addition, these studies used cross-sectional data sets or traditional regression methods, or both, which did not account for the timing and transitions of insurance coverage or the clustering of populations within states. Also, these studies produced conflicting crowd-out estimates, with some finding no evidence of displacement of private insurance by public programs and others reporting high crowd-out estimates.

This chapter analyzes the 1996 panel of the Survey of Income and Program Participation (SIPP), combining both event history and multilevel modeling techniques to examine health insurance transitions and crowd-out under Medicaid/SCHIP. The combined estimation techniques account for the timing of insurance coverage as well as clustering of children within their states of residence, both crucial for the study of health insurance dynamics. Thus, our objectives are to investigate whether the post-1996 Medicaid/SCHIP expansion crowds out private insurance coverage among low-income children in the United States and examine the effect of programmatic features, that is, types of public expansion, and individual, family, and state-specific characteristics on health insurance transitions.

Data and Methods

We used the 1996 panel of SIPP, a nationally representative longitudinal survey of the civilian, noninstitutionalized population, designed for the provision of detailed information on the economic situation of households and persons, and conducted by the Census Bureau. Data contain information on the distribution of income, wealth, and poverty and assess the effects of federal and state programs on well-being.

The interviewed population consists of individuals fifteen years or older at the time of the first interview. Information on younger individuals who live with eligible interviewees is also included in the survey. One-fourth of the sampled households were interviewed each month, and households were reinterviewed at four-month intervals. The 1996 panel consists of twelve interview periods, referred to as waves of data, with the first wave starting in April 1996 and the last in March 2000, which produced forty-eight months of data.

Questions about health insurance and other questions covering the preceding four months were asked at each interview. However, the SIPP data set has what is known as *seam bias* concerning transitions between types of insurance coverage. Seam bias is said to occur when there are a disproportionate number of transitions every fourth month because of the tendency for SIPP respondents to report changes in their insurance status between interviews instead of between months covered by the interview. Other data sets appended to the SIPP data consisted of those collected from the County Business Patterns and City and County Data Books of the Regional Economic Information Service (2005), the Medicaid Statistical

Information System, and the Health Care Finance Administration (HCFA)-2082 reports of the Centers for Medicare and Medicaid Services.

Analytic Samples

The sample for the study consisted of children age nineteen years and younger living in low-income families. Low-income children are defined as those with family monthly incomes below 325 percent of FPL. Following Short and Graefe (2003), our study adopted a long-term measure of family income as a percentage of FPL. This measure sums monthly family income for each individual over the forty-eight months of the survey. Monthly poverty thresholds assigned to each person were also summed up over the forty-eight months. Finally, the summed income was divided by the summed poverty thresholds to obtain a percentage of FPL for each person. An income cutoff point of 325 percent of FPL was chosen after examination of SIPP to include as many children as possible who would have been eligible for SCHIP at some point in time. Children who were identified as married as well as those reported to have no other insurance but Medicare were dropped from the study sample. These selection criteria resulted in a sample of 7,780 low-income, unmarried children who were nineteen years old or younger.

Three different subsamples of children were then created based on insurance status in month 13 of the SIPP: one for children who had private coverage; one for those who had Medicaid/SCHIP; and a third for those who were uninsured. Based on insurance coverage type in month 13, the samples have 4,620, 1,701, and 1,459 observations (person-level files) for children who had private insurance, children who had Medicaid/SCHIP, and children who were uninsured, respectively. We then converted the person-level data files into person-months files, which we organized by type of transition. When transformed to person-month files, the private-to-Medicaid/SCHIP data file has a total of 153,626 person months, while the Medicaid/SCHIP-to-private and uninsured-to-private files are made up of 44,523 and 33,141 person months, respectively.

Estimation Techniques

We used event history (or duration) analysis and a multilevel modeling approach for this study. The events of interest for this chapter are the following three types of transition in insurance coverage: private coverage to Medicaid/SCHIP; Medicaid/ SCHIP to private coverage; and uninsurance to private coverage. Since the window of observation in the SIPP data set is not sufficiently wide to identify the actual starting months of an individual's health insurance history, it is therefore imperative to define an appropriate starting point of analysis, which is the initial time of an episode (or spell) being observed, for each event and for each individual.

For this study, based on results of preliminary regression analyses, month 13 of the SIPP was selected to define the initial insurance status of sampled children.

This was done by first identifying the observed beginning (new spells) of each of the different health insurance spells, namely private, Medicaid, and uninsured spells. Then the probability of ending each spell was modeled as a function of a set of dummy variables that represented the length of spell and other covariates in the regression models, to be discussed in the next section. The time-in-spell dummies were measured in four-month intervals, for example, 1–4, 4–8, . . . , 45–48, yielding twelve dummy variables. The appropriate choice of starting cross-section would be that interval where the effect of two adjacent dummy variables, on the probability of ending a spell, flattens out; that is, the point at which the two adjacent dichotomous variables are no longer different.

The unit of analysis is the person-month. We constructed the event-history data files to accommodate repeated transitions for each of the three insurance coverage types. Multiple transitions were accounted for in our analyses because repeated events ensured that maximum information from every observation was used. Compared with models that allow only a single transition per person-month, models of repeated events had greater probabilities of an event occurring, and also had better statistical fit based on the log likelihood ratio and other tests. The transition probabilities from one type of insurance coverage to another were then estimated using discrete-time logit models, which specified random effects for the intercepts, that is, transition rates and the approximated Medicaid/SCHIP eligibility variable. The three logit models incorporated both time-invariant and time-varying covariates.

Further, since children in each state of residence might have state-specific transition rates, we employed a multilevel modeling approach, which corrects for clustering of children within states and nonconstant variance in the error term. Children were considered the level-1 unit of analysis, while states, within which samples of children are clustered, made up the level-2 unit of analysis.

Econometric Models

For each insurance spell, empirical models were specified to estimate the effects of explanatory variables on health insurance transition decisions. The discrete-time hazard rate is defined as

$$P_{it} = Pr[T_i = t \mid T_i \geq t, X_{it}] \tag{1}$$

where T is the discrete random variable that gives the uncensored time of event occurrence. Equation (1) is the conditional probability that an event occurs at time t, for individual i, given that the event has not already occurred.

Following Phillips et al. (2004) to illustrate the estimation of the multilevel regression model, we consider some data in which there are two levels of information: at the individual (or children) level and at the state of residence level. Let J be the number of states of residence and N_j the number of children (level 1) in each state (level 2). The dependent variable, which is a level-1 variable, is Y_{ij} and the independent variable X_{ij}, and on level 2, there is the independent variable Z_j. Then we have a separate regression equation in each state of residence, which expresses a child's outcome (transition from one type of coverage to another) as the sum of an intercept for the child's state of residence β_{0j}, and a random error e_{ij}, associated with the ith child in the jth state, as follows:

$$Y_{ij} = \beta_{0j} + \beta_{1j}X_{ij} + e_{ij} \tag{2}$$

where $e_{ij} \sim N(0,\sigma^2)$.

At level 2 (the state level), the β_j are modeled by explanatory variables at the state level:

$$\beta_{0j} = \gamma_{00} + \gamma_{01}Z_j + U_{0j} \tag{3}$$
$$\beta_{1j} = \gamma_{10} + \gamma_{11}Z_j + U_{1j} \tag{4}$$

Substituting Equations (3) and (4) into Equation (2) yields the multilevel (mixed) model:

$$Y_{ij} = \gamma_{00} + \gamma_{10}X_{ij} + \gamma_{01}Z_j + \gamma_{11}Z_jX_{ij} + U_{ij}X_{ij} + U_{0j} + e_{ij} \tag{5}$$

where γ_{00} is the overall (grand) mean.

Specifically, the estimated discrete-time logistic regressions, which are the individual-level equations, defined identically for each type of transition, were of the form:

$$Ln[P_{t(is)} / (1-P_{t(is)}] = \alpha_{is} + \beta_{is}MedSCHIPElig_{t(is)} +$$
$$\beta_{is}OldMedElig_{t(is)} + \beta_{is}PrePost + \beta_{is}MedSCHIPElig_{t(is)}*Prepost +$$
$$\beta_{is}OldMedElig_{t(is)}*PrePost + \beta_{is}X_{t(is)} + \ldots + \beta_{ks}X_{kt(is)} + \varepsilon_{t(is)} \tag{6}$$

The dependent variable in Equation (6) represents the logit of the probability of transition from, say, private insurance to Medicaid/SCHIP in time interval t for child i living in state s, given that the child was in private coverage at the beginning of time interval t; α_{is} (γ_{00} in Equation [5]) is the estimate of the natural log of the baseline hazard of transition from one coverage type to another during each interval t; $Elig_{t(is)}$ is the imputed Medicaid/SCHIP eligibility variable for a child i living in state s at time t; $Elig_{t(is)}*PrePost$ is the interaction term between public program eligibility and state-specific SCHIP program implementation dates; $X_{t(is)}$ represents the matrix of individual and parent or family characteristics in state s and interval t; and $X_{kt(is)}$ represents the matrix of programmatic and state-specific variables, which vary across both states and time. The discrete-time hazards specification above will give an estimate of the baseline hazard of transitions from one health insurance state to another.

Variations in odds of transition across states are estimated by the level-2 equation below:

$$\beta_{ks} = \theta_{k0} + \theta_{k1}Z_{1s} + \theta_{k2}Z_{2s} + \ldots + \theta_{kq}Z_{qs} + \mu_{ks} \tag{7}$$

The individual- or family-level parameters, β, are assumed to vary across states as a function of state-level characteristics, Z_s, as well as the random variations μ_s. The level-2 error terms, μ_s, represent the random effects that model the correlation between the timing of transitions for children within the same state.

Dependent Variables

The first step was to identify types of insurance coverage. Mutually exclusive and exhaustive categories of coverage types are defined as follows: (1) private, including military-related coverage; (2) Medicaid/SCHIP coverage; and (3) no coverage.

Three transitions, starting in month 13, were estimated: (1) private coverage to Medicaid/SCHIP; (2) Medicaid/SCHIP to private coverage; and (3) uninsured to private coverage. Each spell defines a dependent variable, the conditional probability of switching from one insurance coverage type to another whenever such a transition occurred between months 13 and 48.

Independent Variables

Explanatory variables included in specified models are children's and family demographic characteristics, Medicaid/SCHIP, and state factors (see Table 18.1).

The Medicaid/SCHIP eligibility variable was approximated by a dichotomous variable representing whether or not a child was eligible for Medicaid/SCHIP. Potential eligibility for the post-1997 Medicaid/SCHIP expansion was imputed by using yearly eligibility criteria in each state. The eligibility variable incorporates the age of children and their state of residence; monthly family income; family size–adjusted FPL; and states' SCHIP upper income thresholds on a month-to-month basis. The approach used to create this variable is similar to those used by Ham and Shore-Sheppard (2000) and Rosenbach et al. (2001). The state-specific values of a year's imputed eligibility variable were then assigned to every month in that particular year. (See Table 18.2 [p. 372] for Medicaid/SCHIP expansion dates.)

Similarly, a dummy variable representing eligibility for the pre-SCHIP Medicaid was created. Lastly, a dichotomous variable was created for the third group of sampled children who were not eligible for either pre-SCHIP Medicaid or post-1997 Medicaid/SCHIP because their family income levels were too high to qualify for Medicaid/SCHIP in a given month. Further, in order to capture changes in health insurance status attributable to Medicaid/SCHIP eligibility, while isolating external market factors such as the economic expansion and welfare reforms that took place in the mid- to late 1990s, an interaction term between the imputed

Table 18.1

Source, Level, Type, and Description of Variables

Variable	Source/Level	Type	Description
CONTEXTUAL*			
Medicaid/SCHIP eligibility	SIPP/Individual	Time-varying (monthly)	Imputed Medicaid/SCHIP variable (1,0) with 1 indicating a child is eligible for the expansion.
Old Medicaid eligibility	SIPP/Individual	Time-varying (monthly)	Imputed pre-SCHIP Medicaid variable (1,0) with 1 indicating a child is eligible for the old Medicaid.
Income eligibility	SIPP/Individual	Time-varying (monthly)	Imputed eligibility variable (1,0) with 1 indicating a child is not eligible for the public insurance due to family income.
Medicaid/SCHIP eligibility* Pre-Post	SIPP/Individual	Time-varying (monthly)	Interaction between Medicaid/SCHIP eligibility and states' SCHIP implementation dates.
Old Medicaid eligibility* Pre-Post	SIPP/Individual	Time-varying (monthly)	Interaction between Old Medicaid eligibility and states' SCHIP implementation dates.
Income eligibility*Pre-Post	SIPP/Individual	Time-varying (monthly)	Interaction between Income eligibility and states' SCHIP implementation dates.
Pre-Post	SIPP/Individual	Time-varying (monthly)	Binary variable (0,1) with 1 representing the implementation of SCHIP program.
Income disregards	CMS/Program	Time-invariant	Binary variable (0,1) with 1 indicating that state uses income disregards.
Medicaid expansion	CMS/Program	Time-invariant	Binary variable (0,1) with 1 indicating that state increases eligibility by Medicaid expansion versus stand alone SCHIP program.
Mixed expansion	CMS/Program	Time-invariant	Binary variable (0,1) with 1 indicating that state increases eligibility by both Medicaid expansion and new SCHIP program versus stand- alone SCHIP program.
Retail-service employment ratio	REIS/State	Time-invariant	Continuous variable representing share of state's total employments in the retail or service sector.
Percap_Mcd_exp	CMS/Program	Time-varying (yearly)	Continuous variable for state per capita Medicaid/SCHIP expenditure for children under age 21, computed as the ratio a state expenditure to the number of beneficiaries.

Unemployment	ARF/State	Time-varying (yearly)	Continuous variable representing state's unemployment rates.
Emp_small_firm	REIS/State	Time-varying (yearly)	Continuous variable measured by the ratio of employments in firms with less than 20 employees to that of total employments in all firms.
Per capita income	ARF/State	Time-varying (yearly)	Continuous variable representing a state's per capita income.
Min_ratio	ARF/State	Time-varying (yearly)	Continuous measuring state's proportion of minority population.
PARENT/FAMILY*			
Mom works fulltime	SIPP/Parent	Time-varying (monthly)	Dummy variable (0,1) with 1 indicating that parent works fulltime.
Mom works part-time	SIPP/Parent	Time-varying (monthly)	Dummy variable (0,1) with 1 indicating that parent works parttime.
Mom works other	SIPP/Parent	Time-varying (monthly)	Dummy variable (0,1) with 1 indicating that parent works full or part time.
Not a high school graduate	SIPP / Parent	Time-invariant (initial value)	Binary variable (0,1) with 1 indicating attainment of some schooling but less than a high school diploma.
Some college	SIPP / Parent	Time-invariant (initial value)	Binary variable (0,1) with 1 indicating less than 4 years of college education.
College graduate	SIPP / Parent	Time-invariant (initial value)	Binary variable (0,1) with 1 indicating four years of college, i.e., a college graduate.
Graduate education	SIPP / Parent	Time-invariant (initial value)	Binary variable (0,1) with 1 indicating postgraduate education.
Family stability	SIPP/Family	—/—	Continuous variable indicating the number of months, within the window of observation, during which a child lives in a two-parent family. Updated monthly.
Income-poverty ratio	SIPP/Family	Time-varying (monthly)	Continuous variable representing family income as a percentage of FPL
AFDC Receipts	SIPP/Family	Time-varying (monthly)	Binary variable (0,1) with 1 indicating AFDC receipt.
Number of children under 18	SIPP/Family	Time-varying (monthly)	Continuous variable for number of children under 18 years old in family.

(continued)

Table 18.1 (*continued*)

Variable	Source/Level	Type	Description
Resides in Northeast	SIPP/Family	Time-varying (monthly)	A regional, binary variable (1,0) with 1 indicating residence in the Northeast.
Resides in Midwest	SIPP/Family	Time-varying (monthly)	A regional, binary variable (1,0) with 1 indicating residence in the Midwest.
Resides in West	SIPP/Family	Time-varying (monthly)	A regional, binary variable (1,0) with 1 indicating residence in the West.
INDIVIDUAL (CHILD)*			
Age_6–12 years	SIPP/Individual	Time-varying (monthly)	Binary variable (0,1) with 1 indicating children between 6 and 12 years old.
Age_13–19 years	SIPP/Individual	Time-varying (monthly)	Binary variable (0,1) with 1 indicating children older than 12 years.
Poor health status	SIPP/Individual	Time-varying (monthly)	Binary variable (0,1) with 1 indicating fair or poor health.
Black	SIPP/Individual	Time-invariant (initial value)	Binary variable (0,1) with 1 indicating African American.
Hispanic	SIPP/Individual	Time-invariant (initial value)	Binary variable (0,1) with 1 indicating Hispanic.
Other minority	SIPP/Individual	Time-invariant (initial value)	Binary variable (0,1) with 1 indicating other minority racial groups.
Seam_month	SIPP/Individual	Time-varying	Variable to capture "seam effect" in SIPP: equals 1 every fourth month, 0 otherwise.
Duration_1–3months**	SIPP/Individual	Time-varying	Dummy duration variable (0,1) with 1 indicating between 1-and 3-month long coverage spell.**

Duration_4–6months**	SIPP/Individual	Time-varying	Dummy duration variable (0,1) with 1 indicating between 4- and 6-month long coverage spell.**
Duration_7–9months**	SIPP/Individual	Time-varying	Dummy duration variable (0,1) with 1 indicating between 7- and 9-month long coverage spell.**
Duration_10–12months**	SIPP/Individual	Time-varying	Dummy duration variable (0,1) with 1 indicating between 10- and 12-month long coverage spell.**
Response Variables			
$P(t=Ev1|Ev1>=t$	SIPP/Individual	Time-varying	Conditional probability of an event representing transitions from private coverage to Medicaid/SCHIP coverage.
$P(t=Ev2|Ev2>=t$	SIPP/Individual	Time-varying	Conditional probability of an event representing transitions from private coverage to being uninsured.
$P(t=Ev3|Ev3>=t$	SIPP/Individual	Time-varying	Conditional probability of an event representing transitions from Medicaid/SCHIP to private coverage.
$P(t=Ev4|Ev4>=t$	SIPP/Individual	Time-varying	Conditional probability of an event representing transitions from Medicaid/SCHIP to being uninsured.
$P(t=Ev5|Ev5>=t$	SIPP/Individual	Time-varying	Conditional probability of an event representing transitions from being uninsured to private coverage.
$P(t=Ev6|Ev6>=t$	SIPP/Individual	Time-varying	Conditional probability of an event representing transitions from being uninsured to Medicaid/SCHIP coverage.

*Explanatory variables are in bold, capitalized letters.

**The spell variable varies depending on the model under consideration. For example, for the subsample that started with private insurance in month 13, it is the length of prior spell of private coverage before making a transition to another coverage type. Medicaid/SCHIP and uninsured spell variables were similarly measured for subsamples that started with Medicaid/SCHIP and being uninsured, respectively.

Table 18.2

Effective Dates of Medicaid/SCHIP Expansion by State

State	Effective date
Alabama	February 1, 1998
Alaska	March 1, 1999
Arizona	October 1, 1997
Arkansas	October 1, 1998
California	July 1, 1998
Colorado	April 22, 1998
Connecticut	October 1, 1997
Delaware	October 1, 1998
District of Columbia	October 1, 1998
Florida	April 4, 1998
Georgia	September 1, 1998
Hawaii	January 3, 2000
Idaho	October 1, 1997
Illinois	January 5, 1998
Indiana	October 1, 1997
Iowa	July 1, 1998
Kansas	July 1, 1998
Kentucky	July 1, 1998
Louisiana	November 1, 1998
Maine	July 1, 1998
Maryland	July 1, 1998
Massachusetts	October 1, 1997
Michigan	May 1, 1998
Minnesota	September 30, 1998
Mississippi	July 1, 1998
Missouri	October 1, 1997
Montana	January 1, 1998
Nebraska	May 1, 1998
Nevada	October 1, 1998
New Hampshire	May 1, 1998
New Jersey	February 1, 1998
New Mexico	March 31, 1999
New York	April 15, 1998
North Carolina	October 1, 1998
North Dakota	October 1, 1998
Ohio	January 1, 1998
Oklahoma	December 1, 1997
Oregon	July 1, 1998
Pennsylvania	June 1, 1998
Rhode Island	October 1, 1997
South Carolina	October 1, 1997
South Dakota	July 1, 1998
Tennessee	October 1, 1997
Texas	July 1, 1998
Utah	August 3, 1998
Vermont	October 1, 1998
Virginia	October 26, 1998
Washington	January 1, 2000
West Virginia	July 1, 1998
Wisconsin	April 1, 1999
Wyoming	April 1, 1999

Table 18.3

An Illustration of Difference-in-Differences Hypothesis Tests for Crowd-out

	Medicaid/SCHIP minus Ineligible	Old Medicaid minus Ineligible	Medicaid/SCHIP minus Old Medicaid
Model	1	2	3
Private-to-Public	A	B	A–B
Public-to-Private	A	B	A–B
Uninsured-to-Private	A	B	A–B

Medicaid/SCHIP eligibility variable and state-specific SCHIP implementation dates was created. This interaction term represents a difference-in-differences framework similar to the approach used by Blumberg, Dubay, and Norton (2000). Similarly, interaction terms were created between states' SCHIP implementation dates and the other two categories of sampled children just discussed above. The eligibility variable for the third group of children and its interaction term is the reference (omitted) category. Therefore, the interaction term of "Medicaid/SCHIP eligibility*Pre-Post," as described in Table 18.1, represents differences in the change before and after Medicaid/SCHIP eligibility expansion, between Medicaid/SCHIP-eligible children and those ineligible due to too-high family income levels ("A" in Table 18.3). The interaction term of "Old Medicaid eligibility*Pre-Post" ("B" in Table 18.3) represents differences in the change before and after Medicaid/SCHIP eligibility expansion, between pre-SCHIP Medicaid-eligible children and those ineligible due to too-high family income levels. Finally, the differences between A and B, as shown in Table 18.3, capture the overall (or net) difference in the change before and after Medicaid/SCHIP eligibility expansion between pre-SCHIP-eligible and SCHIP-eligible children, regarding health insurance transitions in the relevant models.

Extent of Substitution of Medicaid/SCHIP Expansion (Crowd-Out) for Private Insurance

Crowd-out is measured as the proportion of increase in the people enrolled in Medicaid/SCHIP that would have remained in private coverage in the absence of the Medicaid/SCHIP expansion (Blumberg, Dubay, and Norton 2000; LoSasso and Buchmueller 2002).

The coefficient for the variable representing the interaction of Medicaid/SCHIP eligibility and SCHIP implementation dates approximates the difference between newly eligible children for the enhanced Medicaid/SCHIP and ineligible children regarding likelihood of making transitions from one type of insurance coverage to another coverage type. For example, in the model of transitions from private insurance to Medicaid/SCHIP coverage, the interaction term of Medicaid/SCHIP eligibility and SCHIP implementation dates tests whether change in transitions for the target group of sampled children, that is, newly eligible for Medicaid/SCHIP, is different from change for ineligible children, that is, the reference group. According to Blumberg, Dubay, and Norton (2000), differences between newly eligible and ineligible children, while controlling for measurable factors, are due to the public program expansion.

Results

Characteristics of Person-Months in Private, Public, and Uninsured Spells

Tables 18.4, 18.5, and 18.6 present the descriptive statistics for all explanatory variables by insurance coverage type. Some 15.1 percent of the person-months in private coverage spells were months in which the child was Medicaid/SCHIP eligible after the post-SCHIP implementation (Table 18.4). Only 6.2 percent of the person-months in private coverage spells were eligible for pre-SCHIP Medicaid. The proportions of person-months in public insurance coverage spells that were eligible for Medicaid/SCHIP and pre-SCHIP Medicaid coverage are 12.1 percent and 32.7 percent, respectively (Table 18.5), while for person-months in uninsured spells, the proportions are 17.9 percent and 15.9 percent (Table 18.6).

These means demonstrate some potential for crowd-out in the SCHIP program. Effectively, they indicate that a child experiencing a person-month of private coverage was more likely to be eligible for Medicaid/SCHIP coverage than a child experiencing a person-month of public coverage. By comparison, a child experiencing a person-month of public coverage was five times more likely to be eligible for Medicaid under the pre-SCHIP eligibility rules than a child experiencing a person-month of private coverage.

Results of Regressions of Transitions from Private Insurance Coverage to Medicaid/SCHIP

Estimated parameters were obtained from the multilevel models using the logit link discussed below (see Table 18.7). The positive coefficient on the interaction of imputed Medicaid/SCHIP eligibility and states' SCHIP implementation dates indicates that low-income children eligible for the post-1996 Medicaid/SCHIP expansion were more likely to make transitions from private to public insurance, relative to children ineligible due to high family income. The enhanced Medicaid/SCHIP eligibility appears to encourage movements of newly eligible low-income children from private to public insurance. The coefficient on this variable is, however, not statistically significant, indicating that crowd-out is not present.

Table 18.4

Characteristics of Person-months in Private Insurance Coverage Spells

Variable	Mean (N = 153,171)	Std Dev
Contextual Factors		
Medicaid/SCHIP eligibility	0.2777	0.4479
Old Medicaid eligibility	0.1213	0.3264
Medicaid/SCHIP*Pre-Post	0.1511	0.3581
Old Medicaid Elig*Pre-Post	0.0620	0.2412
Pre-Post	0.5519	0.4973
Income disregards	0.5461	0.4979
Medicaid expansion	0.2379	0.4258
Mixed expansion	0.5124	0.4998
Retail-service employment ratio	0.5719	0.0335
Parent/Family Factors		
Mom works full time	0.4735	0.4993
Mom works part time	0.1879	0.3906
Mom works other	0.0328	0.1782
Not a high school graduate	0.0883	0.2838
Some college	0.3938	0.4886
College graduate	0.1298	0.3361
Graduate education	0.0226	0.1487
Family stability	38.3699	18.1646
Income-poverty ratio	226.6466	106.1812
AFDC receipts	0.0024	0.0492
Number of children under 18	2.4150	1.1905
Resides in Northeast	0.1644	0.3706
Resides in Midwest	0.2893	0.4534
Resides in West	0.2138	0.4100
Individual (Child)		
Age 6–12 years	0.4951	0.5000
Age 13–19 years	0.3150	0.4645
Poor health status	0.0137	0.1163
Black	0.1031	0.3040
Hispanic	0.0074	0.0855
Other minority	0.0302	0.1712
Seam month	0.2506	0.4334
Duration 1–3 months	0.0281	0.1653
Duration 4–6 months	0.0256	0.1578
Duration 7–9 months	0.0244	0.1541
Duration 10–12 months	0.0237	0.1520

N = Number of person-months.

These initial results do not provide strong support for a crowd-out effect. If anything, they might suggest that the main effect of expanded eligibility was increasing the likelihood of a transition from private insurance to uninsured status. It is possible that this is an indirect result of requirements in some SCHIP programs designed to prevent crowd-out. Some states required that individuals have a lapse

Table 18.5

Characteristics of Person-months in Public Insurance Coverage Spells

Variable	Mean (N = 43,969)	Std Dev
Contextual Factors		
Medicaid/SCHIP eligibility	0.2341	0.4235
Old Medicaid eligibility	0.6953	0.4603
Medicaid/SCHIP*Pre-Post	0.1212	0.3264
Old Medicaid Elig*Pre-Post	0.3270	0.4691
Pre-Post	0.4831	0.4997
Income disregards	0.5702	0.4951
Medicaid expansion	0.1810	0.3851
Mixed expansion	0.5780	0.4939
Retail-service employment ratio	0.5718	0.0282
Parent/Family Factors		
Mom works full time	0.2165	0.4119
Mom works part time	0.1451	0.3522
Mom works other	0.0417	0.1999
Not a high school graduate	0.4275	0.4947
Some college	0.1975	0.3981
Family stability	20.0086	22.4259
Income-poverty ratio	92.9550	75.8126
AFDC receipts	0.3572	0.4792
Number of children under 18	2.7597	1.6587
Resides in Northeast	0.1900	0.3923
Resides in Midwest	0.1802	0.3844
Resides in West	0.3121	0.4633
Individual (Child)		
Age 6–12 years	0.4946	0.5000
Age 13–19 years	0.2877	0.4527
Poor health status	0.0681	0.2520
Black	0.2753	0.4467
Hispanic	0.0484	0.2146
Other minority	0.0501	0.2181
Seam month	0.2505	0.4333
Duration 1–3 months	0.0818	0.2741
Duration 4–6 months	0.0652	0.2469
Duration 7–9 months	0.0554	0.2288
Duration 10–12 months	0.0496	0.2172

N = Number of person-months.

of coverage or waiting period prior to SCHIP enrollment, which might have resulted in parents declining private coverage for a child and experiencing a short-term uninsured period, in expectation of future SCHIP coverage.

The positive sign on the variable representing the Medicaid expansion variable suggests that a child who lives in a state that chose to expand its existing Medicaid program, relative to states that opted for new stand-alone SCHIP programs, on average, is more likely to make a transition to public insurance; however, this

Table 18.6

Characteristics of Person-months in Uninsured Spells

Variable	Mean (N = 32,236)	Std Dev
Contextual Factors		
Medicaid/SCHIP eligibility	0.3851	0.4866
Old Medicaid eligibility	0.3733	0.4837
Medicaid/SCHIP*Pre-Post	0.1793	0.3836
Old Medicaid Elig*Pre-Post	0.1595	0.3662
Pre-Post	0.4687	0.4990
Income disregards	0.6815	0.4659
Medicaid expansion	0.1613	0.3679
Mixed expansion	0.6410	0.4797
Retail-service employment ratio	0.5743	0.0334
Parent/Family Factors		
Mom works full time	0.3748	0.4841
Mom works part time	0.1674	0.3734
Mom works other	0.0357	0.1856
Not a high school graduate	0.4380	0.4961
Some college	0.1763	0.3811
College graduate	0.0421	0.2008
Graduate education	0.0101	0.0998
Family stability	34.5092	20.6904
Income-poverty ratio	142.5205	111.0242
AFDC receipts	0.0308	0.1729
Number of children under 18	2.6899	1.7614
Resides in Northeast	0.1214	0.3266
Resides in Midwest	0.1333	0.3399
Resides in West	0.2772	0.4476
Individual (Child)		
Age 6–12 years	0.4772	0.4995
Age 13–19 years	0.3658	0.4817
Poor health status	0.0229	0.1495
Black	0.1527	0.3598
Hispanic	0.0179	0.1326
Other minority	0.0414	0.1992
Seam month	0.2545	0.4356
Duration 1–3 months	0.0995	0.2994
Duration 4–6 months	0.0792	0.2701
Duration 7–9 months	0.0672	0.2504
Duration 10–12 months	0.0593	0.2363

N = Number of person-months.

effect is not statistically significant. This result is similar to that found by LoSasso and Buchmueller (2002) showing that Medicaid expansions and new stand-alone programs did differ in their effects on public insurance take-up.

The sign on the variable measuring the share of a state's total employment in the retail or service sector is positive and statistically significant. These results indicate

Table 18.7

Multilevel Logit Models of Transitions from Private Insurance

	Private to Medicaid/SCHIP	
Variable	Estimated coefficient (.) Std Error	t-Value
Intercept	−10.1051*** (1.6107)	−6.2738
Contextual Factors		
Medicaid/SCHIP eligibility	−0.0982 (0.2613)	−0.3757
Old Medicaid eligibility	0.8638*** (0.2746)	3.1455
Medicaid/SCHIP*Pre-Post	0.3496 (0.3390)	1.0314
Old Medicaid Elig*Pre-Post	−0.3755 (0.3246)	−1.1567
Pre-Post	0.2407 (0.2026)	1.1877
Income disregards	−0.0527 (0.2511)	−0.2098
Medicaid expansion	0.2317 (0.3198)	0.7244
Mixed expansion	0.1134 (0.2868)	0.3956
Retail-service employment ratio	4.4961* (2.7697)	1.6234
Parent/Family Factors		
Mom works full time	−0.3172** (0.1425)	−2.2256
Mom works part time	−0.3000* (0.1731)	−1.7335
Mom works other	−0.1392 (0.3115)	−0.4471
Not a high school graduate	0.5178*** (0.1667)	3.1057
Some college	0.0661 (0.1312)	0.5042
College graduate	−0.5804** (0.2535)	−2.2894
Graduate education	−0.3619 (0.4935)	−0.7333
Family stability	−0.0148*** (0.0031)	−4.8197
Income-poverty ratio	−0.0032*** (0.0010)	−3.0809
AFDC receipts	1.6247*** (0.3195)	5.0852
Number of children under 18	0.0711* (0.0416)	1.7099

Table 18.7 *(continued)*

Variable	Private to Medicaid/SCHIP	
	Estimated coefficient (.) Std Error	t-Value
Resides in Northeast	0.9019*** (0.3370)	2.6761
Resides in Midwest	0.0327 (0.3239)	0.1009
Resides in West	−0.0315 (0.3461)	−0.0909
Individual (Child)		
Age 6–12 years	−0.1073 (0.1466)	−0.7314
Age 13–19 years	0.0322 (0.1581)	0.2036
Poor health status	0.5164 (0.3427)	1.5069
Black	0.4275*** (0.1576)	2.7126
Hispanic	0.9679** (0.4253)	2.2758
Other minority	−0.0804 (0.3066)	−0.2622
Seam month	3.1000*** (0.1636)	18.9531
Duration 1–3 months	−0.3307 (0.2885)	−1.1463
Duration 4–6 months	1.8427*** (0.1444)	12.7576
Duration 7–9 months	1.1414*** (0.1938)	5.8903
Duration 10–12 months	0.1454 (0.5170)	0.2812
LLR	1,638,946	
AIC	1,638,954	
Person months (N)	153,626	

*Significant at the 10 percent level.
**Significant at the 5 percent level.
*** Significant at the 1 percent level.

that the larger the share of a state's employment in the retail or service sector, the greater the odds of a child switching from private coverage to Medicaid/SCHIP, all else remaining constant. In general, availability of private health insurance coverage tends to be lower for workers in the retail and service sectors.

The results also show that a parent's employment status and educational attainment, family stability, and a child's race are likely to affect transitions from private coverage to Medicaid/SCHIP. The positive signs on the duration variables that measure the length of time of private insurance coverage before making transitions to public coverage suggest that the longer a child remains in private coverage, on average, the less likely the child is to switch to public coverage.

Results of Regressions of Transitions from Medicaid/SCHIP to Private Coverage

Results of transitions from Medicaid/SCHIP to private coverage are presented in Table 18.8. There is a negative sign on the coefficient of the interaction of imputed Medicaid/SCHIP eligibility and states' SCHIP implementation dates, suggesting that low-income children who were made eligible for expanded Medicaid/SCHIP, relative to children ineligible for SCHIP due to too-high family income levels, were less likely to transition from public insurance to private coverage, all else constant. This coefficient is, however, not statistically significant, suggesting that the model does not identify crowd-out due to delaying or preventing transitions out of public coverage.

The negative sign on the Medicaid expansion suggests that children who live in a state that chose to expand its existing Medicaid program, relative to states that opted for new stand-alone SCHIP programs, on average, are less likely to make transitions out of Medicaid/SCHIP coverage to private insurance. The negative sign on the income-disregards variable suggests that a child who lives in a state where certain types of income are excluded in determining eligibility for the Medicaid/ SCHIP expansion, relative to a child who lives in a state with no income disregards, on average, has decreased odds of becoming privately insured.

Thus, while the Medicaid/SCHIP expansion itself does not appear to have created crowd-out in this way, those states that relied on expanding the existing Medicaid program do appear to have had a problem with reduced levels of transition to private insurance. It is important to recall that those states that created a new stand-alone SCHIP program were given greater latitude to regulate participation, which might affect transitions to private insurance.

Results of Regressions of Transitions from Being Uninsured to Private Coverage

The logit estimates of making transitions from being uninsured to private coverage are presented in Table 18.9. The sign on the coefficient of the interaction of imputed Medicaid/SCHIP eligibility and states' SCHIP implementation dates is negative, but it is not statistically significant. This result suggests that the expanded program eligibility did not significantly decrease the odds of children making a transition out of uninsured status. However, the sign on the coefficient of the interaction of imputed pre-SCHIP Medicaid eligibility and states' SCHIP implementation dates is positive. Uninsured children eligible for pre-SCHIP Medicaid coverage,

Table 18.8

Multilevel Logit Models of Transitions from Medicaid/SCHIP

	Medicaid/SCHIP to Private	
Variable	Estimated coefficient (.) Std Error	t-Value
Intercept	−6.1904*** (1.7728)	−3.4919
Contextual Factors		
Medicaid/SCHIP eligibility	0.0319 (0.2094)	0.1521
Old Medicaid eligibility	−0.6262*** (0.2291)	−2.7327
Medicaid/SCHIP*Pre-Post	−0.3567 (0.2704)	−1.3190
Old Medicaid Elig*Pre-Post	−0.1655 (0.2705)	−0.6118
Pre-Post	0.0877 (0.2178)	0.4028
Income disregards	−0.4849* (0.2756)	−1.7596
Medicaid expansion	−0.7601** (0.3511)	−2.1650
Mixed expansion	−0.2034 (0.3052)	−0.6665
Retail-service employment ratio	0.1783 (3.1132)	0.0573
Parent/Family Factors		
Mom works full time	0.7920*** (0.1012)	7.8258
Mom works part time	0.2038 (0.1284)	1.5874
Mom works other	1.0391*** (0.1696)	6.1265
Not a high school graduate	0.1082 (0.1043)	1.0369
Some college	0.3933*** (0.1036)	3.7951
Family stability	0.0041* (0.0022)	1.8574
Income-poverty ratio	0.0014* (0.0007)	1.9194
AFDC receipts	−1.5465*** (0.1427)	−10.8392
Number of children under 18	0.0686** (0.0284)	2.4146
Resides in Northeast	0.0838 (0.4054)	0.2067
Resides in Midwest	0.5695	1.5949

(continued)

Table 18.8 *(continued)*

Variable	Medicaid/SCHIP to Private	
	Estimated coefficient (.) Std Error	t-Value
	(0.3571)	
Resides in West	−0.2544	−0.6405
	(0.3972)	
Individual (Child)		
Age 6–12 years	−0.0406	−0.3932
	(0.1032)	
Age 13–19 years	−0.2350**	−1.9595
	(0.1199)	
Poor health status	−0.3135*	−1.6309
	(0.1922)	
Black	0.2589**	2.3503
	(0.1101)	
Hispanic	0.7269***	3.0854
	(0.2356)	
Other minority	−0.3161	−1.2629
	(0.2503)	
Seam month	3.0492***	27.2457
	(0.1119)	
Duration 1–3 months	−1.7847***	−7.5111
	(0.2376)	
Duration 4–6 months	0.7387***	6.9525
	(0.1063)	
Duration 7–9 months	0.3889***	2.9564
	(0.1315)	
Duration 10–12 months	0.3247	1.3417
	(0.2420)	
LLR	388,481	
AIC	388,489	
Person months (N)	44,523	

*Significant at the 10 percent level.
**Significant at the 5 percent level.
***Significant at the 1 percent level.

relative to other children, are more likely to make transitions to private coverage as a result of the implementation of the SCHIP program. These results might be due to individuals reporting public insurance as private coverage. Also, enforcement of measures to curb crowd-out, such as waiting periods, cost sharing, and enrollment caps, especially by states that operate stand-alone SCHIP programs, might discourage movement of children into public insurance coverage. Variables measuring a parent's employment status and educational attainment, family stability, and a child's characteristics likely influence transitions out of uninsured status (see Table 18.9).

Table 18.9

Multilevel Logit Models of Transitions from being Uninsured

	Uninsured to Private	
Variable	Estimated coefficient (.) Std Error	t-Value
Intercept	−4.6031*** (1.0684)	−4.3085
Contextual Factors		
Medicaid/SCHIP eligibility	−0.5187*** (0.1158)	−4.4791
Old Medicaid eligibility	−1.1097*** (0.1429)	−7.7631
Medicaid/SCHIP*Pre-Post	−0.0370 (0.2194)	−0.1687
Old Medicaid Elig*Pre-Post	0.4748* (0.2478)	1.9160
Pre-Post	−0.1821* (0.1098)	−1.6581
Income disregards	0.0560 (0.1800)	0.3109
Medicaid expansion	−0.1746 (0.2255)	−0.7743
Mixed expansion	0.0239 (0.1912)	0.1249
Retail-service employment ratio	0.1391 (1.8749)	0.0742
Parent/Family Factors		
Mom works full time	0.6864*** (0.0890)	7.7106
Mom works part time	0.3342*** (0.1110)	3.0097
Mom works other	0.1213 (0.1962)	0.6182
Not a high school graduate	−0.4386*** (0.0934)	−4.6989
Some college	0.2975*** (0.0887)	3.3559
College graduate	0.4650*** (0.1531)	3.0361
Graduate education	−0.4827 (0.3747)	−1.2880
Family stability	0.0000 (0.0019)	−0.0019
Income-poverty ratio	0.0005 (0.0003)	1.4590
AFDC receipts	−1.1517** (0.4964)	−2.3199
Number of children under 18	−0.0263 (0.0261)	−1.0079

(continued)

Table 18.9 *(continued)*

Variable	Uninsured to Private	
	Estimated coefficient (.) Std Error	t-Value
Resides in Northeast	0.1500 (0.2677)	0.5603
Resides in Midwest	0.3987* (0.2234)	1.7848
Resides in West	0.2426 (0.2351)	1.0318
Individual (Child)		
Age 6–12 years	−0.1100 (0.0966)	−1.1388
Age 13–19 years	−0.3518*** (0.1059)	−3.3221
Poor health status	−0.3600 (0.2799)	−1.2861
Black	0.1714 (0.1079)	1.5888
Hispanic	−0.8695*** (0.3316)	−2.6218
Other minority	−0.3845** (0.1823)	−2.1092
Seam month	2.1706*** (0.0753)	28.8250
Duration 1–3 months	−1.1358*** (0.1657)	−6.8549
Duration 4–6 months	1.1428*** (0.0867)	13.1808
Duration 7–9 months	0.5068*** (0.1131)	4.4796
Duration 10–12 months	0.3650** (0.1842)	1.9812
LLR	243,393	
AIC	243,401	
Person months (N)	33,141	

*Significant at the 10 percent level.
**Significant at the 5 percent level.
***Significant at the 1 percent level.

Estimating the Crowd-Out Effect of Medicaid/SCHIP Eligibility on Private Insurance

Table 18.10 presents the difference-in-differences, which approximates the overall differences in the change regarding health insurance transitions, before and after Medicaid/SCHIP eligibility expansion between pre-SCHIP-eligible and SCHIP-eligible children. The coefficient on the variable that represents the

Table 18.10

Summary Table of Difference-in-Differences Hypothesis Tests for Crowd-out

Model	Medicaid/SCHIP Eligible minus Ineligible		Medicaid/SCHIP Eligible minus Old Medicaid Eligible	
	Estimated coefficient (.) Std Err	t-value	Estimate coefficient (.) Std Err	t-value
Private-to-Public	−0.3496 (0.3390)	1.0314	0.7251 (0.3736)	1.9411*
Public-to-Private	−0.3567 (0.2704)	−1.3190	−0.1912 (0.2388)	−0.8008
Uninsured-to-Private	−0.0370 (0.2194)	−0.1687	−0.5118 (0.2943)	−1.7390*

*Significant at the 10 percent level.

interaction of imputed Medicaid/SCHIP eligibility and states' SCHIP implementation dates, in each of the estimated models, approximates the difference in health insurance transitions between the target group of sampled children, that is, those who were potentially eligible for the expanded public insurance program, and the comparison group, that is, children who were ineligible because they had too-high family income levels. In order to capture only transitions in health insurance attributable to the Medicaid/SCHIP eligibility, it is important to net out the effect of other market factors such as the 1996 welfare reform and the economic expansion that characterized the period under analysis. Following an approach similar to that of Blumberg, Dubay, and Norton (2000), we used a difference-in-differences estimation framework that serves to capture health insurance transitions while isolating relevant external factors. Changes between Medicaid/SCHIP-eligible children and ineligible ones due to too-high family income levels, and in the period before and after the implementation of SCHIP, were approximated by the interactions between the imputed Medicaid/SCHIP eligibility and states' SCHIP implementation dates (see second column of Table 18.10). Further, overall (or net) changes are captured by difference-in-differences just discussed: difference in the change before and after Medicaid/SCHIP eligibility expansion between pre-SCHIP-eligible and SCHIP-eligible children. The differences in the coefficients on the interaction terms, that is, "Medicaid/SCHIP*Pre-Post minus Old_Medicaid_Elig*Pre-Post," for the regression models, give the net changes, which approximate the effect of Medicaid/SCHIP eligibility on the displacement of private insurance. These differences in changes estimates, presented in the fourth column of Table 18.10, provide further tests of the effect on Medicaid/SCHIP program eligibility expansion on the relevant health insurance transitions.

Therefore, if there was crowd-out during the period under analysis, one would expect a statistically significant correlation and (1) positive signs on the variable representing the interaction of the imputed Medicaid/SCHIP eligibility and states' SCHIP implementation dates and also on the differences between the interaction terms in the model predicting the odds of private-to-Medicaid/SCHIP transitions; (2) negative signs on the variable in the equation predicting whether a child would switch from Medicaid/SCHIP to private coverage; and (3) negative signs on both the interaction term and the differences between the interaction terms in the model predicting the odds of transitions from uninsurance to private coverage.

The sign on the coefficient of the variable representing the interaction between the imputed Medicaid/SCHIP eligibility and states' SCHIP implementation dates is positive. The direction of effect indicates that the post-1996 Medicaid/SCHIP expansion increases the likelihood of eligible low-income children, relative to ineligible ones, switching from private to public insurance. The coefficient on this variable is, however, not statistically significant (the coefficient is –0.3496 and the t-value is 1.0314). As expected however, the coefficient measuring the difference between the interaction terms is positive and is weakly statistically significant at the 10 percent level (the coefficient is 0.7251 and the t-value is 1.9411). The difference between the interaction terms, that is, logit estimates in the fourth column of Table 18.10, can be transformed into probability estimates by using the following relationship: Probability $= 1/1 + e^{-logit}$. Transforming the logit coefficient of 0.7251 using this mathematical expression gives a probability estimate of 0.6737, interpreted as follows: The relative odds of transitioning from private coverage to public insurance increase by approximately 67 percent after Medicaid/SCHIP expansion, relative to pre-SCHIP-eligible children, all else remaining constant.

Also, in the model predicting the odds of transitions from public to private coverage, both the coefficients on the interaction term and the difference between the interactions are negative, suggesting that low-income children who were made eligible by the Medicaid/SCHIP expansion, relative to ineligible children, are less likely to make the transition from public insurance to private coverage. However, neither of the two estimates is statistically significant.

Finally, in the model predicting the odds of uninsured children becoming privately insured, the signs on the coefficients of both the interaction term and the difference between the interactions are negative, indicating that the Medicaid/SCHIP-eligible children, relative to ineligible ones, on average, have a smaller likelihood of making the transition from being uninsured to private coverage. While the coefficient on the interaction term on the Medicaid/SCHIP-eligibility variable is not statistically significant, the difference in the interaction terms is. The degree of statistical significance for this estimate is, however, weak (the coefficient: –0.5118; t-value, –1.7390). Using the mathematical expression as stated above, the equivalent probability estimate is 0.3748, which suggests that the relative odds of making the transition from being uninsured to private coverage decrease by approximately 37 percent after the Medicaid/SCHIP expansion, relative to pre-SCHIP-eligible children, all else remaining constant.

Coefficient signs measuring the interaction between Medicaid/SCHIP eligibility and states' SCHIP implementation dates, and the difference between the interactions are suggestive of crowd-out, but there is no clear evidence of the displacement of private coverage by the enhanced Medicaid/SCHIP eligibility.

The results are similar to that of LoSasso and Buchmueller (2002), who did not find clear evidence of crowd-out owing to Medicaid/SCHIP among low-income children. Finally, using the 1996 panel SIPP, Dubay and Blumberg (2006) concluded that the Medicaid/SCHIP expansion did not seem to have an adverse effect on private coverage; that is, there was no evidence that SCHIP expansion caused significant movement of low-income children from private to public coverage. Although findings in this study indicate that the enhanced Medicaid/SCHIP eligibility might have resulted in movements of low-income children from private to public coverage, the results do not give conclusive evidence that eligibility for the Medicaid/SCHIP expansion has had an adverse effect on private coverage.

Conclusion

In this study, we took advantage of the longitudinal structure of the SIPP data, using an event history and multilevel modeling technique to estimate whether or not crowd-out of private insurance resulted from the period immediately following the post-1996 Medicaid/SCHIP eligibility expansion for low-income children. We also examined the effect of the form of public program expansion on the odds of health insurance transitions, while controlling for an array of individual, family, and state-level factors, among sampled children.

Implementation of SCHIP has had some effect of increasing the likelihood of transitions from private to public coverage among SCHIP-eligible low-income children, relative to other children. Results also indicate that the expanded public program may have decreased the odds of SCHIP-eligible children making the transition from being uninsured to private coverage. While the size of these effects is substantial (a 67 percent increase and a 37 percent decrease), both are only weakly significant in statistical terms. Thus, it is difficult to argue that they provide clear and convincing evidence of crowd-out of private insurance by the Medicaid/SCHIP expansion. The economic expansion, especially between 1998 and 2000, might have provided employment opportunities for parents, which created greater opportunities for employer-provided insurance coverage for families. Finally, preliminary analysis shows that private coverage increased from 58 percent to approximately 64 percent in the last wave, while uninsurance declined from 18 percent to 16 percent for sampled low-income children during the period under analysis, that is, between the first and last waves of the SIPP data set.

Furthermore, results suggest that key characteristics of the public programs can have significant impacts on transitions. One major decision that states faced in the SCHIP program was whether they would create a new, stand-alone program or simply expand the old Medicaid program. The latter had certain advantages of simplicity, at the cost of retaining the potential social stigma and other negative aspects of Medicaid. The former gave states the advantage of establishing new rules that could limit crowd-out and reduce stigma, but the problems of putting a new program in place. Children in states that used a Medicaid expansion, relative to their counterparts in states that opted for new stand-alone SCHIP programs, are less likely to make the transition from public insurance to private coverage. To the extent that expanding the Medicaid program leads to greater crowd-out than a stand-alone SCHIP program, it does this not through transitions from private to public coverage, but by reducing transitions from public coverage to private coverage (and by increasing the likelihood that those moving out of uninsured status move into public coverage).

One explanation is that it reflects the presence of some measures such as waiting periods, enrollment caps, and other monitoring mechanisms that stand-alone SCHIP programs could impose to curb crowd-out. These measures can potentially discourage parents from enrolling their children in such stand-alone SCHIP programs, whether they are moving from private coverage or uninsured status. These administrative roadblocks may offset the effects of reduced stigma enough to decrease enrollment in the new separate SCHIP programs.

The characteristics of the family, the parents, and the individual child as well as a state's share of employment in the retail or service sector are likely to affect transitions into and out of private insurance. Therefore, it might be worthwhile to focus attention on creating enabling environments for factors such as employment creation, better education, family stability, and so forth, that encourage retention in private coverage in order to reduce the rates of uninsurance. Also, policy makers who are expanding public insurance coverage and want to limit crowd-out might want to explore some incentives to encourage employers, especially those in the retail and service sectors, to offer affordable insurance coverage to their employees. Provision of health insurance for low-income individuals has implications for access to needed medical care, and it can be cost-effective to society. For example, it is estimated that poorer health due to uninsurance costs the United States between $65 billion and $130 billion yearly (Institute of Medicine 2004).

There are some limitations in the data and analysis that caution against drawing definitive conclusions from these results. A potential caveat to the results is that the imputed eligibility variable used in this study does not incorporate every state rule concerning expanded Medicaid/SCHIP. Some of this stems from a lack of precise variable measurements based on information that is available in the SIPP data set. For example, to calculate the amount of income disregards, information is needed on income deductions, such as amount of child support received, work expenses, and child care expenses. However, SIPP does not provide information on the actual amount of child care expense.

In spite of SIPP's limitations, this study contributes to the literature by addressing gaps in the methodological approach generally used in examining the dynamics of health insurance: Unlike previous studies of the effect of Medicaid/SCHIP expansions on private coverage and uninsurance rates, this study combines both event history and multilevel modeling approaches, thereby incorporating the timing of health insurance transitions, as well as adjusting for clustering of children within their states of residence.

There are several important areas for future research. Detailed measures of insurance coverage and the program features should be developed to assess whether the weak evidence of crowd-out found in this study holds up under closer scrutiny. Improved measures could also help identify which aspects of programs increase or decrease crowd-out. Future work could also examine the effects of policy interventions on employment or family stability on insurance transitions and compare those to the effects of insurance programs like SCHIP.

References

Blumberg, L.J., L.C. Dubay, and S.A. Norton. 2000. "Did the Medicaid Expansion for Children Displace Private Insurance? An Analysis Using the SIPP." *Journal of Health Economics* 19: 33–60.

Cunningham, P.J., J. Hadley, and J. Reschovsky. 2002. "The Effect of SCHIP on Children's Health Coverage: Early Evidence from the Community Tracking Study." *Medical Care Research and Review* 59 (4): 359–83.

Cutler, D.M., and J. Gruber. 1996. "Does Public Insurance 'Crowd-Out' Private Insurance?" *Quarterly Journal of Economics* 111 (2): 391–430.

———. 1997. "Medicaid and Private Insurance: Evidence and Implications." *Health Affairs* 16 (1): 194–200.

Dubay, L., and L.J. Blumberg. 2006. "The Dynamics of Health Insurance Coverage: 1996 to 2000." *Findings Brief* 9 (3): 5.

Ham, J.C., and L. Shore-Sheppard. 2000. "The Effect of Medicaid Expansions for Low-Income Children on Medicaid Participation and Insurance Coverage: Evidence from the SIPP." Working paper. Joint Center for Poverty Research/University of Chicago, University of Pittsburgh, and NBER.

Institute of Medicine. 2004. "Insuring America's Health: Principles and Recommendations." *Shaping the Future for Health*. www.iom.edu/uninsured. (Accessed 11 August 2008.)

Kronick, R., and T. Gilmer. 2002. "Insuring Low-Income Adults: Does Public Insurance 'Crowd-Out' Private?" *Health Affairs* 21 (1): 225–39.

Long, S.H., and M.S. Marquis. 2003. "Public Insurance Expansions and 'Crowd-Out' of Private Coverage." *Medical Care* 41 (3): 344–56.

LoSasso, A.T., and T.C. Buchmueller. 2002. "The Effect of the State Children's Health Insurance Program on Health Insurance Coverage." Working paper w9405. Cambridge, MA: National Bureau of Economic Research.

Phillips, J.A., J.E. Miller, J.C. Cantor, and D. Gaboda. 2004. "Context or Composition: What Explains Variation in SCHIP Disenrollment?" *Health Services Research* 39 (4): 865–86.

Regional Economic Information Service. 2005. "County Business Patterns." fisher.lib. virginia.edu/collections/stats/ (Accessed 17 November 2008).

Rosenbach, M., M. Ellwood, J.L. Czajka, C. Irvin, W. Coupe, and B. Quin. 2001. "Implementation of the State Children's Health Insurance Program: Momentum Is Increasing After a Modest Start." First Annual Report, Washington, DC: 22 Mathematic Policy Research.

Shore-Sheppard, L.D. 2005. "Stemming the Tide? The Effect of Expanding Medicaid Eligibility on Health Insurance Coverage." Working paper 11091. Cambridge, MA: National Bureau of Economic Research.

Short, P.F., and D.R. Graefe. 2003. "Battery-Powered Health Insurance? Stability in Coverage of the Uninsured." *Health Affairs Data Watch* 22: 244–55.

U.S. General Accounting Office. 1997. "Children's Health Insurance 1995." GAO/HEHS-97–68R. Washington, DC: U.S. General Accounting Office.

Yazici, E.Y., and R. Kaestner. 2000. "Medicaid Expansions and the Crowding Out of Private Health Insurance Among Children." *Inquiry* 37 (1): 23–32.

About the Editors and Contributors

Editors

Terry F. Buss, PhD, is currently distinguished professor of public policy at the Heinz School of Public Policy and Management, Carnegie Mellon University, in Adelaide, Australia. Buss earned his doctorate in political science and mathematics at Ohio State University. Over the past thirty years, Buss has built his career in both academe and government. In his immediate past position, he served as program director at the National Academy of Public Administration for five years. Buss has managed schools and programs at Youngstown State University, University of Akron, Suffolk University, and Florida International University. On the government side, he has served as senior adviser at the Council of Governors Policy Advisors, the Congressional Research Service, the World Bank, and the U.S. Department of Housing and Urban Development. From 1987 to 1997, Buss was director of research at the St. Elizabeth Hospital Medical Center and adjunct faculty at the Northeast Ohio College of Medicine. Buss has published twelve books and nearly three hundred professional articles on a variety of policy issues, many of them on health care policy and practice.

Paul N. Van de Water is vice president for health policy at the National Academy of Social Insurance and senior fellow at the Center on Budget and Policy Priorities. Previously, he served in senior executive positions at the Social Security Administration and the Congressional Budget Office. Van de Water has written extensively on health and retirement policy and governmental finance and has testified before several congressional committees. He holds an AB with highest honors in economics from Princeton University and a PhD in economics from the Massachusetts Institute of Technology.

Contributors

Jill Bernstein, PhD, is a consultant in health care policy.

John M. Bertko, FSA, MAAA, is the recently retired chief actuary of Humana Inc.

Lawrence D. Brown, PhD, is professor of public health at the Department of Health Policy and Management, School of Public Health, Columbia University.

Xiuwen Dong, DPH, is director of the Center for Construction Research and Training, Center to Protect Workers' Rights, (CPWR) in Silver Spring, Maryland.

Bryan Dowd, PhD, is a professor of health policy and management at the Division of Health Policy and Management, University of Minnesota.

Lynn Etheredge, PhD, is a health policy consultant in Chevy Chase, MD, working on the Health Insurance Reform Project at the George Washington University in Washington, D.C.

Alissa Fujimoto is a research analyst at the CPWR-Center for Construction Research and Training in Silver Spring, Maryland.

Daniel P. Gitterman, PhD, is associate professor of public policy and director of graduate studies at University of North Carolina–Chapel Hill.

Christen Holly is a doctoral candidate at the Department of Public Policy at the University of North Carolina–Chapel Hill.

Timothy Stoltzfus Jost, JD, holds the Robert L. Willett Family Professorship of Law at the School of Law, Washington and Lee University.

Sandy Matava is director of the Center for Public Management, Suffolk University, in Boston, Massachusetts.

Mark Merlis is a consultant with thirty years' experience in the health policy and management field.

Judith Moore, JD, is a senior fellow at the National Health Policy Forum at the George Washington University in Washington, D.C.

Catherine M. Murphy-Baron is vice chairperson of the Unemployed Work Group at the American Academy of Actuaries and a consulting actuary with Milliman-New York.

Kieke G.H. Okma, PhD, is adjunct associate professor at the Wagner School of Public Service, New York University.

Adetokunbo B. Oluwole, PhD, is assistant professor of public health administration at the Martin School of Public Policy and Administration, University of Kentucky at Lexington.

F. Stevens Redburn, PhD, is a fellow and project director at the National Academy of Public Administration and National Academies of Science in Washington, D.C.

Knut Ringen is a consultant in Seattle, Washington, specializing in disease management, environment, safety and health risk management, workers' compensation, and group health insurance.

Nicole Rivers is a senior research associate at the Center for Public Management, Suffolk University, in Boston, Massachusetts.

Sonya Schwartz, JD, is a program manager at the National Academy for State Health Policy in Washington, D.C.

Dennis G. Shea, PhD, is department head and professor, Department of Health Policy and Administration, College of Health and Human Development, Pennsylvania State University, in University Park, Pennsylvania.

C. Eugene Steuerle, PhD, is a senior fellow and codirector of the Urban-Brookings Tax Policy Center at the Urban Institute in Washington, D.C.

Cori E. Uccello is a senior health fellow at the American Academy of Actuaries.

Alan Weil, JD, MPP, is executive director of the National Academy for State Health Policy in Washington, D.C.

Elliot K. Wicks, PhD, is an economist and policy analyst with twenty-five years' experience in the field of health policy.

Michael Wroblewski is project director, strategic planning and information services, at the Consumers Union, in Yonkers, New York.

Index

Italic page references refer to tables and figures.

Accreditation organizations, private, 77
Adjusted community rating, 38–39
Administration on Aging, 109
Administration of health insurance
  administrative costs
    "black box" of, 285
    classifying and defining, 267–268
    estimating, 268, *269*, 270–273, *270*
    private insurance, 271–272
    reducing, potential, 48–50
    reform proposals with implications for,
      279–280
    types of, 48–50
  employer costs, 273
  market efficiency and, 4
  national health expenditures and, 268, 270–271
  overview, 267, 285
  provider costs, 272–273
  simplifying transactions
    HIPAA and Administrative Simplification
      Compliance Act, 275–276
    overview, 273
    policy options, 278–284
    pre-HIPAA initiatives, 274–275
    progress and barriers, 276–277
Administrative costs. *See* Administration of
  health insurance
Administrative Simplification Compliance Act
  (2001), 275–276, 278
Adverse selection, 6–7, 36–38, 42, 81
Advertising information, 63–64
Aetna Health Inc. v. Davila, 91
Age Discrimination in Employment Act, 92
Agency for Healthcare Research and Quality
  (AHRQ), 203, 218
Agency-related nonprofit organizations, 215
Agents, recruiting, 28–29
Aggregate claims, 16
Aggregate reinsurance, 44–45
AHRQ, 203, 218
Aid to Families with Dependent Children, 362
All-payer system, 258
Altenstetter, Christa, 137
Americans with Disabilities Act, 92
America's Health Insurance Plans, 270, 276
Amtrak, 211
Antifraud activities, 49
Any willing provider (AWP) laws, 87
Application in administrative process, 170,
  171–172, 173
Arizona, 128
Ashenfelter, Orley, 186

Automatic enrollment, 37, 66, 198–199
Automobile insurance, 191–192
AWP laws, 87

Balanced Budget Act (1997), 57, 345
Behavior-based premiums, 252
Benefit packages
  designing, 27–28
  hybrid, 41
  market and, 42
  requirements, for regional health market, 40–42
  services to include in, 41–42
  standardized, 12–14, 40–41, 61–63
  summary of, *232*, 233–234
Beveridge model (United Kingdom), 146
Blue Cross and Blue Shield plans, 80–81, 84,
  271–272, 280
Blumberg, Linda, 42, 198
Boren Amendment, 131
Boston Eligible Metropolitan Area (EMA),
  303–305, 307–308, 310, 312, 317
Boston Public Health Commission, 303,
  305–306, 310–317
Boston Public Health Commission Performance
  Initiative
  overview, 304–305
  Phase I, 305–307
  Phase II, 308, *309*, 310–311
  Phase III, 311–313, *314*, 315–317
"Bounded rationality" of insurance purchasers, 82
Bowsher v. Synar, 205, 213
Breaux, John, 206
Breaux-Thomas proposal, 206–207
Brokers, recruiting, 28–29
Bundled payments, 256
Bureau of Prisons, 211
Bush, George W., 131, 345
Busse, Reinhard, 137

C-SCHIP, 344–345, 347
Cafeteria plans, 3, 18–19, 89
California
  CalPERS, 21, 41, 167, 176
  car insurance, 191
  coverage mandates, 81, 182
  eligibility in high-risk pools, 8
  exchange, 20
  health care reform and, 125–126
  SCHIP model, 354, 357–358
  SCHIP study and choosing model, 354, 357–358
  standardized benefit plans, 12
  workers' compensation, 187

California Integrated Healthcare, 254
California Low Cost Automobile Insurance
    Program, 191
California Public Employees' Retirement
    System (CalPERS), 21, 41, 167, 176
Canada Health Act (1984), 134
Canadian health care system, 133–136, 258
Canadian Medical Association, 134
Capitated payment, 79, 256
Caps, out-of-pocket, 116–118, 128
Car insurance, 191–192
CARE, 301–302
Care coordination costs, 49–50
CBIA, 20
Centers for Disease Control and Prevention, 301
Centers for Medicare and Medicaid Services
    (CMS), 55, 64, 69–70, 109, 126, 204, 255,
    268, 277, 298
Chernew, M.E., 119
Child Tax Credit, 107
Children. *See also* State Children's Health
    Insurance Program (SCHIP)
    background information, 344–345
    overview of health care, 344, 360
    private insurance and low-income
        data, 363–365
        econometric models, 365–367, *368–373,*
            373–374
        methodology, 363–365
        overview, 362–363, 387–389
        results, 374–376, *375, 376, 377, 378–379,*
            379–380, 381–382, 382, *383–384,*
            384–387
    SCHIP study
        administrative choices, 347–351, *349,*
            355–359
        analytical approach, 345, *346,* 347
        contextual characteristics, 350–351
        expanding, 351–359
        Medicaid regulation and, 344, 349–350
        program separation, 344
        reauthorizing, 359–360
        selection of states, 345, *346,* 347
Children's Health and Medicare Protection Act
    (2007), 203
Choice of insurance, 4, 64–66, 175–177, *176*
Christianson, Jon, 57
CIGNA's HealthPass program, 276, 278, 284
Claims
    adjudication, 49
    aggregate, 16
    review, 77
Clinton, Bill, 131
Clinton, Hillary, 127–128
Clinton (Hillary) health reform plan (1993–94),
    125, 127
CMS, 55, 64, 69–70, 109, 126, 204, 255, 268,
    277, 298
COBRA coverage, 8–9, 91, 184
Coinsurance, 113–117, 119
Colorado, 20, 125, 191
Commercial health insurance market, 51. *See*
    also Government-run health plan; Market,
    health
Committee for Economic Development, 205

Common-law rights of insureds, 77
Community-rated premium from one job to
    another, guarantee of, 59
Community rating, 6–7, 38–39, 85, 281
Companion documents, 277
Comparative Effectiveness Research Trust
    Fund, 203
Competition, 5, 45–47, 122
Competitive pricing, 57–58
Congressional Budget Office, 201, 213
Congressionally chartered organizations,
    215–216
Connecticut, 20
Connector, 246–247
Consolidated Omnibus Budget Reconciliation
    Act (COBRA) coverage, 8–9, 91, 184
Consumer choice, 4, 64–66, 175–177, *176*
Consumer demand, modifying, 252–254
Consumer information, 63–64
Consumers Union study on individual health
    insurance
    findings
        attributes affecting selection, 228–230
        information sources used to purchase,
            227–228
        overview, 226–227
        reasons for purchasing, 227
    methodology, 226
    overview, 224–226
    policy implications and recommendations
        comparison of plan-summary prototype to
            other plan disclosures, 230, *231–232,*
            234–236
        overview, 230
        plan-summary prototype, 230, 233–234
    starting point, 224
Contra preferentum doctrine, 76–77
Contributions
    Employer's to premiums, 66–68, 100
    fixed, 109–110
    wage-related, 110–111
Conyers, John, 282
Cooper, Philip F., 67
Copayments, 113–117, 119–120, 192
COSE, 20
Cost-containment approaches
    interplay with coverage-expansion
        approaches
        controlling prices, 257–259
        instrumental measures, 259–262
        modifying consumer demand, 252–254
        modifying provider behavior, 254–257
        reducing need for services, 251–252
    overview, 241, 249, *250,* 251, 262–263
Cost and coverage questions, *231,* 233
Cost sharing
    differential, 254
    Medicaid and, 120
    in paying for health care and insurance,
        100–102, 112–117, 120, 122
    progressive, 253
    tiered, 253–254
Coulam, Robert, 55
Council on Affordable Quality Healthcare,
    276–277

Court, Jamie, 66
Coverage-expansion approaches
    connector, 246–247
    health spending and, 242–244
    interplay with cost-containment approaches
        controlling prices, 257–259
        instrumental measures, 259–262
        modifying consumer demand, 252–254
        modifying provider behavior, 254–257
        reducing need for services, 251–252
    overview, 241, 244–248, *245*, 262–263
    play-or-pay, 247–248
    public program expansion, 248
    single-payer, 248
    subsidized nongroup coverage, 245–246
Coverage mandates, 37, 81, 182, 190
Coverage policies, 257
Current Population Survey, 186
CUSIP (Committee on Uniform Security
    Identification Procedures), 176

Daschle, Tom, 205–207
Debt collection, federal, 192
Deductibles, 115–116
"Deemer" clause, 97
Default enrollment, 37, 66, 198–199
Defense Health Care, 295
Deficit Reduction Act (2005), 350
Dekker committee, 148
Dekker, Wisse, 148
Deregulation of private health insurance,
    88–89
Differential cost sharing, 254
Dirigo health reforms, 107
Disclosure of risks, full, 76
Dowd, Bryan E., 55, 57
"Downstreaming" risk, 79
"Drive-through-delivery" laws, 87
"Dutch disease," 147
Dutch health care system, 145–148
Dutch health insurance
    decision making, shifting, 150–151
    health care in Netherlands and Europe and,
        145–148
    health care reform (1980s and 1990s),
        148–150
    Health Insurance Law (2006), 245
    managerial changes in, 152–154
    mandates and, 182
    overview, 144–145, 157–160
    patient roles, new, 155–156
    uninsured and, 154–155
    voluntary compliance and, 194
"Dutch miracle," 147–148

Early Periodic Screening, Diagnosis, and
    Treatment Program, 130, 132
Earned Income Tax Credit (EITC), 107, 170,
    193, 196
Econometric models, 365–367, *368–373*,
    373–374
Economic Policy Institute, 53
Efficiency, market, 4
Efficiency problems, 51–52
EITC, 107, 170, 193, 196

Electronic filing, 278
Eligibility
    exchange, 33–34
    high-risk pools, 8–9
    income-based, 169
    rules, 168–170, *169*, 178–179
Emanuel, Ezekiel J., 205
Employee Retirement Income Security Act
    (ERISA), 11, 19, 24, 82–83, 90, 94, 96–97,
    184, 186
Employer costs, 273
Employer mandates, 183–189
Employer-sponsored insurance
    fixed contributions, 109–110
    overview, 109
    tiered premiums, 111–112
    wage-related contributions, 110–111
Employer's contribution to premiums, 66–68
Enforcement penalties, 194–195
Enrollment
    in administrative areas
        exchange, 33
        Medicaid-plus-tax-credits initiative, *169,*
            170, 173–174
    automatic, 37, 66, 198–199
    default, 37, 66, 198–199
    importance of, to success of plan, 178–179
ERISA, 11, 19, 24, 82–83, 90, 94, 96–97, 184,
    186
Established Program Financing (Canada), 135
European health care system, 145–148
Exchange
    in California, 20
    eligibility, 33–34
    major tasks
        choosing plan administrator, 24–26
        defining plan's tasks, 24–26
        designing benefit packages, 27–28
        getting participation of plans, 26–27
        marketing and education, 29
        overview, 24
        rating practices, 29–31
        recruiting agents and brokers, 28–29
        risk adjustment, 31
    in Massachusetts, 19
    national, 31–34
    in New York, 20
    overview, 19–20
    price taker versus negotiator, 22
    public versus private, 22–24
    risk-rating challenges, 32–33
    size, 20–21
    start-up issues, 24
Executive departments, 207, 210
"Experimental care" exclusions, 82

Fair Labor Standards Act, 186
Fair Share Contribution, 184–186
Fairness problems, 51–52
Fannie Mae and Freddie Mac, 217
Federal Advisory Committee Act, 219
Federal Deposit Insurance Corporation, 211
Federal Employees Health Benefit (FEHB)
        Program, 21, 31, 61, 70, 121, 167, 176,
        205, 246–247, 280, 298

Federal executive agencies, 207, *208–209,*
    210–213
Federal health insurance regulation, 88–92
Federal Housing Administration, 211
Federal Open Market Committee, 213
Federal poverty line (FPL), 362
Federal Prison Industries, 211
Federal Reserve Board, 70, 206
Federal Reserve for Health, 201. *See also*
    Health-related organizations, new
Federal Reserve System, 205, 212–213
Federal Retirement Thrift Investment Board,
    206, 212, 219
Federal Trade Commission, 225
Federalism, foreign
    Canada, 133–136
    Germany, 133, 136–139
    overview, 132–133
    Switzerland, 133, 139–141
Federally funded research and development
    centers (FFRDCs), 214–215
Fee-for-service (FFS) Medicare plan, 54–57,
    59–60, 69
FEHB program, 21, 31, 61, 70, 121, 167, 176,
    205, 246–247, 280, 298
Feldman, Roger, 55, 57
Fendrick, A.M., 119
FFS Medicare plan, 54–57, 59–60, 69
Financial responsibility, 79–80
Fixed contributions, 109–110
Florida, 20, 125, 128
Free Rider Surcharge, 186
Fuchs, Victor R., 203, 205

Generalizability, 127
Generating resources to pay for health care and
    insurance, 100–101
Georgia, 191
German health care system, 133, 136–139, 259
Glaser, William, 137
Government Accountability Office, 78
Government corporations, 211
Government Performance and Results Act
    (1993), 289, 305
Government-run health plan
    designing and running
        administration , 69–70
        advertising and consumer information,
            63–64
        choice environment, 64–66
        employer's contribution to premiums,
            66–68
        mandatory participation and default
            enrollment, 66
        overview, 60
        pool versus health plan, 60–61
        provider payment rates, 68–69
        reasons for, 58–60
        risk selection and adjustment, 64
        standardized benefit package, 61–63
        tax effects, 68
    Medicare lessons, 51, 54–58
    overview, 51, 70–71
    premiums in, 59
    problems in market and, 51–52

Government-run health plan *(continued)*
    proposal, 53–54
    term of, 69
Graetz, Michael J., 198
Group Health Association, 86
Guaranteed issue, 281
Guide to Health Plans for Federal Employees,
    63

Hacker, Jacob, 53, 62, 64, 207
Hasse, Leif, 204
Hawaii, 110, 182, 185–186
HCAP, 53–54, 59, 61–69
HCTC, 106–107, 121, 166, 175–177
HDHPs, 115, 252–253, 284
Health cards, personal, 174
Health Care for America Plan (HCAP), 53–54,
    59, 61–69
Health Care Choice Act (2005), 97
Health care costs. *See* Medical costs
Health care efficiency, promoting, 101–102
Health Care Financing Administration, 206
Health care reform. *See also* Health-related
    organizations, new
    California and, 125–126
    Colorado and, 125
    Dutch, 148–150
    federalism and, foreign
        Canada, 133–136
        Germany, 133, 136–139
        overview, 132–133
        Switzerland, 133, 139–141
    Florida and, 125
    focus of, 244, *245*
    generalizability and, 127
    level of government and, 96–98
    managed care, 86–88
    mandates and, 127–129
    Medicaid and, 127–132
    Medicare and, 129
    models and, 127–129
    national, 125–127
    New York and, 125–126
    overview, 125–126, 141–142
    rating, 83–86
    regulation of health care and, 93–96
    regulation of health insurance and, 93–98
    state, 125–127
    underwriting, 83–86
    Vermont and, 125
Health Centers, 295–296
Health Choices Menu, 127
Health Connector, 35, 45–48, 176
Health Coverage Tax Credit (HCTC), 106–107,
    121, 166, 175–177
Health information technology, 259–260
Health insurance. *See also* Administration
    of health insurance; Government-run
    health plan; Regulation of private health
    insurance; *specific program*
    exchange
        major tasks, 24–31
        national, 31–34
        overview, 19–20
        price taker versus negotiator, 22

Health insurance. *See also* Administration
    of health insurance; Government-run
    health plan; Regulation of private health
    insurance; *specific program (continued)*
exchange
    public versus private, 22–24
    size, 20–21
    start-up issues, 24
governance of, 76–78
interstate sale of, 283–284
issuing, 38–40
job lock and, 52
market characteristics, 4–5
overview, 6, 34
public, 206–207
purpose of, 3–4
rating rules, 38–40
reality of, versus ideal, 5–6
relationship, 73–76
structural change options
    high-risk pools, 8–11
    overview, 6
    public reinsurance, 14–18
    rate compression, 6–8
    Section 125 plans, 18–19
    standardized benefit plans, 12–14
suboptimal, 52
Health Insurance Law (ZVW) of 2006
    (Netherlands), 245
Health Insurance Portability and
    Accountability Act (HIPAA), 58, 84,
    91–92, 126, 273–277
Health insurance purchasing cooperatives
    (HIPCs), 19
Health maintenance organizations (HMOs), 4,
    13, 54–55, 61, 79, 86, 88, 247, 271
Health promotion activities, 251–252
Health-related organizations, new
    federal executive, 207, *208–209,* 210–213
    issues in choosing appropriate
        funding authority, 216
        management structure, 218–220
        operational flexibilities, 217
        overview, 216
        political independence and accountability,
            217–218
        public versus private, 220
    legislative branch, 213–214
    overview, 201, 221
    proposals
        coverage decisions, 204–205
        information on comparative effectiveness,
            202–204
        marketplace for health insurance, 205–206
        public health insurance plan, 206–207
    public-private, 210–213, 214–216
Health risk reassessment after illness or injury,
    protection against, 58–59
Health savings accounts (HSAs), 88–89, 115,
    119, 284
Health-status rating, 37–38
Healthcare Effectiveness Data and Information
    Set Act, 77
HealthPass (New York City), 20
Healthy Families Program, 354

Healthy New York program, 16–17, 117
Healthy Start, 352
High Coverage Tax Credit (HCTC), 106–107,
    121, 166, 175–177
High-deductible health plans (HDHPs), 115,
    252–253, 284
High-risk pools, 8–11
HIPAA, 58, 84, 91–92, 126, 273–277
HIPCs, 19
Hispanic construction workers and their children
    study
    data, 322–323
    findings
        access to health services, 323, *324–326,*
            327
        medical costs and types of services, 327,
            328–332
        perceived health status, 338, *339–340,*
            341–342
        profile of workers, 323
        sources of payment, 333, *334–337*
    Medicaid and, 323
    methodology, 322–323
    overview of health care and, 321–322, 338
    SCHIP and, 323
HIV/AIDS epidemic, 301–302
HMOs, 4, 13, 54–55, 61, 79, 86, 88, 247, 271
Holahan, John, 198
Hospital Insurance Act (Canada), 134
HSAs, 88–89, 115, 119, 284

ID cards, 49, 276
Illinois, 110
Income-related, term of, 100
Income tax credits, 105–107
Indemnity plans, 4, 13
Independent regulatory commissions, 210–213
Indian Health Service, 295
Individual health insurance plan information.
    See Consumers Union study on individual
        health insurance
Individual mandates, 126, 183, 189–198, 224
Individual reinsurance, 45
Institute of Medicine, 204
Instrumental measures, 249, 259–262
Insurance exchange. *See* Exchange
Insurance Research Council, 191
Insurers
    behavior, modifying, 254–257
    costs, 272–273
    market domination by a few, 5–6
    model of competition from both, 47
    payment rates, 68–69
    reinsurance and risk limitations, 44–45
    as "repeat players" in litigation, 77
    role in high-risk pools, 9–10
    survey of (1995), 274
Internal market within social health insurance,
    148–149
Internal Revenue Code (1954), 89
Internal Revenue Service (IRS), 19, 103–104,
    106, 166, 170, 187
Interstate sale of health insurance, 283–284
IRS, 19, 103–104, 106, 166, 170, 187
Issuing health insurance, 38–40

Job lock, 52
Jost, Timothy Stoltzfus, 204, 218

Kaiser/HRET survey, 110, 116
Kazee, Nicole, 128
Kentucky Association of Health Plans v. Miller,
    87, 90
Kupersmith, Joel, 203

Legislative branch agencies, 213–214
Lewin Group, 242
Liability, 353–354
Litigation, 77–79, 87, 90–91, 205
Loss ratio, minimum, 281–282
"Lunatics movement" (1960s), 156

M-SCHIP, 344, 347–350
MA program, 54–55, 59–60, 62, 90, 105, 113,
    121, 270–271
Maine, 107
Managed care reforms, 86–88
Mandates
    administering
        agencies for, 195–197
        automatic enrollment, 198–199
        considerations, initial, 183–184
        employer mandates, 184–189
        individual mandates, 189–198
        overview, 182, 199
    coverage, 37, 81, 182, 190
    employer, 183–189
    health care reform and, 127–129
    individual, 126, 183, 189–198, 224
    participation, 66
    premium, 183
    purpose of, 183
Mannheim, Karl, 66
Market, health. *See also* Government-run health
    plan; Regional health markets
    benefit packages and, 42
    dynamics of, 74–75
    efficiency, 4
    existing, 47–48
    Health Connector, 47–48
    large-group, 83
    managing, 205–206
    Medicare lessons and, 51, 54–58
    mixed public and private insurance system
        designing and running, 58–70
        proposal for, 53–54
    nongroup, 83
    pooling risk, 5
    problems, 51–52
    reasonable choice and, 4
    small-group, 83–86
    types of, 47
    useful competition and, 5
Marketing, 29, 59
Mashaw, Jerry L., 198
Massachusetts
    Boston Eligible Metropolitan Area, 303–304
    coverage mandates, 182, 190
    employer mandates, 186
    enforcement penalties, 194
    exchange, 19

Massachusetts *(continued)*
    Fair Share Contribution, 184–186
    Health Connector, 35, 45–48, 176
    health insurance model, 127
    individual mandates, 126
    mean-tested premium assistance, 107–108
    Medicaid in, 107–108
    penalties for mandate incompliance, 194
    Section 125 plans, 18
    voluntary compliance, 194
    wage-related contributions, 110
Massachusetts Commonwealth Care program,
    197
Massachusetts Commonwealth Choice program,
    113–114, 176
Massachusetts Commonwealth Health Insurance
    Connector Authority, 219–220, 234–236
McCarran-Ferguson Act, 89
Means testing, 100, 107–109
Medicaid
    beneficiary categories, 129
    compliance enforcement, 130–131
    copayments and, 119–120
    cost sharing and, 120
    coverage mandates and, 128
    creation of, 89, 129
    delivery patterns, 130
    enrollment in 2003, 117
    expansion of, 107–108, 248
    federal versus state authority and, 90
    flexibility and innovation, 131
    fraud and abuse, 130
    generating resources for, 101
    growth in, 126
    health care reform and, 129–132
    Hispanic workers and, 323
    income thresholds, 129
    instability of insurance coverage and, 196
    mandated/optional benefits, 129
    in Massachusetts, 107–108
    matching formulas, 130
    Oregon Plan and, 14
    payment policies, 131
    premium increases and, 120
    risk adjustment and, 43
    safety net, 130
    State Children's Health Insurance Program
        regulations and, 344, 349–350
    targeted market, 295–296
    waivers, expanded use of, 178
Medicaid expansion (M-SCHIP), 344, 347–350
Medicaid-plus-tax-credits initiative
    administrative areas
        administrative costs, 177
        application, 170–172, *173,* 174
        consumer choice, 175–177, *176*
        eligibility rules, 168–170, *169,* 178–179
        enrollment, 170–172, *173,* 174, 178
        federal government's role in, *166, 167*
        nonworkers, 175
        overview, 168, *169*
        premium payment, 174, *174*
        state government's role in, *166, 167*
        uninsured workers and, 168, *168*
        workers, 174–175

Medicaid-plus-tax-credits initiative (continued)
  advance planning suggestions, 180–181
  legislative drafting suggestions, 180–181
  lessons learned from recent coverage
      expansions, 177–180
  overview, 165
  scenario, 165–166
Medicaid Services Web site, 49
Medical Care Insurance Act (Canada), 134
Medical costs
  administrative
    "black box" of, 285
    classifying and defining, 267–268
    estimating, 268, 269, 270–273, 270
    reducing, potential, 48–50
    reform proposals with implications for,
        279–280
    types of, 48–50
  controlling
    cost-containment approaches, 241, 249,
        250, 251
    coverage-expansion approaches,
        241–248
    overview, 241, 262–263
    prices, 257
    problem of, 34
  coverage policies, 257
  incurrence by U.S. population, 16
  new technology and, 96
  percentage of income and, 42
  reinsurance and, 16
Medical errors, reduced, 252
Medical Expenditure Panel Survey, 322
Medically necessary services, 74
Medicare. See also Medicare Advantage (MA)
    program, Fee-for-service (FFS) Medicare
    Plan
  Canada's version of, 135
  creation, 89
  funding of, 89–90
  health care reform and, 129
  lessons, 51, 54–58
  level playing field in, lack of, 56
  limits on supplemental benefits, 12
  market and, health, 51
  moving toward model of, 16
  NHE estimates (1966–2005), 270–271, 270
  out-of-pocket caps and, lack of, 116
  Part B, 103–104, 109
  Part D, 40, 44, 46, 49, 56, 103, 107–109, 170,
      195–196
  payment by insurees, 103–105
  private plans in, 54–55, 57–58, 64
  risk adjustment and, 43
  standardized benefit packages in, 62
Medicare+Choice systems, 70
Medicare Advantage (MA) program, 54–55,
    59–60, 62, 90, 105, 113, 121, 270–271
Medicare Choice initiative, 170
Medicare Modernization Act (2003), 57
Medicare Payment Advisory Commission
    (MedPAC), 57, 202–203, 213–214
Medicare Savings Programs (MSPs), 107–108
Medigap policies, 41, 54, 62, 94, 248,
    281–282

MedPAC, 202–203, 213–214
Merlis, Mark, 211, 218
Meyer, Jack, 278
Minimum benefits, 40–41
Minimum Benefits Law, 81
Minimum wage, 186
Minnesota, 114, 126, 274–275
Minnesota Advantage, 114
Modified community rating, 38–39
Moral hazard, 74–76, 113
MSPs, 107–108

NAIC, 79, 81
National Academy of Public Administration,
    215–216, 221
National Academy of Sciences, 216
National Association of Insurance
    Commissioners (NAIC), 79, 81
National clearinghouse, 278
National Council for Quality Assurance, 77
National Drug Code (NDC), 277
National exchange, 31–34
National Governors Association, 129
National health care reform, 125–127
National health expenditures (NHE), 241–242,
    268, 270–271
Netherlands. See Dutch health insurance
New Jersey, 12
New Mexico, 110, 128
New York
  coverage mandates, 81
  exchange, 20
  health care reform and, 125–126
  Healthy New York program, 16–17, 117
  reinsurance and, 117
  Universal New York Health Care, 274
New York State Conference of Blue Cross and
    Blue Shield Plans v. Travelers' Ins. Co., 91
NHE, 241–242, 268, 270–271
Nichols, Len, 183, 203, 205
Nondiscrimination provisions of Internal
    Revenue Code, 89
North Carolina, 20, 354–355, 358–359
Nyman, John, 68

Obama, Barack, 127–128
Office of the Comptroller of the Currency, 216
Office of Federal Housing Enterprise Oversight,
    217
Office of Federal Student Aid, 217
Office of Management and Budget, 106, 220,
    289. See also Program Assessment Rating
    Tool (PART)
Office of Personnel Management, 280
Office of Thrift Supervision, 216
Ohio, 20, 352–353, 356
Oklahoma, 128
Omnibus Budget Reconciliation Acts, 350
Open-enrollment periods, 64
Oregon Plan, 14
Orszag, Peter, 202
Osborne, David, 301
Out-of-pocket maximums, 116–118, 128
Outcomes Measurement System, 307, 311–312,
    316–317

P4P, 254–256, 258
Pacific Business Group on Health, 205
PART. *See* Program Assessment Rating Tool
Participation mandates, 66
Participation of plans, getting, 26–27
Patent and Trademark Office, 217
Patient safety, 252
Paul v. Virginia, 78
Pauly, Mark V., 62, 113, 182, 194–195, 196
Pay-for-performance (P4P), 254–255, 258
Paying for health care and insurance
    background information, 99–102
    cost sharing, 100–102, 112–117, 120, 122
    course for, plotting, 120–122
    efficiency in health care, promoting, 101–102
    employee-sponsored insurance, 109–112
    overview, 99
    policy goals and, achieving, 118–120
    public programs, 103–109
    resources, generating, 100–101
    social and political goals and, contributing to
        broader, 102
PBO concept, 217
Penalty for delay in purchasing insurance,
    37–38
Performance-based management
    Boston Eligible Metropolitan Area and,
        302–304
    Boston Public Health Commission
        Performance Initiative and
        overview, 304–305
        Phase I, 305–307
        Phase II, 308, *309,* 310–311
        Phase III, 311–313, *314,* 315–317
    challenges of, 304
    overview, 301, 317–318
    Ryan White programs and, 301–302
Personal health record (PHR), 259–260
Plan administrator, choosing, 24–26
Plan-summary prototype, 230, *231–232,* 233
Play-or-pay provisions, 193–194, 247–248
Point-of-service (POS) plans, 86
Points of transition, 173–174
Polder model, 147
Policy goals, achieving, 118–120
Pooling risk, 5, 35–36, 117
Portability of coverage, guarantee of, 59
POS plans, 86
PPOs, 4, 13, 42, 86, 115
Preexisting conditions, 10
Preferred provider organizations (PPOs), 4, 13,
    42, 86, 115
Premium support approach, 57–58
Premium
    adjusting, 112
    administration, 33
    behavior-based, 252
    community-rated from one job to another,
        guarantee of, 59
    competition, 121
    employer's contribution to, 66–68, 100
    in government-run health plan, 59
    for high-income enrollees, 100
    in high-risk pools, 10–11
    lowering, 14–16

Premium *(continued)*
    mandated, 183
    mean-tested assistance, 107–109
    payments, 174–175, *174*
    rating, 38–40
    risk pooling and, 5, 35–36, 36, 117
    "standard rate," 10
    subsidies, 37
    taxes, 50
    tiered, 111–112
Prepaid Health Care Act, 185–186
Preventive services, 251–252
Price transparency, 261–262
Private insurance
    administrative costs, 271–272
    low-income children and
        data, 363–365
        econometric models, 365–367, *368–373,*
            373–374
        methodology, 363–365
        overview, 362–363, 387–389
        results, 374–376, *375, 376, 377, 378–379,*
            379–380, *381–382,* 382, *383–384,*
            384–387
Private-sector monopoly model, 46
Program Assessment Rating Tool (PART)
    final observations, 299–300
    performance of federal programs and
        effectiveness and incentives, 297–298
        final observations, 299–300
        organizational responsibility and authority,
            296–297
        outcomes and measures, 294–296
        overview, 291, *292, 293*
        process, 289–291
        strategies for program improvement,
            overview, 298–299
Progressive cost sharing, 253
Provider-sponsored organizations (PSOs), 86
Providers. *See* Insurers
PSOs, 86
Public insurance system, 206–207. *See also
    specific name*
Public-private entities, 214–216
Public program expansion, 248
Public programs for paying for health care and
    insurance
    income tax credits, 105–107
    means-tested premium assistance, 107–109
    overview, 103
    social insurance models, 103–105
Purchasing entity. *See* Exchange
Pure community rating, 6–7, 38–39

Qualified bidder model, 46–47

RAND Corporation studies, 225, 242
Rate compression, 6–8
Rating
    practices, 29–33
    reforms, 83–86
    rules, 38–40
Regional health markets
    administrative cost reduction, potential,
        48–50

Regional health markets *(continued)*
  adverse selection, 37–38
  benefit package requirements, 40–42
  competition, 45–47
  existing insurance markets, 47–48
  issue and rating rules, 38–40
  overview, 35, 50
  risk-pooling issues, 35–36
  risk sharing, 42–45
Regulation of private health insurance
  balance sheet, interim, 92–93
  federal, 89–92
  governance of health insurance and, 76–78
  health care reform and, 93–98
  health insurance relationship and, 73–76
  overview, 73
  state
        coverage mandates, 81–83
        deregulation and, 88–89
        early efforts, 78–79
        financial responsibility, 79–80
        managed care reforms, 86–88
        other concerns, traditional, 80–81
        underwriting and rating reforms,
           83–86
Regulatory compliance, 49
Reinhardt, Uwe, 203
Reinsurance
  aggregate, 44–45
  challenges, 283
  individual, 45
  medical costs and, 16
  New York and, 117
  out-of-pocket maximums and, 117
  private, 15
  public, 14–18
  risk limitations to insurers, 44–45
"Repeat players" in litigation, 77
Research, effective, 260
Retail Industry Leaders Association v. Fielder,
   90
Risk adjustment, 31, 38, 43, 64
Risk corridors, 44
Risk pooling, 5, 35–36, 117
Risk rating, 32–33
Risk selection, 64
Risk sharing, 42–45
Robert Wood Johnson Foundation, 165, 274
Romney, Mitt, 127
Rosen, A.B., 119
Royal Commission on Health Services
   (Canada), 134
Rush Prudential HMO, Inc. v. Moran, 90
Rush v. Parham, 79
Ryan White Comprehensive AIDS Resources
   Emergency (CARE) Act, 301–302
Ryan White HIV/AIDS Treatment
   Modernization Act, 302
Ryan White programs, 301–302

S-SCHIP, 344, 347–348
Salary-reduction plans, 4, 18–19
Savings clause, 90
SCHIP. *See* State Children's Health Insurance
   Program

Schwarzenegger, Arnold, 182
Seam bias, 363
SEC, 70, 206
Section 125 plans, 3, 18–19, 89
Securities and Exchange Commission (SEC),
   70, 206
Selective Service System, 190
Self-insurance, 90
Sickness Fund Decree (Netherlands), 146
Sickness Fund Law (ZFW) of 1962
   (Netherlands), 146
Silow-Carroll, Sharon, 278
Single-payer plan, 248, 282–283
Smith, Robert S., 186
Social health insurance, internal market within,
   148–149
Social insurance models, 103–105
Social Security, 103–104
Social Security Administration (SSA), 104, 109,
   192, 212
SSA, 104, 109, 192, 212
"Standard rate" premium, 10
Standardized benefit packages, 12–14, 40–41,
   61–63
Stanton, Thomas H., 207, 218–220
Stark, Fourtney, 282
State Children's Health Insurance Program
   (SCHIP), 95, 101, 107–108, 120
  creation of, 126, 345, 362
  expansion of, 185, 248, 351–359
  federal parameters and, 347
  growth in, 126
  Hispanic workers' children and, 323
  instability of insurance coverage and, 196
  legislation, 347–348
  program separation, 344
  study
        administrative choices, 347–351, *349,*
           355–359
        analytical approach, 345, *346,* 347
        contextual characteristics, 350–351
        expanding, 351–359
        Medicaid regulations and, *344,* 349–350
        program separation, 344
        reauthorizing, 359–360
        selection of states, 345, *346,* 347
State health care reform, 125–127
State health insurance regulation
  coverage mandates, 81–83
  deregulation and, 88–89
  early efforts, 78–79
  financial responsibility, 79–80
  managed care reforms, 86–88
  other concerns, traditional, 80–81
  underwriting and rating reforms, 83–86
Steuerle, C. Eugene, 194, 196
Subsidized nongroup coverage, 245–246
Suffolk University, 210–317, 305–308
Survey of Income and Program Participation
   (SIPP) panel (1996)
  data, 363–365
  econometric models, 365–367, *368–373,*
     373–374
  methodology, 363–365
  overview, 363

Survey of Income and Program Participation (SIPP) panel (1996) *(continued)*
results
characteristics of person-months in private, public, and uninsured spells, 374, *375, 376, 377*
estimating crowd-out effect of Medicaid/SCHIP eligibility on private insurance, 384–387, *385*
transitions from being uninsured to private coverage, 380, 382, *383–384*
transitions from Medicaid/SCHIP to private coverage, 380, *381–382*
transitions from private insurance to Medicaid/SCHIP coverage, 374–377, *378–379*
Swiss health care system, 133, 139–141, 182, 194

Tax credits, 105–107
Tax Equality and Fiscal Responsibility Act (TEFRA), 70
Taxes, 50, 68, 105–107, 128, 187–188, 192–193
TEFRA, 70
Tennessee Valley Authority, 211
Texas, 20, 128, 353–354, 356–357
Thatcher British National Health Service, 267
Thomas, Bill, 206
Thorpe, Kenneth, 268, 285
Thrift Savings Plan, 212
Tiered cost sharing, 253–254
Tiered premiums, 111–112
Title XXI of Social Security Act. *See* State Children's Health Insurance Program (SCHIP)
Total replacement, 46
Transactions, simplifying insurance-related
HIPAA and Administrative Simplification Compliance Act, 275–276
overview, 273
policy options, 278–284
electronic filing, required, 278
guaranteed issue and community rating, 281
health savings accounts, 284
high-deductible plans, 284
interstate sale of insurance, 283–284
minimum loss ratio, 281–282
national clearinghouse, 278
open FEHB Program or similar exchange, 280
reform proposals with implications for administrative costs, 279–280
reinsurance, 283
single payer, 282–283
standardized transactions, fully, 278–279
pre-HIPAA initiatives, 274–275
progress and barriers, 276–277

Transition points, 173–174
Tuohy, Carolyn, 135–136

Underwriting, 38, 49, 50, 59, 83–86
Unemployment insurance, 187
Uniform pricing, 254, 258
Uninsured, 52, 131, 154–155, 191
United States v. Southeastern Underwriting Association, 78
UnitedHealth Group, 6
Universal New York Health Care, 274
University of Michigan, 114
University of Rochester, 110
U.S. Bureau of Labor Statistics, 100
U.S. Commerce Department, 217
U.S. Congress, 69, 87, 89, 130, 197, 207, 305
U.S. Constitution, 133
U.S. Education Department, 217
U.S. Health and Human Services Department, 178, 203, 275, 296, 302
U.S. Housing and Urban Development Department, 211, 217
U.S. Justice Department, 211
U.S. Postal Service, 211, 219
U.S. Supreme Court, 78, 91, 205
U.S. Treasury Department, 103, 106, 178
Utah, 274, 278
Utah Health Information Network, 274

Value, promoting, 114
Varied pricing, 254
Vermont, 125
Veterans Health Administration, 117, 295, 298
Veterans Health Service, 298
Vistnes, Gregory S., 67
Vistnes, Jessica P., 67
Voices of Experience (research studies), 314–316
Voinovich, George, 352
Voluntary compliance, 193–194
Vulnerable populations, protecting, 113–114

Wage-related contributions, 110–111
Wal-Mart, 119
Washington State, 126
Welch, W. Pete, 56
"Welfare medicine," 129
WellPoint, 6
West Virginia, 110
White, Ryan, 295
Wicks, Elliot, 278
Wilensky, Gail, 203
Wilson, Woodrow, 212
Wisconsin ETF program, 111, 114
Wisconsin Group Health Insurance program, 111
Withholding tables, 196
Workers' compensation, 187